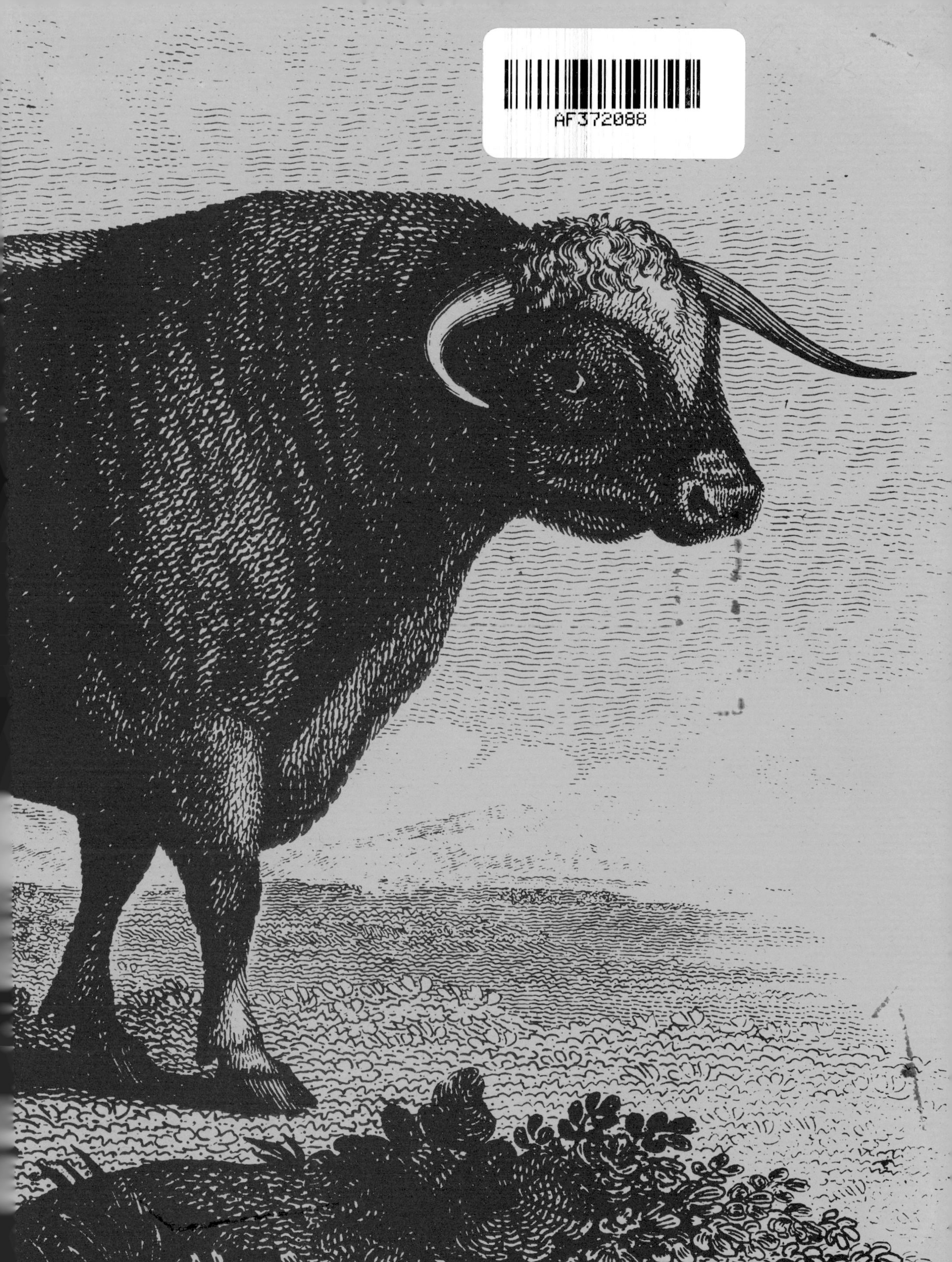

The Bull

The

Allan Fraser

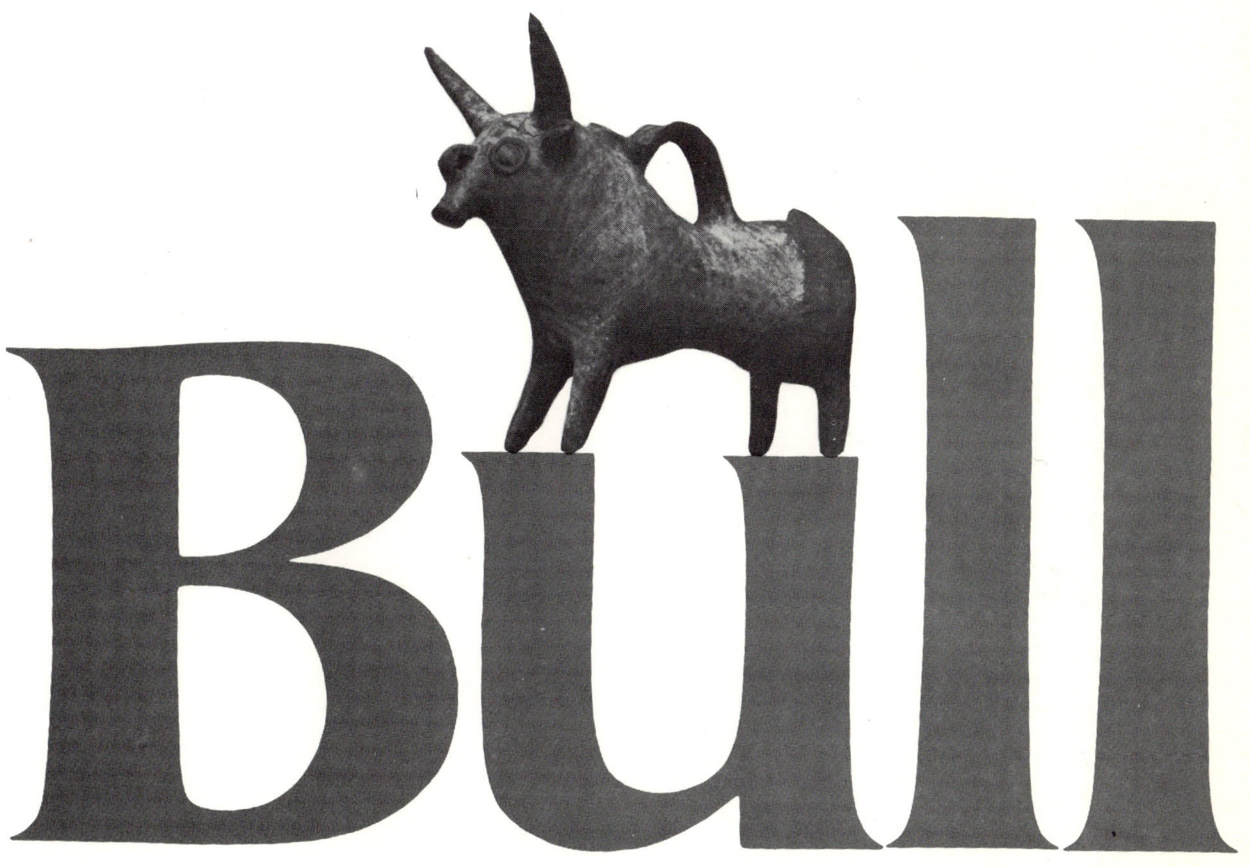

Bull

⊕ Osprey

Published in 1972 by
Osprey Publishing Ltd, P.O. Box 25,
707 Oxford Road, Reading, Berkshire

Designed by Behram Kapadia

SBN 85045 072 1

Photoset by BAS Printers Limited, Wallop, Hampshire
and printed in Great Britain by
The Berkshire Printing Company Ltd., Reading, Berkshire

The author acknowledges Hodder & Stoughton Ltd.
for permission to reproduce extracts from *The Crystal
Cave* by Mary Stewart, and Jonathan Cape Ltd. for the
inclusion of passages from *Death in the Afternoon* by
Ernest Hemingway.

For Peter

Contents

1   The Bull at Large   9

2   The Bull in Mythology   25

3   The Bull in Religion   47

4   The Bull in Art   69

5   The Bull in Sport   89

6   The Bull in Pedigree   113

7   The Bull in Farming   131

8   The Bull in Technology   157

9   The Bull in Review   177

  References   197

  Index   203

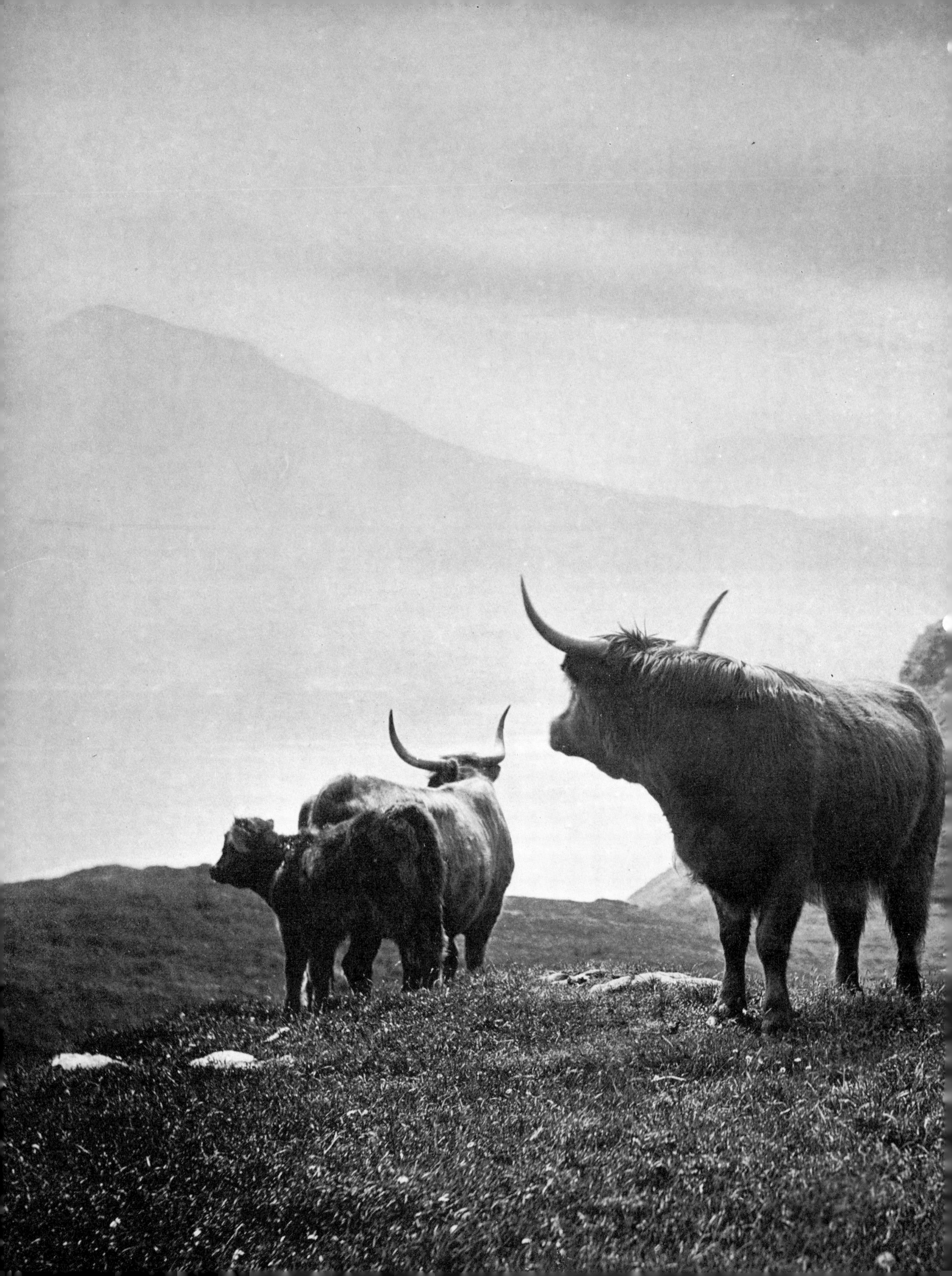

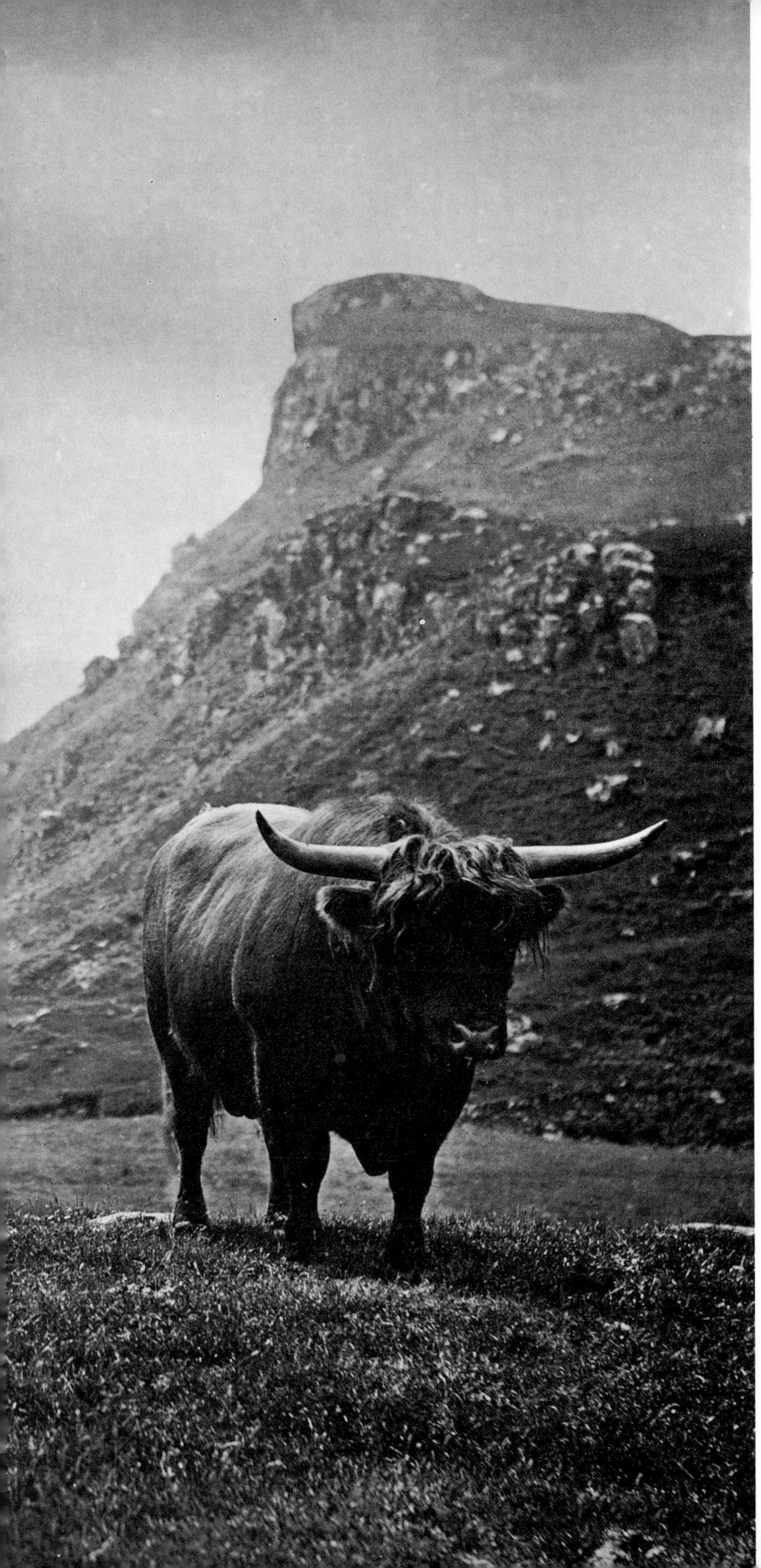

1 The Bull at Large

Highland bull with cows and calf: the dual duty of procreation and protection.

§ This story of the Bull begins with the wild bull of fabulous strength, ferocity and virility – the bull called the aurochs – long extinct, but from which all the domesticated cattle of Europe, of the Americas and of Australasia are said to be derived. Its pictorial representation can be seen scratched by prehistoric man on the cave walls of Lascaux, in south-west France. Its bones have been found in the soils of western Asia, throughout Europe and in northern Africa. Its distribution extended westwards into Britain but was brought to a halt by the Irish Sea. The last known survivor died two and a half centuries ago in a remote forest in Poland, called Jaktorowka.

Far beyond the bounds of written history, in the palaeolithic or stone age period of man's emergence, certain prehistoric and anonymous artists carved and painted representations of both man and animals on the walls of caves. In addition to the artistic merit of these drawings – reckoned by experts to be of the highest order – they show with apparent fidelity the species of animals on which these prehistoric people of hunting culture had to depend for their livelihood.

In these deep and tortuous subterranean caves there is no evidence of continuous habitation. Rather it would seem that the cavemen went there periodically for sanctuary or for a secret place in which to practise their primitive magical rites. For, although these animal artists displayed considerable skill they did not practise their art for art's sake but, according to archaeologists, in pursuit of what is termed hunting or sympathetic magic. In this – the representation of an animal – say a bull or a bear – and sometimes its symbolical destruction by perforations or scratchings – was supposed to give power to the hunter in facing and overcoming the more dangerous reality. It was the same sort of idea as sticking pins in the clay image of an unpopular person or private enemy and then leaving it in running water to waste away, a practice common enough in remote places, even in this century. As the image wasted away, or so people believed, the person the image represented would waste away also. These prehistoric cavemen deserved and required all the confidence their magic gave them. For, armed only with the primitive weapons of his era, the human hunter had to confront the vastly greater physical power, the brute strength and merciless ferocity of the animals he slew. His food, clothing and the implements he fashioned from bone depended upon the proceeds of his hunting. The survival and safety of his family were linked with his success. No prize of the successful hunt could have provided greater reward than the slain aurochs. With its wealth of meat, its tough and shaggy hide, its strong bones and sharply pointed horns, the carcass of a slain bull aurochs must have been a fitting reward for valour. Yet, since every aurochs herd, as every herd of wild cattle even to this day, lived under the domination and protection of the supreme king bull, any attempt to kill a weaker member of that herd – a calf or heavily pregnant cow – might bring the wild king bull down upon the hunter with the force of a ton weight of furious charge, in blind passion of destruction, determined to crush anything that might threaten the safety of the herd. Even with the domesticated cattle of today it is a rash and foolish herdsman who will come between the bull and the cows he closely guards, since the bull in nature has the dual duty of procreation and protection.

The most famous prehistoric pictures of the aurochs are those on the cave walls of Lascaux in France. The Abbé Breuil described and reproduced them in his wonderful book *Four Hundred Centuries of Cave Art*. The vitality of these drawings is so very remarkable that it is difficult not to believe that here was an artist who at times may have forgotten magic in the perfection of his art. Whether these prehistoric artists sublimated their magic into religion and whether the wild bull so brilliantly drawn on the walls of subterranean sanctuaries became enshrined in their mythology, remains an unsolved query, perhaps for ever insoluble. It is more probable, perhaps, when the hunt was over and the aurochs slain, that the hunter, devouring the flesh of the mighty bull, felt himself strengthened by the vigour and potency of the beast he had conquered. He may have laid down upon, or wrapped himself in the slain bull's hide believing that, by so doing, the strength and fertility of the bull would refresh and invigorate his own body – a belief that explains certain curious customs in the Scottish Hebrides persisting almost to this day.

The genealogy of cattle is an involved affair with authorities in conflict as to whether our domesticated cattle as we know them today arose from one wild species or from several. There has been a vast amount of printer's ink spilt over this somewhat academic question with numerous wild speculations hidden in the technical jargon of scientific dissertations. Victorian zoologists who followed perhaps rather too closely in the footsteps of Charles Darwin were quite pre-pared and imagined themselves perfectly capable of reconstructing an extinct bovine from the somewhat slender evidence of a crumpled horn. It appears to be agreed, however, that the aurochs, also called the urus or *Bos primigenius*, was the predominant if not the exclusive ancestor of *Bos taurus*, which includes all European cattle and those introduced from Europe into North America, South America and Australasia. *Bos indicus* of India and many parts of Africa, the hump-backed zebu or brahman, may be a rather different story.

It can be accepted, then, that the aurochs was the species of wild cattle hunted by cavemen from the Urals to the Irish Sea.

Julius Caesar described it, rather incidentally perhaps, as he was primarily concerned in relating events which led to the conquest of Gaul and, without cavil, Julius Caesar was more of a soldier than an authority on natural history. He was inclined to accept fable as fact

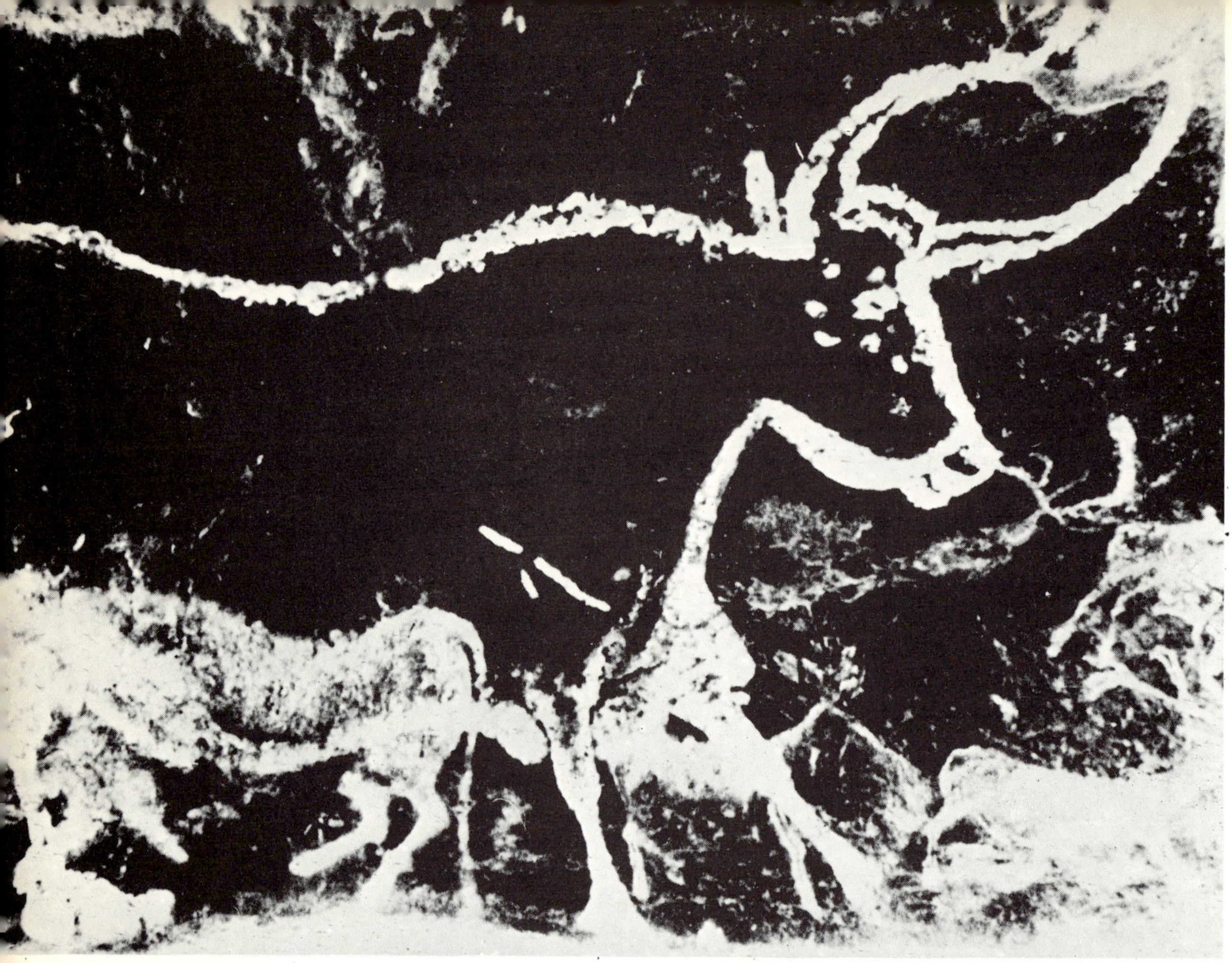

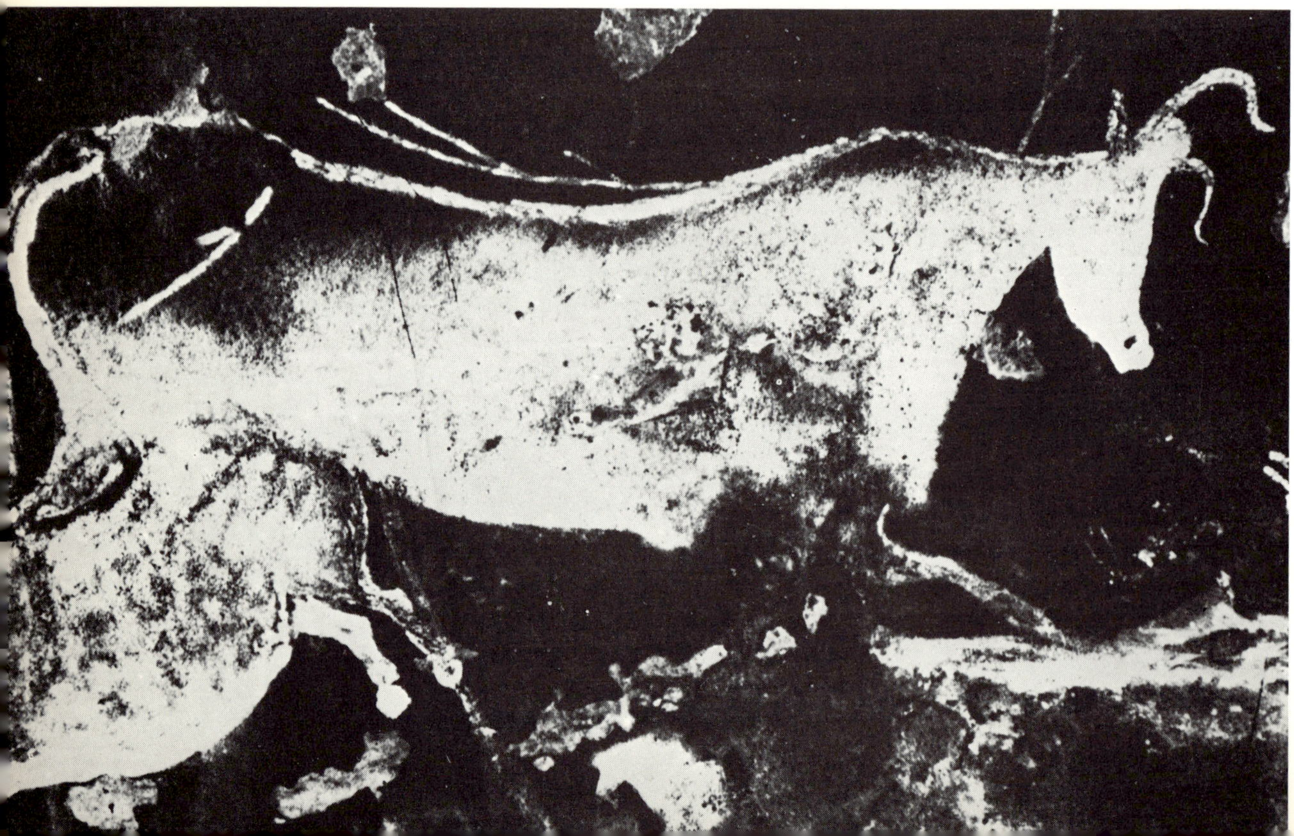

as many have since done and continue to do. He wrote of

an elk which apparently had no joints in its legs, with the result that it
could not lie down. If it happened to fall down by accident it was unable to
rise again. The unfortunate animal, therefore, had to recline against trees
to take its rest, a habit which, we are told, was its undoing, for the hunters
of those days weakened the trees in such a manner that when the elks leant
against them they fell down.[1]

It might be wiser, then, to accept Caesar's description of the aurochs,
although superficially far more credible, with a cautionary pinch of
salt. It runs as follows:

There is a third kind of these animals which are called uri. In size these
are but little inferior to elephants, although in appearance, colour, and form
they are bulls. Their strength and their speed are great. They spare neither
men nor beast when they see them. In the expanse of their horns, as well as
in form and appearance, they differ much from our oxen.[2]

The uri or aurochs that Caesar described were those inhabiting the
vast Hercynian forest which at that time – 65 BC – covered most of
Germany and included the Black Forest.

Pliny the elder, who was a professed naturalist of classical times
mentions the aurochs in his writings some hundred years later (AD 77).
A century had not sufficed to eliminate palpable fable from possible
fact. He described, for example a creature called the bonasus, which
had, at least according to Pliny

the mane of a horse, but is, in other respects, like the bull, with horns,
however, so much bent inwards upon each other as to be of no use for the
purposes of combat. It has, therefore, to depend upon its flight, and, while
in the act of flying, it sends forth its excrements, sometimes to a distance of
even three jugera [104 Roman feet], the contact of which burns those who
pursue the animal, just like a kind of fire.

Pliny also refers to the urus in more credible terms as being 'possessed of remarkable strength and swiftness'.[3]

The naturalist Lydekker, in his book *The Ox and its Kindred*, collected and analysed all the available information on the aurochs. It is
of interest to learn that the Emperor Charlemagne in the ninth
century hunted it in the forests near Aix-la-Chapelle.

In ancient Egypt the hunting of wild bulls in the Nile valley swamps
was also a sport of kings:

The most famous scene of wild-bull hunting is that carved on the mortuary
temple of Rameses III at Medinet Habu. Here the Pharoah is shown hunting
in reed marshes; he is standing in a chariot drawn by two galloping horses
and shooting with bow and arrow. One bull is shown transfixed with arrows,
lying on its back dying, and another is brought to its knees wounded, while a

Opposite: the extinct
aurochs, presumed
progenitor of domestic cattle,
portrayed on the cave walls
of Lascaux, France. *Above,* a
bull; *below,* a cow.
(*Barnaby's Picture Library*)

third lies on its back dead. These animals appear to have been genuine wild aurochsen.[4]

The aurochs apparently became extinct in western Europe some time about the year 1400 but survived in Poland until a much later date, lingering on until 1627 when the last cow died. During the course of its extinction, however, it left a trail of skeletal remains behind it:

From skulls and bones that have been discovered, it is apparent that the aurochs formerly occurred on the Continent in Denmark, Scandinavia, France, Switzerland, Austria, Italy and Russia. When the aurochs disappeared from Britain is not known. A considerable number of prehistoric skulls and other remains have been dug up from time to time in various parts of England and Scotland, but not in Ireland. Sixteen skulls were discovered during the excavation of a dock near Preston between 1884 and 1892, while a fine articulated skeleton was found in Burwell Fen, Cambridge. A skull, measuring a yard in length and with the points of the horn cores three and a half feet apart, was discovered near Blair Atholl in Perthshire – and other bones have been found throughout the length of Scotland from Caithness to Wigtownshire . . .[5]

From its skeletal remains it is evident that the aurochs was a sufficiently large brute to strike fear and admiration if ever encountered. Its height was between 16 and 18 hands – 6 feet tall – and built in proportion, huge indeed, although hardly up to Caesar's elephantine standards.

What did these extinct wild cattle most resemble? According to F. E. Zeuner[6] 'The external appearance of wild cattle is well known' – possibly a slight exaggeration. The animal has long been extinct and it is difficult to reconstruct a reliable portrait from old bones and classical speculations. It is true that a British zoologist called Hamilton Smith came by chance upon a picture of an aurochs in an Augsburg shop early in the nineteenth century. The original was lost but a reproduction, credible enough, survives. According to Zeuner[7] 'The colour of the hair coat of the bull was black with a white stripe along the back and white curly hair between the horns; the muzzle was white or greyish. The summer coat was more sleek, especially in the southern races, whilst the winter coat was thick and somewhat curly.' Possibly both coat colour and horn formation varied fairly widely as they still do in all domesticated breeds of cattle. Certainly that would seem to be the case in the cave wall drawings at Lascaux. Such variability also occurred in the not too remotely related American bison. M. S. Garretson[8] described colour variation in this wild species, never in any way influenced by human selection. The prairie bison or buffalo, as everyone knows, was generally brown. Yet, pied individuals, light-grey, creamy, white with dark head, did occur, exceptionally, and

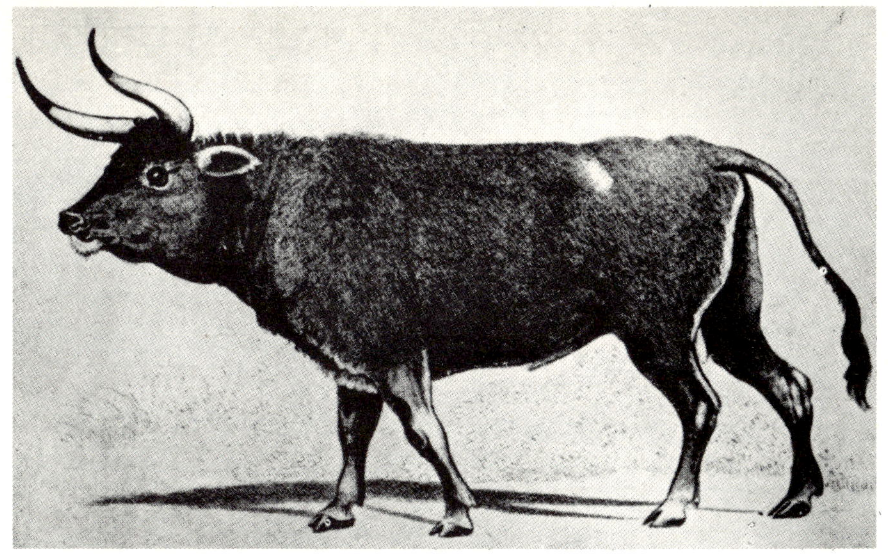

Reproduction from a painting of an aurochs discovered in an Augsburg antique shop in the early nineteenth century.

in the earliest known paintings of the aurochs in the caves of Lascaux the hide markings also appear to be variable. In cattle, it is, in fact, as unjustifiable to speculate on the basis of hide coloration as it is on horn formation. Nobody can be certain as to what the wild aurochs actually looked like.

In an effort to solve the problem and, indeed, to bring this extinct species back to life, two German zoologists, Lutz and Heinz Heck conceived a new approach, based on genetics. By breeding methods they aimed to 'reconstitute' the aurochs. Their experiments were founded on the assumption of genetical science that while a wild species may die out, its genes which control heredity must persist in its domesticated descendants. Consequently, if these surviving genes could be suitably combined by cross-breeding of domesticated breeds, the wild species would, as it were, be reborn. It has long been known that in rabbits, for example, if two fancy breeds with unusual fur coloration are cross-bred, the original fur colour of the wild rabbit reappears in their offspring. On the same principle, the Heck brothers went to work in the zoological gardens of Berlin and Munich, to reconstruct the aurochs. They claimed to have succeeded in doing so within a relatively short time. Something fairly wild and primitive certainly emerged but since no genuine aurochs survives with which a fair comparison can be made, the case differs substantially from that of the rabbits. One is inclined to agree with G. K. Whitehead[9] who commented, 'One wonders, however, if the experiments carried out by Professor Heck in breeding back the aurochs have really proved his point.'

Although the precise shape, form, size, coat coloration and horn curvature of the extinct aurochs may be speculative there can be no

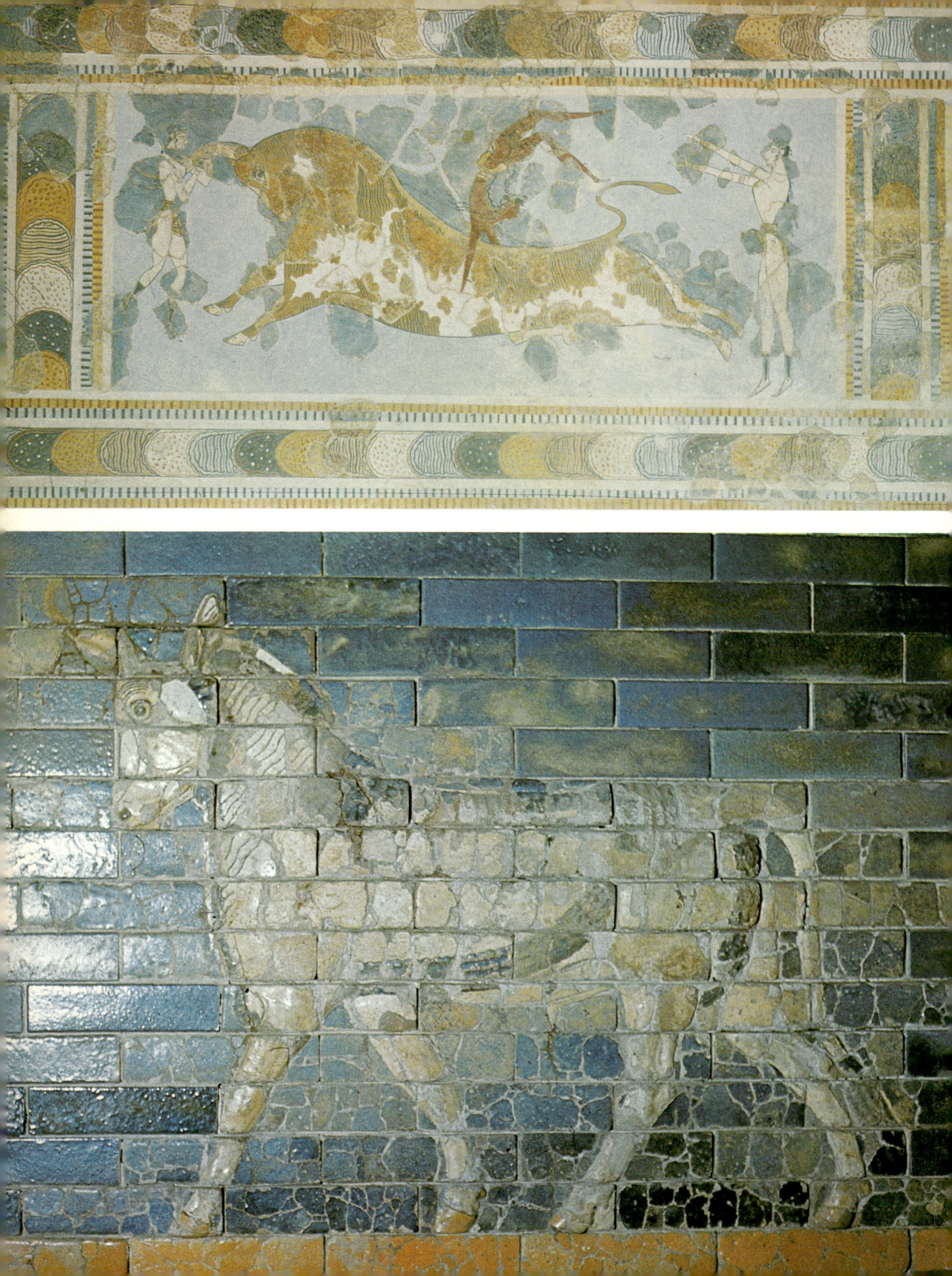

other White Park cattle they should not be confused with albinos: indeed the muzzle, hoofs and horn tips are black, the ears black or red. Moreover, in contrast to most other cattle breeds in which, in Mendelian terms, white is recessive and likely to be hidden when crossed with black or red, white is dominant in White Park cattle. The White cattle herd in Chillingham Park is available to the public for inspection at a safe distance. It is improbable that many members of the public desire closer acquaintance. I have seen these cattle for myself – at a safe distance – and, to be entirely honest, I was not greatly impressed. The herd looked peaceful enough grazing in the afternoon sunshine and one old cow approached the party in a leisurely and almost confiding manner as though in hopes that some kind person might offer her food. Whitehead noted a resemblance to Ayrshire cattle, the domesticated milking breed native to this country and my impression was the same. I happened to be in the company of Andrew Biggar, the well-known agriculturist broadcaster, and he confided to me that these reputedly wild cattle made him feel a humble man.

Opposite, above: Bull-leaping fresco from the Palace of Knossos, Crete. (*Ronald Sheridan*)

Opposite, below: Mural of a bull from the Ishtar Gate, Babylon. (*Peter Clayton*)

Below: Ancient White cattle of Chartley Park, Staffordshire. In 1905 the Chartley herd was transferred to Woburn Park, Bedfordshire, where they were crossed with Longhorn cattle, the descendants of which still remain there. (*Mansell Collection*)

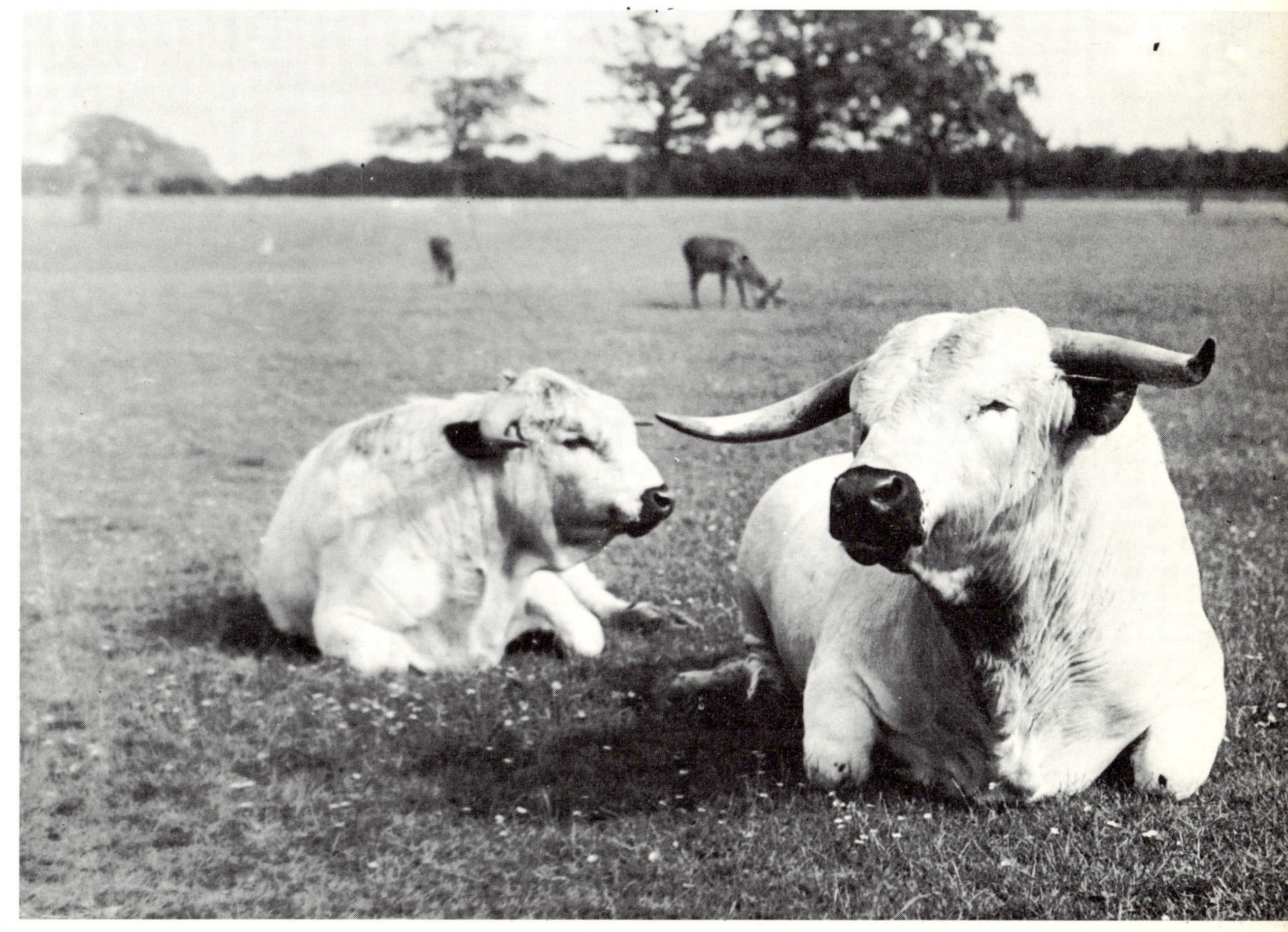

Being a breeder of Ayrshire cattle himself he failed to see very much improvement in their conformation in comparison with the Wild White cattle of seven centuries of unselected breeding!

Although, in appearance, the Wild White cattle of Chillingham Park may be more suggestive of modern dairy cattle than of aboriginal aurochs, there are certain aspects in their husbandry that are of peculiar interest. Whereas among domesticated cattle breeding is controlled by separating the bull from the cows except at artificially defined breeding seasons, at Chillingham both sexes run together all the year round just as they were born. Since the sexes, male and female, arrive in equal numbers, there are likely to be just as many bulls as cows within the herd. Since cattle are polygamous, the strongest bull, called the king bull appropriates the entire cow harem to himself, leaving the other bulls in enforced frustration. Doubtless, as wherever polygamy occurs, the excluded bulls find alternative recreation among themselves and may even, in the darker evenings, appropriate a straying cow. Yet, in general and in daylight the king bull reigns supreme. At intervals one or other of the younger bulls will challenge his supremacy. A fight occurs, more akin to a heavy-weight boxing championship than a duel to the death, for once one bull has established his superiority the conflict ends. The old king bull is not dead, but the new king bull reigns.

Associated with this system of mating – genuinely a thing of the wild – calves may be born at all seasons of the year, since there is no natural rutting season in cattle as there is in deer. The cows hide their calves among the bracken just as their wild ancestors would certainly have done, and they can be genuinely dangerous at such times. Certainly, in their organisation and probably in their ancestry as well, the Chillingham herd has, of any cattle existent today, the best title to be called Wild White cattle.

Yet there are several other herds of the same type in this country, all white with distinctive black markings, all enclosed in the parks of great manors, none maintained for purposes other than historical interest, aristocratic pride, sentiment or show. Evidently a survival of a distant past, but a survival of what? There are almost as many theories as there are herds.

Direct descent from the extinct aurochs is, of all, the least probable. Neither in size nor in dominant coloration do they seem to resemble them. Feral herds of a breed once domesticated are perhaps more likely. Some say the breed was introduced to Britain by the Romans since there are many domesticated white cattle of similar type in Italy to this day. Yet another theory is that they were a special breed reserved for Druidic sacrifice in ancient Britain. Unfortunately, there is even less reliable information about the Druids than there is about Wild White cattle. From the little information available, chiefly from Latin

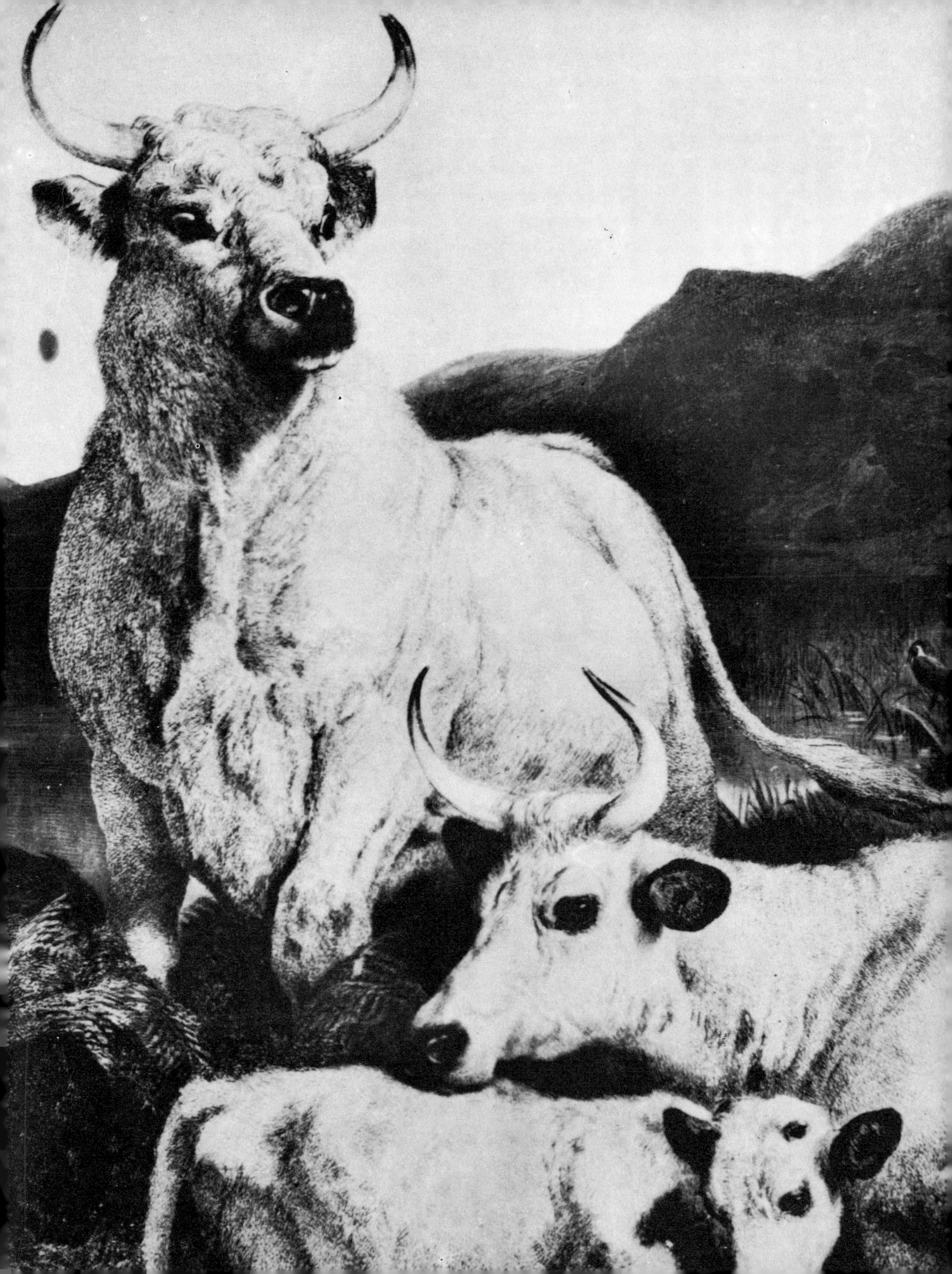

scripts, it seems that the Druids rather specialised in human sacrifice. One unpleasant Druidic ceremony, according to Roman writers, was to stuff a hollow tree trunk, presumably an oak, with sacrificial victims and then set the whole thing alight, rather as the worshippers of Baal slid unwanted babes off inclined metal plates into a fiery furnace while their parents piped on high-pitched wind instruments to drown their cries. On the whole, sacrifice is inclined to be a disagreeable custom.

Possibly, the Druids, when human victims were hard to come by, used bulls instead and, indeed, there is written evidence to that effect. The Romans, to their credit, did all they could to suppress human sacrifice. As Pliny wrote, 'Therefore we cannot too highly appreciate our debt to the Romans for having put an end to this monstrous cult whereby to murder a man was an act of the greatest devoutness, and to eat his flesh most beneficial.'[11]

Pliny, in another passage from his copious writings describes one such Druidic sacrifice, in which bulls replaced men as sacrificial victims:

Having made preparation for sacrifice and a banquet beneath the trees, they bring thither two white bulls, whose horns are bound then for the first

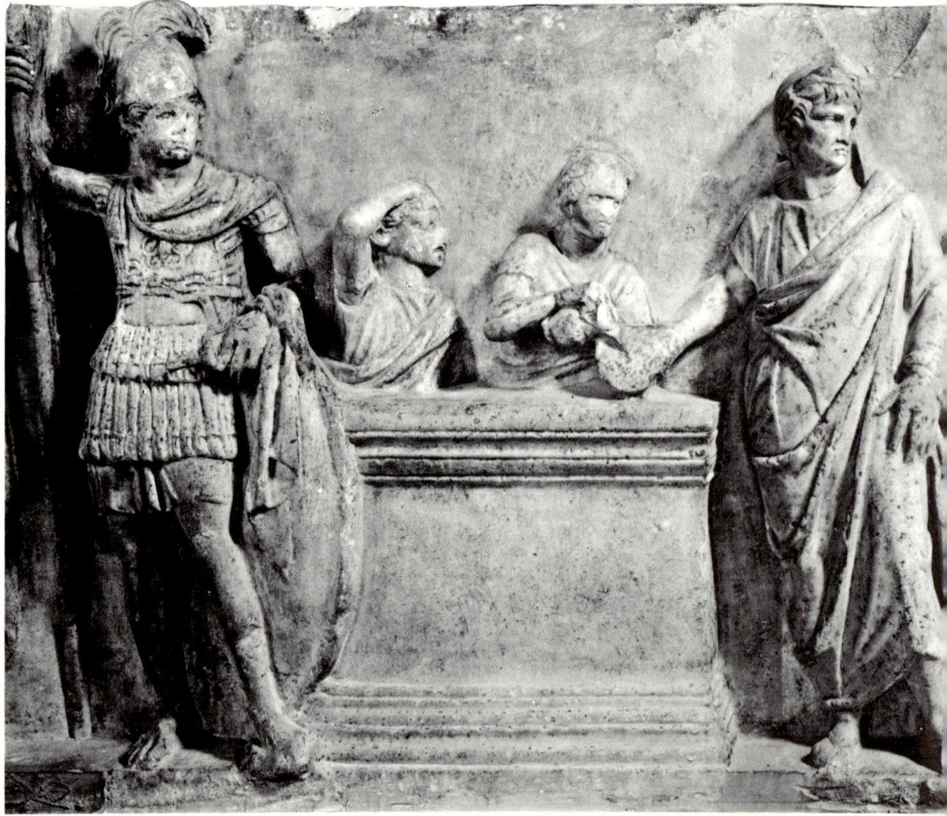

Relief of a classical bull sacrifice from the walls of the Villa Medici, Rome. (*Mansell Collection*)

time. Clad in a white robe, the priest ascends the tree and cuts the mistletoe with a golden sickle, and it is received by others in a white cloak. They then kill the victims, praying that God will render this gift of his propitious to those to whom he has granted it.[12]

As will become evident in succeeding chapters there was clearly something deemed peculiarly holy in a white bull, and that from the earliest times. The bull that Mithra sacrificed for the redemption of mankind was a white bull. The bull with which the Cretan queen Pasiphaë became hopelessly enamoured was a white bull. The Druids, it seems, preferred to sacrifice a white bull. It is not inconceivable, therefore, that the 'Ancient White Cattle of Britain and their Descendants' are the remnant of an old breed reserved specifically for pagan sacrificial rites.

Since the whiteness of these cattle is dominant in breeding they could be expected to breed true to type in this important respect, to have a sacrificial utility and even to have attained a degree of religious respect. Lewis Spence made this suggestion in his book *The History and Origins of Druidism*[13], and Whitehead, who gave more critical consideration to the problem than anyone had given before or is ever likely to do again, apparently came to the same conclusion.

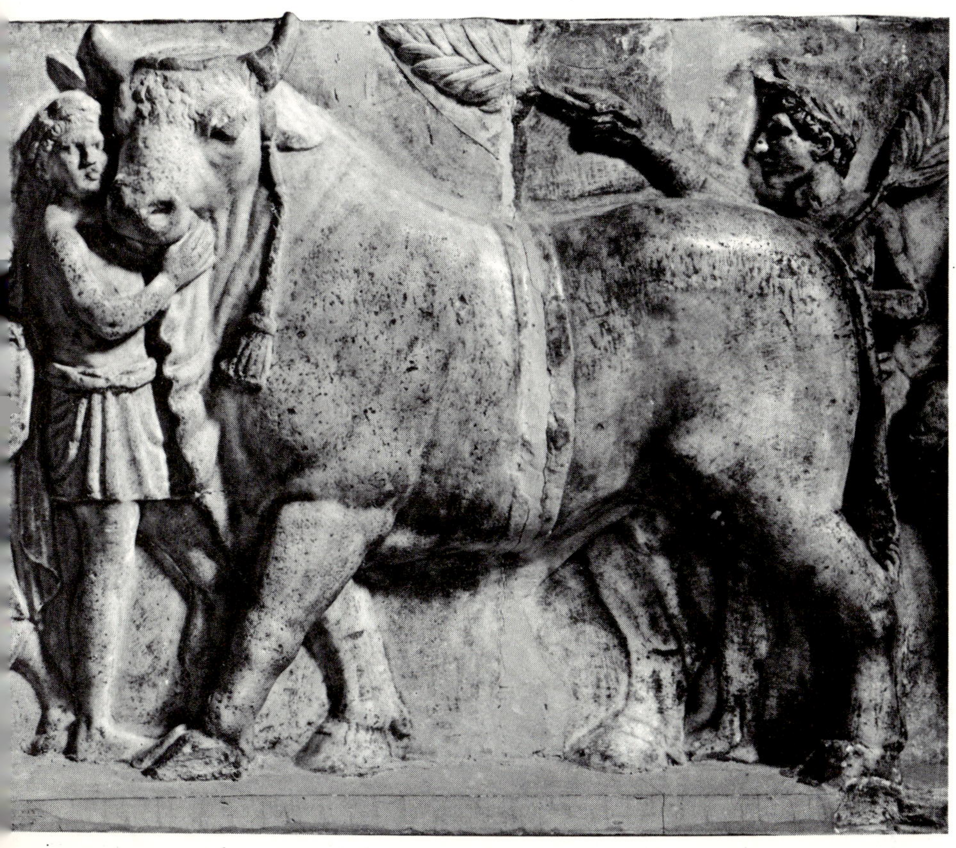

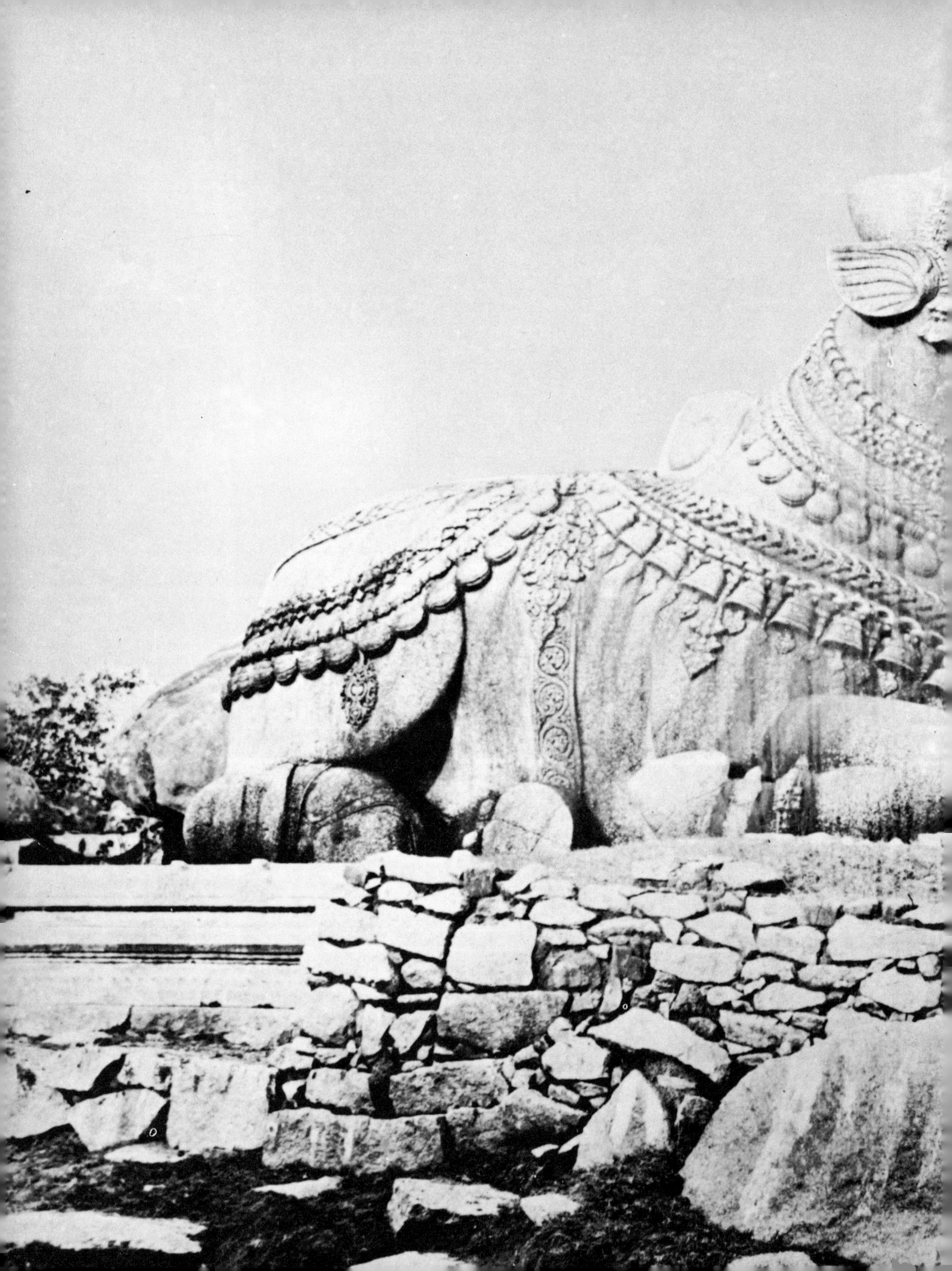

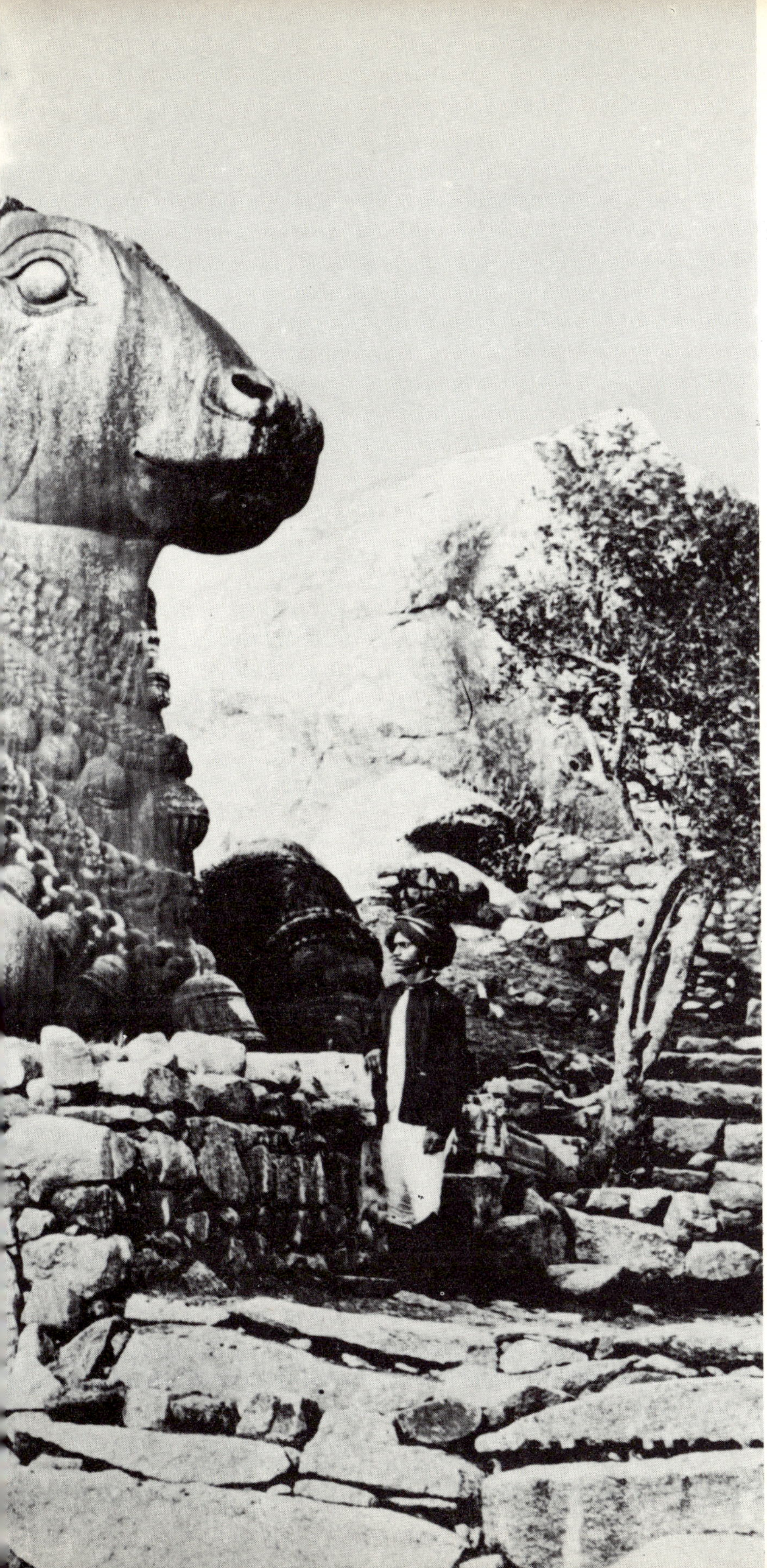

2
The Bull
in
Mythology

Statue of a sacred bull, Mysore, India. (*Radio Times Hulton Picture Library*)

§ Throughout the mythologies of Asiatic and European peoples, the cult of the Bull keeps recurring, like the theme of a symphony or the refrain of a song.

As in so much of the mystic of religion and legend, it began in the deserts and lonely places of the East, spreading westwards over Asia Minor and over Europe like succeeding waves of an advancing tide. Some say that the cult originated with the Aryans who were a cattle-raising people and daily witnesses of the bull's majesty as protector and progenitor of the herd since 'To a pastoral people a bull is the most natural type of vigorous reproductive energy.'[1]

The prominence of the bull in mythology is perhaps more easily understood today because of the current questioning of Christian values and the evident revival of those inherent in most pagan faiths. Christianity is associated in men's minds with peace, humility and chastity; with the shepherd's crook and the innocent lamb. If the present age is – as is so often proclaimed – one characterised by violence and sex, then it is no longer a Christian age. It has come closer to those faiths and ages in which aggression, power, courage and sexual vigour – the admired qualities of the warrior rather than those of the saint – were most revered. It was in such creeds that the bull, as a symbol of power, fertility and aggressive courage, became equated with divinities and confused with kings. 'Power, irresistibility, brute force, these were the bull qualities that held the greatest appeal for the people who thought of their king as a god.'[2]

Naturally, it was only in those countries where bulls were found, either wild or domesticated, that the bull could become involved in the mythology of a people. As Robert Graves wrote in his introduction to the *Larousse Encyclopedia of Mythology*,[3] 'One constant rule of mythology is that whatever happens among the gods above reflects events on earth.' It follows that unless an object or event occurs on earth it cannot be reflected among the gods above. Only within the terrestrial distribution of cattle, especially of that particular species of cattle, the aurochs and its domesticated derivatives, could mankind include the bull among his pantheon. Since the distribution of cattle was wide, so also was the bull cult extensive: from India, through Persia, Mesopotamia, Egypt, the Levant, Greece and Rome to the Spanish bullfight of the present day. It has contributed little or nothing to the mythologies of those continents devoid of cattle before their introduction by European colonists – the Americas and Australasia. Nor has it an important part in the mythologies of the Far East or Oceania. Where cattle were indigenous, however, the bull became an object of worship as a god or the symbol of gods, as a king or a symbol of kings, as an emblem of fertility, as a victim for sacrifice. Finally, in certain developments of the cult the actual or symbolic eating of the flesh of the bull and the drinking of its blood were believed to confer the bull's properties upon those partaking of this strange sacrament.

Both gods and kings – and in many instances the two were united in the king-god – were frequently compared to the bull as being the primal source of power and reproduction:

... Parjanya, the old Indian god of thunder and rain ... was conceived as a deity of fertility, who not only made plants to germinate, but caused cows, mares, and women to conceive. As the power who impregnated all things, he was compared to a bull, an animal which to the primitive herdsman is the most natural type of the procreative energies. In a hymn of the Rigveda, it is said of him –

The Bull, loud roaring, swift to send his bounty, lays in the plant the seed for germination.

He smites the trees apart, he slays the demon; all life fears him who yields the mighty weapon.

From him the exceeding strong flees, e'en the guiltless when thundering Parjanya smites the wicked.

And again in Hymn 101:

May this my song to sovran lord Parjanya come near unto his heart and give him pleasure.

May we obtain the showers that bring enjoyment, and god-protected plants with goodly fruitage.

He is the Bull of all and their impregner: he holds the life of all things fixed and moving.[4]

The emblems of the chief Hittite deity were the thunderbolt and the bull. So also were they the signs of divine power of the Assyrian god, Adad.

The name Hittite is sufficiently familiar to those still conversant with the Hebrew scriptures. Yet in the Old Testament it is little more than a name. Only within more recent times has the importance of the Hittite Empire been revealed. Archaeology, rather than written history, is the main source of modern knowledge. An ancient civilisation has, as it were, been dug out of its grave. Its home was in Asia Minor, now called Turkey, and in particular in that vast elevated central plateau called Cappadocia, bordering Syria and Mesopotamia – a bleak, inhospitable, volcanic region, with harsh climate and infertile soil, primarily pastoral, the home of a hardy and aggressive people, a people that worshipped the bull. The capital city was called Bogazköy, near the Black Sea and the chief evidence of bull worship comes from excavations at the palace of Euyuk in north-western Cappadocia.

On one of the reliefs at the palace of Euyuk we see the priest with his characteristic dress and staff followed by a priestess, each of them with a hand raised as in adoration; they are approaching the image of a bull which stands on a high pedestal with an altar before it.[5]

In ancient civilisations there are many evidences of the bull cult but frequently, as in ancient Egypt, the bull appears among a multitude of other animals accorded religious significance. But 'the Hittites never bestowed divinity upon any other animal but the bull'.[6]

It is of importance, perhaps, that Asia Minor, like Crete, is a volcanic region. The rumble of the earthquake has often been likened to the distant bellow of an angry bull. It was a common superstition in volcanic areas that the shaking of the earth's surface was due to a monstrous bull that held the world between his horns, tossing it from side to side when moved to anger. With the wild aurochs still threatening the lone hunter on the surface of the earth; with an enraged bull causing death and destruction to mankind from the earth beneath, little wonder, perhaps, that the Hittites sacrificed rams before the image of a bull above the earth. For the whole basis of sacrifice is the propitiation of a god given to vengeful passion, and where the fear was great so also was the sacrifice bountiful.

On the island of Crete, with its strange pictures of bull-sports and legends of the Minotaur, half-bull, half-man, 'the bull was at once the king's crest and an emblem of the sun'.[7]

In ancient Egypt, it was believed that the bull might be the abode of a dead king's soul. 'An unusually fine head of cattle is also recognised as the abode of the great king's soul; for example he once appeared in the shape of a white bull, whereupon the living king commanded special sacrifices to be offered in honour of his deified predecessor.'[8]

In ancient Egypt, animals of all shapes and sizes were idolised. Herodotus wrote that the Egyptians were the most religious of men and their devotion to animals both alive and dead was such that animal worship formed an important part of that religion. Animals deemed sacred included the bulk of the Nile valley fauna. There were sacred rams, dogs, falcons, frogs, jackals, hippopotami, crocodiles, cats and ibis. It was a capital offence to kill a cat. There was a special cemetery for cats, so well patronised that in modern times it was deemed economic to excavate it and use the feline dust as a source of manure. Yet, above all these varied species the sacred bull was supreme. The most famous of these sacred bulls was one called Apis, said to be a reincarnation of the god named Ptah. According to Egyptian theology, Ptah, assuming the disguise of a celestial fire, inseminated a virgin heifer and from this union there resulted a black bull calf with certain mystical markings which was Ptah reincarnated and returned to earth. The priesthood, and it only, claimed to be able to interpret and recognise the mystical markings which distinguished Ptah in bovine form from all other black bull calves. The sacred bull Apis was kept in a temple at Memphis opposite the temple of Ptah. Honoured throughout Egypt and under regal patronage and care, Apis was a centre of attraction to devout pilgrims. At a fixed hour each day he was watered and fed in a court-

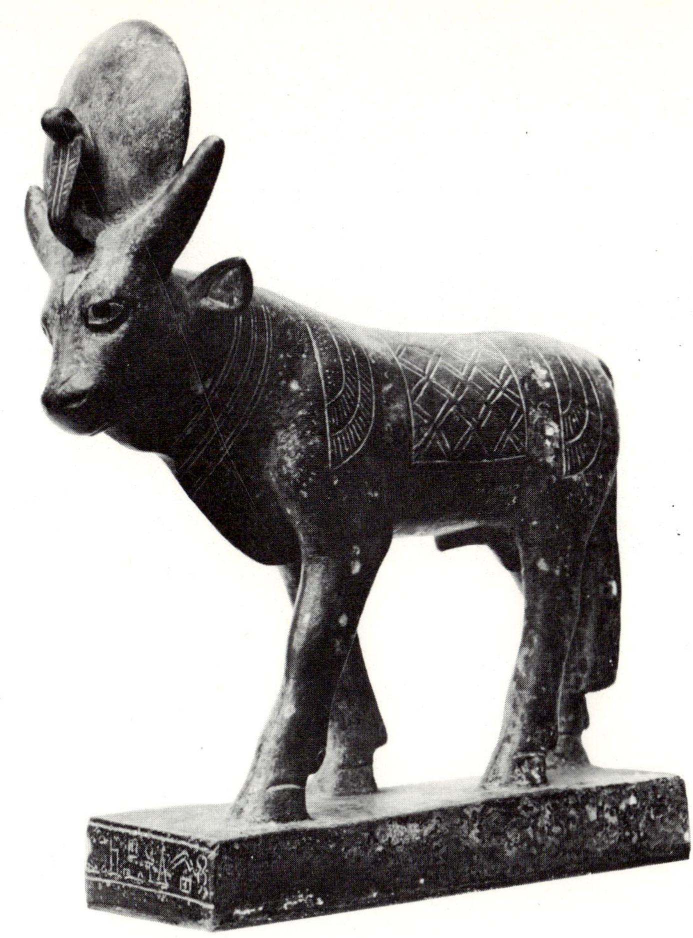

Apis – bronze statuette. In ancient Egypt the most famous of the sacred bulls was one called Apis, said to be a reincarnation of the god named Ptah. (*British Museum*)

yard attached to his temple while the devout watched and wondered. Apis, in keeping with his divine origin, received every care and comfort his worshippers could provide. When he died of old age he was mummified and laid in a sarcophagus. According to the priests he died only to be born again and after diligent search for a black bull calf with the appropriate mystical markings, one was always conveniently discovered.

Although Apis was the chief and most sacred bull in Egyptian mythology, there were others. There was, for example, the bull Buchis, whose hide was said to change colour every hour. These sacred bulls, supposedly notable for their wisdom and prophetic gifts, living in regal luxury, even provided conveniently with a harem of concubine cows, mummified with ceremony, buried with expensive dignity, were very far remote from the wild aurochs once upon a time hunted and slain by the arrows of the Pharoahs amid the reedy swamps beside the Nile. While there may have been at one time a symbolic relationship between the irresistible power and sexual vigour of the wild bull and the qualities sought for and admired in human rulers, it would seem that in ancient Egypt both bulls and kings tended to grow soft together.

The mythologies of Assyria and Phoenicia had many similarities and relationships to those of ancient Egypt.

As in many other Asiatic religions or mythologies the bull, from earliest times, had become the symbol of strength and creative energy and, as such, incorporated in ancient conceptions both of gods and kings. So also was it in the Aegean when mythology emerged from the even more primitive worship of stones, pillars, animals and trees. The ancient Mediterranean civilisation known as Minoan and centred in Crete, preceded that of Greece, and much of the elaborate mythology of classical times, both Greek and Roman, was based upon and influenced by that of Crete.

'Crete was indeed a land dedicated to the worship of the bull.'[9] There is ample evidence from Sir Arthur Evans's archaeological researches in the ancient Cretan palace of Knossos to support that claim, although its precise interpretation may differ according to the opinions of various experts. That there was bull sacrifice and bull worship is admitted by all, although the details of ceremonial and the significance of rites, particularly the spectacular bull-leaping acrobatics from the mural paintings of the palace of Knossos, must remain hypothetical. It has been maintained that the horn grappling by the acrobats had a fertility-rite significance since ancient peoples imagined that the fertilising power of a bull was concentrated in its horns. Others prefer to regard the spectacle as acrobatic feats performed by trained acrobats and trained bulls with the sporting element paramount and the religious significance of secondary import. Particularly is there a division of opinion as to the nature of the bulls. Were they wild bulls? Were they aurochs? Were they domesticated and tamed? In support of the contention that the bulls were wild bulls, the various artistic representations of the bulls being captured by the allurement of cows in heat, by nets or by ropes are cited as evidence. Yet, nobody has ever suggested that the ranch cattle of the North American prairies or of the South American pampas were wild cattle although without lasso or bolas they could hardly have been captured and controlled. Nor do the mural paintings of piebald and skewbald bulls suggest that they were aurochs which, so far as can be gleaned from other evidence, were of very different appearance and predominant colour scheme. Again, since it is known that the Irish Sea formed a sufficient water barrier to the aurochs's westward distribution, it seems highly improbable that the wild aurochs ever reached Crete, a theory also subscribed to by F. E. Zeuner.[10]

It seems altogether probable that the Cretan bulls were of a domesticated variety, possibly of a breed specially maintained for ceremonial purposes, as are the fighting bulls of Spain and Mexico today. Whether

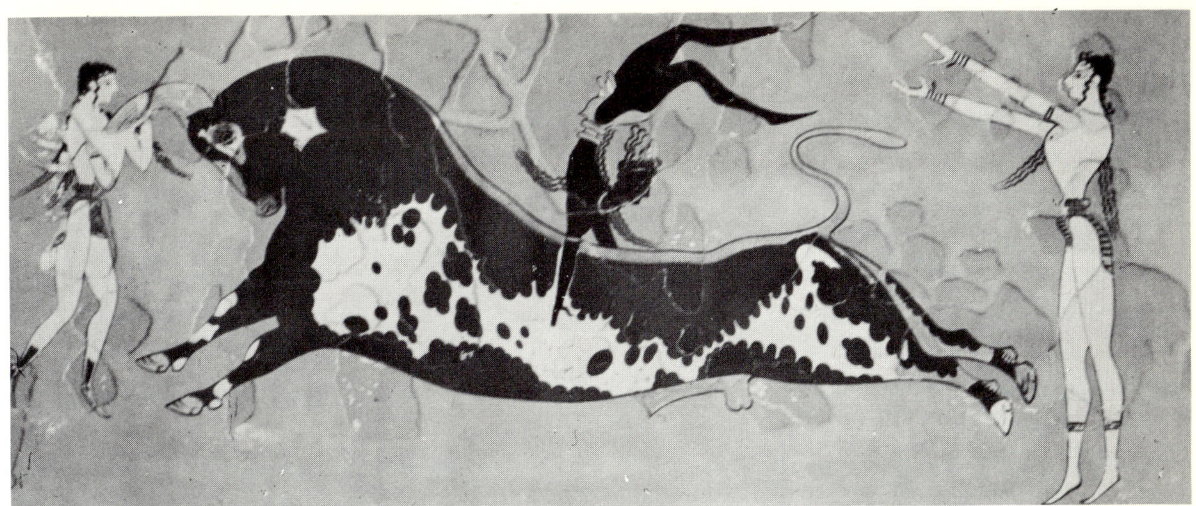

Bull-leaping fresco reconstructed from the walls of the palace of Knossos, Crete. (*Barnaby's Picture Library*)

they were more or less ferocious must remain a matter for speculation. It is true that on a Cretan rhyton or libation cup there is a vivid representation of an acrobatic performer who, having lost his grip, is shown impaled upon a bull's left horn. The whole attitude of the bull suggests that this was no accident but was done by intention. On the other hand, to quote Zeuner, '. . . steer-throwing experts maintain that the feats performed by the acrobats seizing the bull by the horns were possible only with beasts specially bred or trained'.[11] Might it not even be that the Cretan murals represent an ideal perfection that was never achieved? It is sometimes salutary to reflect that so much of the evidence accepted by archaeologists would hardly satisfy a court of law.

In any case, whatever the interpretation of detailed evidence may be, it is incontestable fact that the bull cult reached notable development in Crete; that this Minoan cult had an important influence on the mythology and legends of classical Greece, through Greece to Rome, and through Rome to western Europe. From whence did the bull cult reach Crete? According to Zeuner,[12] it is probable that it originated in western Asia, and this is made more likely by the fact that, without doubt, that is where the bull cult began. In any event, since the Minoan culture preceded that of Greece and since Crete and Greece were so closely linked both by geography and trade, it is not surprising that so many of the bull legends of Crete became interwoven in Greek mythology.

The supreme god of Greek mythology and ruler of Olympus was called Zeus, who became the Jupiter of the Romans. His chief attributes were irresistible power and uninhibited sexuality. In his lusts he frequently outran permission. What he failed to achieve by persuasion or deceit he secured by force. Usually he attempted persuasion

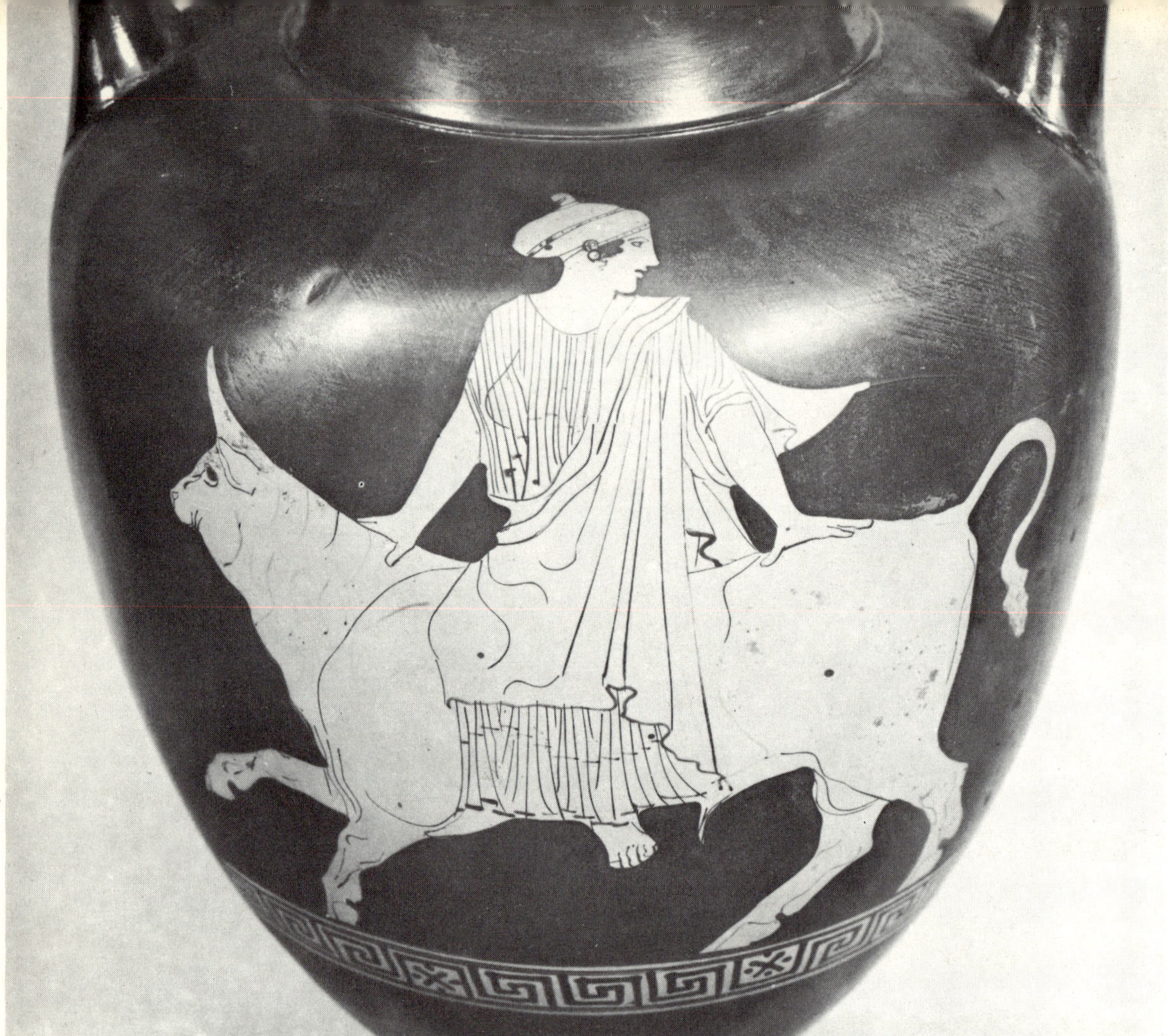

The rape of Europa. Zeus, disguised as a bull, swam across the open seas to Crete carrying the terrified virgin with him on his back. There, in Crete, Europa was raped by Zeus. From a Greek amphora. (*British Museum*)

first and in doing so had the divine advantage of being able to assume a variety of disguises. During the course of his manifold seductions he appeared to the objects of his passion as a dove, a cuckoo, an eagle, a swan, a flame, a satyr, a cloud, a horse or a shower of gold. He also, on several occasions took the form of a bull and it is notable that that was his favoured disguise when intent on rape. For example, Zeus became enamoured of the goddess Demeter. She would have none of him so that, to achieve his desires, he changed himself into a bull and then violated her. From this union was born the goddess Persephone who dwelt in Hades.

Again Zeus became a bull in the somewhat hackneyed myth of the rape of Europa. It may be recalled that this innocent maiden, daughter of the King of Phoenicia, was out with her companions gathering flowers on a sun-kissed meadow by the sea. She noticed a strange yet beautiful bull among her father's herd and approaching him trustingly climbed upon his back and proceeded to wreathe fresh flowers about his horns. Of a sudden the bull reared to his feet, leapt into the waves

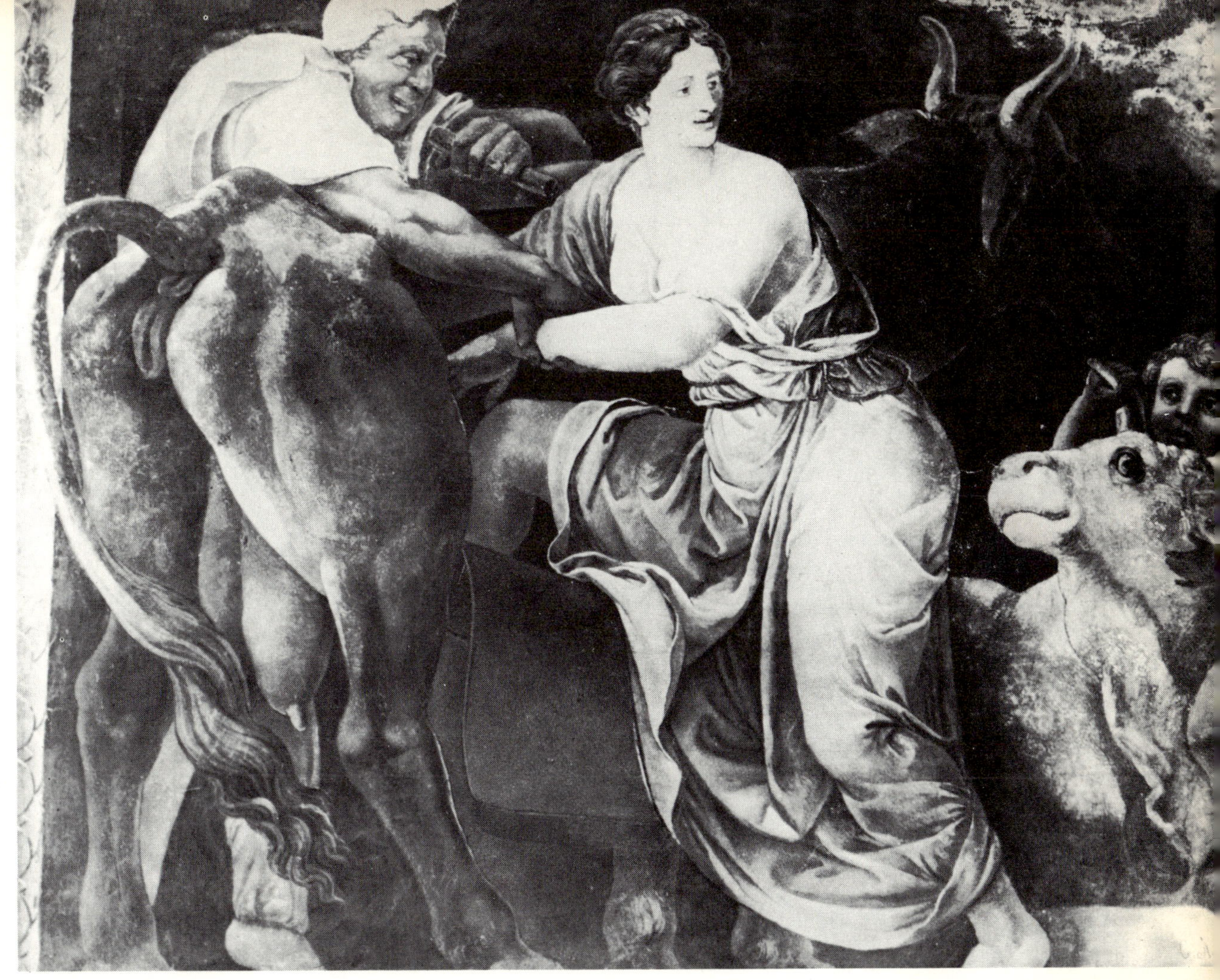

and swam across the open seas to Crete carrying the terrified and protesting virgin with him on his back. There in Crete, Europa was raped by Zeus, although whether still disguised as a bull or in some other form the legend does not relate. In any event as a result of this violation Europa gave birth to Minos who became king of Crete.

Perhaps because of the circumstances of his conception, Minos himself became, as it were, somewhat bull-haunted. His queen was called Pasiphaë. She had borne him several normal children when in revenge for some slight connected with a sacrificed bull, the god Poseidon inspired Pasiphaë with somewhat the same monstrous passion for a bull that Titania had for the weaver Bottom. Her passion, however, was a trifle less poetical. She desired actual intercourse with the chosen bull and to that end commanded Daedalus, the master craftsman of Crete at that time, to fashion a dummy cow in which she hid herself, lying in wait to seduce the bull. This mythical exercise of technology in the service of bestiality succeeded. The infatuated Pasiphaë became pregnant to the bull. From this unnatural union

Paisphaë being disguised as a cow by Daedalus. From a painting by Giulio Romano. (*Radio Times Hulton Picture Library*)

33

was born the far-famed Minotaur, half-human and half-bull. Pasiphaë's husband Minos, tyrant of Crete, very naturally wished to get this revolting monster out of sight and to that end condemned it to life imprisonment in an underground labyrinth at Knossos, capital of Crete.

The Minotaur could survive only upon a diet of human flesh and this was provided by the annual tribute of seven Athenian youths and seven Athenian maidens, a tribute which came to a timely end when the hero Theseus met and slew the Minotaur in its labyrinthine maze, escaping by retracing the thread he had unwound behind him.

The hero, in Grecian mythology, was a sort of intermediary between gods and men. The most famous hero was Heracles, the personification of physical strength and sexual vigour. The legends connected with his muscular prowess are too familiar to require repetition. Those connected with his manly prowess are perhaps less well known. Yet they were no less remarkable. Once, it was related, when only eighteen years of age, he was in pursuit of a ferocious lion. While awaiting the brute's appearance, Heracles took shelter in the palace of a king called Thespius who had fifty daughters. During the course of the night, the hero lay with each daughter in turn, yet arose next morning to slay the lion. Bodily strength and sexual vigour were heroic virtues to the Greeks as indeed to most pagan peoples. It was these same values possessed by the bull among the beast creation that led these pagan peoples to make bulls into heroes or even into gods. Because, throughout mythology, the bull is the symbol of violence and sex, of sex and violence.

These classical legends, these prizes of scholarship, these fruits of archaeological research, have long been familiar to all educated people. The question that most concerns us here is why in so many of them the bull had such a leading part to play. Surely the answer was given by Sir James Frazer in *The Golden Bough* when he wrote, 'To a pastoral people a bull is the most natural type of vigorous reproductive energy . . .'[13] and before the advent of mechanised industry, all peoples were primarily pastoral. That is why, presumably, the shepherd, the lamb, the crook figure so largely in Christian belief and why, in pagan creeds, the bull is supreme.

Now, the Celts were, and indeed, when left to themselves as they seldom are today, still are an especially pastoral people. They were also, throughout their history, a cattle-raising people, herdsmen rather than shepherds in their chosen calling. In Celtic mythology, therefore, as in classical mythology, the bull, although far less copiously documented, played a noble part:

Bull sacrifices were common among the Celts with whom the bull had been a divine animal.[14]

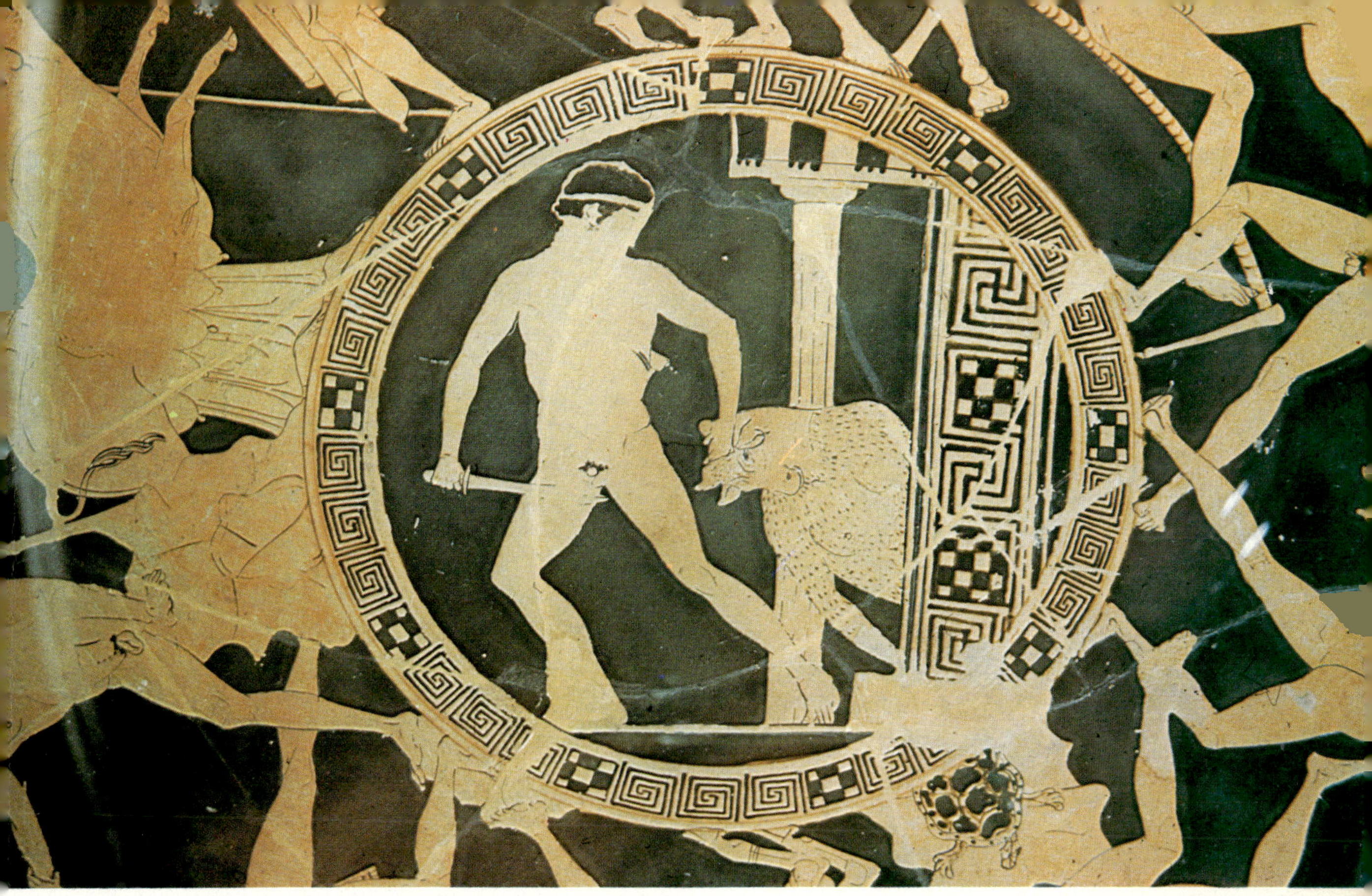

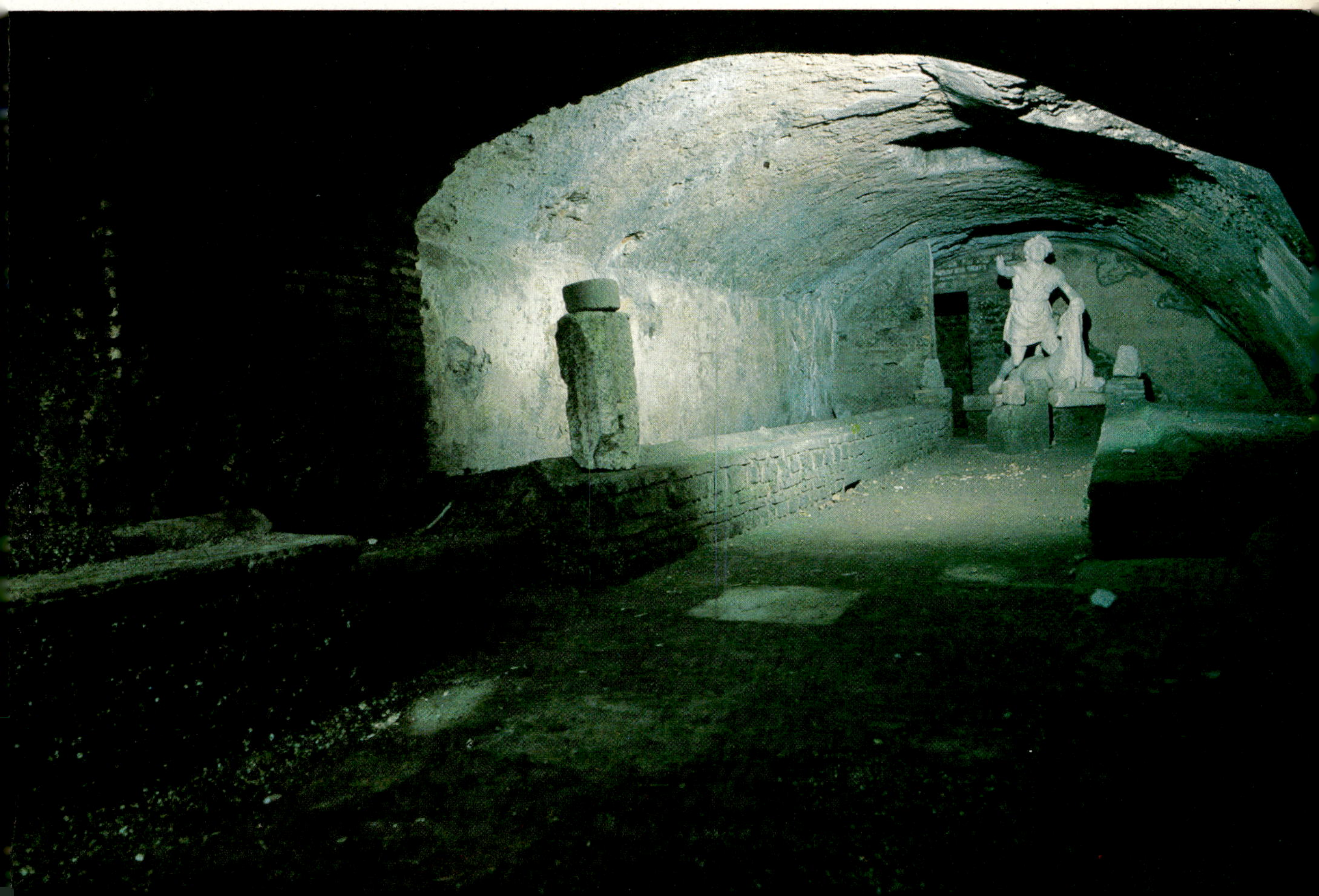

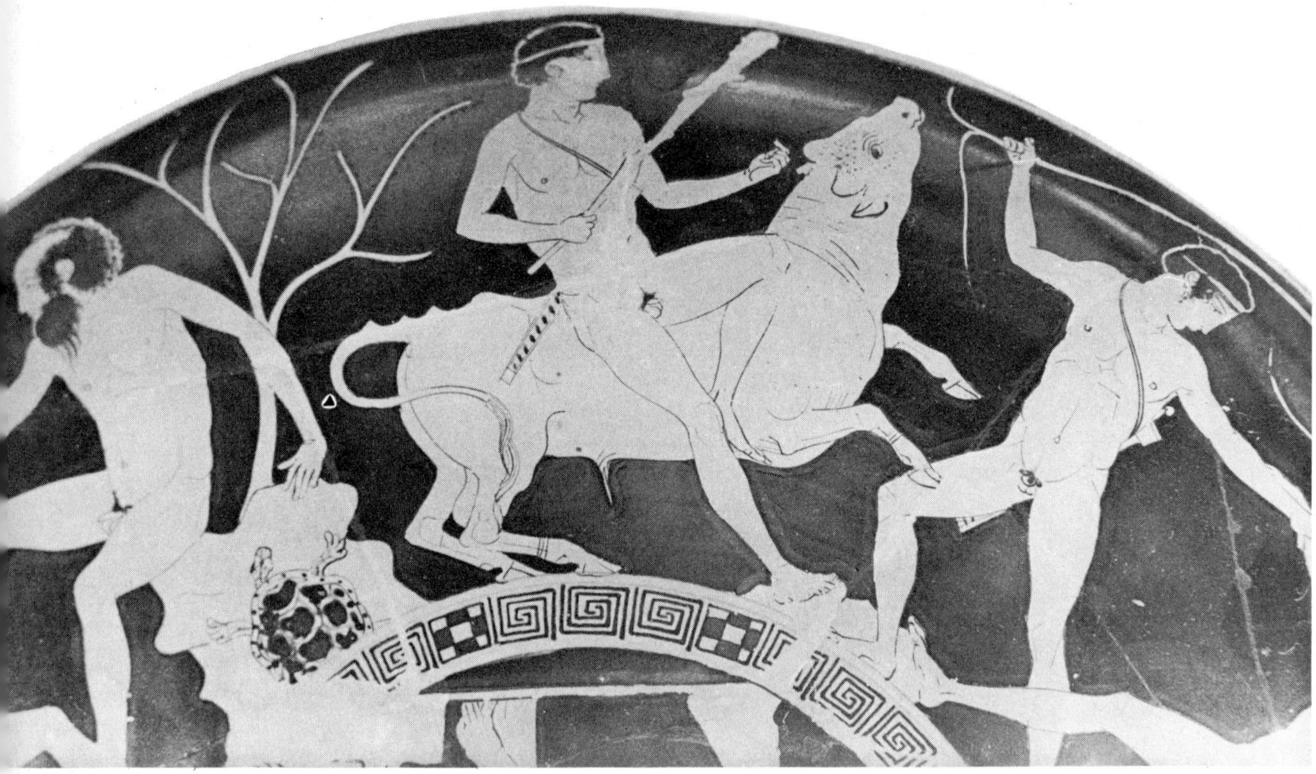

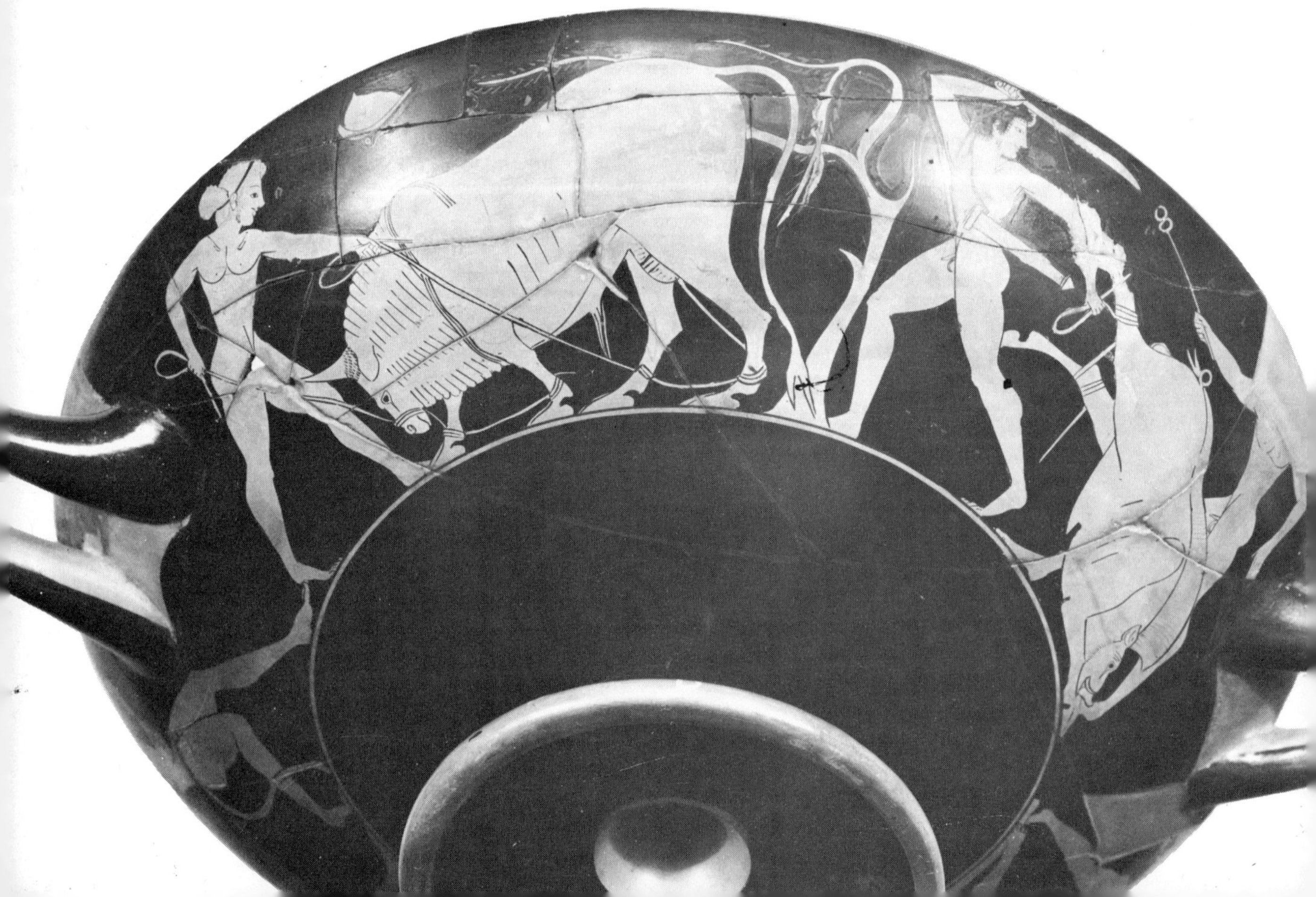

The strength and fighting courage of the bull, of the fighting bull of Spain or even more of the untamed aurochs, are so clearly evident that the pagan admiration for the bull's individual and physical prowess can be appreciated and easily understood. To accept the bull as a symbol of fertility is certainly more debatable. Cattle as a species are far from fertile since one calf to each cow in one year is its maximum production. Virility and masculinity are features of the bull that are prominent and easily observed. Yet it was also as an emblem of fertility, clearly defined, that the bull was thought of by herdsmen of pastoral tribes. The belief has some quaint and interesting survivals as in '. . . the old Hindoo rule that when a bride reached the house of her husband . . . women should seat the bride on a bull's hide. . . . Here the ceremony of seating the young wife on a bull's hide seems plainly intended to make her fruitful through the generative virtue of the bull.'[19]

Again,

. . . when the corn is thick and strong in one spot, they say in some parts of East Prussia, 'The Bull is lying in the corn'. When a harvester has over-strained himself, they say in the Grandenz district of West Prussia 'The Bull pushed him'; in Lothringen they say – 'He has the Bull.' The meaning of both expressions is that he has unwittingly lighted upon the divine corn-spirit, who has punished the profane intruder with lameness.[20]

At times, it would seem that the generative power of the bull persisting in its hide was deemed so potent that it could restore life, if not in this world, then in another. This would seem the most probable interpretation of certain funeral rites in ancient Egypt:

In one of the ceremonies of the 'Opening of the Mouth' the deceased was temporarily placed in a bull's skin . . . From this skin the deceased obtained further power, and his emergence from it was the visible symbol of resurrection.

In this solemn drama of death and resurrection – the celebrant . . . formally opened the eyes and mouth of the dead man by rubbing or pretending to rub them four times with the bleeding heart and thigh of a sacrificial bull . . .[21]

In all mythology and religion sacrifice of life, human or animal, is a recurrent rite. It is strange, and a problem perhaps best left to the theologian and anthropologist why, so frequently, an object of worship should also be a victim of sacrifice as was the fate of the bull. At times, worshipped as a god, at other times sacrificed to other gods, no animal was more frequently destroyed at the behest of priesthoods.

It is generally agreed that the sacrifice of animals is a substitute for that of people. The Druids, that particular priesthood, the subject of so much speculation based on a somewhat slender foundation of fact, were definitely given to human sacrifice of a particularly disagreeable nature. Forecasts of future events, for example, were made on the

Opposite: Contest of Theseus with the Marathon Bull. *Above:* like Heracles, the Greek hero Theseus fought and captured a wild bull. This bull had been devastating Attica. Theseus captured it near Marathon, brought it back to Athens and sacrificed it to Apollo Delphinios. *Below:* the method of capture. The bull's head is tied down to one forefoot; both fore and hind legs are hobbled. A cord is attached to the nose, hind feet, and scrotum, and Theseus draws this tight. (*British Museum*)

convulsions of the dying sacrificial victim. At least that is certain, since the Romans, who forbade the practice, took particular pains to suppress it during their conquest of Gaul. In all probability, the human sacrifice was deemed the most effective. Thus, for example, among the Awemba, a Bantu tribe of what used to be Northern Rhodesia:

> Among the Awemba, who form the aristocracy of the country, when a diviner announced that a drought was caused by the spirits of dead chiefs or kings buried at Mwarulc, a bull would be sent to be sacrificed to the souls of the deceased rulers; or, if the drought was severe, a human victim would be despatched, and the high priest would keep him caged in a stoutly woven fish-basket, until the preparations for the sacrifice were complete.[22]

When men were forbidden as a sacrifice, the bull had to suffice, and in ancient Greece bulls were sacrificed in numerous places on innumerable occasions. Sometimes the bull sacrifices had a certain classic dignity as in the solemn ceremonial at Plataea in memory of the men who died fighting for Greece:

> At Plataea down to the second century of our era might be seen the graves of the men who fell in the great battle against the Persians. Sacrifices were offered to them every year with great solemnity. The chief magistrate of Plataea, clad in a purple robe, washed with his own hands the tombstones and anointed them with scented oil. He slaughtered a black bull over a burning pyre and called upon the dead warriors to come and partake of the banquet and the blood. Then, filling a bowl of wine and pouring a libation, he said, 'I drink to the men who died for the freedom of Greece.'[23]

On the contrary, other ancient sacrificial rites, with the bull as victim, might descend to the lowest depths of barbaric bestiality. Such a one was the ceremony of the *taurobolium* (bath of bull's blood):

> The barbarous custom of allowing the blood of the victim slaughtered on a latticed platform to fall down upon the mystic lying in a pit below, was probably practised in Asia from time immemorial. According to a widespread notion among primitive peoples, the blood is the vehicle of the vital energy, and the person who poured it upon his body and moistened his tongue with it, believed that he was thereby endowed with the courage and strength of the slaughtered animal.[24]

In Greece the ritual became more elaborate and formal. This was the ritual of Attis the priest of Cybele, a goddess of Asiatic origin and character:

> In the baptism the devotee, crowned with gold and wreathed with fillets, descended into a pit the mouth of which was covered with a wooden grating. A bull, adorned with garlands of flowers, its forehead glittering with gold leaf, was then driven on to the grating and there stabbed to death with a concentrated spear. Its hot reeking blood poured in torrents through the apertures, and was received with devout eagerness by the worshipper on every part of his person and garments, till he emerged from the pit drenched, dripping and scarlet from head to foot, to receive the homage, nay the

40

adoration of his fellows as one who had been born again to eternal life and had washed away his sins in the blood of the bull.[25]

The cult spread from Greece to Rome and thence throughout the Roman Empire:

Inscriptions found in Gaul and Germany prove that provincial sanctuaries modelled their ritual on that of the Vatican. From the same source we learn that the testicles as well as the blood of the bull played an important part in the ceremonies. Probably they were regarded as a powerful charm to promote fertility.[26]

The final degradation was achieved in the rites of Dionysus or Bacchus, the personification of the vine. According to legend, this god, in attempting to escape from his enemies, repeatedly changed shape, as was a privilege of the gods, finally assuming the form of a bull. It was while in that particular disguise that his enemies overtook him, when he was cut to pieces by their murderous knives:

. . . the Cretans celebrated a biennial feast at which the passion of Dionysus was represented in every detail. All that he had done or suffered in his last moments was enacted before the eyes of his worshippers, who tore a live bull to pieces with their teeth and roamed the woods with frantic shouts.[27]

The cult of the bull and its seemingly inevitable sacrifice survived in Europe long after the Roman legions had been withdrawn and classical culture and mythology submerged. Paganism persisted until our day and, indeed, is not yet dead. Many were surprised when that typical Scottish Highlander, Colin MacDonald, in his book *Echoes of the Glen* drew the veil aside. Born on 28th January 1882 on a croft near Strathpeffer in Ross-shire, he told how in his early youth a live cock was entombed beneath the threshold of a neighbour's cottage as a means of curing a child of epilepsy. Not so far from Colin's home, in a hamlet called Tarvie, there were rumours of secret bull sacrifice about the same period. Earlier bull sacrifice in Scotland has been more fully documented.

Mitchell, in his curious book *The Past in the Present*, quotes Robertson who described the sacrifice of a bull in Galloway in the year 1164, at a time when Gaelic was the language still spoken in that area:

A writer of the twelfth century, Reginald of Durham, sometimes called Reginald of Coldingham, takes occasion, in his lively *Book of the Miracles of St Cuthbert* to relate certain incidents which befell the famous St Aelred of Rievaux in the year 1164, during a journey into Pictland – that is Galloway it would seem, or perhaps, more generally, the provinces of Scotland, lying to the south of the Forth and Clyde. The Saintlie Abbot happened to be at 'Cuthbrichtis Kirche', or Kirkcudbright, as it is now called, on the feast day of its great patron. A bull, the marvel of the parish for its strength and ferocity, was dragged to the church, bound with cords, to be offered as an alms and oblation to St Cuthbert.[28]

Bull sacrifice to the saints – presumably christianised pagan divinities – occurred in the more remote Scottish Highlands until a very much later date. Mitchell tells of a discovery he made when in the vicinity of Loch Maree in a summer of the 1870s:

The man who accompanied me as a driver in the district happened to be a person of intelligence, and it was he who first informed me, that in the Presbytery Records allusion was made to the superstitions of Loch Maree. I afterwards obtained, through the Rev Dr Maclean, of Kiltearn, the extracts from these records, which follow. The date of the most relevant extract is dated 'At Appilcross, 5th. Septemb; 1656' when –
'The name of God incalled. Interalia, The Minister being inquired be his brethren of the maine enormities of the parochin of Lochcarrone and Appilcross, declaires some of his parochiners to be superstitious, especiallie the men of Auchnascallach – findeing among uther abhominable and Heathenishe practises that the people in that place were accustomed to sacrifice bulls at a certain tyme upon the 25th of August, which day is dedicate, as they conceive, to St Mourie, as they call him . . .'

Mitchell remarked that 'The most interesting feature of these extracts is the finding so complete and formal a sacrificial ceremony *commonly* practised in our country at so late a period as within 200 years of our own day.'[29]

MacCulloch, however, when he extended the existence of the practice to a much later date, was certainly correct: 'These rites, occurring in the seventeenth century, were condemned by the Presbytery of Dingwall, but with little effect, and some of them still survive.'[30]

The especially magical qualities believed to reside in the bull's hide are a feature of all bull cults. The ancient Egyptians wrapped their dead in them as an aid to the soul's resurrection. Mithraists lay on them to renew both bodily and spiritual strength. The practice continued in the Scottish Highlands long after its meaning and significance had been forgotten. The eve of 'Calluinn' or New Year's Day is still full of superstitious customs, the jetsam of ancient pagan faiths washed up on a Christian shore. Alexander Carmichael, who devoted forty-four years of his life to the salvage of such jetsam, has recorded a rune he heard recited in the Western Isles in the latter part of the nineteenth century. In Gaelic it runs:

> *Calluinn a bhuilg*
> *Calluinn a bhuilg*
> *Buail am boicionn*
> *Buail am boicionn.*
> *Calluinn a bhuilg*
> *Calluinn a bhuilg*
> *Buail an craicionn*
> *Buail an craicionn.*

and in English:

> Hogmanay of the sack
> Hogmanay of the sack
> Strike the hide
> Strike the hide.
> Hogmanay of the sack
> Hogmanay of the sack
> Beat the skin
> Beat the skin.

In Carmichael's time the 'black house' of peculiar structure was typical of the Hebrides. The walls of these houses were five to eight feet thick. The roof of the house being raised from the inner edge of the wall, a broad terrace was left on the outside. Two or three stones projected from the wall at the door forming steps. On these the inmates ascended for purposes of thatching and securing the roof in time of storm. This is how Carmichael describes an ancient ceremony which had become a modern prank:

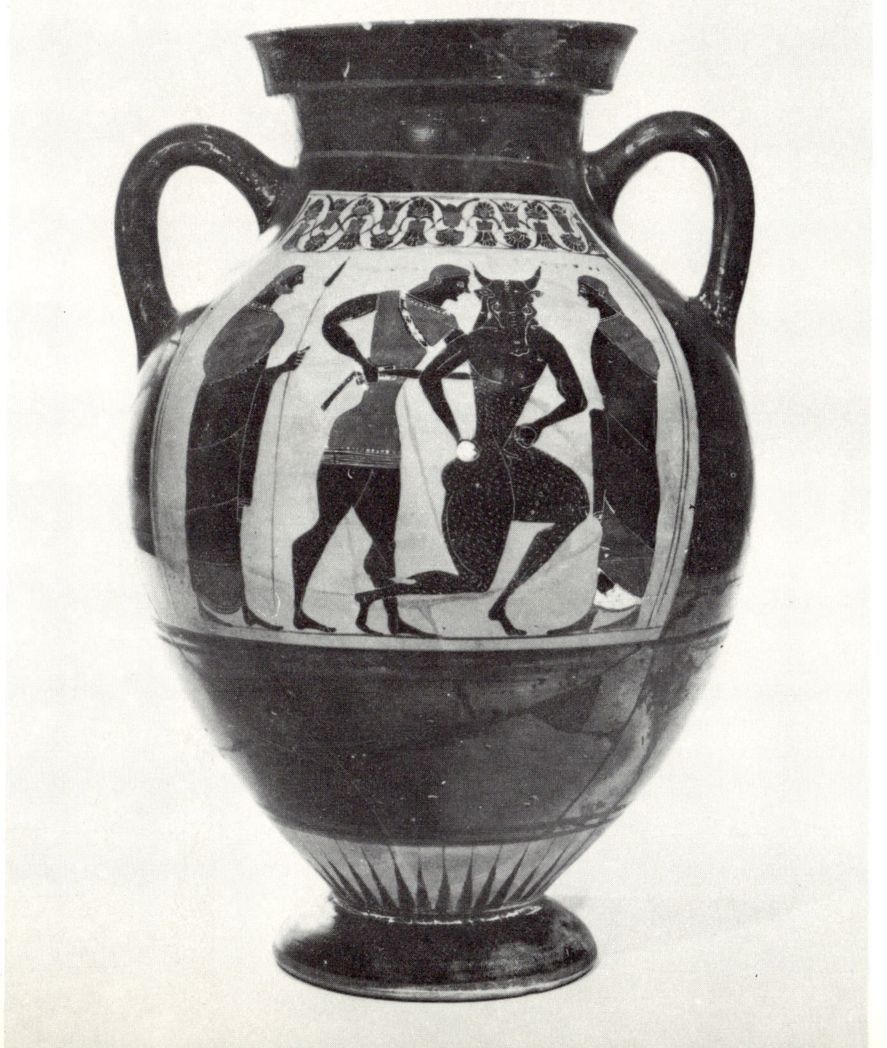

Theseus slaying the Minotaur. From an amphora *c.* mid-sixth century BC. (*British Museum*)

The 'gillean Callaig' carollers or Hogmanay lads perambulate the town-land at night. One man is enveloped in the hard hide of a bull with the horns and hoofs still attached. When the men come to a house they ascend the wall and run round sunwise, the man in the hide shaking the horns and hoofs, and the other men striking the hard hide with sticks. The appearance of the man in the hide is gruesome, while the din made is terrific. Having descended and recited their runes at the door, the Hogmanay men are admitted and treated to the best in the house.

The performance seems to be symbolic, but of what it is not easy to say, unless of laying an evil spirit. That the rite is heathen and ancient is evident.[31]

Certainly the custom, as Carmichael deduced, is both heathen and ancient, in all probability the remnant of a fertility rite of bull sacrifice at the beginning of a new year.

Sacrifice had variable significance and both man and beast were sacrificed with different purposes in view. The rite was performed to please and gain favour with beneficent deities; to assuage the wrath of outraged, jealous or malevolent deities; or as a general purging, as it were, of sins or omissions common to the community. The Biblical scapegoat is the classic example, but the bull on occasion could fulfil the same role. 'When the ancient Egyptians sacrificed a bull, they invoked upon its head all the evils that might otherwise befall themselves and the land of Egypt.'[32]

Dionysus, or Bacchus as he was sometimes known, in the form of a bull bringing his mother Semele back from Hades. (*British Museum*)

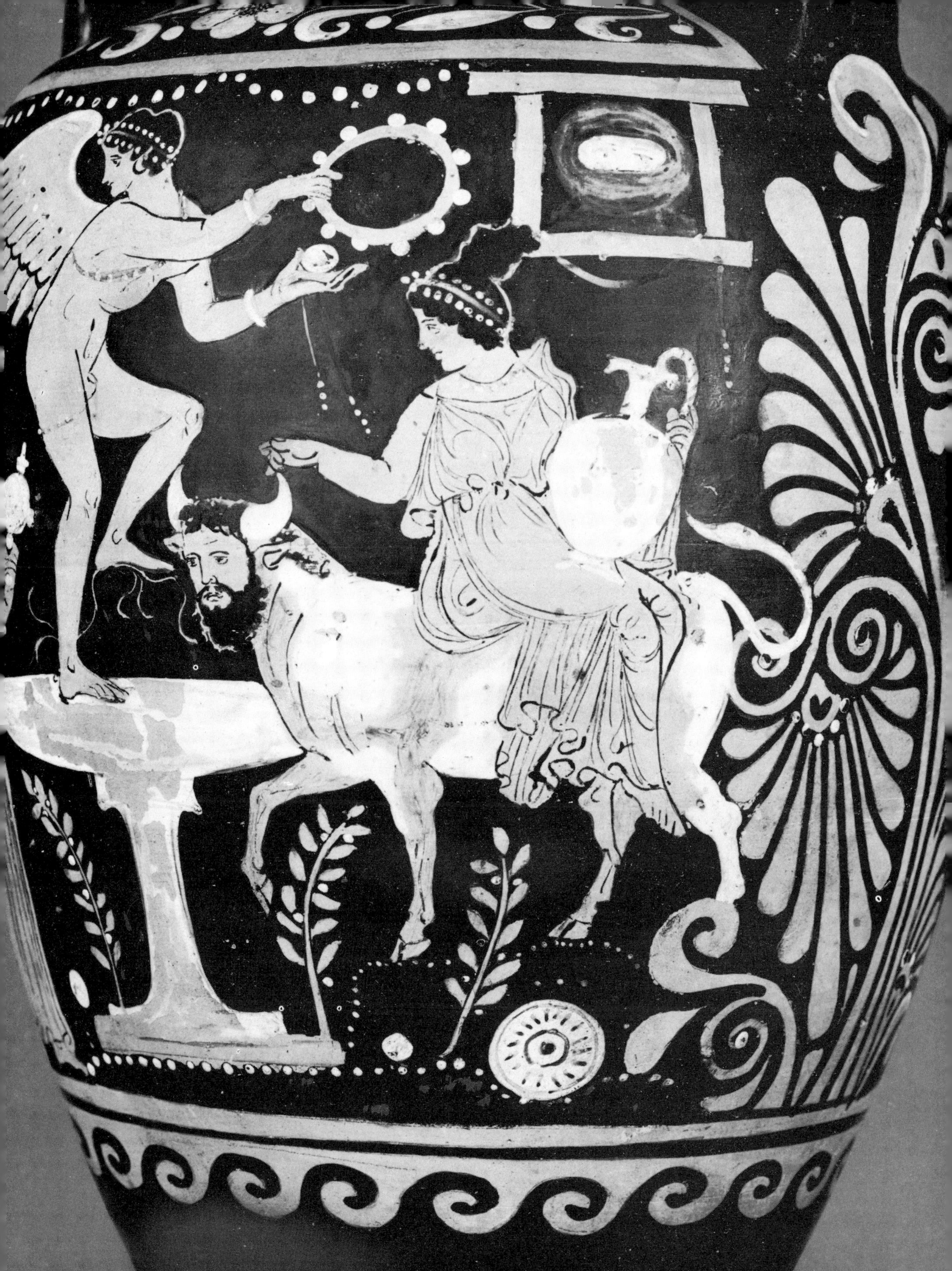

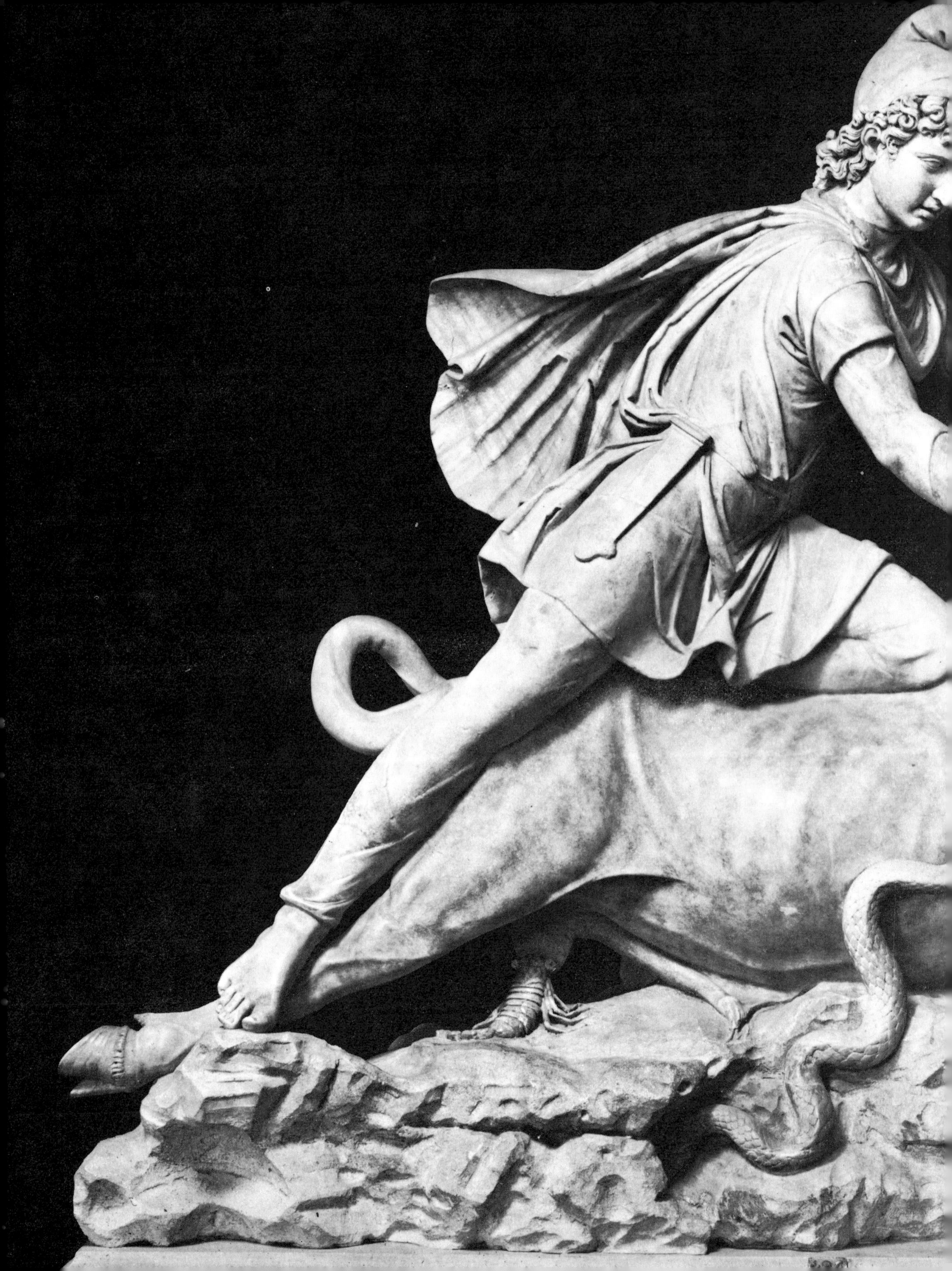

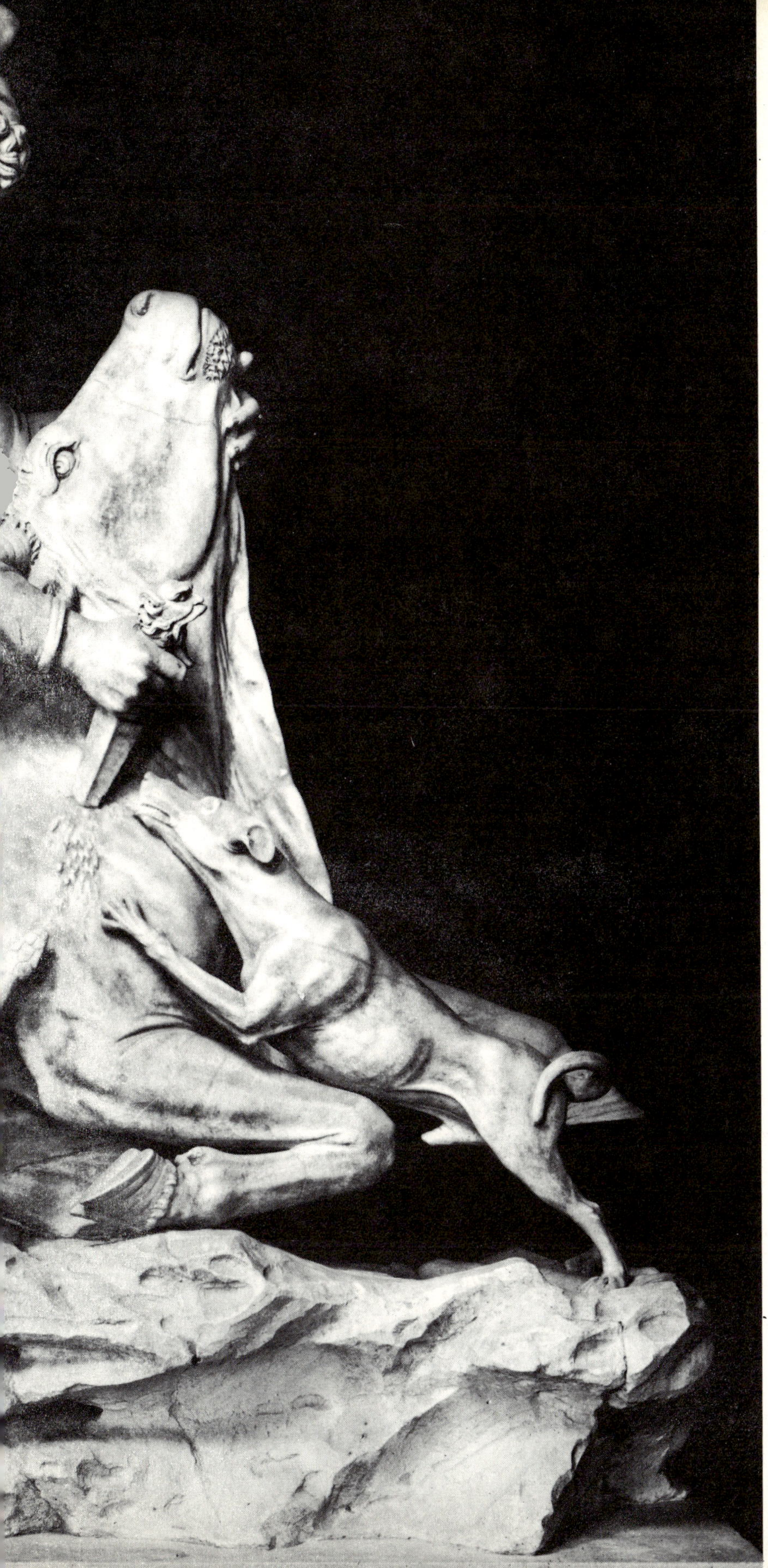

3

The Bull
in
Religion

The bull sacrifice. Mithra
places his left knee on the
back of the bull and,
seizing its horn (or muzzle)
with his left hand, plunges
a knife into its throat.
(*Mansell Collection*)

§ Ahura-Mazda, the supreme God of Good in ancient Persian mythology, created a bull even before he created Gayomart, the first superman. It is natural, therefore, that in Persia first arose the religion of Mithraism, a religion so intimately involved with bull worship.

The religion derived its name from the god called Mithra, of ancient origin.

In that unknown epoch when the ancestors of the Persians were still united with those of the Hindoos, they were already worshippers of Mithra, and the Persians continued to worship him until their conversion to Islam.[1]

Although Mithra gave his name to a religion which for a time threatened to overwhelm Christianity, he was never a central figure in the prolific and involved Persian pantheon. In character he was beneficent, a god of light, of justice and truth, of fertility; a god of hosts, in a sense a 'Redeemer'; a god who came down to earth for a time and after his earthly pilgrimage, ascended into Heaven, from whence on the Final Day of Judgement he was to come again to judge the quick and the dead. This character of Redeemer and final judge of human virtue is only one of the numerous close and strange resemblances between the story of Mithra and that of Christ.

The birth of Mithra was miraculous. He appeared on earth from the face of a rock. 'The birth was in the nature of a miracle, the young Mithras being forced out of a rock as if by some hidden magic power.'[2] The date of his birth was the twenty-fifth day of December, and shepherds watching their flocks heralded his nativity.

Whilst on earth Mithra performed many notable miracles. Like Moses, in time of drought he drew water from a rock, but by shooting arrows against its surface, for he was a famous archer. Presumably it was because of this early miracle that ever afterwards all Mithra shrines were sited beside running water. But it was his adventures with the bull that aroused the greatest admiration and came to be adopted as the sacred symbol of his creed.

Mithra having grown to a splendid and masculine maturity, 'young and supple, strong as Herakles himself',[3] was living in a mountain cave. Because of this early and humble dwelling place every Mithraic shrine was sited either in an actual cave or in underground crypts or cellars artificially designed to resemble caves. He lived alone in the cave except for his dog, his constant companion. One day when walking over hill pastures – one of his divine titles was 'the lord of wide pastures'[4] – he saw a magnificent white bull grazing on the mountainside. For what reason, whether from a desire to test his courage and strength on a worthy opponent, or with dim foreknowledge of events to come, or just in the ecstasy of athletic youth abroad on a fine spring morning, the legend does not relate. In any case Mithra decided to capture the bull alive and that with his own bare hands.

He seized the bull by the horns and like the Cretan acrobats pictured on the friezes of Knossos, succeeded in mounting him. Then the fight began – young god against mighty bull. Mithra was unseated but never relaxed his hold on the bull's horns. He was dragged along, still clinging on until the bull, in the end exhausted by its own efforts, surrendered and collapsed. Then Mithra, seizing it by its hind legs, dragged it captive to his cave. The way home was a rough and rocky one, strewn with obstacles of every description, but to his cave he dragged it. This painful journey (*transitus*) of Mithra became, in Mithraic belief, the symbol of human suffering on earth.

Cumont[5] wrote:

This ingenious fable carries us back to the very beginnings of civilisation. It could never have arisen save among a people of shepherds and hunters with whom cattle, the source of all wealth, had become an object of religious veneration. In the eyes of such a people, the capture of a wild bull was an achievement so highly fraught with honour as to be apparently no derogation even for a god.

Perhaps Mithra, having finalised his capture of the bull by dragging it to his cave, gave it its freedom again, or possibly the bull escaped. In any event it was soon at liberty, roaming freely over the mountain pastures as before. Mithra may well have thought that he was done with the bull.

It was not to be so. One day a message for Mithra came from the Supreme Sun-God (Sol). It was carried by Sol's messenger, the Raven, and the message was a command. Mithra was ordered to pursue the bull once more; and this time not to capture but to slay it. Mithra, with all the soldier's respect for a worthy enemy, with the athlete's admiration for an adversary so difficult to subdue, would fain have disobeyed. Yet the order was from the Supreme God and disobedience was unthinkable. Solemnly, sadly, with his hunting knife at his side and his dog at heel he went out again, to sacrifice the bull.

Mary Stewart, in her book *The Crystal Cave*, has given a wonderfully vivid imaginative vision of the act, as seen through the eyes of the boy Merlin, the seer. He was lying, afraid, among a penned group of cattle, in hiding from a strange rider on a white horse who had arrived at a farm in which he had taken refuge:

. . . suddenly, with no warning, he was there, a tall figure striding across the field, as shadowy and quiet as the wind . . . Then I saw, half in, half out of the shadow of the standing stone, the white animal grazing. His horse must have broken loose.

The grazing animal had lifted its head to watch the man's approach. A cloud swept across the stars, blackening the field. Light ran after the shadow across the frost. It struck the standing stone. I saw that I had been wrong; it was not the horse. Nor – my next thought – could it be one of the young beasts from the shed. This was a bull, a massive white bull, full-grown, with

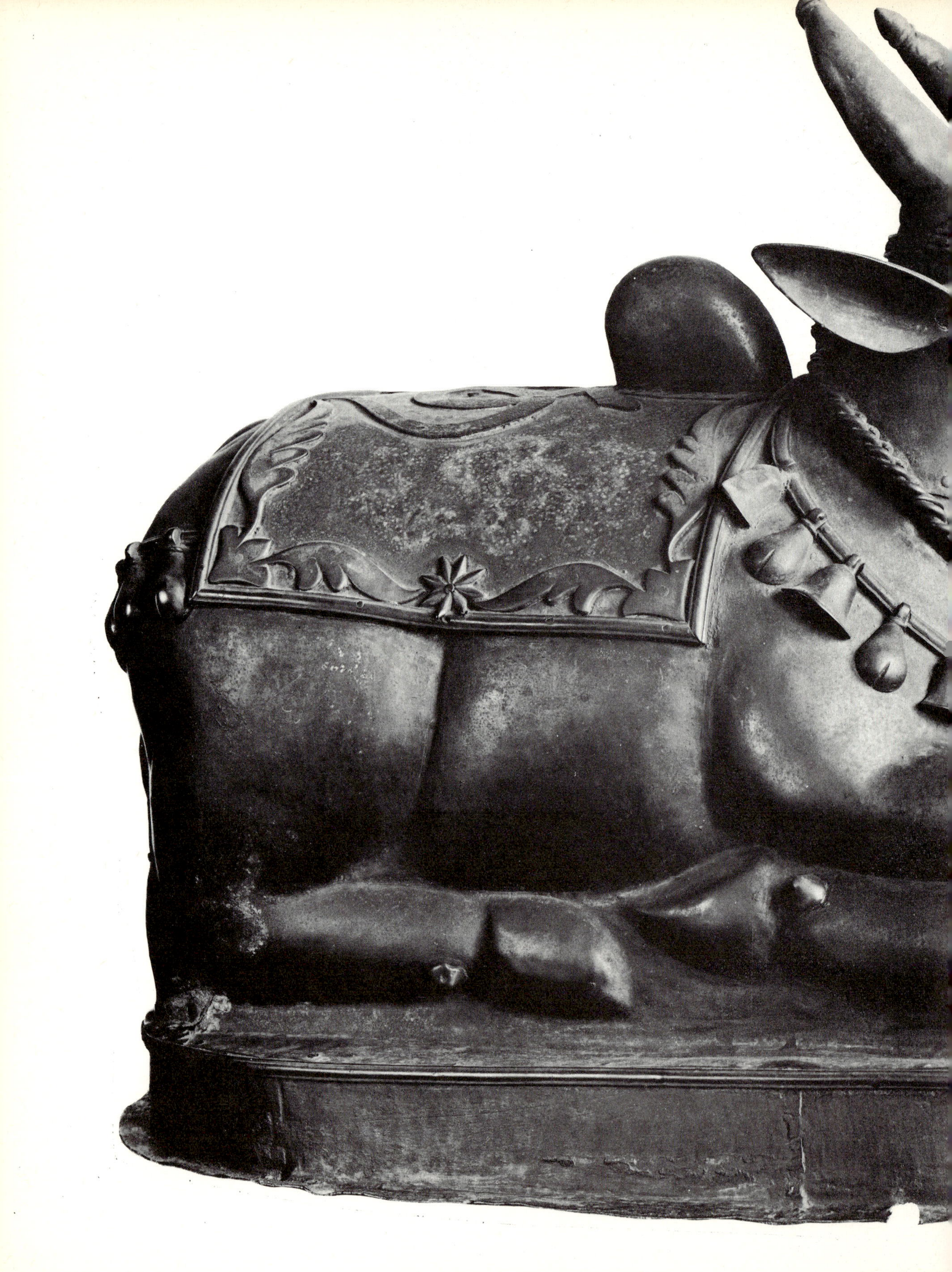

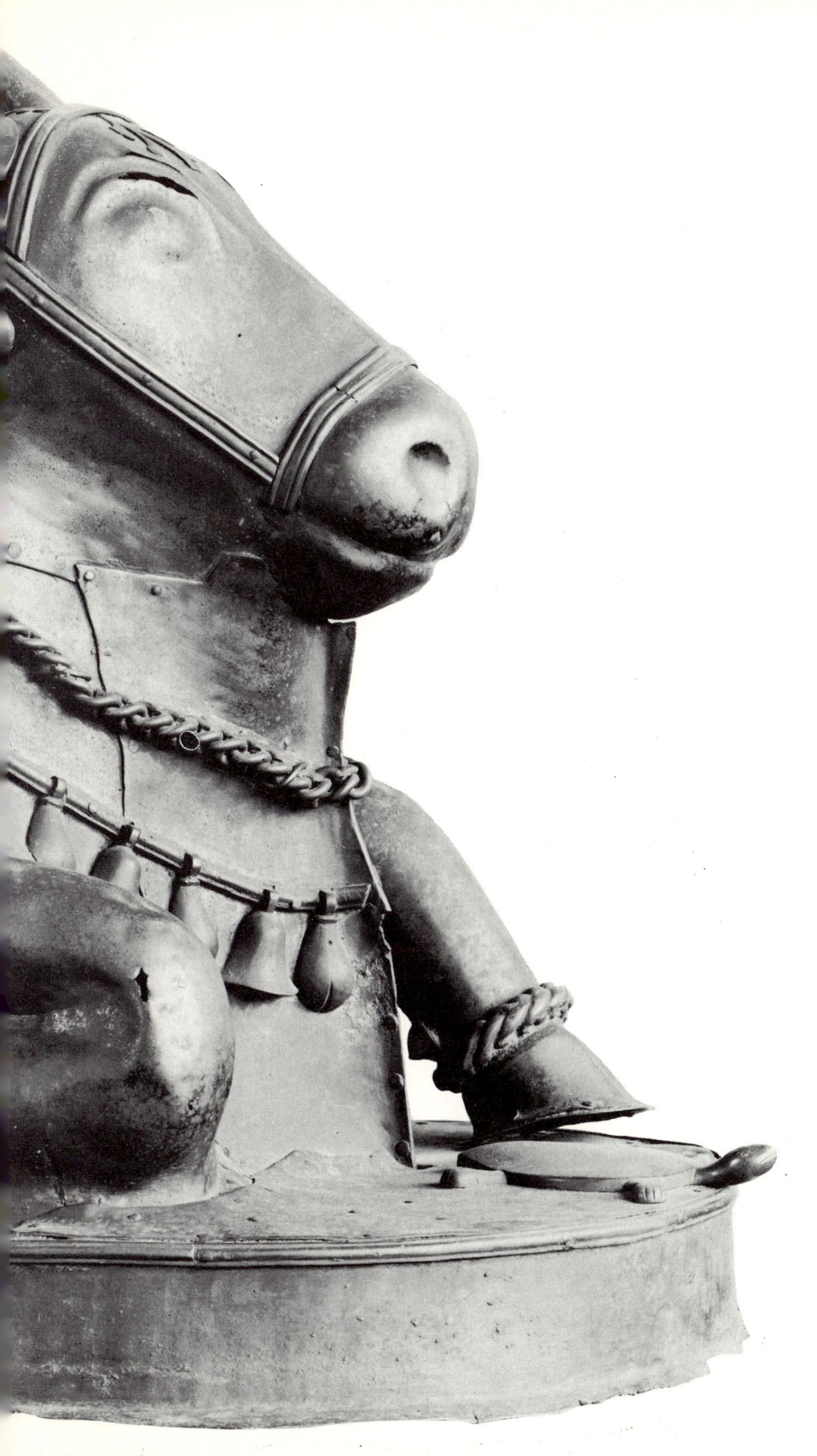

Nandi, the bull-mount of
the Hindu god Siva.
Eighteenth-century copper
figure from South India.
(*British Museum*)

a royal spread of horns and a neck like a thunder-cloud. It lowered its head till the dewlap brushed the ground, and pawed once, twice.

The young man paused. I saw him now, clearly, as the shadow lifted. He was tall and strongly built, and his hair looked bleached in the starlight. He wore some sort of foreign dress – trousers cross-bound with thongs below a tunic girded low on the hips, and a high loose cap. Under this the fair hair blew round his face like rays. There was a rope in his hand, held loosely, its coils brushing the frost. His cloak flew in the wind; a short cloak, of some dark colour I could not make out.

Without warning, and without a sound, the white bull charged. Shadow and light rushed with it, flickering, blurring the scene. The rope whirled, snaked into a loop, settled. The man leapt to one side as the great beast tore past him and came to a sliding stop with the rope snapping taut and the frost smoking up in clouds from the side-slipping hoofs.

The bull whirled, and charged again. The man waited without moving, his feet planted slightly apart, his posture casual, almost disdainful. As the bull reached him he seemed to sway aside, lightly, like a dancer. The bull went by him so close that I saw a horn shear the swirling cloak, and the beast's shoulder passed the man's thigh like a lover seeking a caress. The man's hands moved. The rope whipped up into a ring, and another loop settled round the royal horns. The man leaned against it, and as the beast came up short once more, turning sharp in its own smoke, the man jumped.

Not away. Towards the bull, clean on to the thick neck, with knees digging into the dewlap, and fierce hands using the rope like reins.

The bull stopped dead, his feet four-square, his head thrust downwards with his whole weight and strength against the rope. There was still no sound that I could hear, no sound of hoof or crack of rope or bellow of breath. I was half out of the brushwood now rigid and staring, heedless of anything save the fight between man and bull. . . . But before I could move the cloud had fled, to show me the bull standing as before, the man still on its neck. But now the beast's head was coming up. The man had dropped the rope, and his two hands were on the bull's horns, dragging them back – back . . . up. Slowly, almost as if in a ritual of surrender, the bull's head lifted, the powerful neck stretched up, exposed.

There was a gleam in the man's right hand. He leaned forward, then drove the knife down and across.

Still in silence, slowly, the bull sank to its knees. Black flowed over the white hide, the white ground, the white base of the stone.

The divine order was fulfilled!

Then a miracle which Merlin did not see occurred. All the useful plants that are found in the world sprang from the body of the dying bull. Wheat sprouted out of its spinal cord and its blood turned to wine. The semen from its testicles, after purification in the moon, created all useful animals. By his sacrificial act, Mithra had given new life to the world.

Yet the bull, although its body was slain, retained its immortal soul, and this soul, protected and accompanied by Mithra's dog, ascended into Heaven, '. . . where, receiving the honours of divinity, it became, under the name of Silvanus, the guardian of herds'.[6]

Such is the legend, ignoring time sequences as all legends do. Mithra's bull-slaying feat, in which heroism is so closely linked with tragedy, has all the characters of the primitive fertility rite.

Nor can we doubt that these myths, like so many others, were interpretations of a rite older than mythology, and that the sacrifice of the bull was in origin intended to promote fertility and ensure the annual renewal of life on the earth, the bull being chosen as the victim because of his great generative power.[7]

The terrestrial mission of Mithra was now accomplished. The Great God Sol came down to earth and in company with Mithra feasted off the flesh and blood of the sacrificed bull. Then together they ascended into heaven in the Sun-God's chariot drawn by four swift horses. Although now amongst the gods in heaven, Mithra did not forget his followers on earth. He never ceased to care for and protect those who believed in him and served him.

Yet, according to the myth, Mithra was destined to return to earth once again, when the world should come to an end and final judgement be enacted on mankind. His second coming was to be heralded by the appearance on earth of a marvellous bull, a reincarnation of the bull he had slain. Then Mithra would himself descend and resurrect the dead. In a second supreme sacrifice he would slay the divine bull. He would mingle its fat with consecrated wine and '. . . offer to the just this miraculous beverage which will endow them all with immortality'.[8]

The unjust will perish in a final devastating fire which will destroy all things.

Such was the myth of Mithra which was fated to become the basis of ritual in an organised religion. Indeed a strange story, not without its own fascination and emotional appeal. This religion, called Mithraism, developed in Anatolia, a province of modern Turkey, and from thence spread to western Europe and finally to Rome, where it grew so powerful as to threaten to strangle Christianity at its birth. In its passage from East to West it underwent many changes, with the inevitable tendency to borrow and adopt from other mythologies, as all religions do.

According to the historian Plutarch, Mithraism was first brought to Rome by captured Cilician pirates in the year 67 BC. It rose to its peak, over three centuries later, about AD 308 when Diocletian was Emperor in Rome. It reached its virtual extinction in AD 392 when Christianity triumphed and an Imperial edict suppressing all pagan religions was enacted. Mithraism died. Christianity killed it.

Throughout the first three centuries of our era its spread was

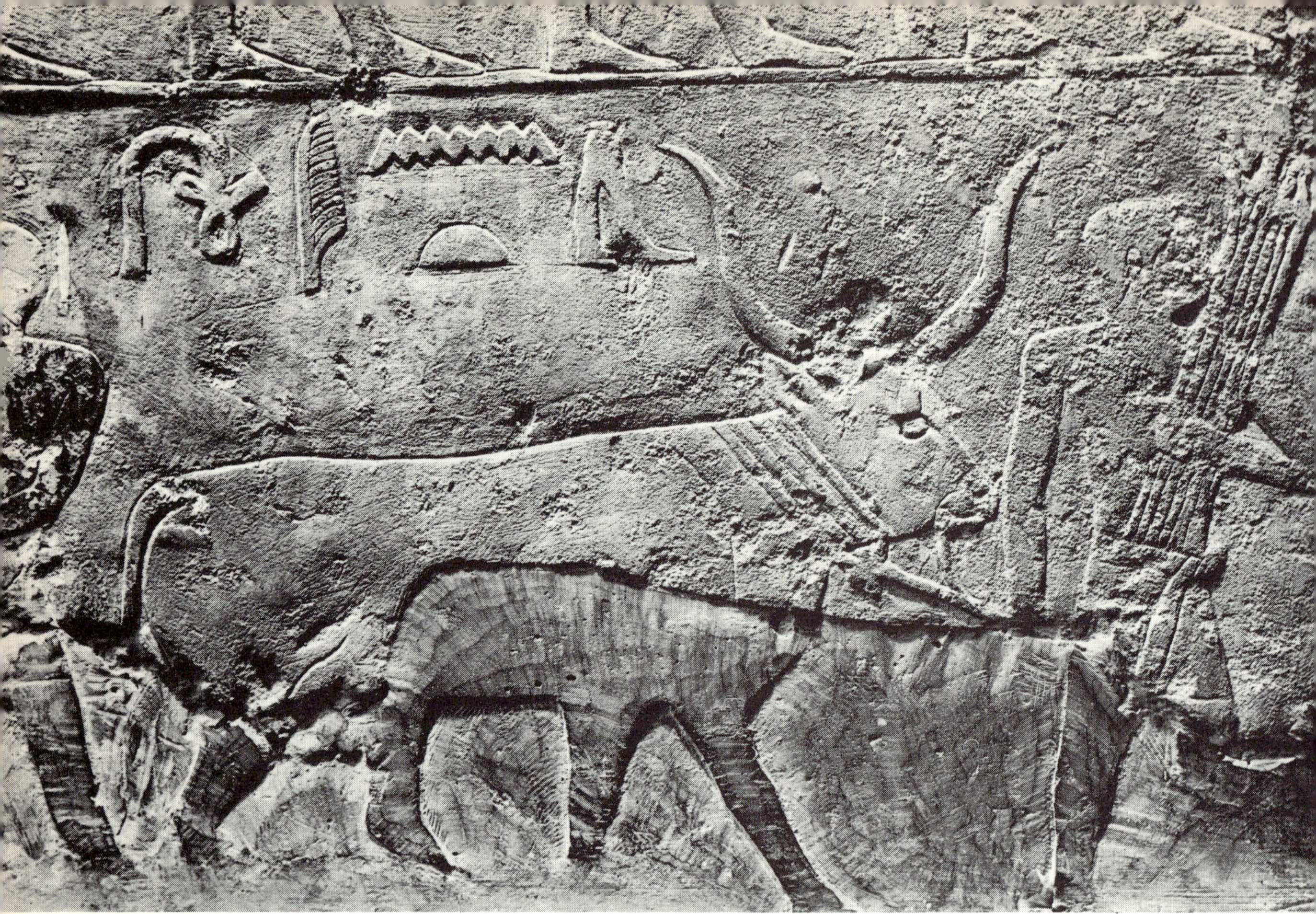

phenomenal. Soldiers, slaves and merchants carried it to the uttermost fringes of the Roman Empire, at that period covering a vast territory, from Hadrian's Wall in Britain to the verge of the Sahara Desert in North Africa. There were very many recruits in the legions that came from Asia Minor and among these were followers of the Mithraic faith. There were missionaries of the faith in every legion, and it was a faith that appealed to the Roman soldier. For Mithra was a god of battles and a Lord of Hosts, leading his followers to victory against every foe.

As the god of armies, Mithra caused his protégés to triumph over their barbarous adversaries, and likewise in the moral realm he gave them victory over the instincts of evil, inspired by the Spirit of Falsehood, and he assured them salvation both in this world and in that to come.[9]

Wherever the Roman legions marched they took this religion with them and wherever they made permanent camps or frontier fortifications they built sanctuaries to their faith. These sanctuaries are found both in Rome itself and on all the distant frontiers of the Roman Empire.

'From the banks of the Black Sea to the mountains of Scotland and to the borders of the great Sahara Desert, along the entire length of the Roman frontier, Mithraic monuments abound.'[10]

Germany beyond all other countries, has the most numerous and richest relics of Mithraic worship. Clearly the hero-god Mithra, the warrior, the athlete, the soldier obedient to the command of a superior divinity, appealed to the Germanic mind. Or, could it be, that the recurrent militarism of that people is a result, rather than the cause of its early history? For, 'certainly no god of paganism ever found in that nation as many enthusiastic devotees as Mithra'.[11]

'Generally speaking, the Iranian cult was in no country so completely restricted to fortified places as in Britain.'[12] York, Chester, Caernarvon, Hadrian's Wall – all camps or forts occupied by the Roman legions – were the only known sites of Mithraic shrines until the year 1954, when a mithraeum was discovered in London. Since Cumont died in 1947, he knew nothing of this important find. It was revealed during excavations around the Mansion House in the very centre of the City, to the east of the course of the Roman Walbrook. Excavators were allowed a short period for exploration before the construction of Bucklersbury House was completed. Founded about AD 150, the shrine was probably in use until the fourth century. The building was small as were all Mithraic shrines, with the usual simple design. A relief showing Mithra the bull-slayer was found very much earlier at the same spot, in the year 1889. It is interesting to speculate as to how many other relics of Mithraism may be hidden under the concrete foundations of Greater London.

The sanctuaries, or mithraeums as they are called, were made to a conventional pattern, one founded upon the adventures of Mithra during his earthly pilgrimage. They were established, wherever possible, close to running water because of Mithra's drought-ending miracle and because in his own terrestrial habitation the sound of running water was ever in his ears. Because Mithra dwelt in a cave, with but two known exceptions, the Mithraic sanctuaries were underground. For preference they were in natural caves but where this was impracticable as in Rome itself, they were artificially adapted to resemble caves. Prominent citizens of Rome sometimes provided cellars in their private houses as places of worship. The two known exceptions to the rule are the Mithraic sanctuaries at Ostia, the port of Rome and at Walbrook in the City of London. There, because of the flat and marshy ground on which they were sited, they were, perforce, built above ground.

The Mithraic sanctuary was invariably small, holding no more than fifty or so people and it was made to a standard plan. In general, steps led down to the cave, or its artificial imitation shaped rather like a tunnel. It was always without windows and dark so that the enemies of Mithraism sneered that 'such is the Sun-god they call Mithras, but

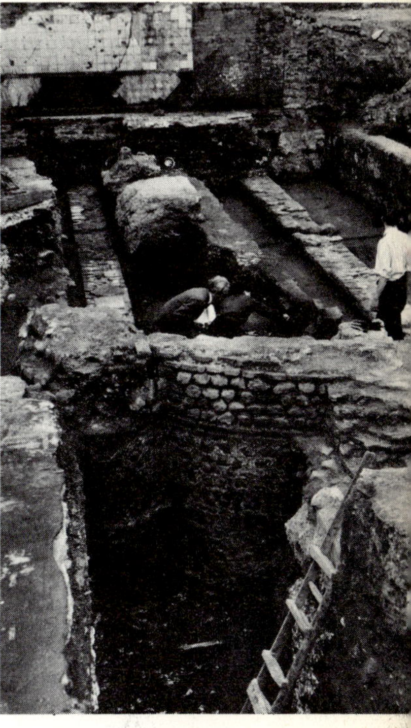

Mithraeum (Mithraic temple) excavated in London during building operations around the Mansion House in the very centre of the city. It lies to the east of the course of the Roman Walbrook. (*Guildhall Museum*)

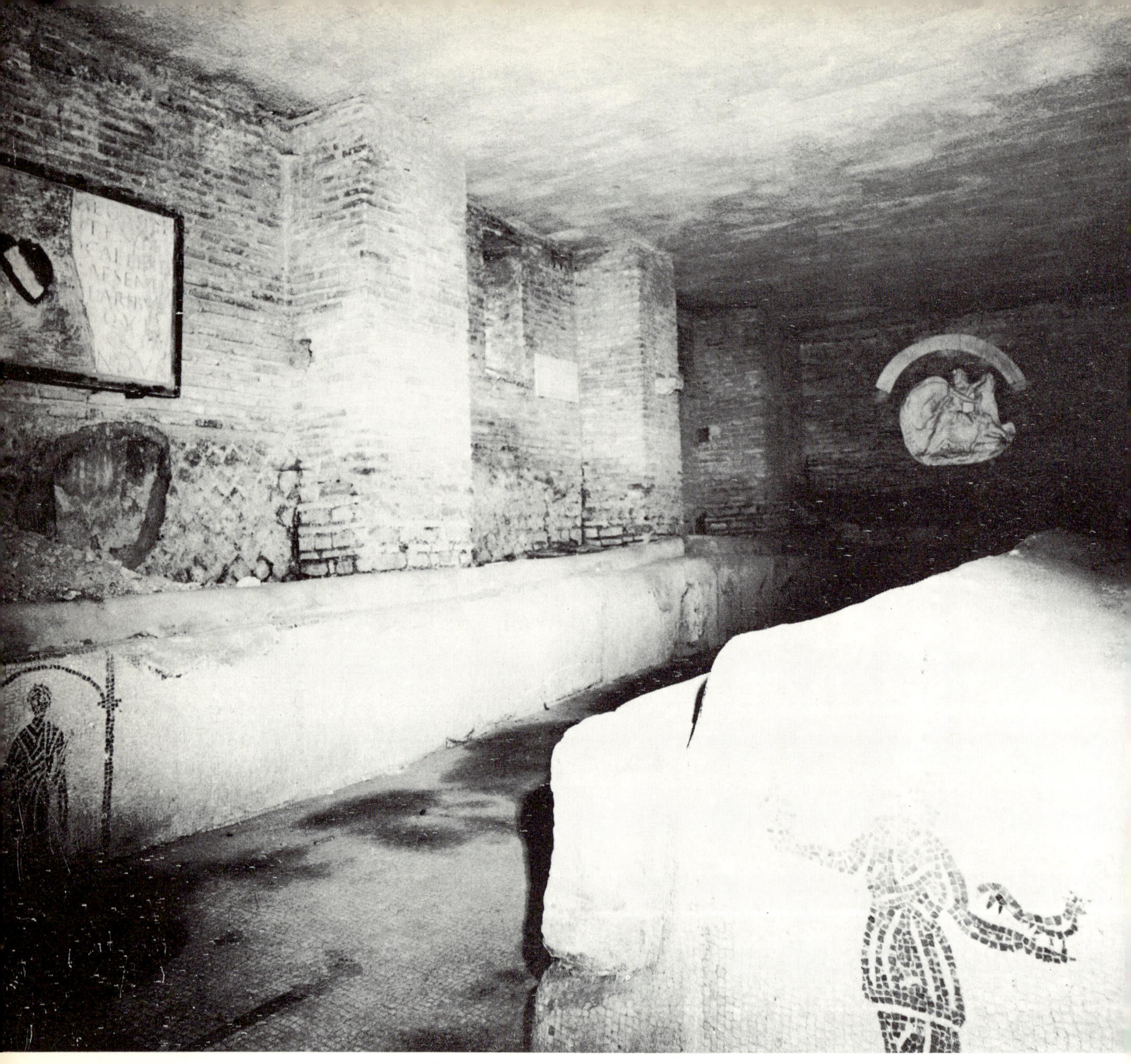

Mithraeum of Ostia, Italy. On either side of the 'aisle' are long benches, decorated with mosaics, and it was upon these that worshippers reclined during mystic ceremonies. (*Ronald Sheridan*)

they celebrate his mysteries in hidden caves, so that ever immersed in the concealing squalor of darkness they shun the beauty of brilliance and clarity of light'.[13] The sanctuaries were, of course, lit by torches, oil-lamps or candles during times of worship.

On either side of a central passageway or aisle were long benches, sometimes decorated with mosaics. There the worshippers reclined during the mystic ceremonies.

At the far end of the aisle in a niche or apse set in the back wall behind two altar fires, was the chief ornament, the central symbol of Mithraic faith. As inevitable as the cross or crucifix in a Catholic church was the representation in marble or paint of the fertility rite enacted by Mithra's sacrifice of the bull. It was present in every Mithraic shrine, it was in miniature form a feature of every Mithraic household. Evidently intended to illustrate the basic tenets of the Mithraic faith, the meaning of some of its symbols is uncertain to this day. The difficulty of interpretation is due to the great gap between the story of Mithra as related in the ancient Persian scriptures and the deserted and despoiled Mithraic shrines still being excavated and explored at the present day. As Cumont, the Belgian savant and the great authority on Mithraism, has said, 'It is as if it were only possible to study Christianity through the Old Testament and the mediaeval cathedrals.'

Practically the only written evidence covering this long interval is references, inevitably derogatory, by Christian critics of the rival faith. It is, therefore, mainly from archaeological evidence that the details of Mithraism, its beliefs and ritual, can be understood. But archaeology has already revealed a great deal and with excavations still in progress may yet reveal a great deal more.

Representations of Mithra slaying the bull are conventional and standardised, artistically seldom of a high standard and at times quite crude. They show how

... Mithra, clothed in the conventional costume which in Greek art signified the Oriental, places his left knee on the back of the bull, and, seizing its horns (or muzzle) with the left hand, plunges a knife into its throat. The scene of the action is a cave. ... A scorpion fastens on the testicles of the dying bull, while a dog and usually a serpent, drink the blood which flows from the death wound. A crow is almost always present, perched either on Mithra's mantle or on the edge of the cave. Finally, we have a significant detail in the ears of corn in which the tail of the bull terminates.[14]

The meaning of Mithra's sacrifice of the bull is sufficiently plain. The significance of the ears of corn sprouting from the end of the bull's tail is also perfectly clear. In some representations vegetation is bursting out of the death wound as well. Did not the flesh and blood of the dying bull originate all vegetables and animals useful to mankind? The 'crow' also must represent Sol's messenger, the raven, who brought his order to Mithra down to earth. But what of the scorpion, the serpent and the dog? Cumont[15] interprets their significance in a particular way, not altogether convincingly:

In vain did the Evil Spirit launch forth his unclean demons against the anguish-wrung animal, in order to poison in it the very sources of life; the scorpion, the ant, the serpent, strove in vain to consume the genital parts and to drink the blood of the prolific quadruped; but they were powerless to impede the miracle that was enacting.

Now, the Mithraic equivalent of the Christian Satan was called

Ahriman, and the scorpion and snake were evil animals in his service. Yet, on the other hand, the dog in ancient Persia, like the cat in ancient Egypt, was held almost sacred and its sacrifice forbidden. It is therefore quite improbable that any dog, whether belonging to Mithra or not, could be involved in an attempt to thwart a miracle inspired by a benign divinity. Again, the snake's attitude like that of the dog's in the conventional representation is not in any way suggestive of aggression against the bull. It seems rather as though they were thrusting their heads forwards and upwards towards the death wound to share in the life-giving virtues of the dying bull's blood.

The scorpion's grip on the testicles of the bull is more in keeping with Cumont's interpretation. It does suggest an attempt at some sort of castration as though to prevent the primary seat of the bull's fertility being used for the benefit of mankind. No doubt, to the Mithraists of Roman times the meaning of these strange symbols was sufficiently clear but today it has to be admitted that their significance is a shade obscure.

The same can be said of those two mysterious figures, the Torch-bearers or Dadophori who, in almost all representations of the bull sacrifice, stand one on each side of Mithra and the dying bull. Their names were Cautes and Cautopates but the meaning of those two names remains unknown. Both are clad in the conventional oriental garb similar to that of Mithra himself. Both carry a flaming torch, of which one is erect, pointing upwards, the other, like a soldier's reversed arms, pointing to the ground. In certain representations one of the torch-bearers, Cautopates, grasps the bull's tail with its terminal sprout of vegetation in his left hand striving, according to Vermaseren, 'to obtain a share in this mysterious power'.[16]

That, then, was the substitute for the crucifix in every Mithraic shrine to which the worshippers may well have bowed the knee in reverence.

What was the ritual of worship in these cave-like sanctuaries? Largely based on the evidence of early Christian authors but more recently supplemented by archaeological researches, particularly at the Aventine Mithraeum in Rome, there is now more certain guidance than there was in Cumont's lifetime. (He died in 1947.)

The two most important points in Mithraic ritual, both reminiscent of Freemasonry, were the vow of secrecy and the exclusion of women.

The wording of the oath has been preserved in a Florence papyrus[17] although a sceptic might question its absolute authenticity. It reads as follows:

In the name of the god, who has divided the earth from the heavens, light from darkness, the day from night, the world from chaos, life from death and creation from destruction, beyond all doubt and in sincere good faith I swear to observe the secrecy of the mysteries, which will be bestowed on me by the most God-fearing Father Serapion and by the most venerable hallowed Herald Ka [merion?], to whom this task falls, and by my fellow initiates and most beloved Brethren. For which cause being true to my oath, I hope for all prosperity, but I commit myself also to all things contrary should I disclose any of this.

Cumont considered that the exclusion of women was the chief cause of the failure of Mithraism in its struggle against Christianity. He may well have been right. The mother's faith, like the mother tongue, is what mankind inclines to cling to. The German philosopher Nietzsche maintained that Christianity was a religion suited only to women. The Mithraist might have argued that that of a bull-slaying god was one fitted only for men.

Mithraism was reputed to be a clean, somewhat ascetic creed, very dissimilar from that of other pagan faiths popular in Rome at the time of its emergence. Yet, because of its Eastern origin, its ritual contained many curious and primitive elements, neither particularly ascetic nor especially clean. Since this ritual was a private one and those initiated to its mysteries vowed secrecy, knowledge of its content remains fragmentary. Until quite recently this knowledge was based on various references, usually uncomplimentary and sometimes vindictive, by Christian authors of the Roman Empire. These accused the Mithraists both of human sacrifice and torture. The first accusation seems highly improbable since both Greeks and Romans were said to abhor human sacrifice and the Romans certainly did everything they could to suppress its practice by the Druids during Caesar's campaign for the conquest of Gaul. The accusation of torture has a sounder foundation for it is known that the initiates to Mithraism were forced to undergo what were termed severe preliminary trials to prove their courage and endurance and such tests, in certain hands, may all too readily acquire a sadistic flavour.

Apart from written evidence, however, certain recently revealed wall paintings in mithraeums, particularly in the grotto at Capua, are suggestive of the type of trials initiates had to undergo.

In one of the scenes a *mystagogus* in charge of the initiates, dressed in a white tunic with red borders, is pushing a naked initiate by the shoulders. The novice has his eyes bound; he is still blind and cannot yet see the secrets of the mysteries. Very unsteadily and slowly he advances with his hands outstretched, not knowing where his guide is going to take him. Next we see him still blindfolded, with hands clasped, kneeling in front of the *mystagogus* while behind him a priest is approaching with a sword or stick. In another representation the novice is kneeling on one knee with a sword on the ground beside him and this time the *mystagogus* is standing behind him and placing both hands on his head. . . .

Another scene shows the same priest, recognisable by his red tunic . . . holding a stick or a sword close to a round object – which is lying on the ground just in front of the novice, who is kneeling with his hands folded together under his chin. The *mystagogus* is standing behind him with one foot on his calves.[18]

A Latin author of the fourth century AD wrote that the followers of Mithras, 'are not even ashamed to be blindfolded – with some their hands are tied together with chicken guts and then they are thrown across pits full of water. Someone approaches with a sword, cuts through the guts and as a result of this act calls himself liberator.' All this ceremonial, although doubtless sufficiently terrifying to the blindfold initiate, may not, in fact, have been so very terrible after all once his eyes were set free to see the familiar faces of his friends again. Yet, who can be certain today? These rites were secret and it all happened so very long ago.

Initiates were branded with hot iron. Of that there can be no doubt. They were branded either on forehead or on hands although the form and meaning of the brand remains obscure.

Were they submitted to a baptism of bulls' blood? Again the evidence is debatable and vague. Certainly, the ceremony could hardly have been enacted in shrines of their own persuasion. These were underground and confined and hardly the place in which to sacrifice a bull. In Rome, certain shrines were sited in private houses of the wealthy and it seems improbable that any influential Roman citizen would have allowed a bull to be brought into his villa for bloody sacrifice no matter how pious his faith in the mysteries of Mithra. Nor is there any mention of the *taurobolium* by those who have excavated and studied ruins of the Mithraic shrines.

On the other hand Cumont writes of Mithraism being involved 'in spite of its austerity, in an equivocal alliance with the orgiastic cult of the beloved of Attis'.[19] The 'beloved of Attis' was the goddess Cybele and the *taurobolium* was a noted feature of her cult. Again according to Cumont,

The most ancient mithraeum known to us was contiguous to the *metroön* (a temple of Cybele) of Ostia, and we have every reason to believe that the worship of the Iranian god and that of the Phrygian goddess were conducted in intimate communion with each other throughout the entire extent of the Empire. Despite the profound differences of their character, political reasons drew them together.[19]

The Iranian god referred to was Mithra and the Phrygian goddess, Cybele. Possibly, the Mithraists used the *taurobolium* of an adjacent *metroön* for baptismal occasions. With the image of the sacrificed bull before their eyes at every ritual service; with the *taurobolium* of a related communion so conveniently at hand, it seems improbable that this ritual was altogether foreign to 'Mithraism, in which the blood of the bull became the pledge of immortality'.[20]

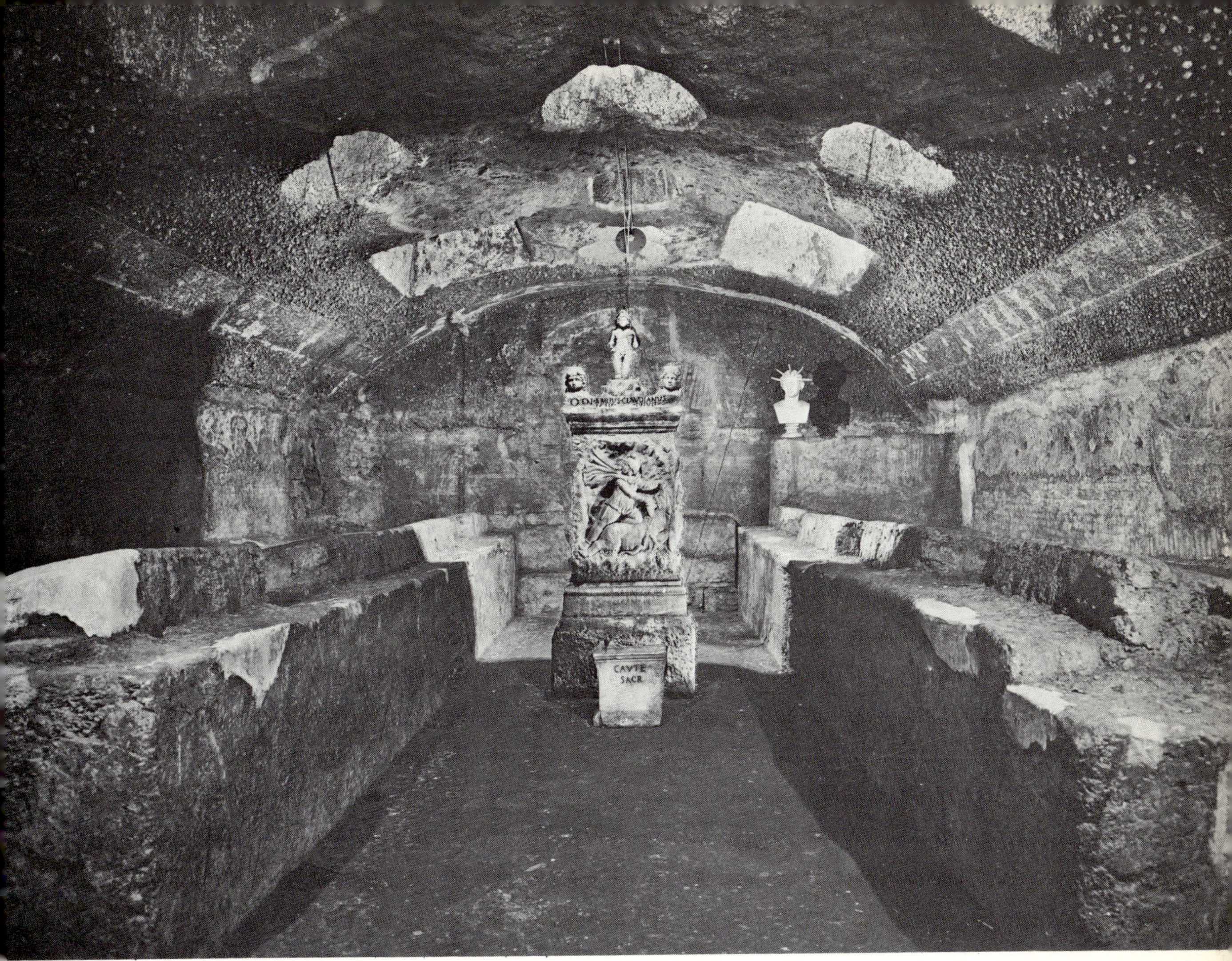

In the Mithraic rites there were seven grades of initiation. After taking the oath of secrecy and passing successfully through the required tests, the novice entered the first grade. Presumably depending on age and ability since there was no class distinction in the creed, he could rise, step by step to the highest grade. These Mithraic grades were perhaps the most clearly Eastern and essentially primitive feature of the Mithraic religion. Mentioned with obvious scorn by Christian writers of the period and illustrated by wall paintings on the ruined shrines, they had the following curious and improbable names: Raven (Corax), Bride (Nymphus), Soldier (Miles), Lion (Leo), Persian (Perses), Courier of the Sun (Heliodromus), and Father (Pater). The sequence of the seven grades was the same throughout the Roman Empire. The exact meaning and functions of these grades remain uncertain. The derivation of the first grade, Raven, is fairly clear. Based on the myth of the messenger to Mithra, bringing the divine command to slay the bull, the Raven, as the wall paintings

Mithraeum from beneath the Church of San Clemente, Rome. At the far end is the central symbol of Mithraic faith – the representation in marble, or sometimes in paint, of the fertility rite enacted by Mithra's sacrifice of the bull. (*Mansell Collection*)

61

show, acted as messenger and servant to the higher grades. The two highest grades, the Father and Herald or Courier of the Sun, certainly controlled the initiation ceremonies as the initiate's oath of secrecy proves. The lowest and the highest grades – Raven and Father – might fairly be equated with the offices of acolyte and bishop in the Catholic Church. What of the Brides, the Soldiers, the Lions, the Persians and the Courier of the Sun? Who were the 'Brides' in a faith excluding women? Possibly with further discoveries in the course of excavations their place in the Mithraic ritual may become clearer. It is known, however, on the evidence both of contemporary writings and of paintings on the walls of shrines that the grades wore masks corresponding to their names. Thus the Ravens wore raven masks, the Lions wore lion masks, and the Brides were veiled. Christian writers mocked at these barbaric customs so reminiscent of the witch doctors in primitive tribes today. The assertion by a Christian writer that 'Some flap their wings like birds, imitating the cry of crows; others growl like lions' is probably the libel of a rival faith. Nevertheless, the rows of weirdly masked worshippers reclining on the benches of a dimly lit cavern, the death agonies of a bull, the most prominent symbol of their faith, was one that no trembling, naked initiate was ever likely to forget.

After the sacrifice of the bull, Sol descended from heaven to share with Mithra a sacred feast on the bull's flesh and blood. This mythological event was commemorated periodically in the Mithraic ritual. As usual, wall paintings and the writings of Christian authors are the main evidence of the ceremony. Apparently the two higher grades, Pater and Heliodromus – the Father and the Courier of the Sun – took the places of Sol and Mithra while Corax – the Raven – and Leo – the Lion – acted as bearers of food and wine. The analogy with the Christian Eucharist is evident and the Christian writers spoke of this Mithraic sacrament as a 'Satanic travesty of holiest rites'.

They [the Mithraics] firmly believed that by eating the bull's flesh and drinking its blood they would be born again just as life itself had once been created anew from the bull's blood. This food and drink were supposed not only to give physical strength but also to bring salvation to the soul which would in time achieve rebirth and eternal light.[21]

It is questionable whether the actual flesh and blood of a sacrificed bull were used. There is no certain evidence to that effect. It seems more probable that meat of any variety was a substitute for bull's flesh and that wine represented the bull's blood. Possibly by a special form of service, a miraculous transubstantiation into the actual flesh and blood of the bull was assumed.

Certain of the Christian writers spoke of a 'sacred meal of bread and water' but there is evidence from wall inscriptions that flesh and wine were the sacramental elements. 'In the Mithraeum at Dura-Europos the expenses of the community are scratched on the walls, and at the head of the list come the charges for meat and wine.'[22]

In refuse pits which have been discovered close to Mithraic sites, the bones of a variety of domestic animals have been unearthed, including those of 'bulls, boars, sheep and birds'.

As mentioned before, the actual sacrifice of a bull within the confined space of a subterranean Mithraic shrine seems, because of physical considerations alone, a highly improbable event.

The Mithraic religion was professedly a man's religion, one, it would seem, peculiarly acceptable to the incomparably fearless and disciplined soldiers of the Roman legions. Throughout the ancient Persian poem called the *Yasht* 'Mithra appears pre-eminently a god of battles; he was, therefore, especially fitted to become, as he did in later times, the favourite deity of the Roman soldier.'[23]

Christianity, at the time, was the only serious rival to Mithraism. To the Roman legionary who might spend the best twenty years of his life on foreign service, the Christian faith may have seemed too gentle, too pacific; out of keeping with the life he led and the duties he had to perform. On the other hand the Mithraists, 'rated strength higher than gentleness, and preferred courage to lenity. From their long association with barbaric religions, there was perhaps a residue of cruelty in their ethics. A religion of soldiers, Mithraism exalted the military virtues above all others.'[24]

Yet, curiously, in many respects, the religions of Mithra and of Christ had much in common both in ethics and in belief:

The resemblances between the two hostile churches were so striking as to impress even the minds of antiquity. From the third century, the Greek philosophers were wont to draw parallels between the Persian Mysteries and Christianity which were evidently entirely in favour of the former. The Apologists also dwelt on the analogies between the two religions, and explained them as a Satanic travesty of the holiest rites of their religion. If the polemical works of the Mithraists had been preserved, we should doubtless have heard the same accusation hurled back upon their Christian adversaries.[25]

Mithraism after its brief Roman flowering, faded into obscurity within three centuries, whereas Christianity has survived nearly two thousand years. Yet, even today, in many men's minds there is an attraction in the brute force, the irresistible power, the unconquerable courage, the sensual pride of the savage bull. The man who could match it, fight it and subdue it was a man indeed – more than a man, a very god – and the young, fearless and athletic god who made the bull prisoner in the joy of his strength and slew it regretfully and only then in obedience to a divine command, was a god that any soldier might well be proud to follow and admire.

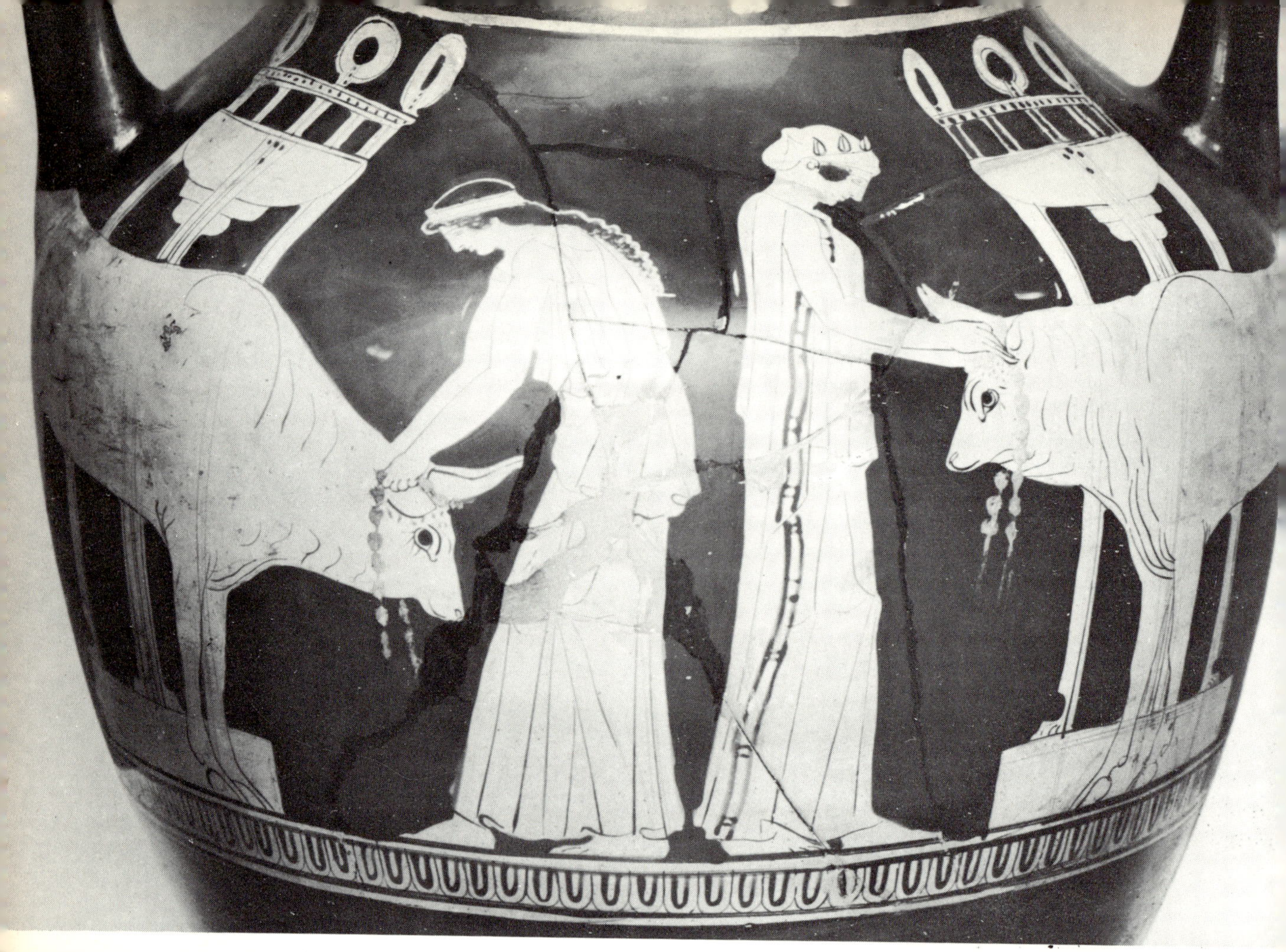

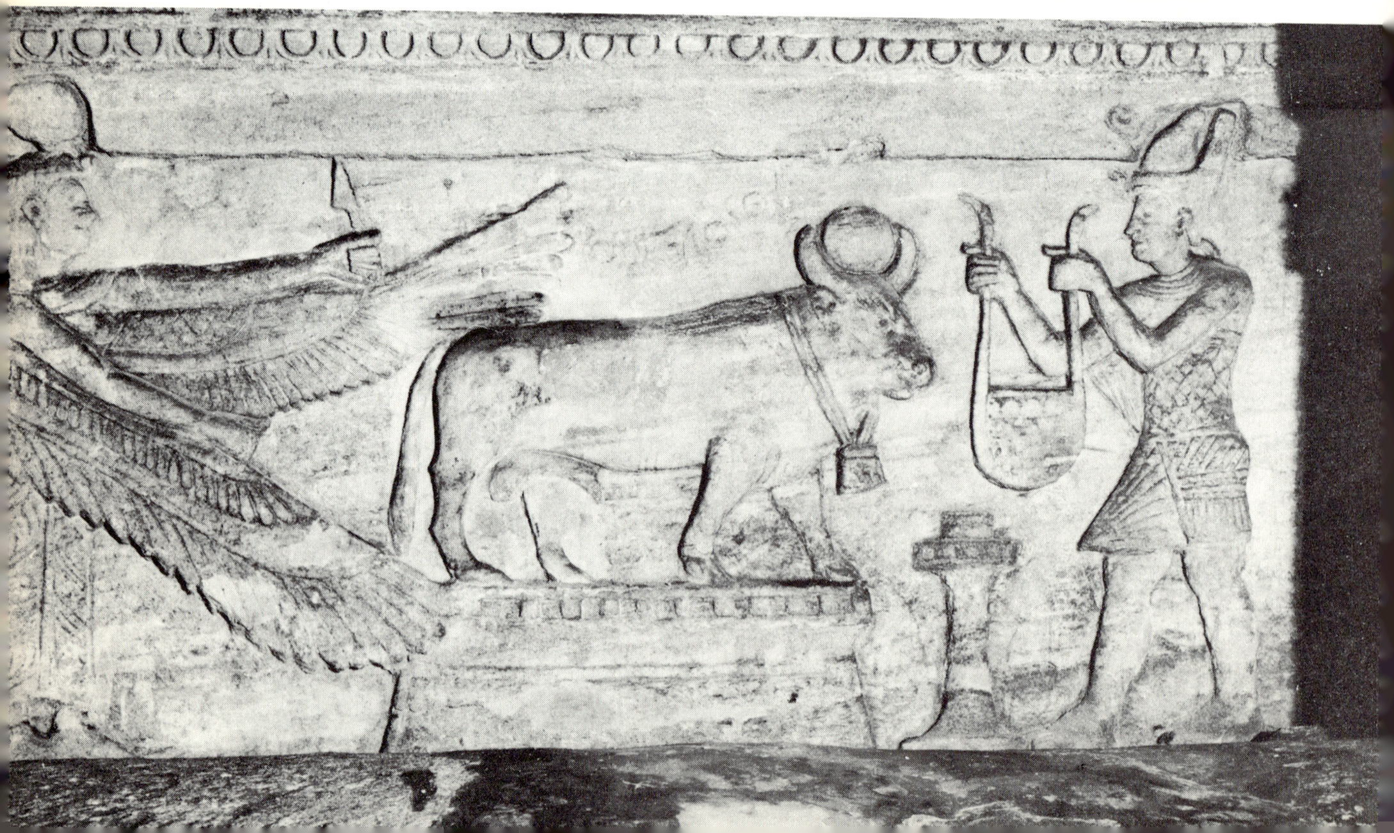

Yet, Mithraism had, and possibly still has, an attraction for other than soldiers. The greatest authority on this exotic cult, Franz Cumont, Professor in the University of Ghent, Belgium, who devoted the best years of his life to its study, wrote this of it:

Perhaps no other religion ever offered to its sectaries in a higher degree than Mithraism opportunities for prayer and motives for veneration. When the initiate betook himself in the evening to the sacred grotto concealed in the solitude of the forests, at every step new sensations awakened in his heart some mystical emotion. The stars that shone in the sky, the wind that whispered in the foliage, the spring or brook that babbled down the mountain-side, even the earth that he trod under his feet, were in his eyes divine, all surrounding nature provoked in him a worshipful fear for the infinite forces that swayed the universe.[26]

One feels that Franz Cumont, himself, was almost persuaded to become a Mithraist!

Running parallel with the bull-cult in pagan religions, there is the echo, the reflection of belief, in the form of art. On the cave walls of Lascaux, in wall paintings of consummate skill, are shown the first reproductions of the wild bull – the aurochs – from which the bull-cult of so many religions and races was derived.

This cult was prominent in the religion and lives of the people of Babylon in Mesopotamia. There, in the year 600 BC, Nebuchadnezzar restored the walls of the city destroyed by the invading Hittites. He had them built of glazed brick in varied colours – blue, yellow, black and white – and their surfaces near the Ishtar Gate were decorated with alternating rows of bulls and dragons in coloured brick relief.

The profile of these bulls, full of grace, vitality and movement, is a monument to their princely animal pride.

Ancient Egypt's strange cult of the Dead was combined with its worship of the bull, and many evidences of the prevailing bull-cult are found on the tombs of kings as well as on the walls of temples. Perhaps the most vivid is that from the twentieth-dynasty temple at Thebes. It shows Rameses III in a horse-drawn chariot hunting with bow and arrow and slaying wild bulls amid the reedy marshes of the Nile. In many Egyptian sculptures also, as in those of Assyria, man and bull are combined with a bull's head on a man's body or a man's head on the body of a bull.

The cult of the bull also comes much nearer home. From the temples of Egypt and Assyria, and from Crete in the Mediterranean, to the small Morayshire coastal village of Burghead in Scotland is a far cry. Yet, in that rather unlikely situation, sandstone slabs have been discovered, sculptured with incised lines on one face. The figures sculptured are those of bulls – conventionalised, diagrammatic, but quite unmistakably bulls, with heads down, tails lashing, prepared to charge. There are six of these sandstone slabs, not very large, 2 ft × 1 ft, and some 4 in

Opposite, above: Two women preparing bulls for sacrifice. From an amphora *c.* 450 BC. These bull sacrifices sometimes had a certain classical dignity. (*British Museum*)

A sarcophagus from Kom el Shugafa, Alexandria, showing the sacred bull being offered a golden necklace by the King whilst being protected by the outstretched wings of a goddess – probably Isis. (*Ronald Sheridan*)

thick, which have all been discovered at intervals in the course of building operations since 1809. Their significance appears to be unknown.. They are recorded in detail and individually illustrated in a publication equally improbable – a huge book of vast learning entitled *The Early Christian Monuments of Scotland.*[27] Whatever these relics signify, the evidence of the bull-cults is plain to see. Indubitably, although early monuments of Scotland, they had nothing whatever to do with Christianity.

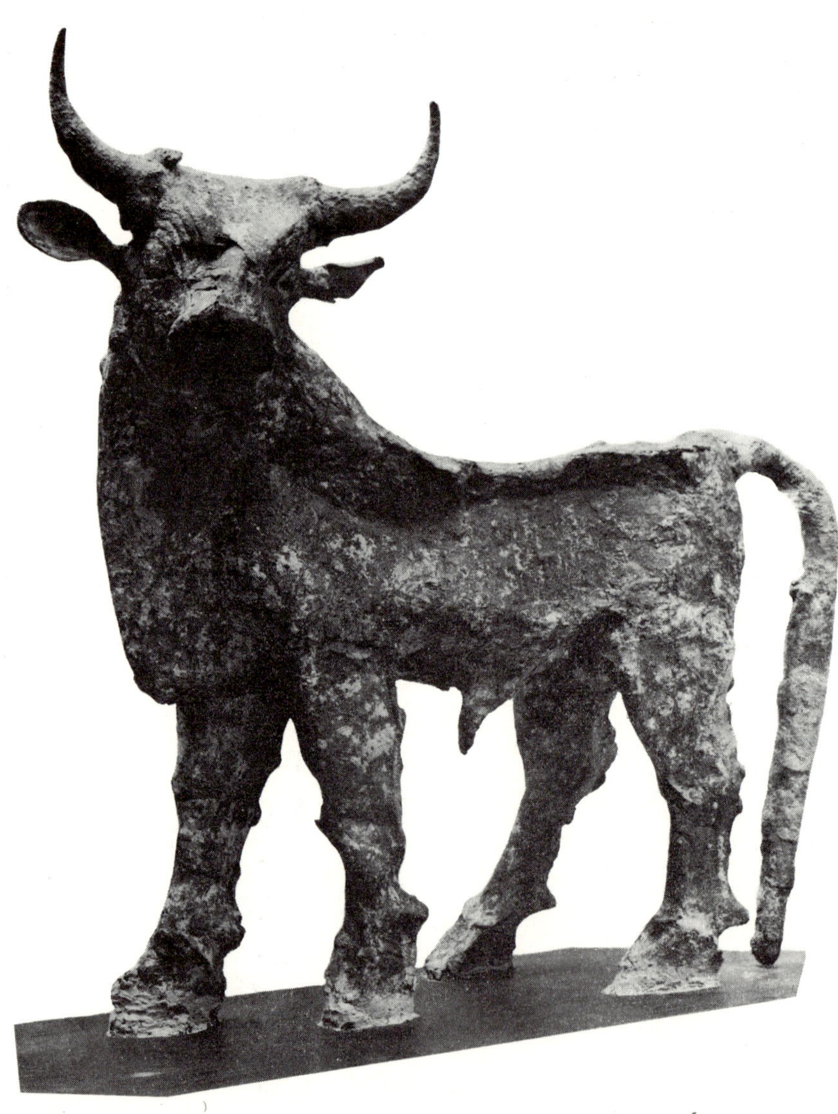

One of a row of copper bulls that stood along the façade of the Sumerian temple at Tell el-Obeid, *c.* 2600 BC. The bull-cult was prominent in the religion and lives of the people of Babylon, and four such copper bulls were discovered in the ruins of the temple wall. (*British Museum*)

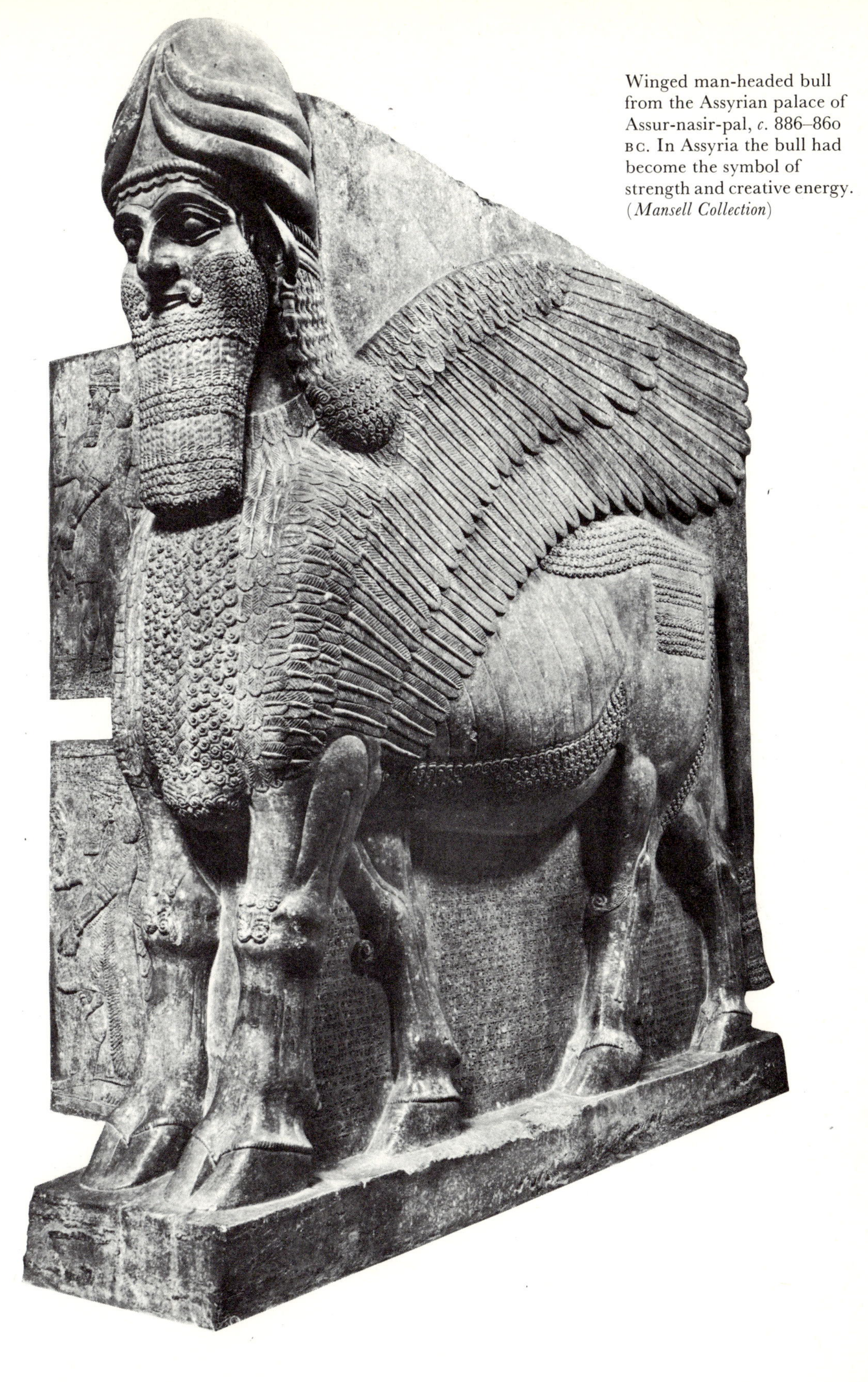

Winged man-headed bull from the Assyrian palace of Assur-nasir-pal, *c.* 886–860 BC. In Assyria the bull had become the symbol of strength and creative energy. (*Mansell Collection*)

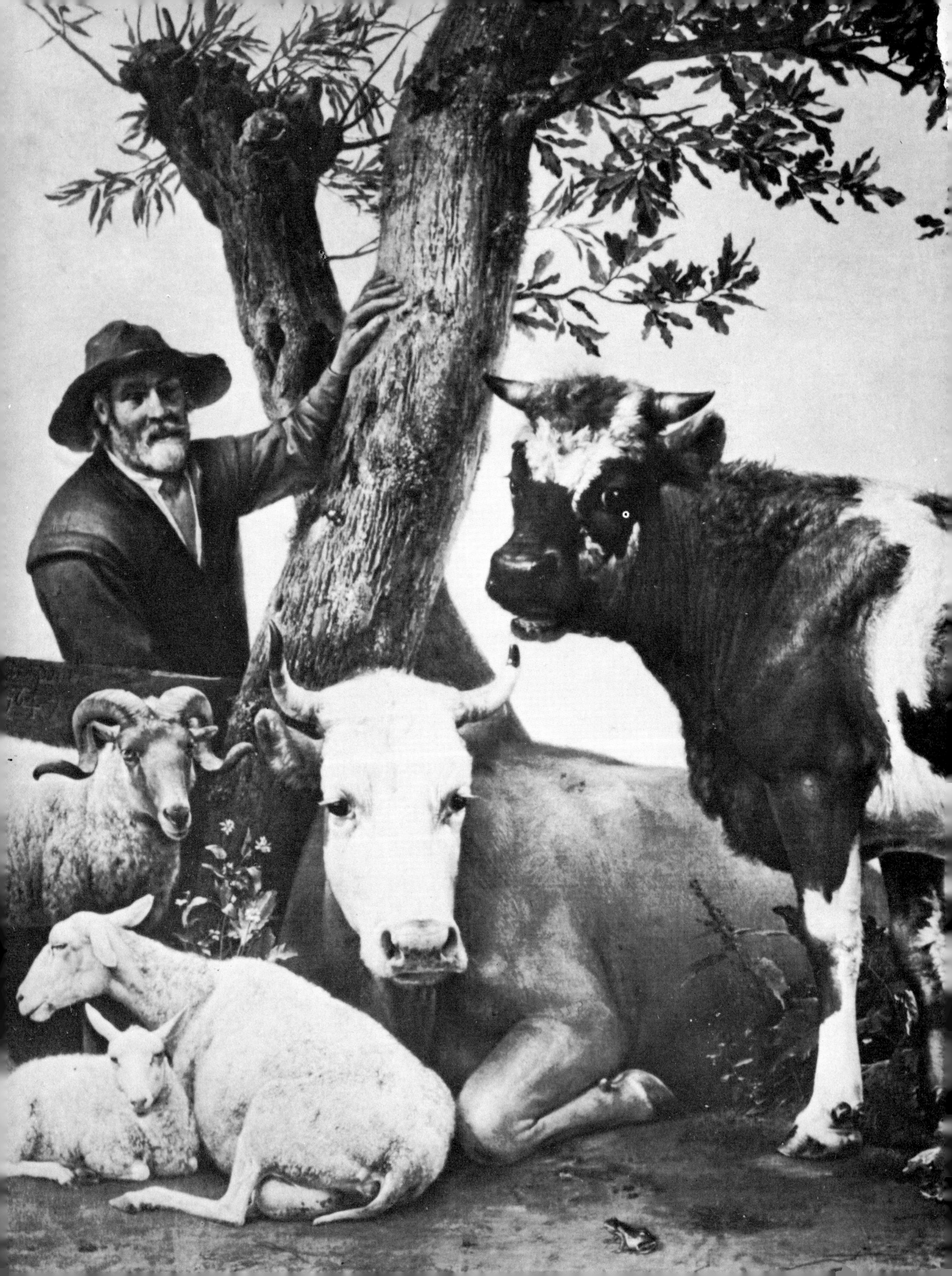

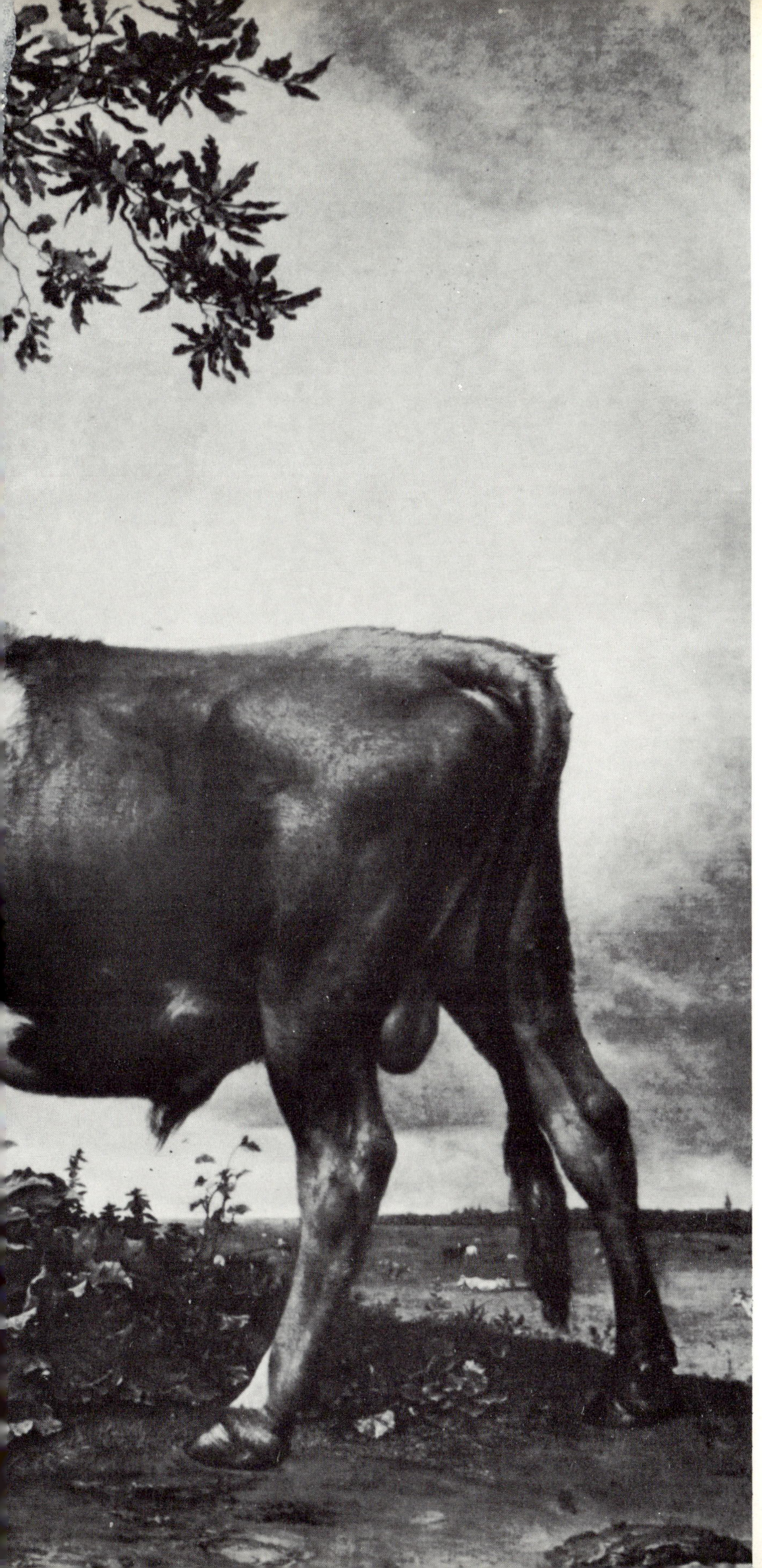

4

The Bull in Art

The Young Bull by Paul Potter
(1625–54). (*Radio Times Hulton
Picture Library*)

§ Art is the reflection of religion or the lack of it. The incomparable artistry of classical Greece elevated a somewhat crude, frequently cruel, occasionally bestial but also poetical mythology into some of the most beautiful artistic achievements mankind has witnessed. The formalised, flat, politically influenced mythology of Rome led to little more than a dull imitation of what Greece had already done. Christianity inspired the best works of the old masters in the service of Christ. Today the failing faith of Western countries and the avowed atheism of Communist States is reflected in the chaotic confusion of modern art.

In the very beginning, in the age of the cave man, the magical rites of the people, so close to if not synonymous with religion, were drawn, sometimes with a rare artistic perfection, on the stone walls of caves. These cavemen artists drew, painted and engraved the wild animals of their era with a fidelity, vitality and beauty of supreme merit. Why such perfection in animal portrayal? Because, according to the Abbé Breuil,[1]

At the base of such artistic creation there must be a profound knowledge of the appearance of animals, which only daily experience in the life of a big game hunter can give; if there is no big game hunting, there is no naturalistic wall art . . . Everywhere it was the big game hunters who produced beautiful naturalistic Art.

These early artists hunted and drew the rhinoceros, the bison, mammoth, deer, horse, bear and many other animals. They also drew and painted the bull.

'Bulls are almost everywhere, but only at Lascaux are there really many.'[2] It is in this cave, in south-west France, that wall paintings of the aboriginal wild aurochs, *Bos primigenius*, are best displayed. The discovery of this cave goes to the credit of two French youths:

The cavern and its paintings, destined to be so celebrated, were discovered on the 12th of September 1940 by two young lads, Ravidat and Marsal, as they were roaming near Montignac with other young companions. They told M. Léon Laval, their old schoolmaster of their discovery; He informed me at once and I visited the cave on the 21st of September. . . .[3]

The cave is situated near the little town of Montignac-sur-Vézère. There, hidden away through thousands of years, there remain the pictures of the aurochs the cavemen drew. These pictures are large, often very large, covering the whole cave wall. One of them is more than five and a half metres in length. They are painted, never engraved, on a thin calcite deposit and the technique of their painting has an interest of its own. In order to paint, the cave artist required light and this was provided by primitive types of lamp. At Lascaux they were probably shavings of pinewood ignited on limestone slabs, since both the slabs and charcoal from conifers were discovered in the cave.

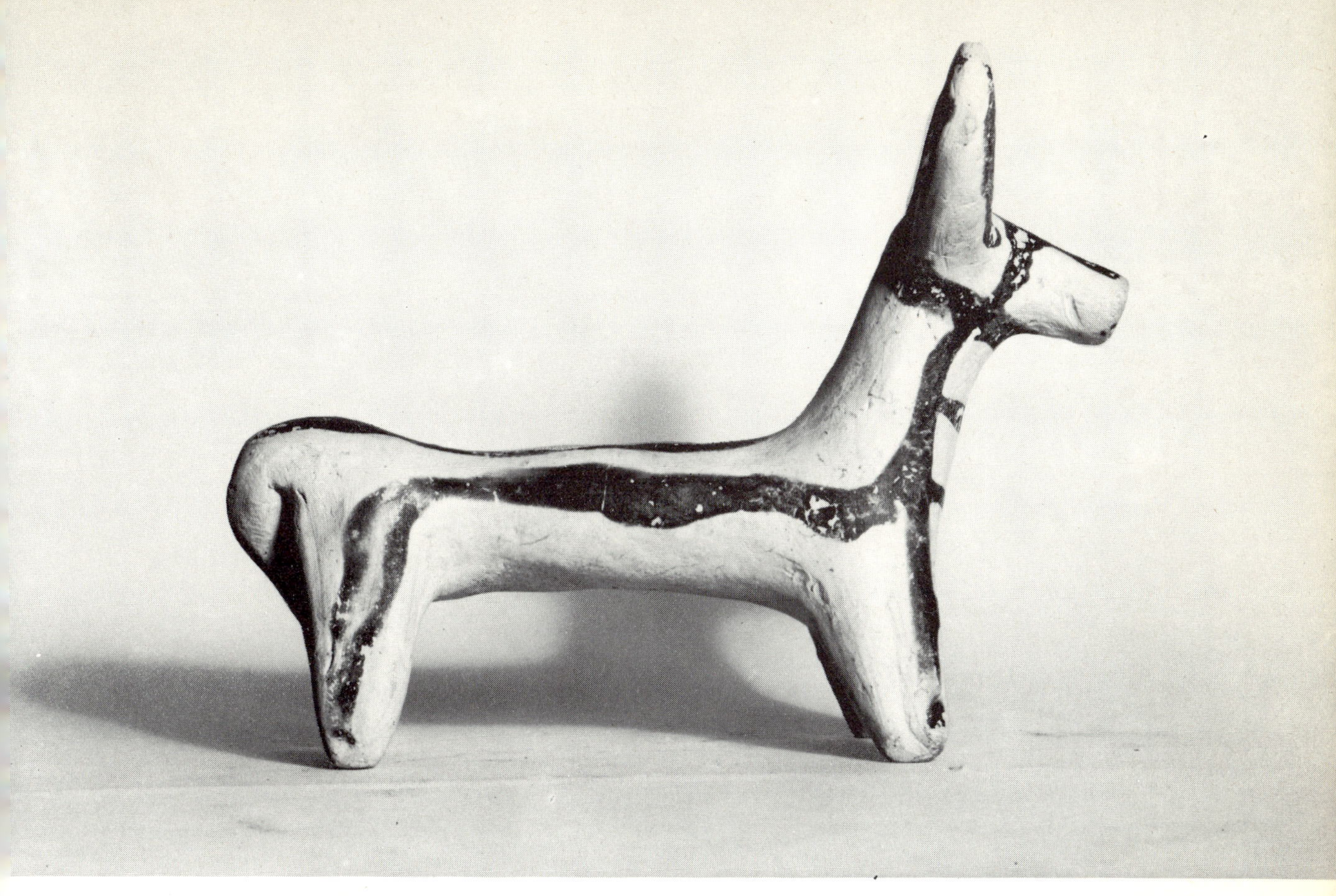

'One thing is certain. Men who explored the great caverns not only knew how to light their way, but were certainly capable of relighting quickly the flame of their lamps, extinguished by a drop of water or gust of air.'[4]

The cave artist used various colouring materials, iron and ochres, and applied the paint either with his fingers, a piece of chewed pine branch or a pad of feathers and fur. The artists of Lascaux improved on this technique, using a kind of blowpipe through which coloured powder was blown.

The artistic reflections of the prevailing bull-cults of Middle Eastern countries – the tomb and temple art of ancient Egypt, Babylon and Assyria – influenced the development of the supreme dedication of artistry to the bull, in its finest flowering in the Minoan art of ancient Crete.

The story of the discovery of this culture and civilisation which preceded that of classical Greece is, in a sense, the story of two men, Heinrich Schliemann who excavated the ruins of the palace of Mycenae in Greece and Sir Arthur Evans who excavated the ruined palace of Knossos in Crete. Working independently and at their own expense, these two Victorians of private means and inspired imagination un-

Terracotta figure of a bull from Rhodes, painted in the Late Minoan period. (*British Museum*)

71

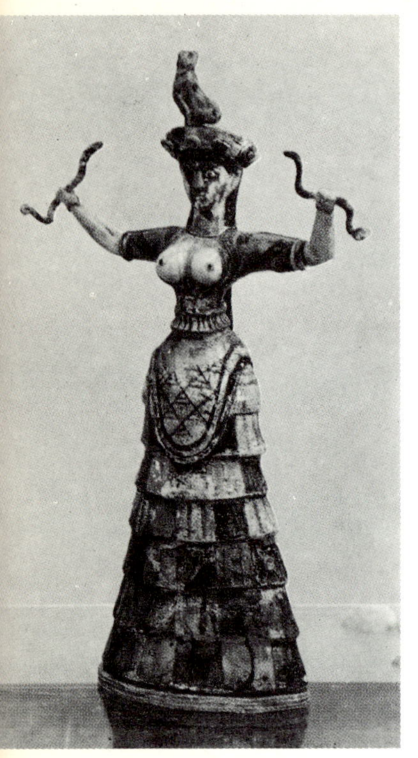

Statuette of Ariadne, daughter of King Minos, Goddess of the serpents and High Priestess of the Cretan bull-cult. From the museum at Heraklion, Crete.

earthed a culture in which the bull, both in religion and in art, reached a prominence in the one and perfection in the other seldom equalled and never surpassed. Sir Arthur Evans wrote of Crete, 'What a part these creatures play here!' Yet, Evans himself was never very certain as to the exact part they did play. During the massive, detailed and costly excavations he controlled at the Palace of Knossos, fragments of certain mural paintings were uncovered which revealed a type of acrobatic bull baiting or bull leaping – Evans preferred the term 'bull-grappling' – which caught the imagination of the world. So much so that it has been used on the postage stamps of modern Greece.

From a restoration of these somewhat fragmentary remains, Evans reconstructed a complete picture and description of what, apparently, was a ceremonial spectacle rather than a sport, probably one with a religious significance. Evans employed a Swiss artist of distinction, E. Gilleron, to make the restorations, of which the best-known and most complete is that of a bull-grappling performance, literally in full swing. The acrobats, both male and female, are in action. One grasps the horns of a gigantic bull in full charge. Another is turning a somersault on the bull's back. A third stands in the rear of the charging bull, evidently prepared to catch the somersaulting acrobat as he returns to earth. The interpretation of the mechanics of this feat, as first put forward was that the acrobat, after grasping the bull's horns, was tossed backwards, performing one or more somersaults before his final descent. According to Evans, the sequence, illustrated diagrammatically, was as follows:

1. Shows the charging bull seized by the horns near their tips.
2. The bull has raised his head in an endeavour to toss his assailant, and at the same time gives an impetus to the turning figure.
3. The acrobat has released his grip of the horns, and after completing a back-somersault has landed with his feet on the hinder part of the bull's back. . . .

In 4. he makes a final leap from the hind quarters of the bull – a risky plunge.[5]

This obvious interpretation of the restored bull-grappling fresco might well have received universal acceptance had it not been for the scepticism of a certain Professor Baldwin Brown who, apparently familiar with bulls in the field as well as on frescoes, doubted the possibility of the acrobatic performance as interpreted by Evans. He made inquiries among American cowboys and rodeo experts. These agreed that to grasp the horns of a charging bull as the start for a somersault was incredible since 'there is no chance of a human person being able to obtain a balance when the bull is charging full against him'. It was also pointed out that were the acrobat successful in performing such a somersault over a charging bull he would have landed, not upon the bull's back, but well to its rear. Evans, no doubt with regret, was compelled to accept the logic of these criticisms and wrote, 'All that can be said is that the performance as featured by the Minoan artist seems to be of a kind pronounced impossible by modern champions of the sport.'[6]

Even in order to adapt the 'bull-grappling frescoes' – 'The Taureador Frescoes' as Evans called them – to the purposes of fiction, Mary Renault in her novel *The King Must Die* had to invent a special breed of bull, huge and strong, superlatively handsome but slow in action and dull in thought. She had also to invent a dummy bull designed by Daedalus, the great artificer who made the dummy cow for the strange pleasures of Queen Pasiphaë. It was on this dummy that the acrobats, the slim youths and the agile maidens learnt to grasp the horns, to perform the somersaults and to land gracefully before the spectators in the packed arena. A lovely and thrilling spectacle, were it true. A pity, perhaps, that Professor Baldwin Brown ever intervened. There is always something particularly sad in the death of a legend.

What, then, did these artistic and original frescoes, the work of the Minoan artist, represent and possibly idealise? A sport, a religious spectacle, an element of sacrifice should an acrobat stumble or a bull grow tired of circus play? Most probably, perhaps, a sport with the occasional accident to please the bloodthirsty, since boxing and wrestling spectacles were held in the same arena. It would be pleasant to believe that the colourful story as told by the novelist held an element of truth; and who dare say after thousands of years that it was not so?

The term 'fresco' means a mode of painting upon walls covered with damp, freshly laid or partially dried plaster, and the Minoan artists used bright colours in their work. Of all the stucco reliefs the excavations at Knossos revealed, that of the head of a charging bull was reckoned by Evans to be the finest:

This head, which is that of a gigantic bull of the Urus breed and measures 64 centimetres from the back of the head behind the ear to the tip of the nose, was incomparably the finest of all the painted stucco reliefs here discovered. It still stands forth as one of the noblest revelations of Minoan art.

It is simple and large in style, but instinct with fiery life. The moulding, though partly in a lower plane, merges into very high relief in the treatment of the eye and forehead, while the upper circuit of the ear is executed in the round. The surface is of a deep ruddy hue with a bluish white spot of cuspid outline on the bridge of the nose. The pupil of the eye is of a yellowish white, and the eye-ball, ringed with coloured bands, is exceedingly prominent.[7]

The colours used were brown madder, pale blue, red and off-white.

Evans went on to say, 'The upstanding ear marks intense excitement; the tongue protrudes, the hot breath seems to blow through the nostrils. The folds of the dewlap show that the head was in a lowered position – it is that of a bull coursing wildly.'[8]

Possibly the original conveys the impression that Sir Arthur Evans so enthusiastically and vividly described. The thrill of unearthing such buried treasure, concealed for thousands of years, must have been an unforgettable experience. Nevertheless, the full-page black and white reproduction in the third volume of his recorded discoveries, *The Palace of Minos at Knossos*, seems to have lost much of its life. It has more than a suggestion of a bull's head hung in a butcher's shop. Possibly, the Minoan artist, like the Victorian artist Joseph Farquharson in his once popular paintings of sheep, employed slaughter-house material to ensure exactitude of detail.

This effigy of the bull is only one of the innumerable reproductions of bulls and of bulls' heads the Cretan excavations revealed. Rhytons or libation vases in the form of heads instead of the whole body were usual in earlier ages. The rhyton is a drinking cup or horn with a hole in the point to drink by, rather similar to the invalid drinking cup in modern usage. It could, of course, quite as easily be used for pouring forth wine or other liquid in honour of a god, in other words, as a libation vessel. One of Evans's most notable discoveries was the greater part of an exceptionally large rhyton 'in the form of a bull's head magnificently inlaid. It was cut and hollowed out of a solid piece of . . . dark steatite [an alternative word for soapstone].'[9]

'But the most beautiful decorative feature of the head was the most perfectly preserved right eye.'[10] The lens was of rock crystal, the pupil painted a bright scarlet, the iris black, the cornea white. 'The crystal setting is itself inserted in a border of red jasper, which surrounds the white field of the eye like the rims of bloodshot eyelids. To add to the effect, the crystal lens of the eye both illuminates and magnifies the pupil and imparts to the whole an almost startling impression of fiery life.'[11]

Was this, in reproduction, the bull that haunted Cottrell when he spent a night alone in the Villa Ariadne that Evans built for himself at Knossos?:

I went back to the fire and then noticed, for the first time the formidable head of the Minoan Bull – a plaster cast – which hung on the wall to the right of the fireplace. It was black, with gold horns, white nostrils and bright, red-rimmed eyes, and as I moved around the room, taking out books from the shelves, examining pictures and ornaments, those little red eyes seemed to follow me. . . .[12]

Of even greater artistry is the silver bull's-head rhyton with a rosette of gold plate attached to its forehead unearthed from the Fourth Shaft Grave at Mycenae. This particular rhyton, as well as being a supreme triumph of the silversmith's art, has an interesting history. Heinrich Schliemann, accompanied by his youthful second wife, a classically beautiful Grecian girl sixteen years old and called Sophia Engastrom-

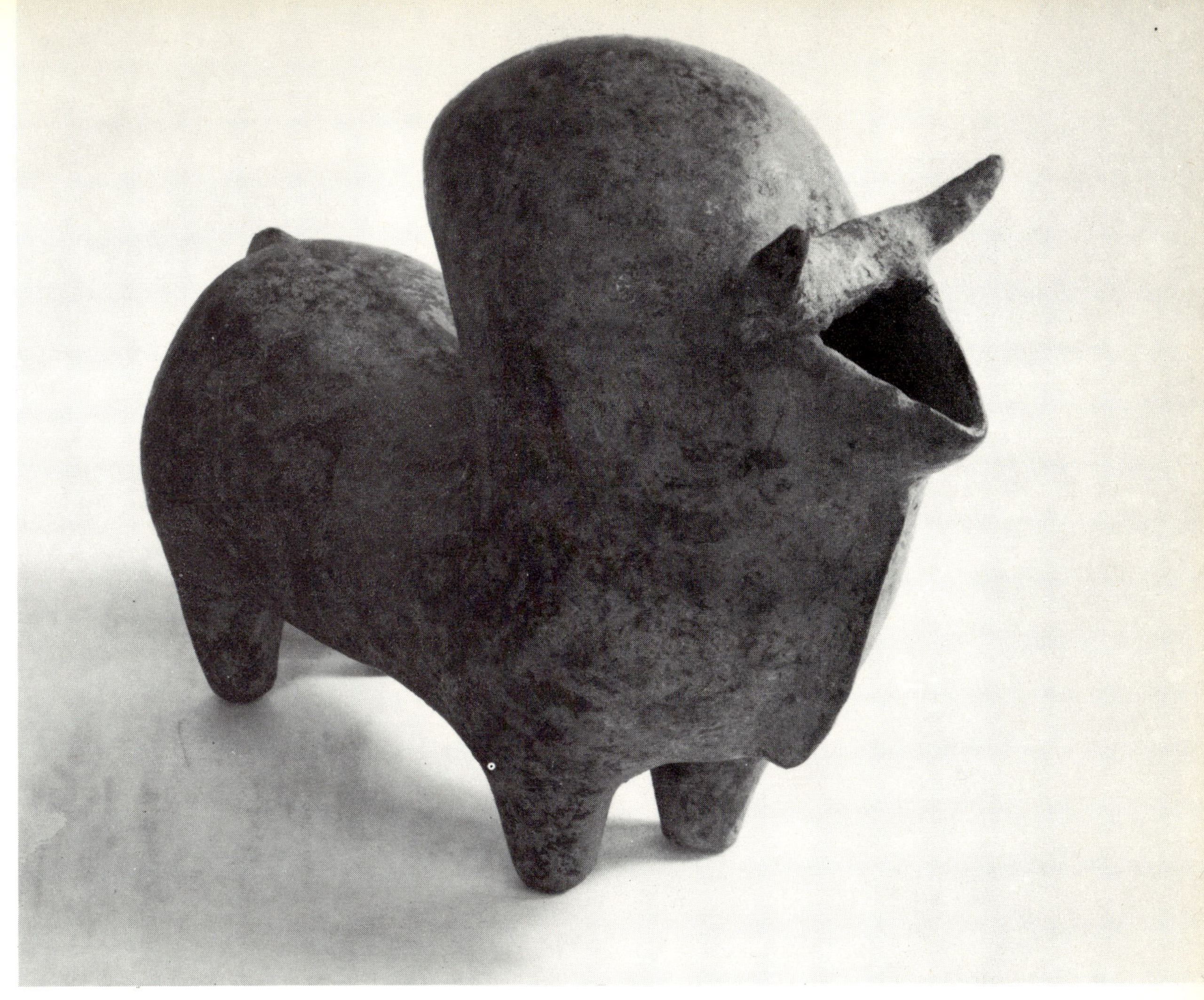

enos, was engaged in excavation of ancient ruins at Mycenae in Greece. Heinrich and Sophia were absorbed in this exhilarating childish pursuit of searching for hidden treasure, dignified in adult years by the title of archaeology, when they struck oil, in the shape of gems and jewellery, of silver and of gold. Schliemann imagined he had discovered relics of the heroic age of Homer's *Iliad*. He even adorned his young wife with what he believed were the jewels of Helen of Troy. He sent a telegram to the King of Greece informing him 'I have gazed on the face of Agamemnon.' Actually, in the shaft graves in the ruined Palace of Mycenae, he had unearthed the buried treasures of a far older epoch called the Aegean Civilisation, to which the Palace of Knossos and the Cretan discoveries of Sir Arthur Evans also belong. In the same grave, the fourth that Schliemann excavated, there were two bulls' heads of very thin gold plate with that ancient and mysterious emblem of divinity, the Double Axe, between the horns. Of this Mycenean bull's-head rhyton Evans wrote, 'In the light of our present knowledge the Mycenae relic must be recognised as Minoan work,

Pottery rhyton in the form of a humped bull. Persian, from Amlash *c.* 800 BC. (*British Museum*)

75

doubtless of the Knossian palatial school. . . .'[13]

The linkages of other artistic treasures found in Greece with the Aegean age and the Palace of Knossos followed swiftly upon the progress of Cretan discoveries. This applied to two very famous gold cups unearthed from the Vapheio tomb near Sparta in Greece. These were known to archaeologists for a decade before Schliemann and Evans established the prehistoric existence of an Aegean civilisation. It is now agreed universally that these two golden cups belong to that age. They may indeed have been the work of the goldsmiths of Knossos itself for one of the two cups shows date palms, which grow in Crete.

These Vapheio cups are decorated with designs illustrating Minoan bull-handling methods that Evans termed the 'cowboy class', as distinct from the acrobatic performances depicted on the frescoes of Knossos. The designs, raised in relief by hammering from within, a technique termed 'repoussé', illustrate two different ways, one forceful, the other more subtle, of entrapping bulls, wild or semi-wild.

These two cups are referred to customarily and for convenience of description as Cups A and B. The first, Cup A, shows the forceful method of capture and the bulls are definitely of the aurochs type. They are being driven into a trap made by a rope cradle stretched between two olive trees and tied to their trunks. Three bulls are shown. One that has escaped is seen galloping off to the right. The central bull is caught and entangled in the rope cradle. The bull to the left has flung one of his trappers to the ground and appears to be about to gore him. Presumably in an attempt at rescue, a girl has locked both her legs and arms about the bull's horns in such a way that it is unable to pierce her. The whole tableau suggests that these 'cowboy' actions, carried out in the midst of harsh reality and deadly danger, may have been the model, as it were, for the more formalised bull-grappling performances in the courtly arena of Knossos in Crete.

The second Vapheio cup, B, shows the capture of a bull by a decoy cow in heat. It is perhaps a shade less realistic. The bull is seen following the scent of the cow but in an attitude more reminiscent of a dog than of a bull. The centrepiece is the same bull in what Evans called 'amorous conversation' with the cow. Previous authorities had interpreted both bovine figures as being bulls, although the more slender head of the cow is quite obviously feminine. Evans based his identification of sex on the raised tail of the cow, visible above the centre of the bull's back, as being an indication of the cow being in heat. The expression on the faces of both bull and cow might be considered rather too anthropomorphic and faintly ridiculous. The left-hand scene is undoubtedly the best. A 'cowboy' has lassoed the bull's left hind-leg preparatory to capture and the frustrated animal is bellowing its impotent rage.

There are in Minoan art many other wonderful representations of

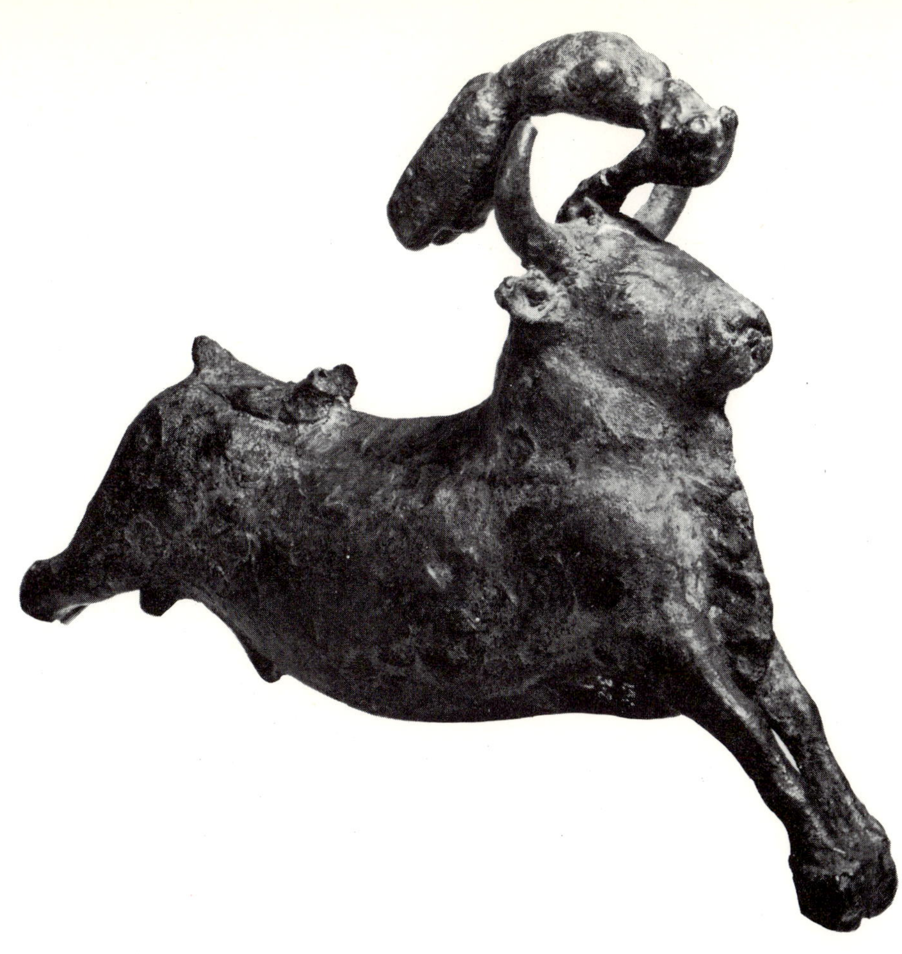

Figure of acrobat and bull
during the performance of
the bull-leap. Late Minoan
period. (*British Museum*)

bulls in action. For example, those illustrating the bull in association
with the slender and graceful Minoan bull-grapplers: on the gold signet
ring from Arkhanes; the bronze group from the Spencer-Churchill
Collection and, perhaps the most vital of all, that of the acrobat between the horns of a bull on the steatite rhyton from Hagia Triada.
These are all echoing corroborations of the 'Taureador Frescoes' of
the Palace of Minos. So also are the innumerable miniatures, intaglios,
clay sealings, signet rings and other ornaments which were found at
Knossos. Many of these have the bull and the acrobat displayed with
great artistic skill on a small surface. The intaglios – figures cut into
any substance, particularly a stone or gem in which the design is
hollowed out (the reverse of cameo) – are especially notable. So also
was the 'art of painting on the back of small crystal plaques or bosses,
which was carried at Knossos to a perfection worthy of the greatest
miniaturists of later times'.[14]

Naturally, Minoan art had many subjects other than bulls and
bull-grappling acrobats. Although it is the 'Toreador Frescoes' as
restored by Gilleron that have attracted the greatest publicity, possibly because of the novelty of the spectacle as much as the artistic

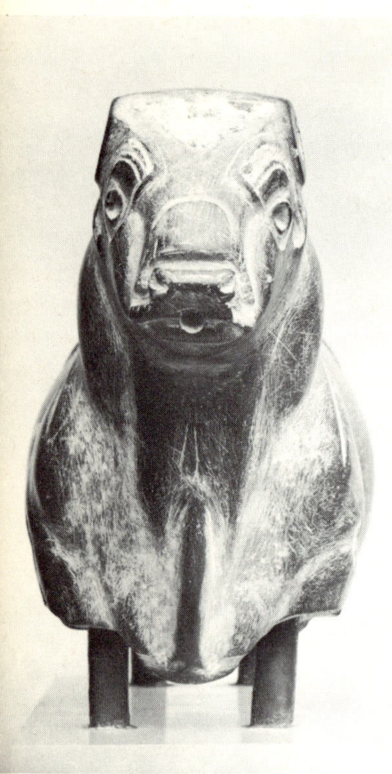

Figure of a bull from the Larsa Dynasty (between 1969 and 1742 BC). The horns, now missing, were probably made of gold. The head was originally decorated with gold and lapis lazuli inlay. (*British Museum*)

merit of the frescoes themselves, the greatest beauty of Minoan art is in the use of marine designs, of the octopus, the starfish, the porpoise, the nautilus, on pottery and faience. For Crete was an island and the ancient Minoans who dwelt there a sea-going people. Even the strange white beautiful bulls that in poetic legend brought Europa from Greece and infatuation to Queen Pasiphaë came out of the sea from amidst the white breakers, and some have asserted that these mythical white bulls were the sun's rising from the ocean that gave life to the world. Yet the bull was a central focus of both Minoan life and religion, of courtly spectacle and sophisticated art. Evans wrote that to the ancient Minoans 'the Bull was quite as much as the lion the King of Beasts'.[15]

The Aegean or Minoan civilisation preceded that of classical Greece, and its mythology came to be incorporated in many a Grecian legend. It is, therefore, no accident that one of the twelve labours of Heracles, in which a bull was concerned, was centred in Crete. The story goes that the god Poseidon had given Minos, king of that island, a bull intended to be sacrificed to him. Minos found another use for the bull and Poseidon in revenge drove the animal mad. Minos appealed for help to Heracles, who was in Crete at the time. The hero succeeded in capturing the bull and took it away on his back over the seas to Argolis. A Greek cup, called 'The Cretan Bull', in the Louvre, shows Heracles in action against the mad bull. Using ropes, he appears to be about to cast the bull in much the same way as is still employed in the 'casting of colts' before their castration. Artistically, the design on the cup has little appeal, the prominent rump of the bull resembling that of a pig. It has none of the realistic vitality of so much of the Cretan work. The exploit itself recalls the more practical adventures of the Persian, Mithra, who became the central figure of a religion.

Mithraism reached its peak in a period of poor artistry. Its phenomenal expansion in the tracks of the Roman legions synchronised with the art of Imperial Rome, universally regarded as unoriginal and uninspired. For the Romans, who as soldiers conquered so much of the world, were only second-rate artists, content to copy what the Greeks had already done. Writing of the monuments of Mithraism Cumont confessed that 'In point of fact, their artistic merit is far below that of their value as historical documents, and their chief worth is not aesthetic but religious.'[16] He goes on to say, almost apologetically, that 'Some of the groups in high and low relief . . . hold a very honourable place in the multitude of sculptured works which the imperial period has left us, and are deserving of some consideration' and concludes, 'It can be proved that all our representations of the tauroctonous Mithra . . . are more or less faithful replicas of a type created by a sculptor of the school of Pergamon, in imitation of the sacrificing Victory which adorned the balustrade of the temple of Athena Nike on the Acropolis.'[17] Even the central decoration of every Mithraic shrine, the standardised representation of the bull sacrifice by Mithra, was a third-hand copy of a Grecian monument.

The centrepiece of every Mithraic shrine corresponded closely to the crucifix in Christian churches. Originality in design was inappropriate to its purpose. Economy of manufacture was frequently of greater importance, since replicas of the bull sacrifice, often extremely crude, were produced in quantity as religious symbols for Mithraic households. 'The ancient manufacturers turned out hundreds of smaller tauroctonous Mithras, just as our image-makers multiply in profusion the very same type of crucifixes and the very same Virgin Mary. It was the religious imagery of the epoch, and it was not more aesthetic than is ours today.'[18]

The swift overthrow of Mithraism by Christianity left the manufacturers of Mithraic symbols with an embarrassing situation and the appalling prospect of profitless dead stock on their hands. They solved the problem in a sufficiently ingenious manner:

A few alterations in costume and attitude transformed a pagan scene into a Christian picture. Mithra discharging his arrows against the rock became Moses causing the waters of the mountain of Horeb to gush forth; the Sun, raising his ally out of the Ocean, served to express the ascension of Elijah in the chariot of fire; and to the time of the Middle Ages the type of the tauroctonous god was perpetuated in the images of Samson rending the lion.[19]

It is of interest to speculate to what high levels of art the idolatry of Mithraism might have attained had not Christianity prevailed. The adventures of Mithra on his earthly pilgrimage, particularly, held seeds of fine flowering. Yet the old pagan worship of the bull, of its power, courage, and virility, seems to have died very hard.

In Raphael's painting *The Vision of Ezekiel* the figure of the brown winged bull is clearly based upon some ancient marble group of the Mithraic bull sacrifice. Again, Michelangelo's statue of Moses holding the ten commandments, in the church of San Pietro in Vincoli, Rome, bears vestigial horns upon its brooding head.

Following the overthrow of Mithraism and the simultaneous triumph of Christianity, the bull faded away into the realms of surreptitious superstition and the secret pagan practices of peasantries. Some would have it that he survived as the Devil in Christian teaching, carrying his horns and his cloven hooves along the road proverbially paved with good intentions. In any event the bull had no place in the Christian Church nor in Christian art. Its divorce from religious practice was complete. Consequently, the bull has come to take only a minor part in all subsequent art. Both in West and East the religions of Christianity and of Islam have pushed all pictorial representations of the bull either into the bullring or on to the farm.

There is, however, one exception to that generalised statement.

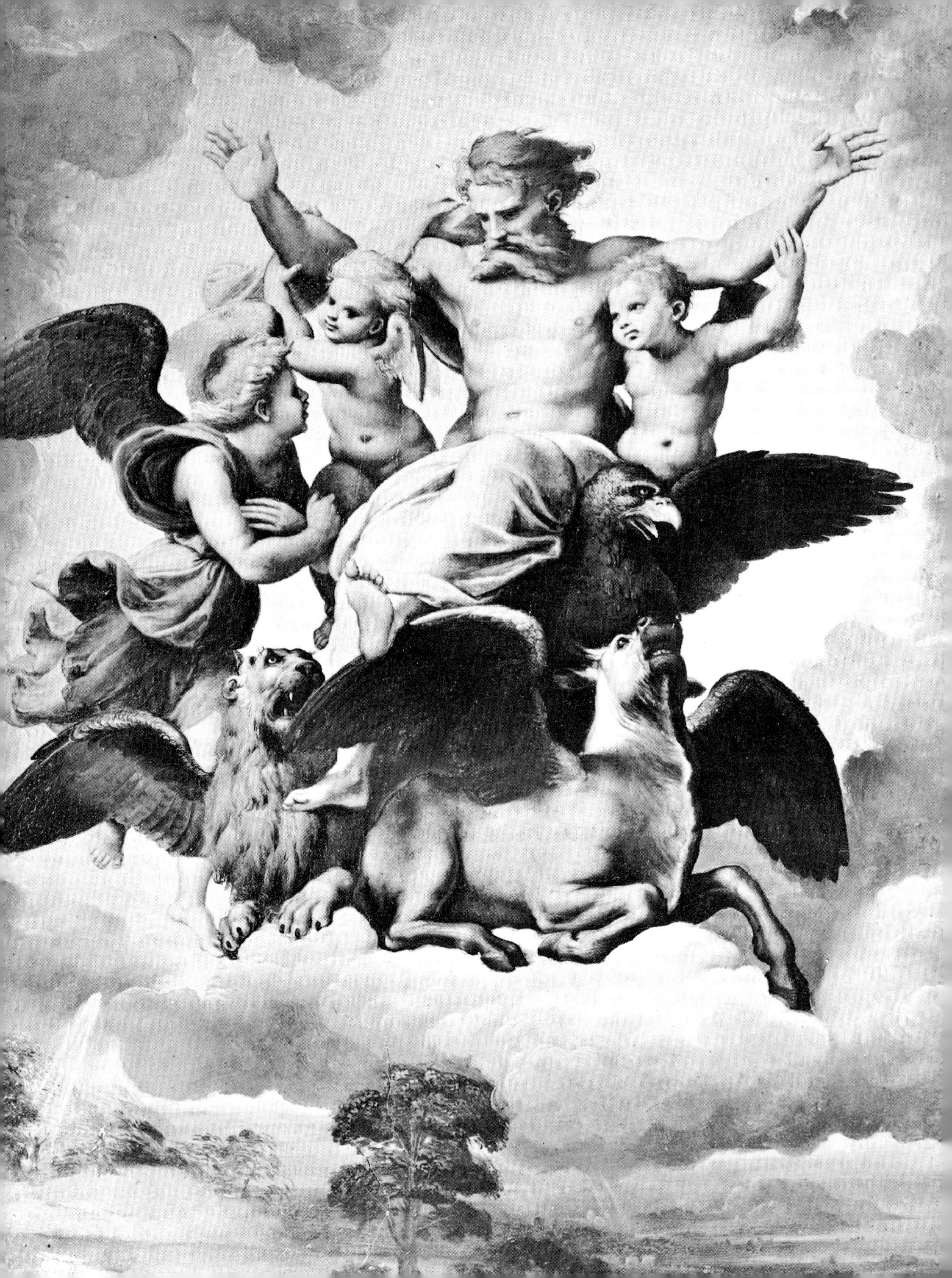

Thomas Bewick, the great eighteenth-century wood engraver, received a commission to do a block of the Chillingham Bull.

This was a bull in a herd of wild cattle belonging to a naturalist correspondent, and Bewick was obliged to stalk the animal in order to make a sketch in the park of Chillingham. This particular bull was a solitary and vanquished rival of the monarch of the herd, which he could not get near enough to sketch.[20]

Bewick, himself, considered this to be the best wood engraving he ever had made.

Animal portraiture was a feature of eighteenth-century English art. Probably due to the greater possibility of patronage and profit, the majority of animal artists, with Stubbs their master, preferred the horse. One English painter, however, James Ward (1769–1859) was attracted by bulls. Partly perhaps because of a measure of ancient paganism in his own character. Rothenstein has written of 'the energy, the richness and masculinity latent in Ward'[21] and John Piper said that 'Tumbled rocks, fighting bulls and prone, gnarled trees were among his subjects.'[22]

Opposite: The Vision of Ezekiel – Raphael. The figure of the brown winged bull is clearly based upon some ancient marble group of the Mithraic bull sacrifice. (*Mansell Collection*)

Detail from the Chillingham Bull. Wood engraving by Thomas Bewick (1753–1828), who considered it to be the best he had ever made. Disastrously, when only a few impressions of this engraving had been taken, the block split. Thus original prints are extremely rare and of considerable value.

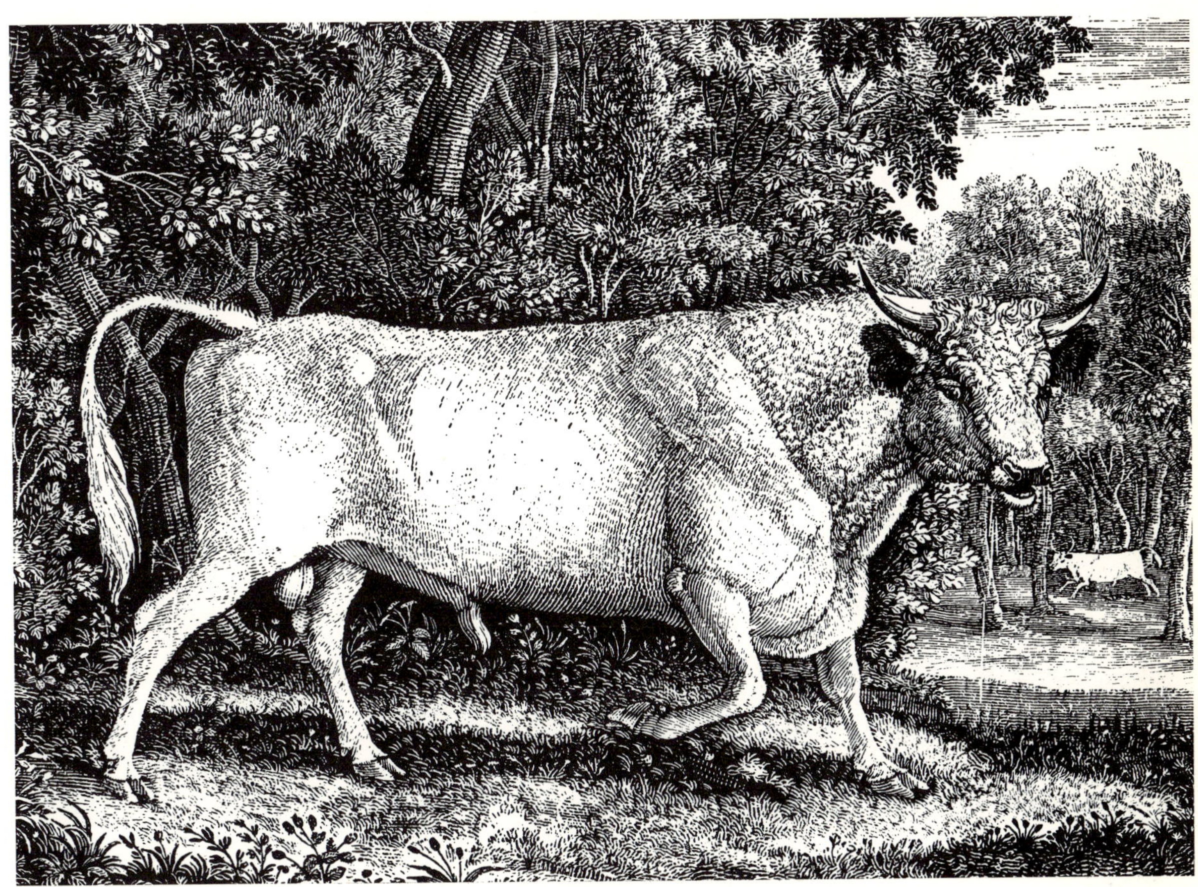

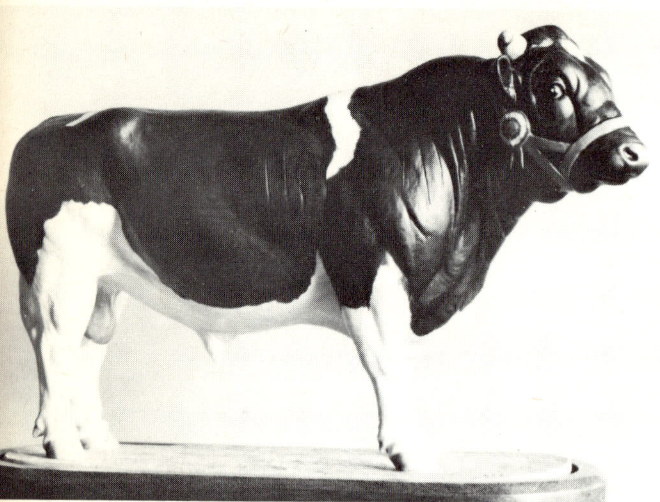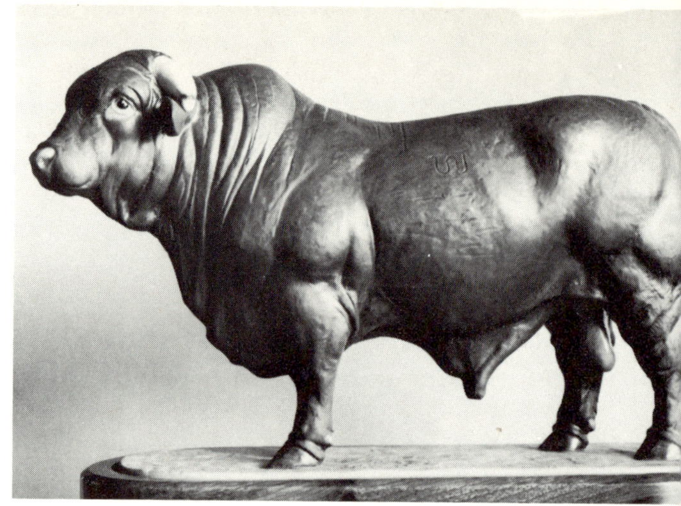

Left: British Friesian bull. One of the series of handmade Worcestershire pottery bulls. *Right:* Santa Gertrudis pottery bull.

Gordale Scar, sometimes called more simply *The Bull*, is his most famous oil painting. So gigantic is its size that it is seldom seen in reproduction. The original is hung in the Tate Gallery. Here, revived in a relatively modern setting, is the age-old combination of Thunder God and Bull. The background is the high, dark, menacing cliffs of the dale; capped by a storm sky at war. In the foreground – proud, valiant, vigilant, menacing – the white bull stands on guard. He stands alone. To his right and beneath him is the cow herd he both protects and rules.

Again, in Ward's *Bulls Fighting* 'a temperamental violence is expressed not only in the actual combat but in the tortured forms of the fallen tree'.[23] Indeed the very landscape seems at war. In this combination of the artist's temperament, agonised landscape and the bull's masculinity, there is more than an echo of the ancient and pagan bull mystique.

In a much softer and more pastoral manner, in the school of Dutch animal painting, Paul Potter is reckoned supreme. His best-known painting, the *Young Bull*, is hung in the Mauritshaus at The Hague. The affectionate pride on the face of the bearded owner is remarkable and as truthful as the developing masculine arrogance of the young bull itself.

At about the same period as Ward in England, the master artist Francisco de Goya (1746–1828), in Spain, was painting his pictures of village bullfights. He was also producing his series of some two score engravings entitled *La Tauromaquia* (bullfighting). Goya, besides being himself an amateur bullfighter was also a passionate follower or *aficionado* of the Spanish national spectacle. This spectacle, sport, sacrifice – call it what you will – was much in vogue in Goya's time, achieving a resurgence of its former glory. In the *Tauromaquia* etchings

Goya sought to illustrate the development of the ritual from the earliest phase until his own day and generation. It has, of course, developed and changed in many ways since Goya's time. It has become far more formalised and, as some would have it, less cruel. The series begins with the ancient Spaniards hunting bulls in open country, either mounted or on foot, armed with spears. – They show how the Moors adopted the Spanish sport. – They show how bulls came to be played with coloured cape in an enclosure. – The spirited Moor Gazul was the first to spear bulls according to rules. – The Moors in the ring played the bull with their burnous. – *Banderillas* were introduced to weaken or to incite the bull. – Casualties were frequent. – Spanish knights, horsed as always, killed the bull with spear or sword. – Even the Spanish king, Charles V, speared a bull in the plaza of Valladolid. – The 'Rabble', the *Canalla*, had their own version of the sport, hamstringing the bull with sickles, lances and other weapons. – The use of the cape and the ballet-dance steps of the matador appear in the bullring. – The famous Martincho throws the bull by grasping horn and tail. – The Moors use donkeys as a barrier against bulls with ball-tipped horns. – Martincho the daring sits on a kitchen chair, playing the bull with sword and hat. – The same hero prepares to jump from a table on to the bull's back. – Juanito Apiñani in the ring at Madrid uses the pole vault to avoid the bull's charge. – Dreadful carnage when a bull broke through into the front rows of the ring at Madrid in which carnage the Mayor of Torrejón was slain. – The manly courage of the famous *torera*, La Pajuelera, a native of Goya's own village, who dressed in man's clothing and mounted, played the bull in the ring at Saragossa. – Mariano Ceballos, called the Indian, kills the bull with his sword without dismounting. – The same Indian, mounted on one bull, charges another. – The dogs are let loose on a cowardly bull. – The role and risk of the mounted picadors are displayed. – *Banderillas* with fire-crackers are used in contempt of a bull without courage to charge. – A bull that was not afraid is throwing two teams of picadors. – Pepe Illo is killed by a bull in the ring at Madrid.[24]

It was much the same story, set in another century and told in words instead of pictures, that Hemingway related. It was then, as it is now, 'Death in the Afternoon'. But in Goya's day, the *corrida* was less highly organised, without the tinsel and the trappings, the ritualised *Paseo*, the spectacular parade that nowadays is a prelude to blood and sand. Curious, however, that bulls as drawn by Goya appear to be smaller than those in use today. Since all modern authors on bullfighting deplore the deterioration in size of the fighting bulls, it would seem either that the criticism is unjustified or that Goya for some reason of art deliberately drew his bulls below scale. Perhaps, in Goya's time, the Spanish bulls like the Spanish people still suffered from *los Desastres de la Guerra*.

One of Goya's series of etchings entitled *La Tauromaquia* (bullfighting). (*Mansell Collection*)

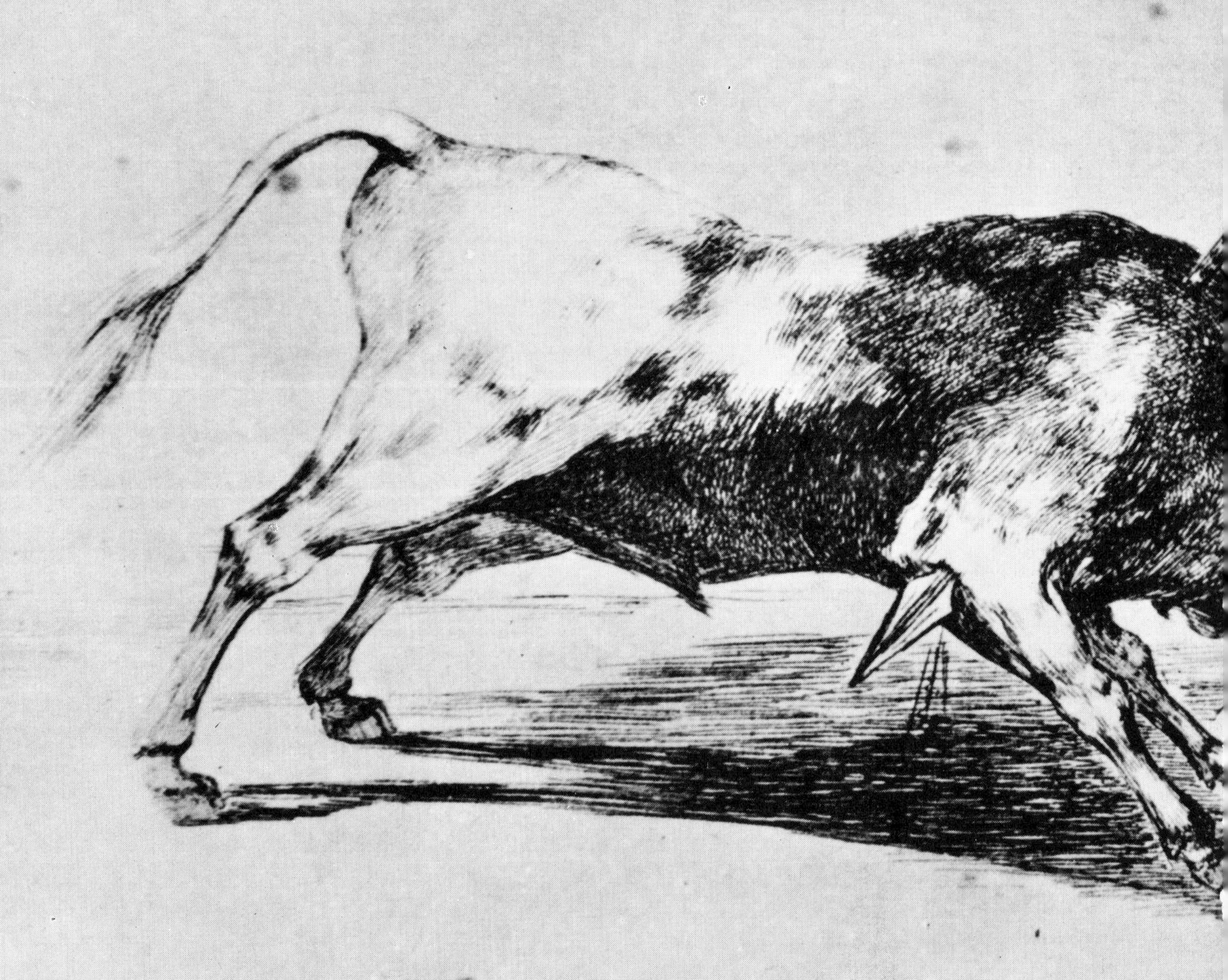

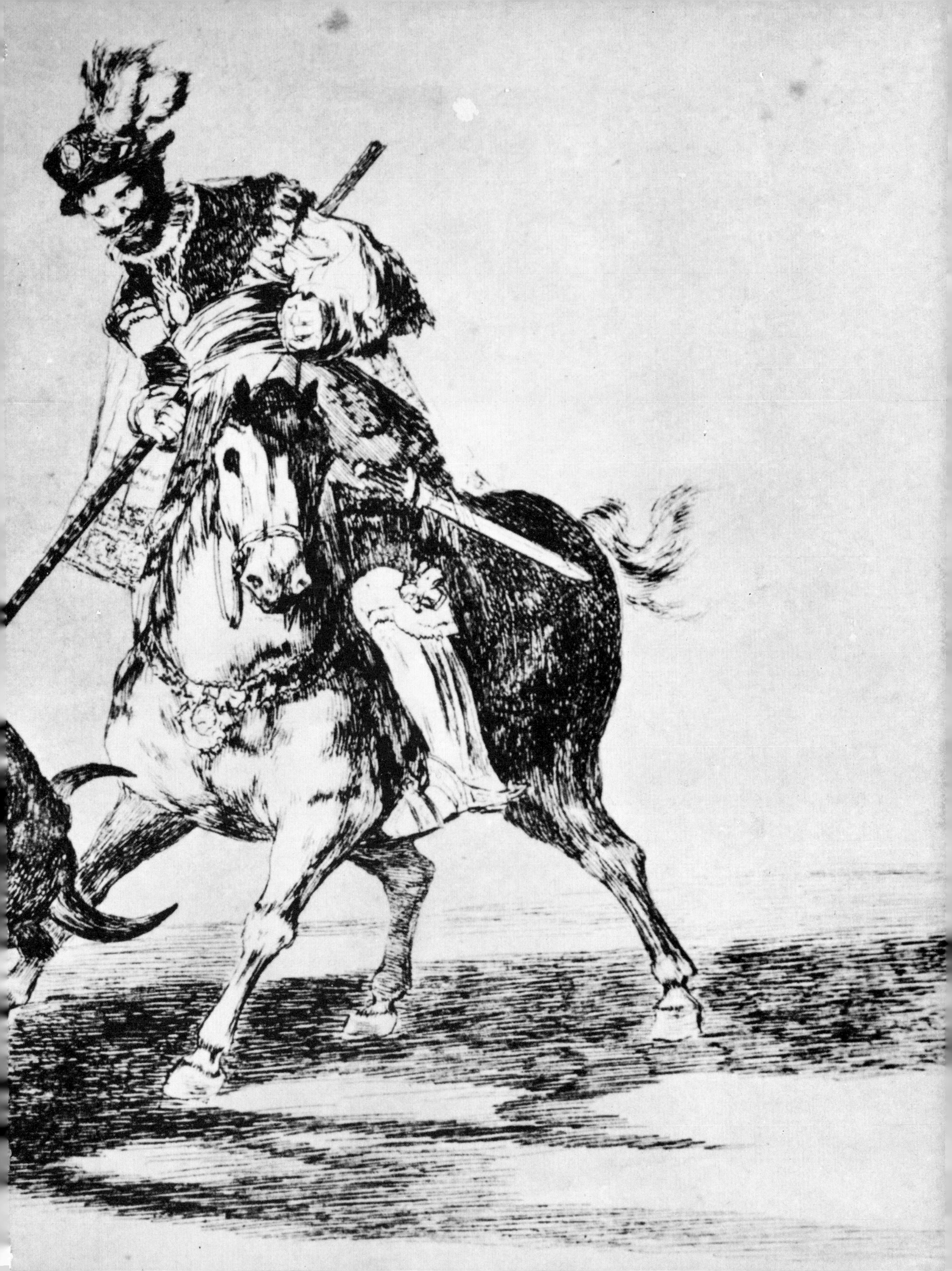

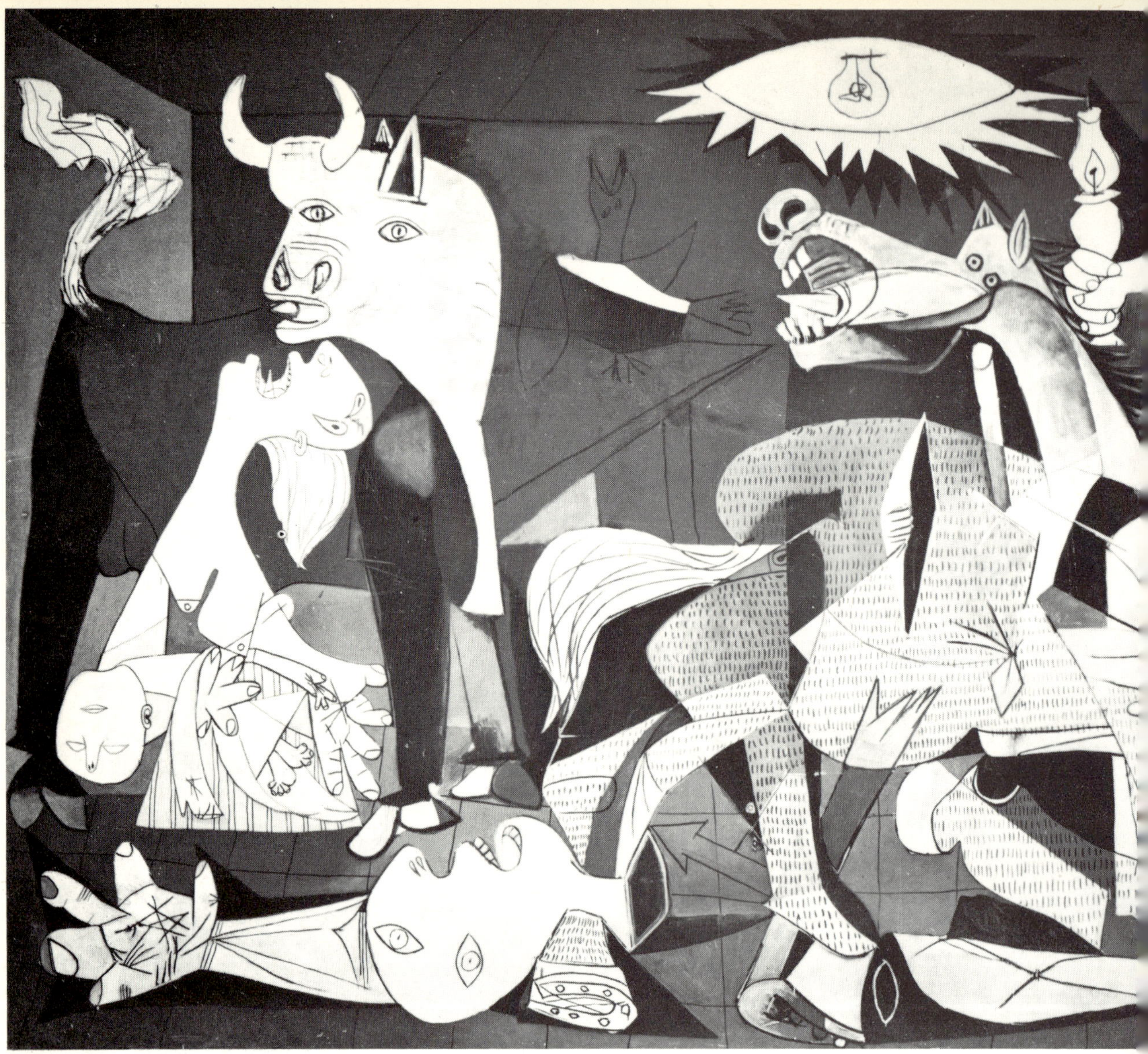

From Goya to Picasso, a long period of time, but not of thought
nor of its expression in art. Both were Spaniards, both lived through
wars, Goya through the Napoleonic, Picasso through the two World
Wars and the Spanish Civil War. It is to the Spanish Civil War that
Guernica belongs, the embodiment and repetition of all that Goya
saw and in seeing suffered, during the Spanish War of Independence.
Los Desastres de la Guerra belong to no particular century, country or
culture. They are basic and inevitable features of every war. Perhaps
Guernica is Picasso's expression, 'not as an artist but as a man profoundly
shocked by war'.[25]

There is no colour in it, it is all black and white and grey, 'like an
elemental diagram of the horrors of war'[26] with its screaming women
and burning house, the corpse, the insane woman with her slain child,

86

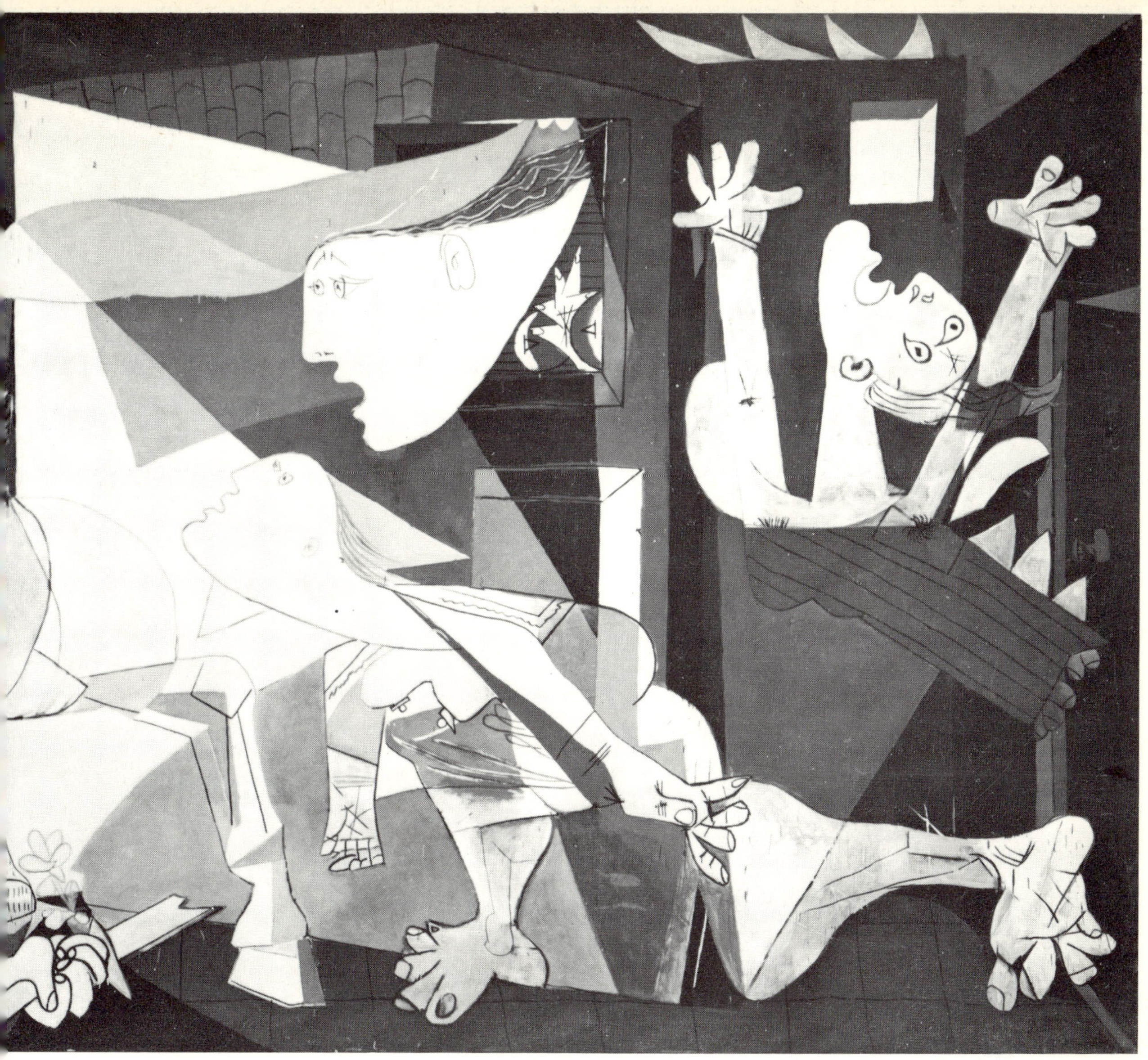

the rearing horse and dominating all – the bull. The head of a bull that is not altogether a bull, for through the face of the bull peers the brutal lust of man maddened and impassioned by the insanity of war. The bull, here again as in so many facets of the bull cult coming down through the ages, is the symbol of irresistible brutal power and force, of mindless destructive instincts, masculine ruthlessness. Some who have seen the bull at peace amid his herd of cows might feel that man, in his search for a scapegoat, has heaped too many human sins upon the bull. For in the sketch, half-man, half-bull, that Picasso made as one of his studies for *Guernica* there is more man than bull. Sir James Frazer was perhaps fairer to the bull when he wrote of 'that proneness to revert to savagery which seems to be innate in most men'.[27]

Picasso's giant mural, *Guernica*, painted at the time of the Spanish Civil War. The bull appears again as the symbol of irresistible brute power and force and masculine ruthlessness; but also through the face of the bull peers the brutal lust of a man maddened and impassioned by the insanity of war. (*On extended loan to The Museum of Modern Art, New York, from the artist*).

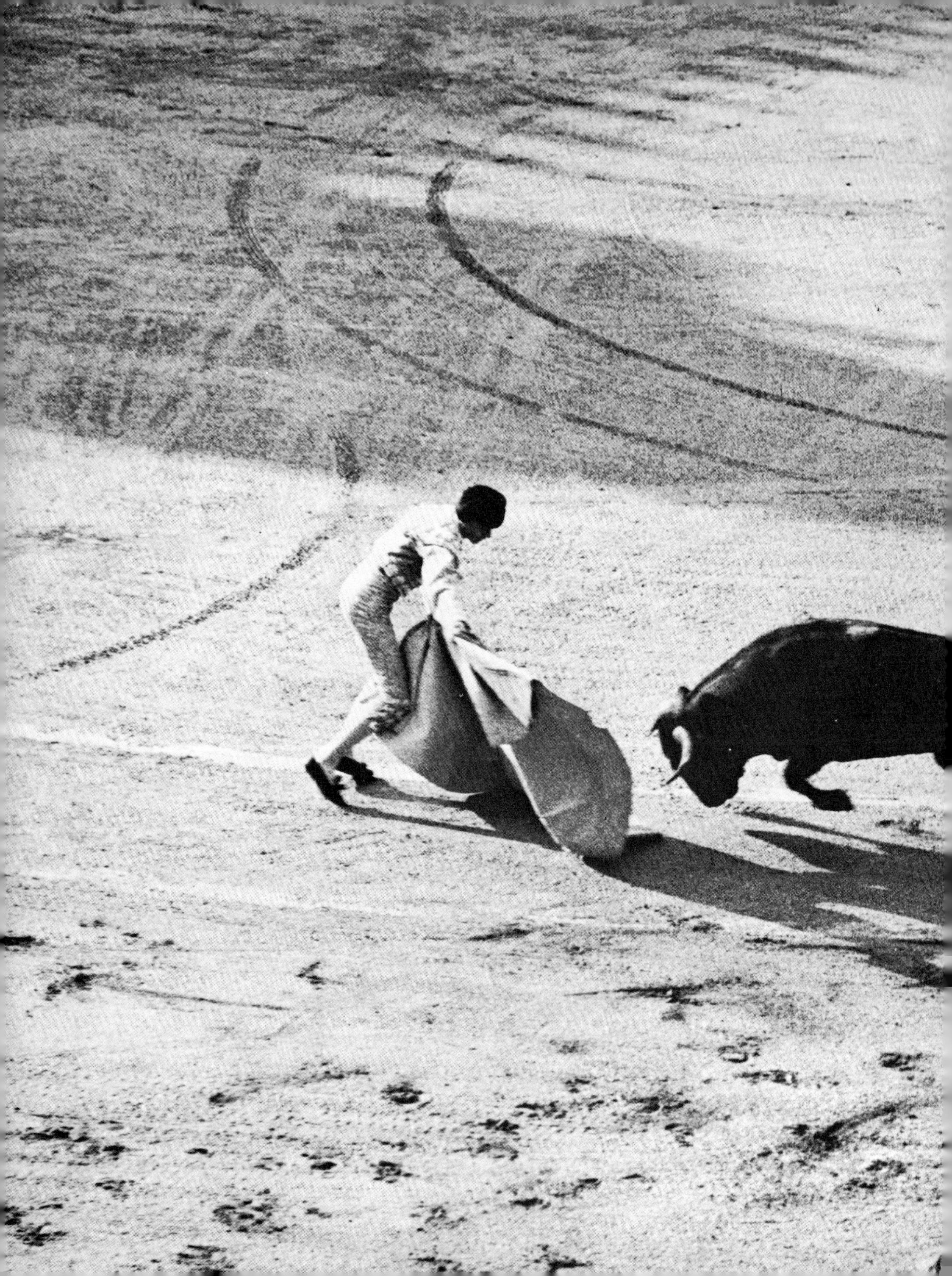

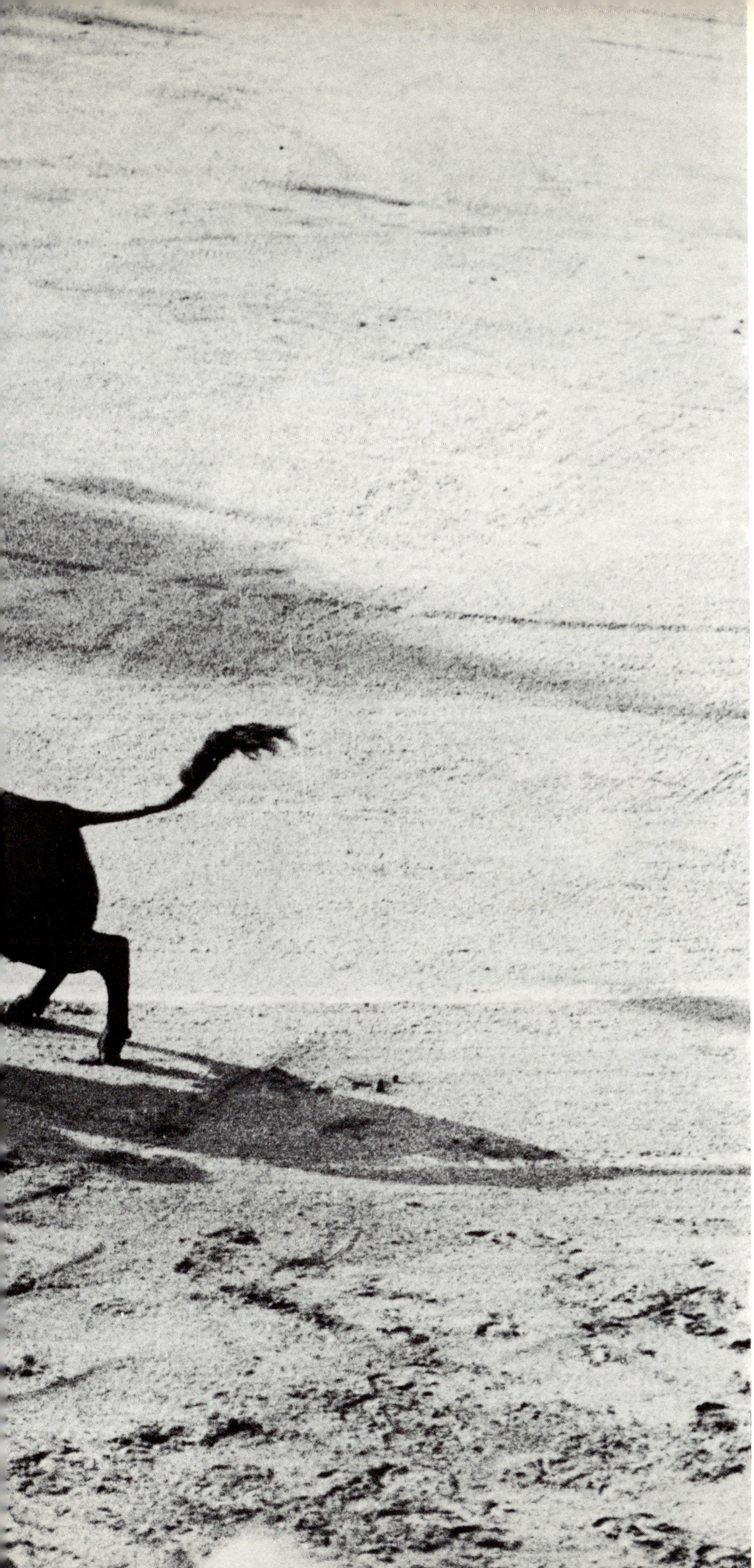

5

The Bull in Sport

Bullfight in progress, Barcelona, Spain. The matador is passing the bull with a *verónica* – a pass with the cape, so called because the manner in which the cape was originally grasped with two hands is similar to the way in which St Veronica is depicted holding the napkin with which she wiped the face of Christ. (*Barnaby's Picture Library*)

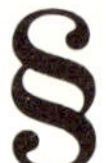 In his immortal classic with that wonderful title *Death in the Afternoon* Ernest Hemingway wrote the following revealing passages:

The bravery of a truly brave bull is something unearthly and unbelievable.[1]

Killing cleanly and in a way which gives you aesthetic pleasure and pride has always been one of the greatest enjoyments of a part of the human race.[2]

It is impossible to believe the emotional and spiritual intensity, and pure classic beauty that can be produced by a man, an animal, and a piece of scarlet serge draped over a stick.[3]

. . . the complete *faena* [the *faena* being the sum of the work done by the matador with the muleta in the final third of the bullfight], the *faena* that takes a man out of himself and makes him feel immortal while it is proceeding, that gives him an ecstasy that is, while momentary, as profound as any religious ecstasy.[4]

Marks in his detailed guide to the technicalities of the bullfight says much the same thing in less vivid prose:

. . . the whole process by which the death of the bull is compassed is nothing but an elaborate ritual.[5]

Trustworthy authorities are agreed that the bullfight is a pagan allegory performed as a solemn rite.[6]

These quotations serve to explain, not only the emotional experiences of the *aficionados* of the bullfight of today, but those of all the millions of people of so many races, countries and times who have offered their homage to the bravery of the bull and, at the same time, found a mystic satisfaction in his sacrificial slaughter. Those who wish to study and understand the bull cults of Mesopotamia, of Egypt, of the Levant, of Crete, of Greece and Western Europe may relive the emotional experience of bull worshippers in the bullrings of Spain, of Portugal, of southern France, of Mexico, Venezuela, Colombia, Ecuador, Bolivia, and Peru. For wherever the Iberian peoples colonised, they took their relics of bull worship with them, and with it the emblems of blood and sand, the red and gold standard which flies above every plaza where modern bull sacrifice persists. Nor were the Spaniards lethargic in establishing the *corrida* in the New World. Thus, it is recorded that the first bullfight in Mexico took place on the thirteenth day of August in the year 1529, only thirty-seven years after the first voyage of Christopher Columbus.

The drama, the emotional tension, the artistry and the techniques of the bullfight, within more recent years, have been so extensively publicised by books, films, and package tours that they are all well nigh as familiar to Britons and Americans as to the Spaniards themselves. A mere summary, therefore, may suffice to inform the few still ignorant.

Opposite: An eighteenth-century engraving of a Spanish bullfight. (*Mansell Collection*)

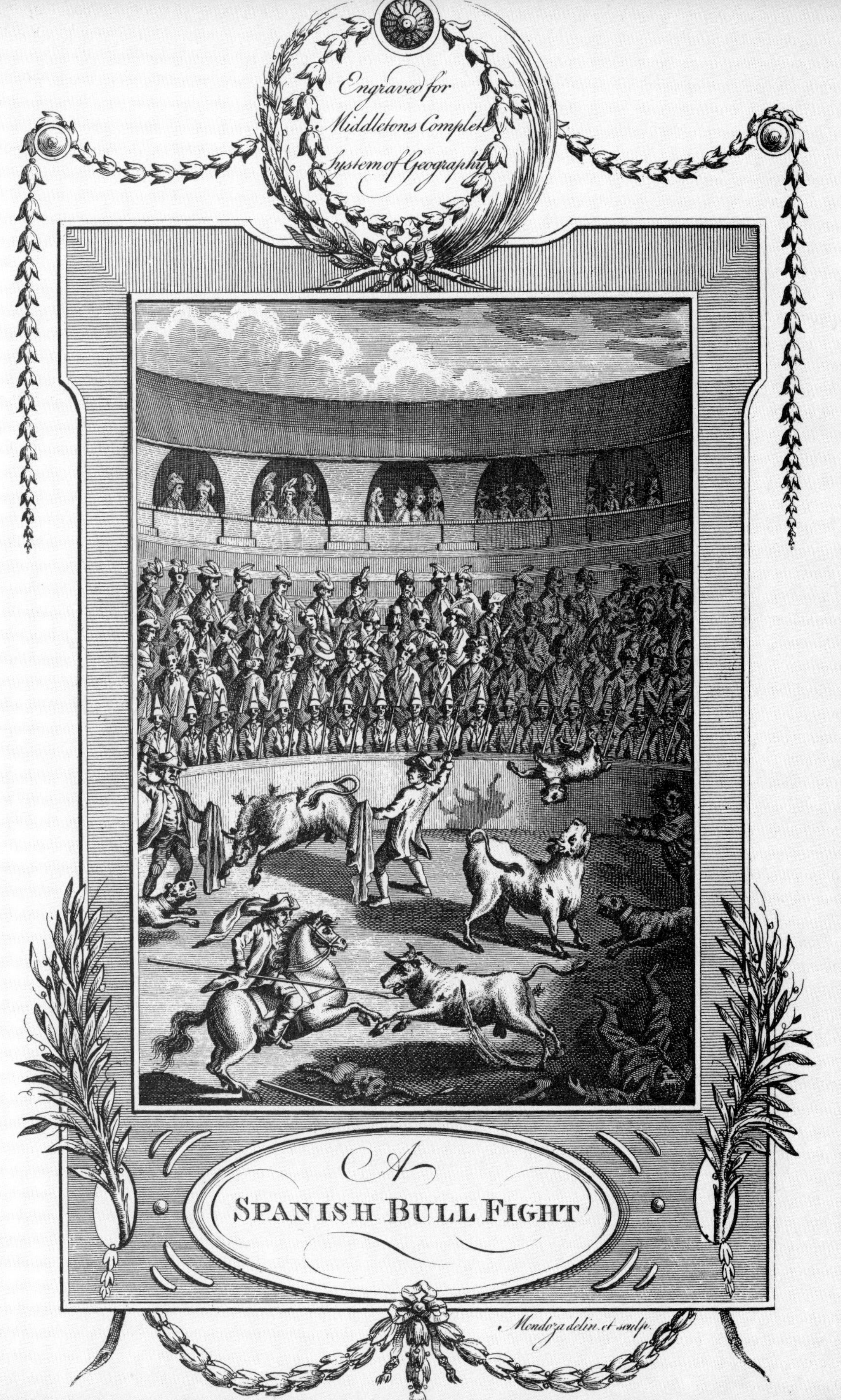

Engraved for
Middletons Complete
System of Geography

A
SPANISH BULL FIGHT

Mendoza delin. et sculp.

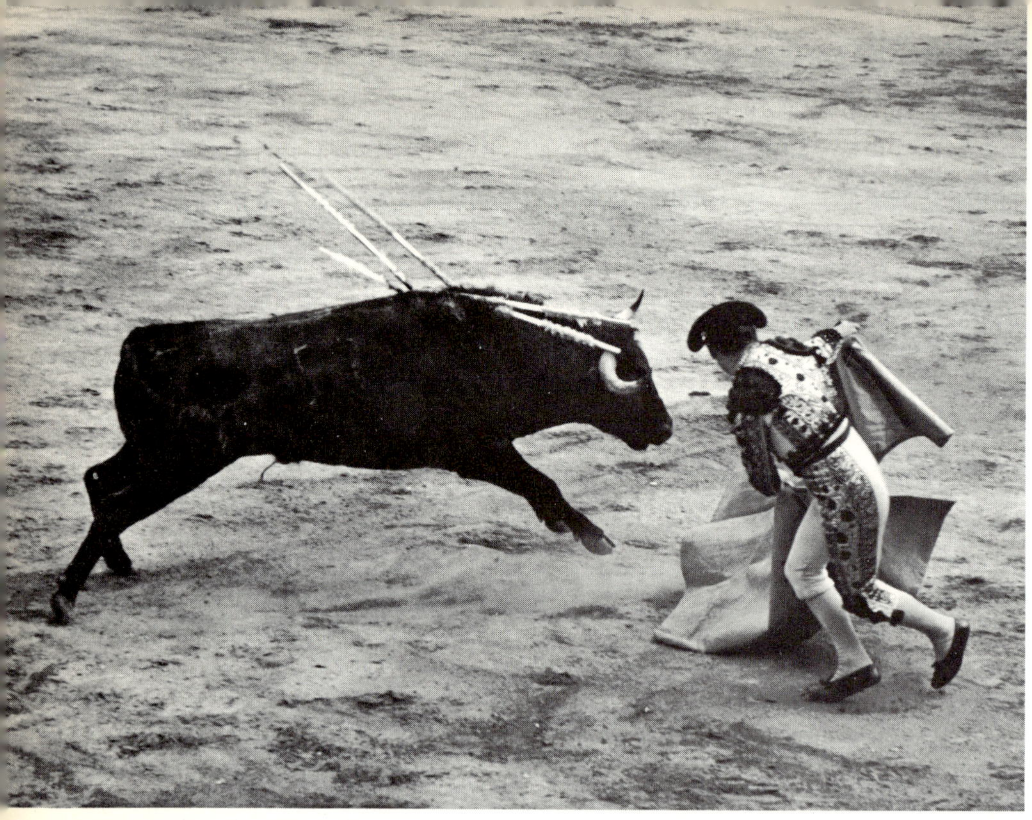

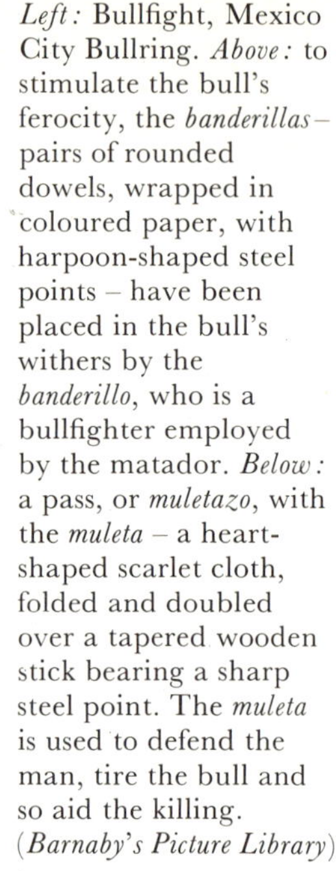

Left: Bullfight, Mexico City Bullring. *Above:* to stimulate the bull's ferocity, the *banderillas* – pairs of rounded dowels, wrapped in coloured paper, with harpoon-shaped steel points – have been placed in the bull's withers by the *banderillo*, who is a bullfighter employed by the matador. *Below:* a pass, or *muletazo*, with the *muleta* – a heart-shaped scarlet cloth, folded and doubled over a tapered wooden stick bearing a sharp steel point. The *muleta* is used to defend the man, tire the bull and so aid the killing. (*Barnaby's Picture Library*)

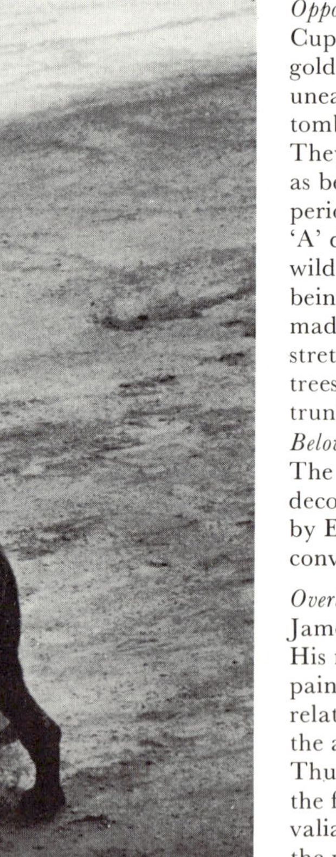

Opposite, above: Vapheio Cup, 'A'. Both this and the gold cup below were unearthed from the Vapheio tomb near Sparta, Greece. They are generally accepted as belonging to the Minoan period. The design on Cup 'A' depicts the snaring of wild bulls in a net, the bulls being driven into a trap made by a rope cradle stretched between two olive trees and tied to their trunks. (*Ronald Sheridan*) *Below:* Vapheio Cup, 'B'. The capture of a bull by a decoy cow in heat, described by Evans as 'amorous conversation'. (*Ronald Sheridan*)

Overleaf: Gordale Scar by James Ward (1769–1859). His most famous oil painting, reviving in a relatively modern setting the age-old combination of Thunder God and Bull. In the foreground – proud, valiant, vigilant, menacing – the white bull stands on guard. (*Tate Gallery, London*)

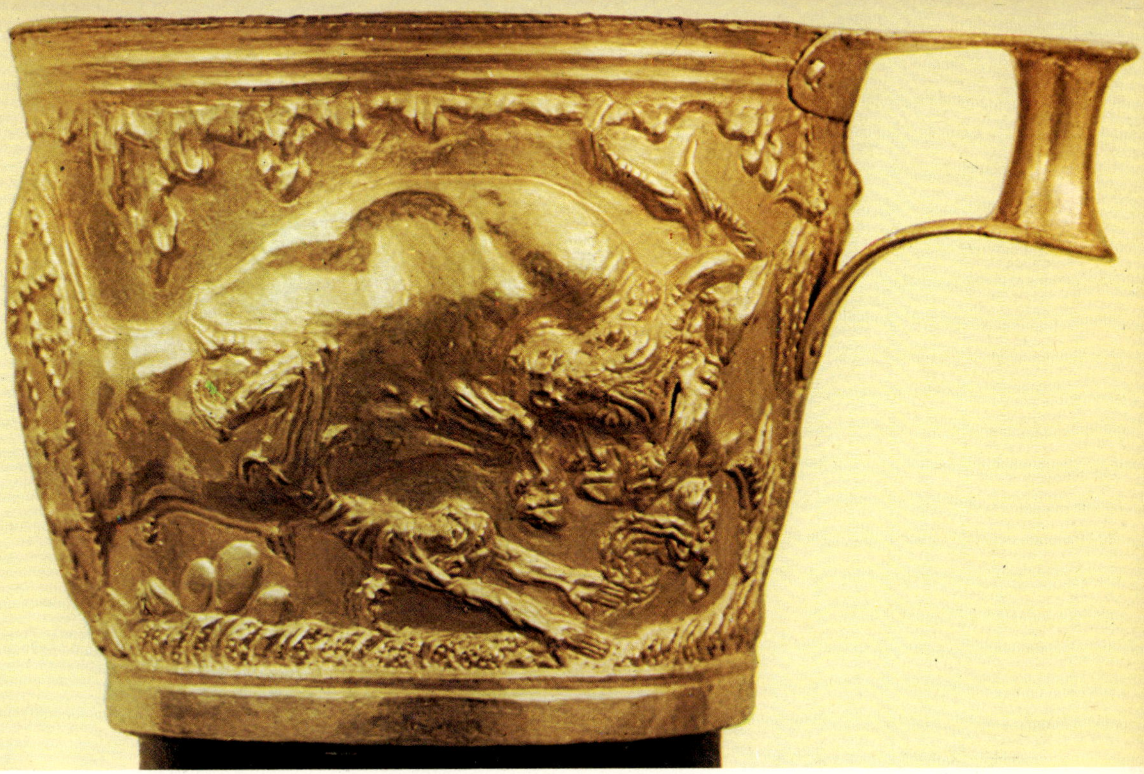

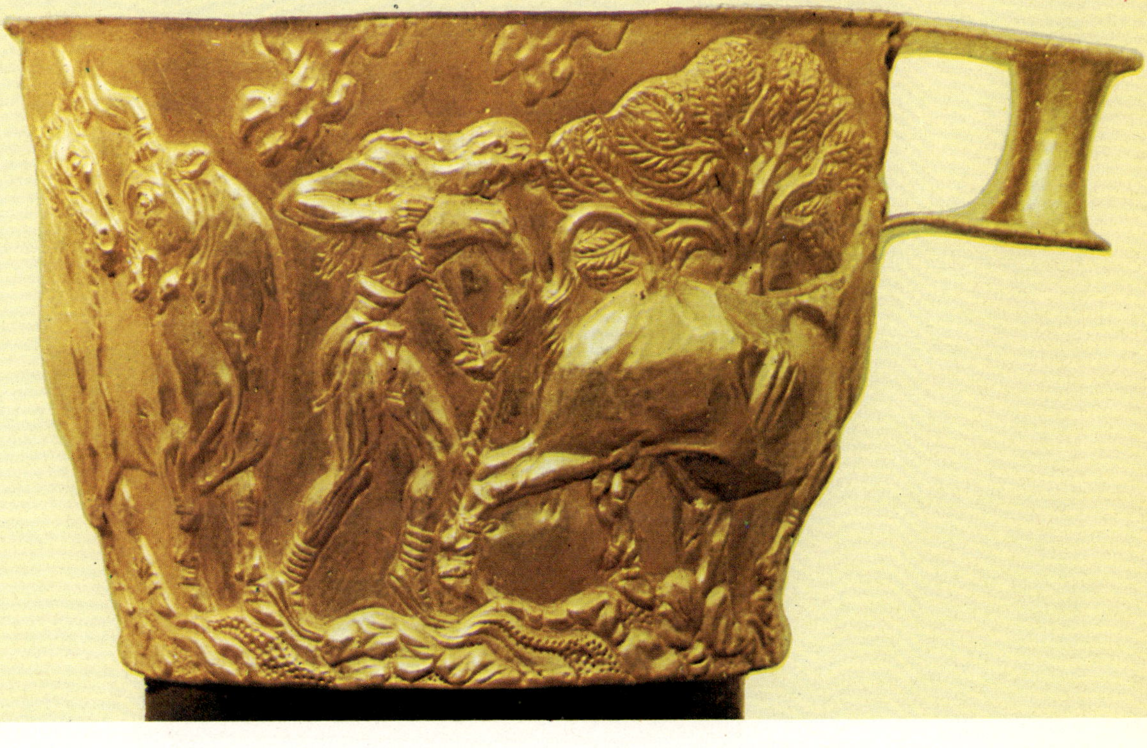

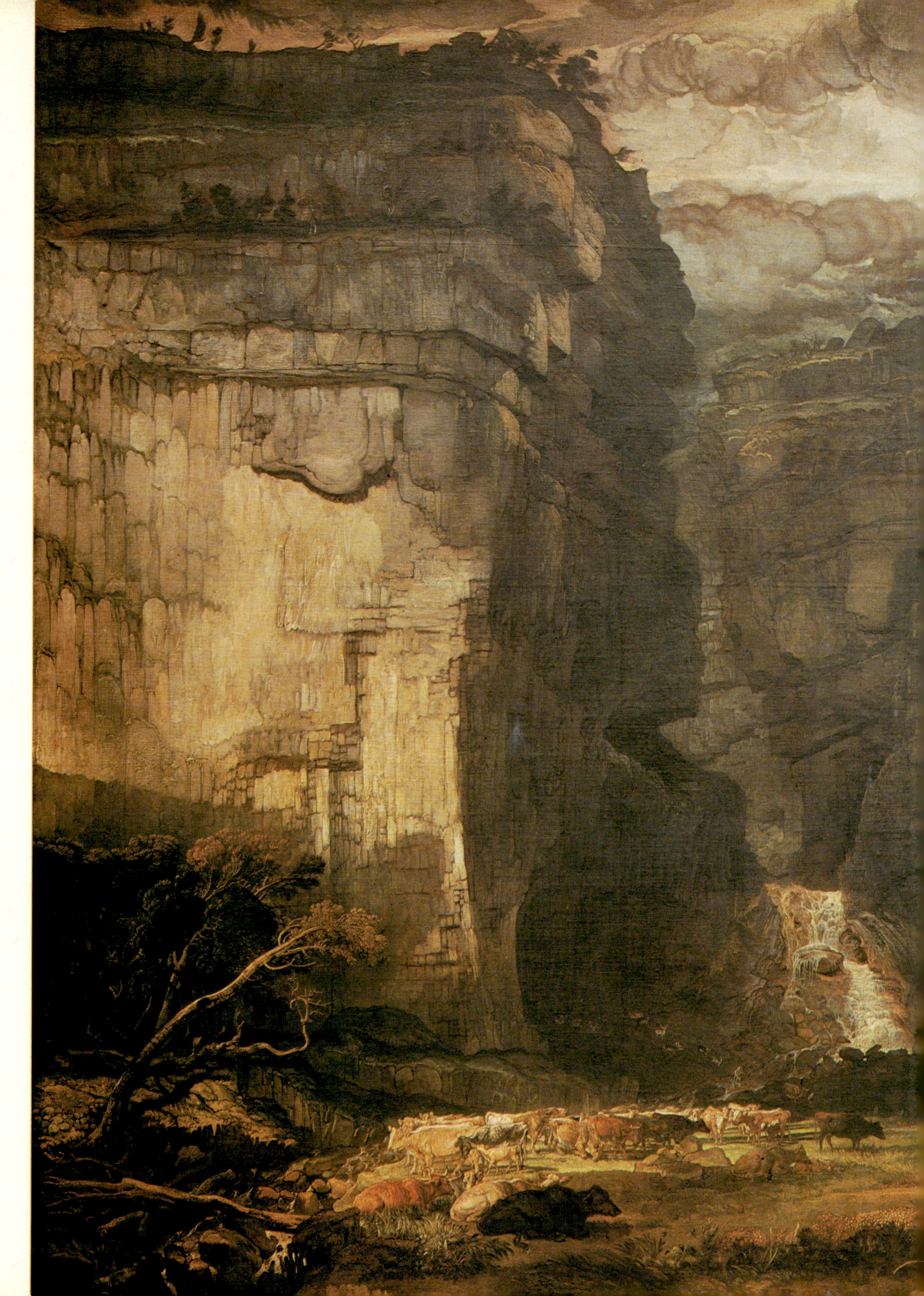

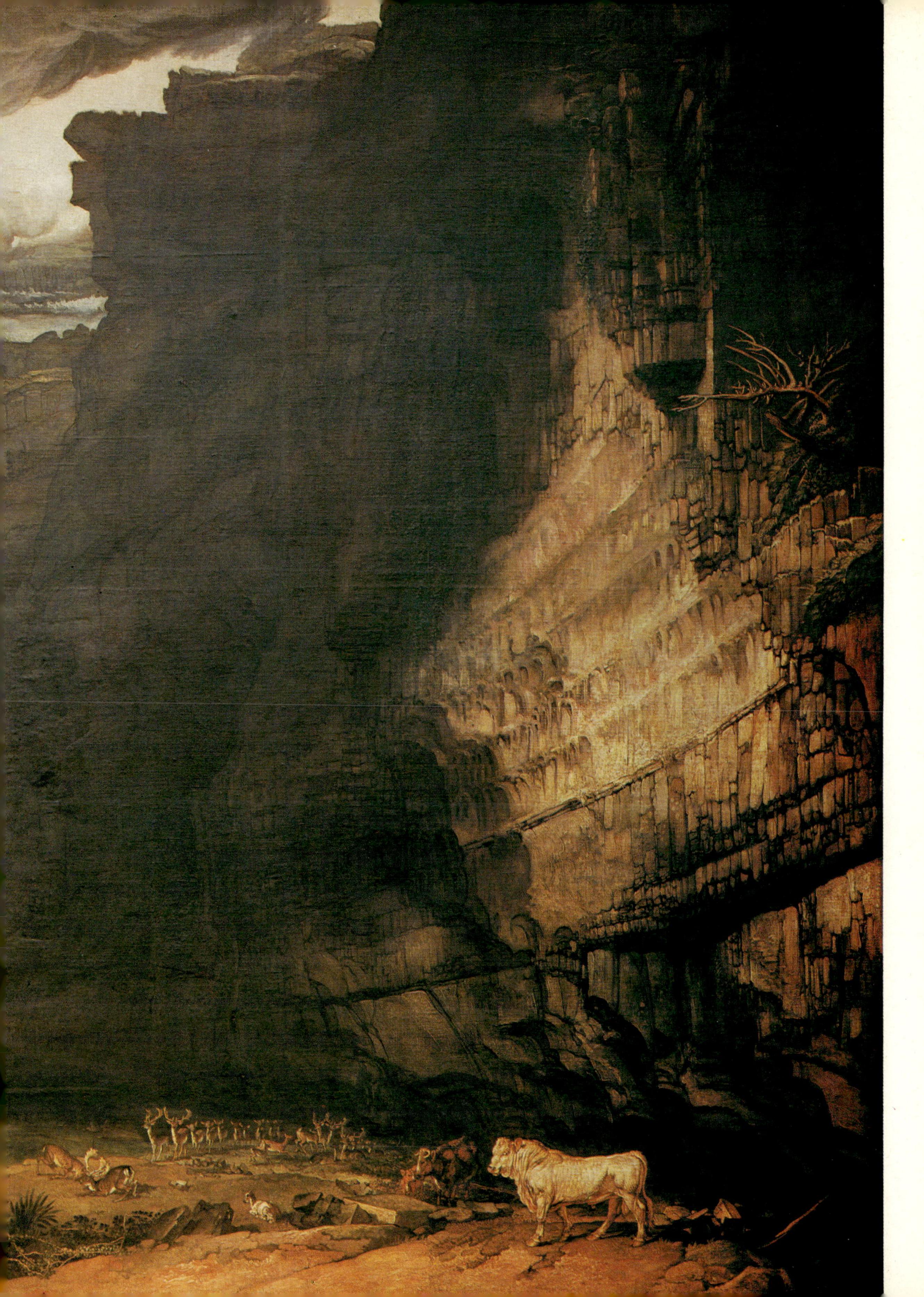

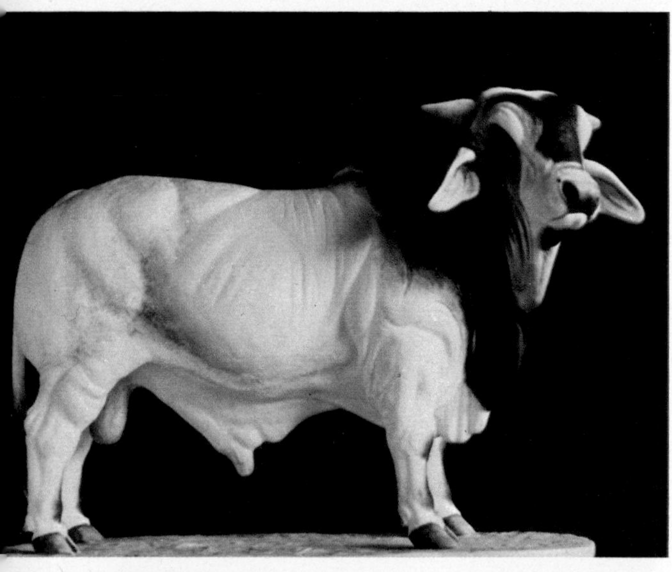
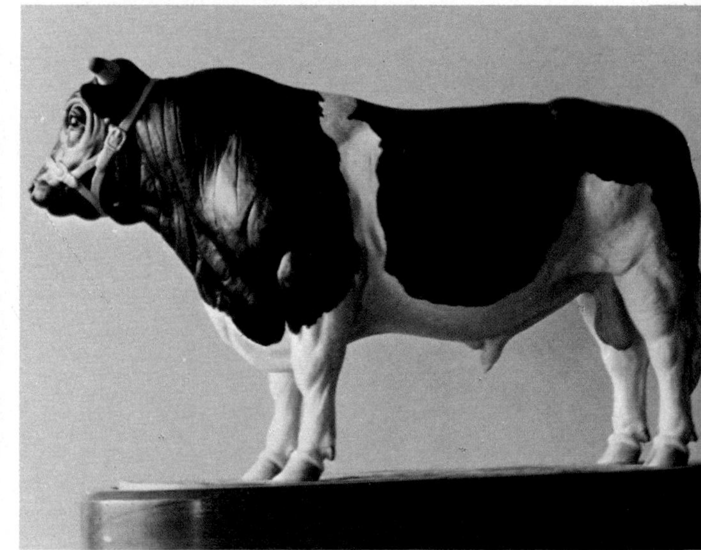
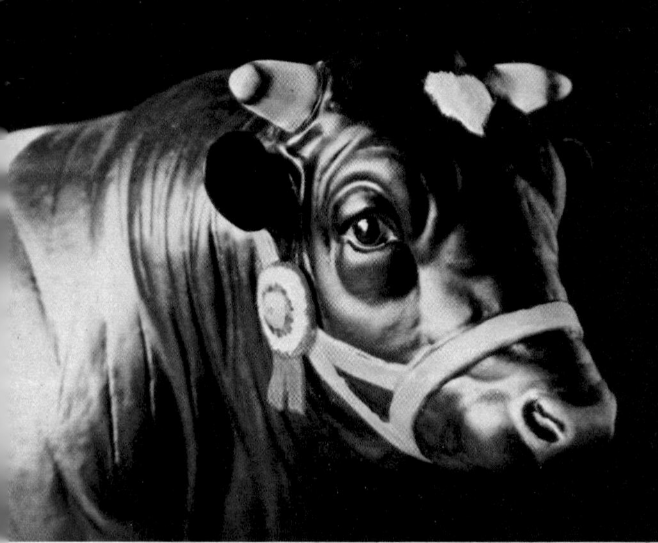
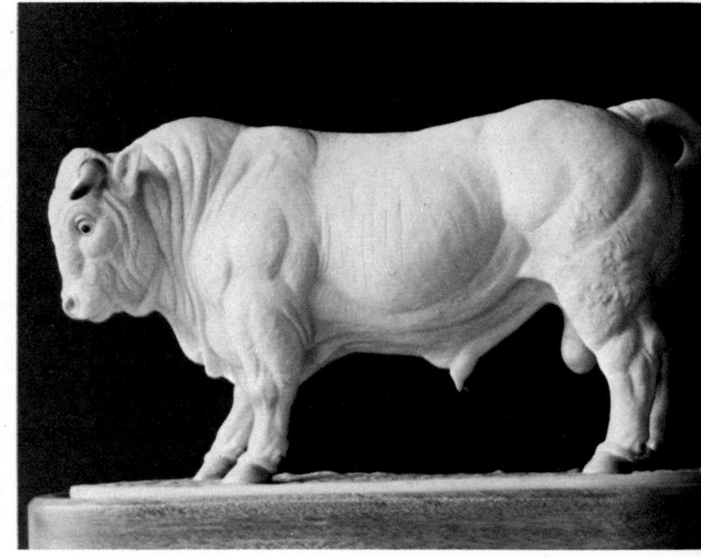

When the bull enters the ring he attacks or is incited to attack first the picadors, mounted men who with pointed lances – actually eight-foot poles with small sharp tips – prick the bull's crest, thereby weakening the muscle with which the bull makes his toss. The horses are frequently sacrificed in this preliminary encounter. The *banderilleros* stick darts in the bull's skin to further stimulate his ferocity. The star performer is, of course, the matador, who plays the bull with his *muleta*, a heart-shaped scarlet cloth folded over a tapered wooden stick, an art with the grace of the ballet which precedes the final act of sacrifice. To kill the bull, the inescapable finale to the tragedy, the matador faces his opponent, 'making him lower his head with the red serge of the *muleta* and killing him with the sword, driving it in high up at the top of the angle between the two shoulder blades'.[7]

The Spanish bullfight, has, of course, a very old history as background to its modern development. The aurochs was at one time native to Iberia and it seems altogether probable that the first contests were between mounted men and wild bulls on the unenclosed pastures of ancient Spain.

Marks wrote that 'The history of bull fighting is divided as neatly as could be, into three stages – primitive, aristocratic, and plebeian – which correspond to the intrinsic development of the contest from a private hunt to a public pageant, and from a pageant to a profession.'[8]

Clearly, an important and organised industry is required to maintain the bullfight as a professional spectacle. In Spain, the bullfighter's year extends from March to October. There are over a thousand bullfights held in some three hundred and fifty bullrings during any one season. There are over two hundred ranches in Spain devoted to the rearing of fighting bulls and to no other purpose. 'Each year about thirty-five hundred fighting bulls from three to five years of age leave these ranches for the corridas of Spain.'[9] The breeding and rearing of these Spanish cattle of fighting breed is a highly specialised and theoretically fascinating aspect of cattle husbandry. Essentially it is an attempt to breed deliberately not for bodily features such as meat and milk, or even muscular development alone, but primarily for a psychological character – courage. What of the exercise and how successfully has it been done? Since it is generally assumed that of all domesticated cattle the Spanish fighting breed is most directly descended from the wild aurochs, the breeders presumably got off to a good start. They have, it would seem, succeeded in preserving the characters of the wild bull so deeply admired in pagan times, at least to an extent that the Spanish fighting breed of cattle, although domesticated in the sense that it is under the domination of man, is yet a very different animal from other domesticated breeds, specialised towards meat or milk or, in older times, as beasts of burden. Hemingway makes a vivid distinction in this description of the fighting breed he

Opposite, top left: Brahman bull, from the series of Royal Worcester pottery bulls by Doris Lindner. This particular model was based on studies of the champion Brahman bull, 'J. D. H. de Ellary Manso' of Hungerford, Texas.

Top right: British Friesian bull, modelled from 'Terling Trusty' the winner of the 1962 Essex and Great Yorkshire shows, and owned by the Lord Rayleigh Estates of Chelmsford, Essex.

Bottom right: Charolais bull, modelled from 'Vaillant', the 1967 champion of the *Concours Général Agricole de Paris.*

Bottom left: Head of a model of the champion Dairy Shorthorn bull, 'Royal Event', from Gayton, Staffordshire.

so greatly admired:

The fighting bull is to the domestic bull as the wolf is to the dog. A domestic bull may be evil tempered and vicious as a dog may be mean and dangerous, but he will never have the speed, the quality of muscle and sinew and the peculiar build of the fighting bull, any more than the dog will have the sinews of the wolf, his cunning and his width of jaw. Bulls for the ring are wild animals. They are bred from a strain that comes down in direct descent from the wild bulls that ranged over the peninsula and they are bred on ranches with thousands of acres of range where they live as free ranging animals. The contacts with men of the bulls that are to appear in the ring are held to the absolute minimum.[10]

The biggest apparent difference between the fighting bull and domesticated bulls is in the distribution of body weight. In this respect he comes closer to the dairy bull than to the beef bull. Compared with, let us say, an Aberdeen-Angus beef bull, the shoulders and forequarters are heavier and the hindquarters lighter. The general result is to emphasise the strength, power and muscular development of the neck and shoulders which the fighting bull uses to toss and to gore. The predominant development of the anterior half of the body, particularly in the male, is, in fact, characteristic of the wild as compared with the domesticated varieties of all mammals. In this, as in so many other respects, the fighting bull displays his more direct descent from the wild aurochs.

Hemingway gives this description of the fighting bull's anatomy:

The physical characteristics of the fighting bull are its thick and very strong hide with glossy pelt, small head, but wide forehead; strength and shape of horns, which curve forward; short, thick neck with the great hump of muscle which erects when the bull is angry, wide shoulders, very small hooves and length and slenderness of tail. The female of the fighting bull is not as heavily built as the male; has a smaller head, shorter and thinner horns; a longer neck, a less pronounced dewlap under the jaw; is not as wide through the chest, and has no visible udder.[11]

The prevailing colour is black but there are numerous exceptions, a point of some interest in view of the conflict of opinion as to whether the Cretan bulls, as depicted on the murals of Knossos, were genuinely wild bulls or domesticated bulls especially trained for acrobatic display. In addition to black, fighting bulls have appeared in the ring that were grey, red, roan or even with broken black and white markings reminiscent of the dairy Friesian and, incidentally of the Cretan bulls also.

As to size, if Julius Caesar's description of the wild aurochs of his time is accurate, which may well be doubted, then the Spanish fighting bull has suffered a sad decline. Caesar stated that the aurochs were as big as elephants whereas the fighting bull of today has not even the weight of many a bull of the fully domesticated cattle breeds. Whereas

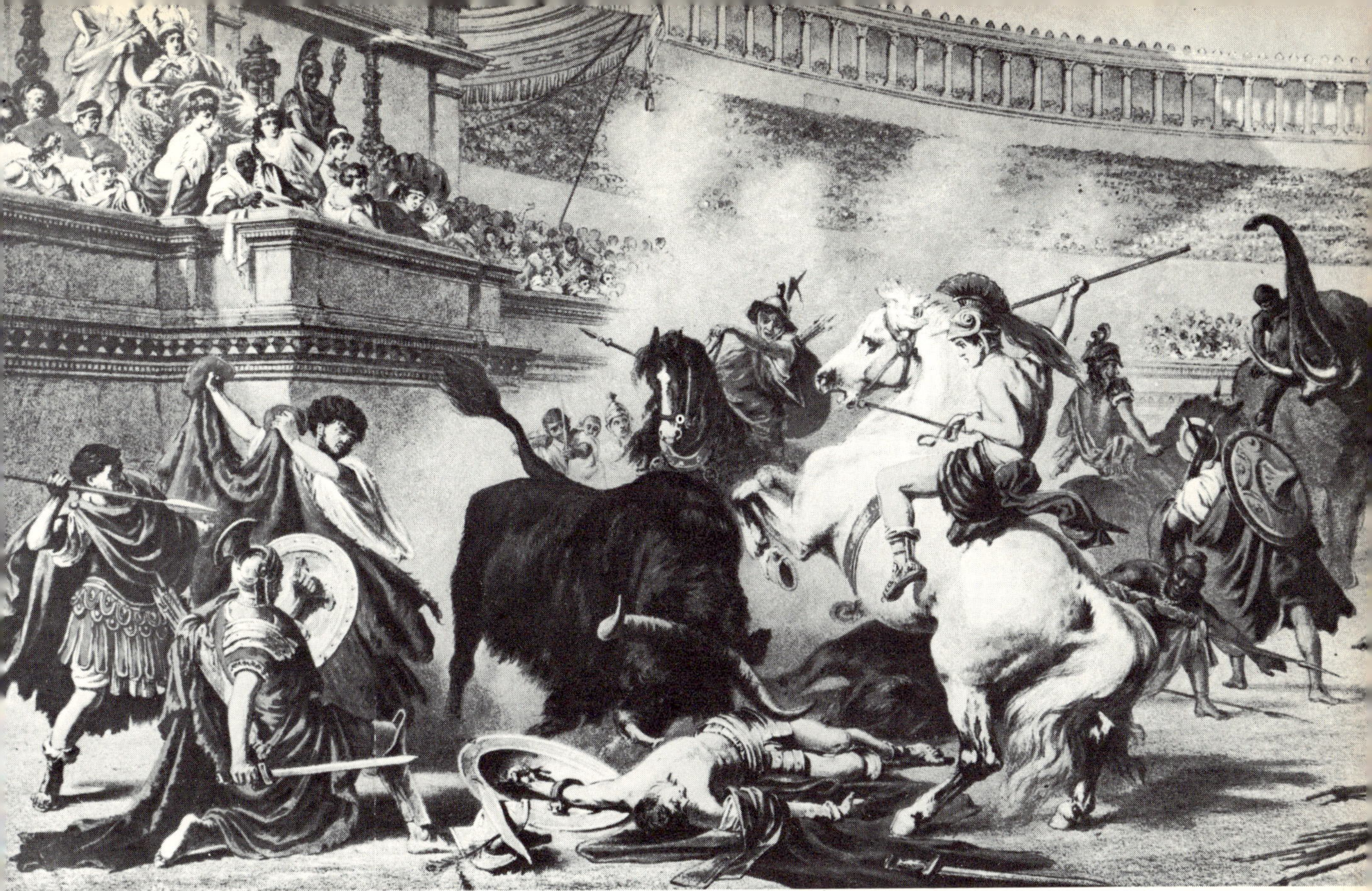

a grown bull of British breeds may reach ton weight (1016 kilos), the fighting bull of between three to seven years of age averages some 14 cwt. (700 kilos). Moreover, the fighting bull has declined in size within recent years. According to Hemingway, 'In the old days the bulls were usually bigger than they are now. . . . They had not been bred down to a smaller size to suit the bullfighters.' The reason for using bulls of lighter weight and younger age is that the star matadors 'were certain to do the wonderful things that the public wanted to see'.[12]

Marks agreed when he wrote, 'Certainly the bulls are younger and less dangerous than they were when the bullfight was still a battle, not a ballet – but it is a mortal ballet, even now . . .'[13]

It appears then, that in the contest between man and bull, although death to the bull is the certain climax, the danger to the man has been reduced by using bulls of younger age and smaller size. A risk to man, reduced no doubt, but far from eliminated since some four per cent of matadors suffer 'death in the afternoon' and certain surgeons special-ise in repairing the injuries caused by the bull's head and horn. Nevertheless, 'It is the decadence of the modern bull that has made modern bullfighting possible,'[14] – giving the matador the opportunity to exhibit the finesse and grace, the hair-splitting passes, even the contemptuous bravado which provides and prolongs the spectacle

A Roman bullfight. From a painting by Professor Wagner. (*Radio Times Hulton Picture Library*)

99

and emotional experience the crowd of *aficionados* have paid their money to see.

Neither age nor weight, however, whether in bull or man, are generally reckoned as conducive to agility, and the fighting bull, according to Hemingway, whatever his decadence in size, remains an athlete of oustanding potentiality:

From a standing start a fighting bull will outrun a horse for twenty-five yards although a horse will beat him in fifty yards. The bull can turn on his feet almost as a cat does, he can turn much quicker than a polo pony, and at four years he has the strength in his neck and shoulder muscles to lift a horse and rider and throw them over his back.[15]

To have the strength, the audacity, the courage to face an armed and mounted man and to lift both horse and rider clear of the ground and to toss them over his back! That is the finished article, the young bull ready to face the ordeal of the *corrida*. How and in what fashion was he prepared?

His courage, that most admired, by no manner of means universal, unpredictable and uncertain of human or animal virtues, was not left to chance. It was the objective of the breeder who bred him on a ranch devoted to that purpose. The ranch may extend for many thousand acres of uncultivated land. On it there are kept from two to four hundred breeding cows and to every fifty cows there is one stud bull. The bulls run with the cows from April to June and, the pregnancy period of a cow being nine months, the calves are born from December to February. Both sire and dam are tested for courage before the calf is even conceived. For it is the custom on ranches to evaluate the pugnacity of both dam and sire. The trials are conducted in the corrals as a rule, but in Andalucia, where it is said the best bulls come from, on the open range. The cows intended for breeding may charge the picador repeatedly to confirm their valour and are tested with both cape and *muleta* to prove their readiness to be, as it were, cheated by red drapery. These characteristics in the cow are deemed by the breeder to be hereditary. Therefore, a cow that fails such examination will be excluded from the breeding herd. The stud bulls are also tested repeatedly in much the same way. The bull calf resulting from the union of stud bull and satisfactory cow is considered worth keeping. He will, of course, be born on the open range and be reared as a suckled calf. He will not have a surfeit of milk from his dam, because cows of the fighting breed have so poor an udder development that stockmen accustomed to more domesticated breeds usually mistake them for steers. Nevertheless, they are presumably capable of producing between the 150 and 200 gallons (675–900 litres), sufficient for the rearing of a single calf. After weaning, the bull calf grows and develops his strength upon the open range. Climate, soil, water and pasture all affect his development. 'So the bulls raised in Navarra, Andalucia and Salamanca differ greatly and this is not due to them coming from differing strains.'[16]

The young bull is tested as his parents were tested, but more sparingly (lest he should learn too much), when he is two years of age. Should he fail such tests he is for the butcher. Should he pass he is destined for the ring. Kept virginal yet freely ranging, he reaches maturity after his fourth year but many, indeed the majority, termed *novillos*, are sent to the ring at three years of age, too young perhaps for fair fight but better suited for the brilliant technical displays by the matador that the modern *aficionado* demands.

To transport a fighting bull from the freedom and privacy of the range where he has spent the first three or four years of his life to the crowded cities where the bullfights are held requires, understandably, a special and elaborate technique. This depends upon the use of trained steers, called *cabestros*, to decoy and accompany the fighting bulls, on the same system by which wild elephants are captured and controlled by those that have already been tamed. Hemingway wrote that, 'It is one of the most interesting of all phases of bullfighting to see the steers work . . . in all the many operations connected with the raising, transporting, and unloading of fighting bulls.'[17]

The great occasion is close at hand. The young bull is ready for his finest and last hour:

He was brought to the bull-ring in a box, he and his fellows were let out into one of the corrals attached to the plaza at night, between two and four o'clock; at noon on the day of the corrida he was inveigled through several doors worked by pulleys and ropes, into his narrow, dark, allotted cell, there to await the order of his release into the arena.[18]

The bull is released, the spectacle has begun, but whatever the brilliance of the matador or the courage of the bull, the end is death.

From time to time a bull refuses to face its enemies: 'It is true, unfortunately, that not all fighting bulls show fight; too many . . . are cowardly.'[19] The condemnation may possibly be a trifle unjust to the bull. While it is acknowledged that 'Every bull fighter has his "on" and his "off" days . . .'[20] the bull has only the one day, his last day. Perhaps he might have done better on another day, since the history of human warfare displays how unpredictable and variable the courage of even a veteran unit may sometimes be. Such bulls are punished for their cowardice:

This punishment takes the place of the now discarded fire-darts; it is applied to bulls who refuse any truck with the picador's lances, and makes up in part for that self-willed immunity by the subsequent use of banderillas with harpoon points, which inflict a deeper wound than the ordinary fish-hook, while at the same time implying a disgrace to the bull-breeder.[21]

The belled steers are brought in and the cowardly bull escorted to the knackery.

Usually, however, the bull is brave and to repeat the encomium that Hemingway conferred, 'The bravery of a truly brave bull is something unearthly and unbelievable.' Yet, whether cowardly or heroic, the bull must die. Should the bull provide the crowd with an unusually striking exhibition of valour he is accorded – but only after his death – the rare distinction of a lap of honour: 'If the bull showed exceptional bravery during the fight, the crowd will insist that the mules drag it round the ring as a posthumous tribute before galloping out with it to the butcher's yard. . . .'[22] A pleasing gesture, no doubt, but the geneticist might add, what a pitiable waste of genetic material! The bull, with an unimpaired potential for leaving courageous offspring, to be sacrificed in this way! Granted that all breeding animals of the fighting breed are tested for courage on their native ranch, that can hardly be the same thing as giving a courageous performance in the strange environment and loneliness of the crowded plaza. In fact, Hemingway acknowledged that 'No one can say, on seeing a fighting bull in the corrals, whether the bull will be brave in the ring. . . .'[23]

Since the end of every bull in the ring must be death, is there no possibility of saving his seed after that death? At least theoretically, the answer is that it could be so saved. In the USSR, when sheep breeders wished to form a new breed of sheep specially suited to high altitudes and harsh environment, they shot rams of a wild species and saved the semen from the still warm corpses; then used the semen to artificially inseminate domesticated ewes. The result was successful and the new breed established. No doubt the artificial insemination of cows of the fighting breed would present difficulties which might prove insuperable even to Spanish herdsmen. Nevertheless the sacrificial slaughter of the proven sire cannot, in the light of modern genetical knowledge, be sensible in breeding. Hemingway wrote that 'fighting bulls are the products of many generations of careful breeding, as race horses are'.[24] That is sacrcely true. The destination of the Derby winner is the stud and not the knackery.

Bullfighting in Portugal differs in several respects from that in Spain. It is less deadly and the older custom of facing the bull with a mounted opponent is to some extent retained. The bull's horns are either padded or tipped with a brass ball. In consequence, horses and bulls are rarely killed and the risk of death or injury to the bullfighters greatly reduced. In Portugal bulls are fought by lancers mounted on highly trained horses. Another special feature is the *salteadores*, men who pole-vault over the charging bull.

For how long is the bullfight – that strange survival of the ancient bull cult and bull sacrifice – likely to survive? Confined mainly to Spanish and Spanish-American countries, illegal in most others, it has to face the competition of other spectacular entertainments. As Marks wrote, 'Spain, herself, like the bullfight, is a survival undergoing change.'[25] Those most knowledgeable about bullfighting always insist that it is a spectacle and not a sport. Yet, are there not many other activities that were wont to be classified as sports, rather rapidly becoming spectacles? Clearly, professional Association Football is the main counter-attraction to bullfighting. Already, in 1953, Marks wrote that in Spain herself there were a million soccer fans for every thousand bullfight enthusiasts.[26] On the other hand the competitive *corridas* between two star matadors in 1959, attracted bigger crowds than ever before. Possibly, were the referee to be sacrificed at a soccer match's conclusion – and some already have but narrowly escaped that fate – the bullring might finally become deserted, since all those who have studied the mysticism of sacrifice appear to be agreed that the immolation of bulls and other animals is a substitute for the earlier sacrifice of human beings.

Additional to the highly organised and commercialised bullfighting in Spanish cities and towns, there is the more informal type of village sport that Goya painted. Something of the same sort was once practised in England. In the Wild White Cattle herd at Chillingham Park in Northumberland, as late as the early nineteenth century it '. . . was the practice to ride out a bull from the herd and then shoot him'.[27]

One of the best and most vivid descriptions of this old method of hunting Chillingham bulls is given by Beilby in his *History of Quadrupeds* published in 1790 and illustrated by Thomas Bewick:

The mode of killing them was perhaps the only modern remains of the grandeur of ancient hunting. On notice being given that a wild bull would be killed on a certain day, the inhabitants of the neighbourhood came mounted, and armed with guns, etc. sometimes to the amount of an hundred horse, and four or five hundred foot, who stood upon the walls, or got into the trees, while the horsemen rode off the Bull from the rest of the herd, until he stood at bay; when a marksman dismounted and shot. At some of these huntings, twenty or thirty shots have been fired before he was subdued. On such occasions, the bleeding victim grew desperately furious, from the smarting of his wounds, and the shouts of savage joy that were echoing from every side. But from the number of accidents that happened, this dangerous mode has been little practised of late years, the park-keeper alone generally shooting them with a rifle, at one shot.

Although England never developed a sacrificial spectacle similar to the Spanish *corrida*, the so-called sports of bullbaiting and bullrunning were popular features of English festivals and entertainments.

Bullbaiting was the more formal and aristocratic diversion, although bearbaiting seems to have been judged the superior sport. It was much harder on the dogs than on the bear. The bear, chained to a pole, was attacked by a succession of dogs let loose upon it. Many dogs

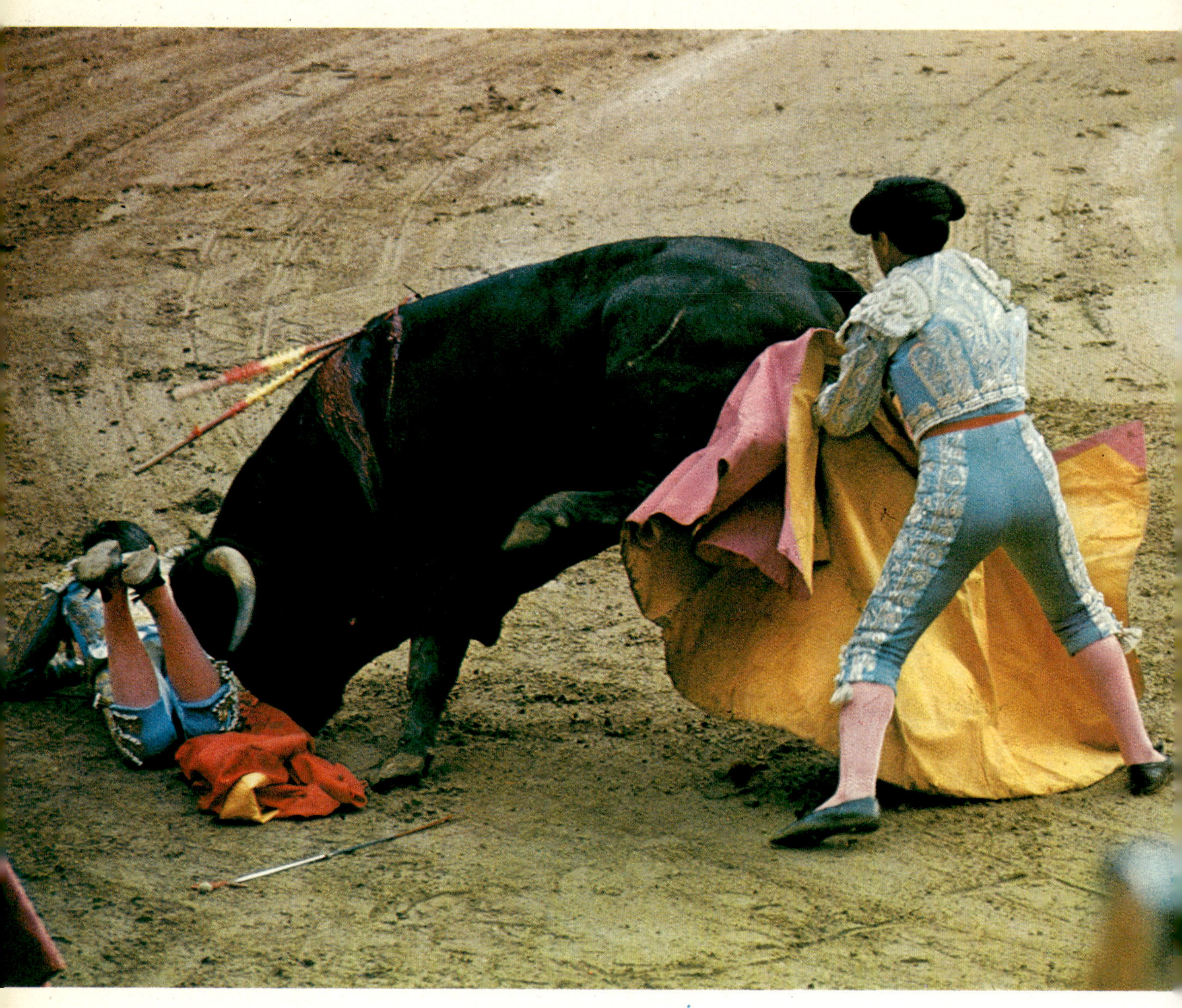

were sacrificed but apparently few bears were killed. Indeed certain bears, the pride and profit of their bear-wards, became popular heroes or heroines. There was, for example, "The famous Middlewich bear, Old Nell' who used to be taken to the ale-house by her master after a bait and there refreshed with beer; there is a story that she once repaid his kindness by chasing away a terrified constable who came to distrain upon his goods for debt.'[28]

The famous bear-garden on Bankside in Southwark was built in 1526. An adjoining circus for bullbaiting was opened over forty years later, in 1570. The bull, although confined to the ring, was not chained like the bear, and at least had freedom of movement to defend itself against mastiffs and bulldogs. The death of the bull was not the inevitable climax to the spectacle as in the Spanish bullfight, and many a fine fighting bull, like many a valiant bear, lived to be baited another day. For 'the animals themselves were the aristocrats of their world, and between baits they were as carefully tended as any English race-horse . . . of to-day'.[29]

In later times bullbaiting became more commercialised and apparently required additional excitements to draw the crowd. An eighteenth-century advertisement for the Eccles September Wake, which stretched over three days, 'spoke of "baiting the bull, Fury"' and 'the additional attraction of a smock race by ladies . . .'.[30]

During the Puritan supremacy of Cromwellian England baits were suppressed, but revived in the permissive period that followed the Restoration. Baiting of both bulls and bears continued until the middle of the nineteenth century. A bill to abolish it was put before Parliament in the year 1802, but was rejected by the small majority of thirteen. In the 1830s, however, when everything in England, including Parliament itself, was being reformed, the abolitionists succeeded in 1835 in making baiting illegal. It lingered on, illegally, for some twenty years longer. The last bullbaiting is said to have been held in 1853 in the village of West Derby, now engulfed by Liverpool. It is rather curious, however, that although bullbaiting gave rise to a special breed of dog, the bulldog, there appears to be no evidence of a special breed of fighting bulls in England such as has persisted in Spain until the present day. Provided the bull was sufficiently ferocious – the term 'mad bull' so frequently used probably meant no more than that – it seems that a bull of any breed would serve its purpose.

Bullbaiting, with royal and aristocratic patronage, was a sport under control and graced with formalities. Bullrunning, on the contrary, was quite literally a free-for-all and, as in Spain, it meant certain death to the bull. A holiday feature in many English villages and towns, that of Stamford in Lincolnshire became most notorious. It all started – or so it is said – far back in English history, in the first half of the thirteenth century when King John of Magna Carta fame sat some-

Opposite: Drama in the bullring. A *banderillero* endeavours to draw the bull away as it tries to gore the fallen matador. (*Barnaby's Picture Library*)

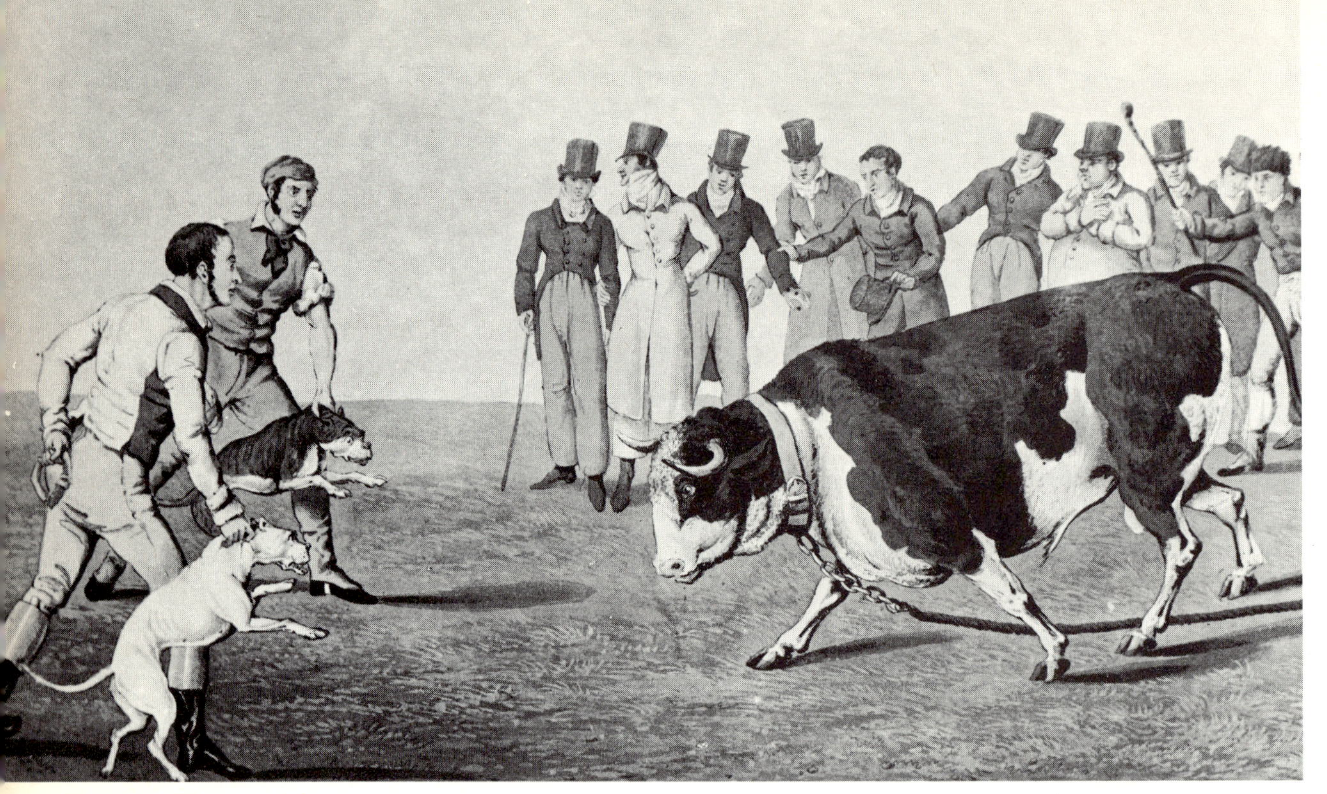

what uneasily upon the English throne. It so happened that a certain lord of the manor, William de Warenne, saw two bulls fighting in one of his fields: 'Some butchers' dogs attacked them and chased one right through the town, and this so delighted de Warenne that he gave the field to the butchers on condition that they provided a bull every year for the running.'[31]

So began the Stamford bullrunning which became an institution, a legend and a proverb. Stamford butchers got their field and for a full six centuries they fulfilled the condition of the gift. Every year, for six hundred years, on each thirteenth day of November, a bull – the madder the better – was let loose in the streets of Stamford. The hunt was well and truly up. Shopkeepers barricaded their shops, all business ceased, while many women, children and dogs flocked on to the streets in pursuit of the bull. The festival had its Queen as is the fashion of all festivals today. She was called the 'Bull Queen' and was made gay with bright ribbons. Yet, in spite of the Queen, selected no doubt as is the modern custom from a panel of beauties, the Stamford bull-running could have been no pretty spectacle. The bull-chasers were called 'bullards' and these heroes 'exerted themselves to the utmost in their efforts to cause the bull pain, madden it, and finally kill it; sometimes the bull was very dangerous and the bullards needed all the protection that could be afforded by a series of hogsheads placed in chosen positions.'[32] 'If a bull would not run it was beaten until it

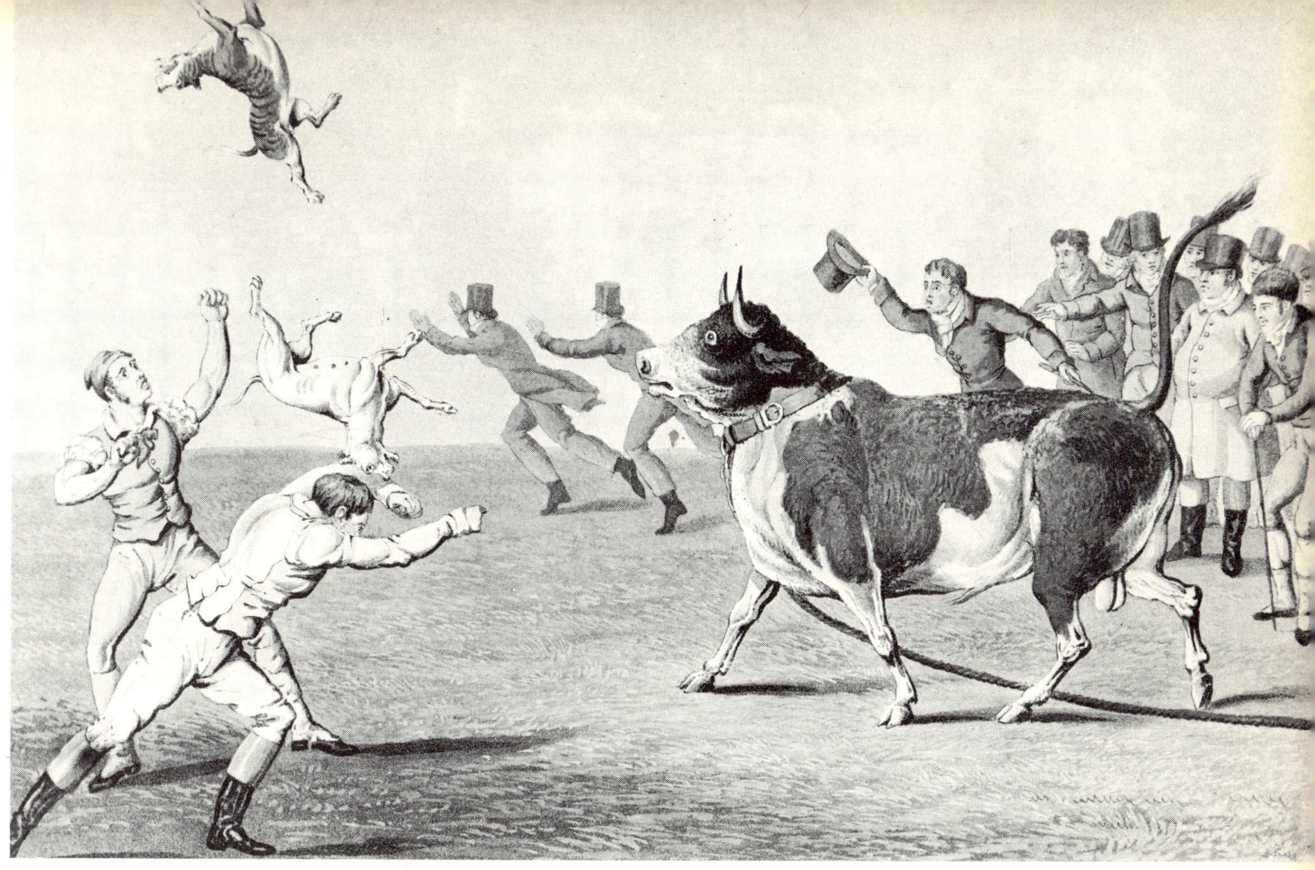

did; the great object of the hunt was to get it on to the bridge and from thence to chase or hurl it into the river and out again over the muddy fields adjoining.'[33]

When the bull became exhausted it was killed and roasted, its beef sold cheap or given gratis to the Stamford poor. The bullard who had shown the greatest daring was presented with the 'Great Gut or Pudding, commonly known as Tom Hodge' as a reward for his gallantry.

Stamford persisted in its annual bullrunning in provincial defiance of national legislation. Let the London Parliament legislate as it wished, on the thirteenth day of November each year, the townspeople of Stamford continued to run the bull. In the year 1788 the town Mayor jointly with Lord Exeter tried to stop the show and 'were openly insulted for their pains'.[34] The years rolled by while the bull ran. Fifty-five years after Mayor and Lord had been openly insulted, the Society for the Prevention of Cruelty to Animals took a hand. Their protests having been flouted, they sent down several of their officers to intervene in person. These were roughly handled and windows smashed in the riot. Arrests were made and the town raised a fund for the prisoners' defence. Of eight bullards arrested, five were acquitted and three released on bail. The following year a bull was run again, to the delight of the populace.

In 1838, matters came to a pretty pass. The Mayor and the town officials, goaded on by the Home Secretary, enlisted special constables,

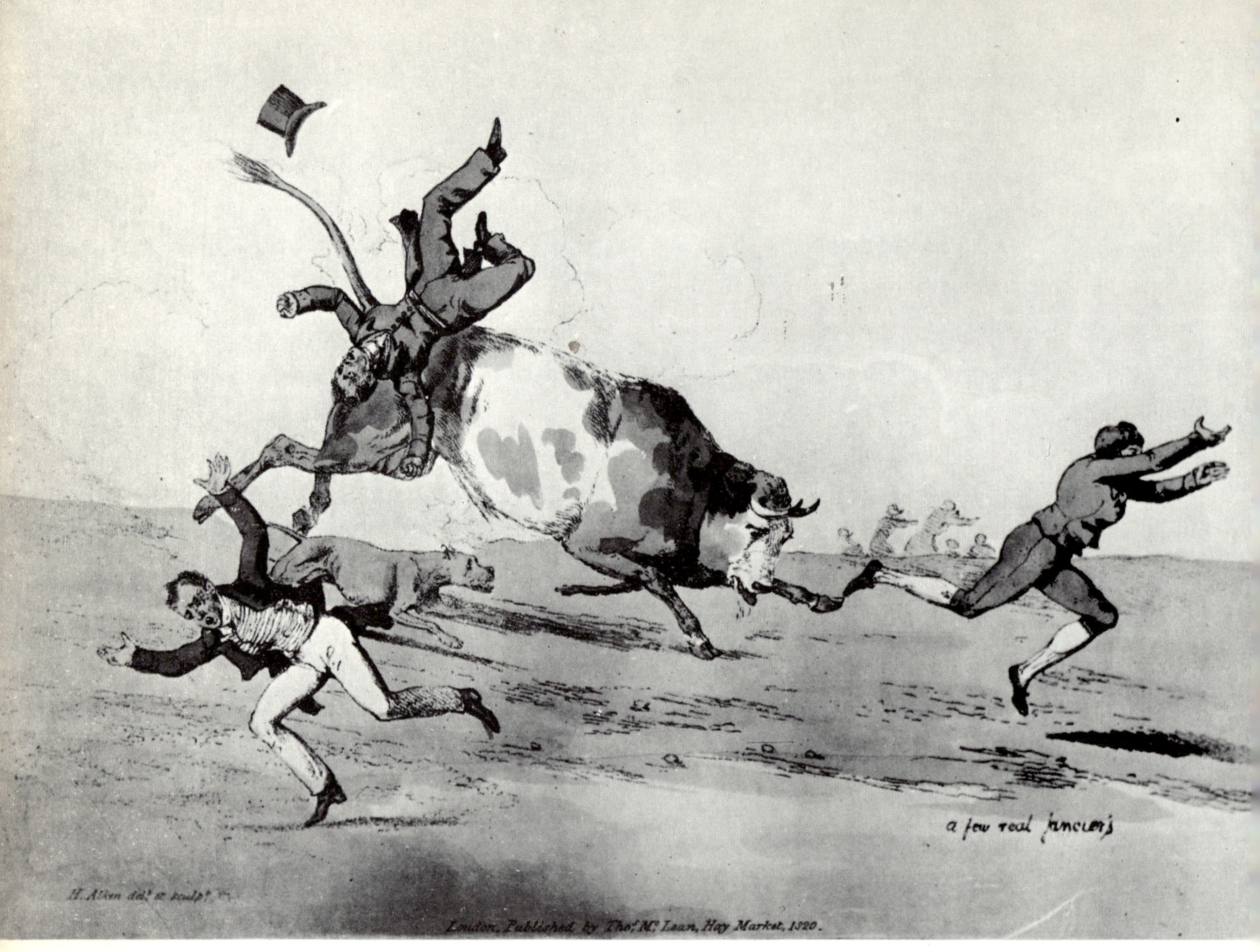

Above: a nineteenth-century print depicting bull-running. When the bull became exhausted it was killed and roasted, but not before it had caused considerable havoc. (*Mansell Collection*)

Opposite, above: Present-day bull-baiting in Villa Franca de Xira, Portugal. *Campinos* (cowboys) parade through the street before the bull-baiting begins. Several bulls are released, but streets are barricaded into sections and only one bull is apportioned to each section. (*Barnaby's Picture Library*)

Opposite, below: 'The end is death.' The sacrificed bull's carcase being dragged from the arena. If the bull has shown exceptional bravery during the fight, the crowd will insist that the mules drag it round the ring as a posthumous tribute before galloping out with it to the butcher's yard. (*Barnaby's Picture Library*)

requested and were granted the support of a company of soldiers and the metropolitan police, thoroughly searched for hidden or smuggled-in bulls. Nevertheless, on November 13th a bull appeared on the streets of Stamford. The bull ran, the townspeople chased it, the troops intervened and 'there was a sharp fight between the soldiers and the people'.[35]

In the following year there was further trouble, but in 1840 wiser counsels prevailed. The townsmen offered to forego their cherished sport on condition that no more soldiers or policemen were imported from outside, or expense incurred by the enrolment of special constables. This spontaneous offer was accepted, and since that time there has been no more bull-running in Stamford or anywhere else in Great Britain.[35]

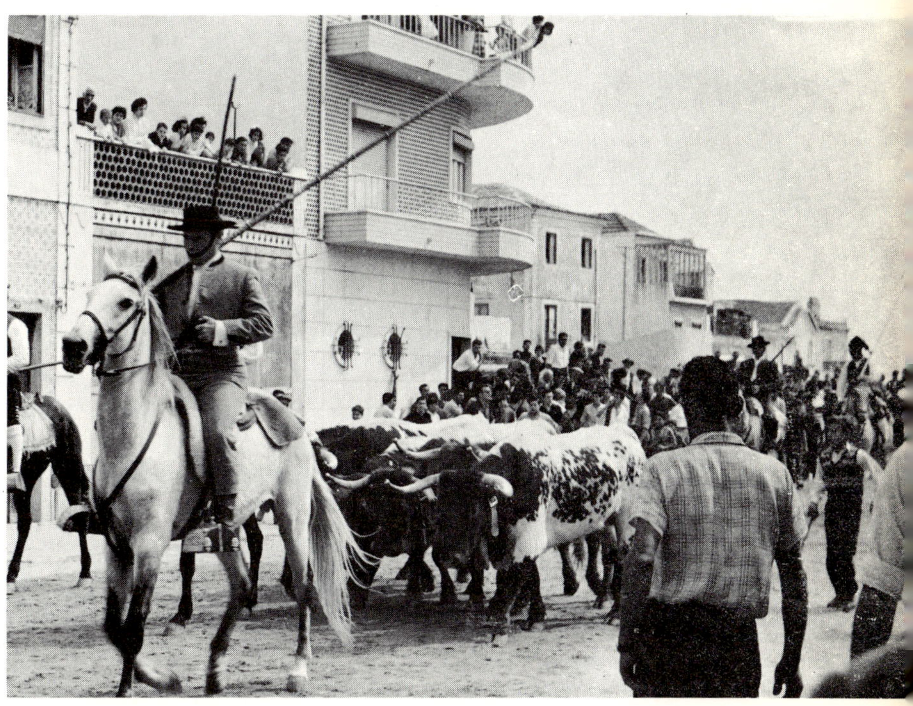

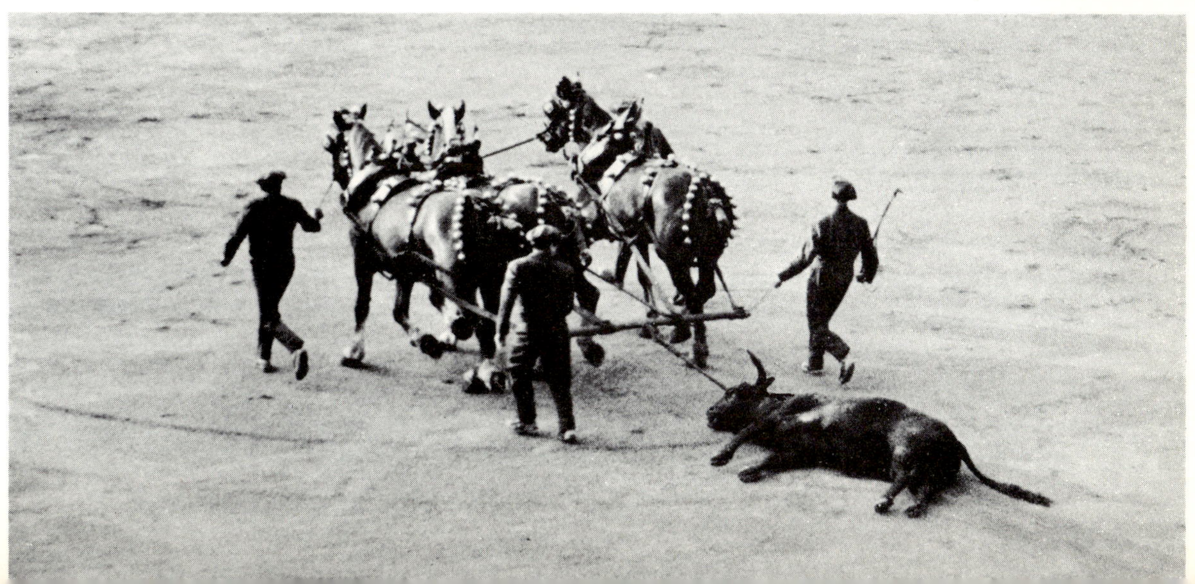

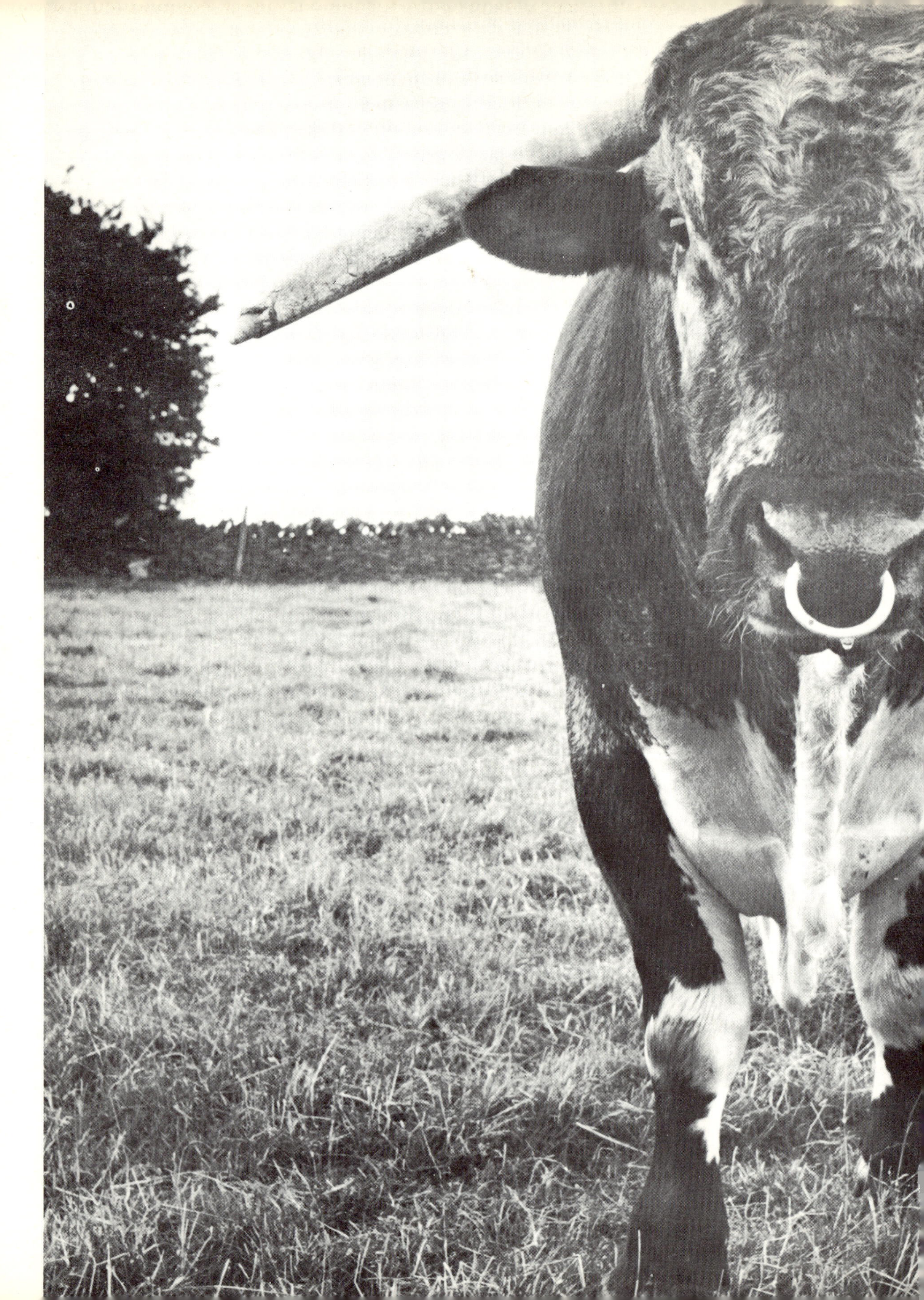

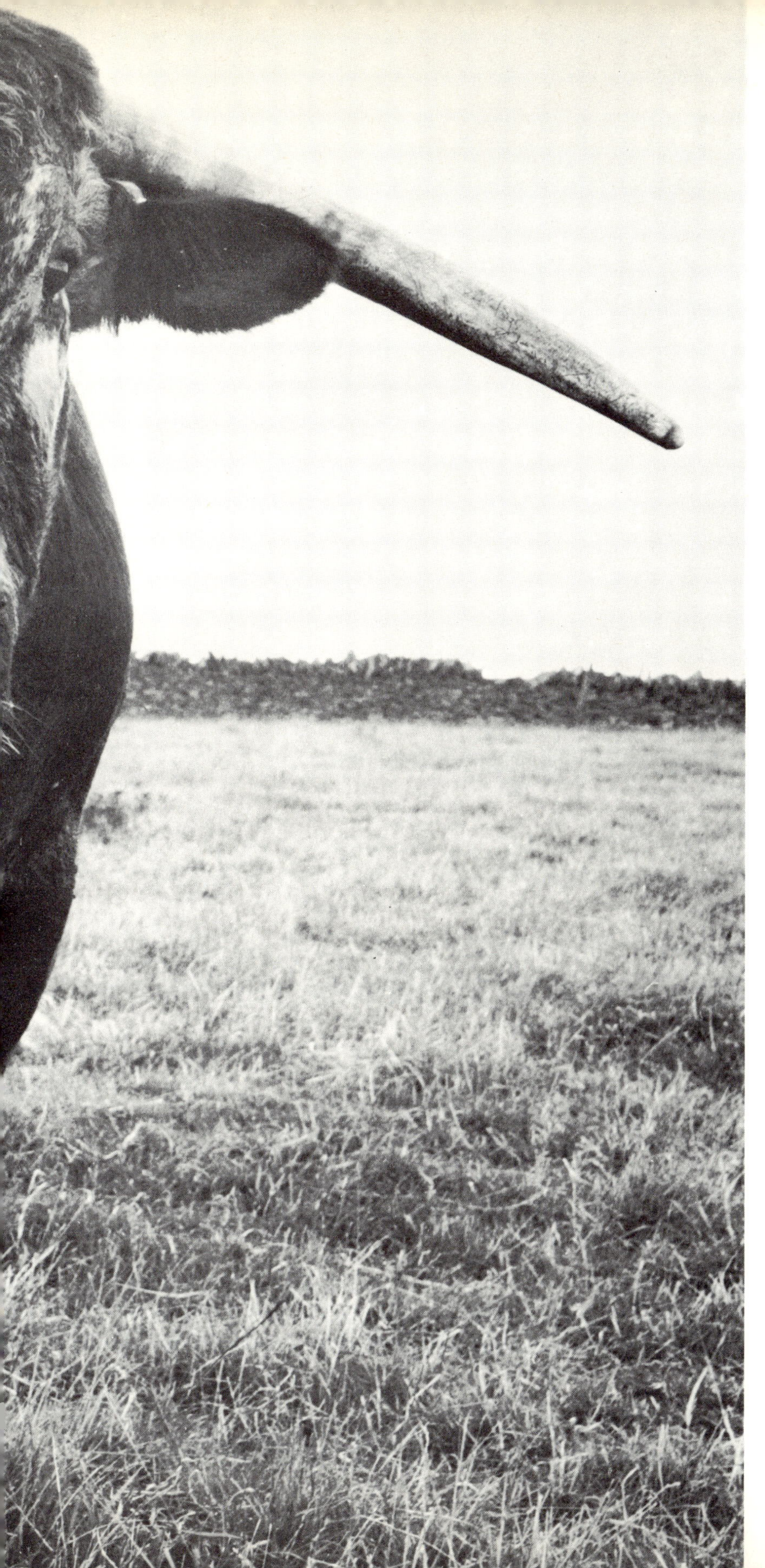

6

The Bull
in
Pedigree

Longhorn bull. Once the dominant cattle breed on the meadow lands of England, and an early object of Bakewell's improvement by in-breeding, it failed in competition with the Shorthorn and, today, only a remnant exists. (*Eagle Photos*)

§ It is an accepted fact that there were many domesticated cattle in Britain long before the days of written history. In medieval times their main use was as plough oxen, with dairy produce, beef and hides of secondary and variable importance. Until the end of the eighteenth century, cattle-breeding appears to have been somewhat haphazard, described with some exaggeration as 'the mating of nobody's son with everybody's daughters'. Surely there must have been some degree of selection and choice, at least as far as the bull was concerned. Castration is an operation as old as man himself and references to the male castrate in cattle – the ox – go back to the beginnings of written history. In medieval England, where farming operations were based upon the village community, selection in some form must have rescued *the* village bull from becoming *a* village ox:

The basis for selection must remain speculative and obscure but undoubtedly, nevertheless, the choice would have fallen upon a bull with both testicles descended, masculine in appearance and nowise imperfect in his private parts. A bull active, freely-moving and firmly set on straight legs, well grown for his age, eager yet controllable, out of a good cow, come of a good family would stand the best chance of avoiding castration.[1]

It is improbable that anybody paid much attention to coat coloration or to horn length and curvature, and, in appearance at least, the cattle herds on the pastures of old England must have been a motley collection of browns and blacks, duns and fawns, piebald and skewbald, horned and polled.

Greater order and uniformity had to await the enclosures of Hanoverian times in the eighteenth century. It was then that cattle herds came under the individual ownership of landlords or tenant farmers and each cattle-breeder could shape his own breeding course without the approval and occasional obstruction of neighbours sharing the village common and the village bull.

Several of such farmers, of whom the name of Robert Bakewell (1725–95) of the farm of Dishley Grange in the county of Leicester achieved greatest fame, aimed to improve animal productivity by the use of a new tool. At least it was a new tool as far as farmers were concerned, although the breeders of the thoroughbred racehorse had used it for some time. The technique employed was deliberate inbreeding. To breed the best to the best, that was the principle, and what was likely to be a better match for an outstanding bull than that bull's own daughters, his sisters or even his dam? Although already adopted by what were perhaps the more sophisticated breeders of racehorses, in-breeding was strenuously opposed by the majority of breeders of farm animals of that day and generation. They called the practice incestuous, sinful and unscriptural and prophesied disaster to such in-bred stock and damnation to those who used in-breeding.

In certain instances their warnings were fulfilled. Bakewell himself, for example, when he tried in-breeding his Berkshire pigs, ended up with litters that, at least according to his contemporary critics, who were numerous, proved to be 'all rickety' or 'all fools'. Whether the prophecy regarding breeders was fulfilled must remain forever unknown! In any event, despite pigs and prophecies, and regardless of his position as a pillar of his local Unitarian church, Bakewell went ahead with his plans, ruining his Berkshire pigs, spoiling his Longhorn cattle, but succeeding admirably with his Longwool Leicester sheep. He became famous; royalty and nobility paid visits to his farm; and, perhaps most important of all, he taught and entertained certain imitative disciples. At the suggestion of George Culley (author of *Observations on Live Stock* and a great admirer of Bakewell), Charles Colling of Ketton Hall, near Darlington (1750–1836), made in the year 1783 a prolonged visit to Dishley Grange and was for a time joined there by his brother Robert. The brothers Colling were converted:

After their visit to Bakewell about 1783 they returned with the determination to do for the Shorthorns what they conceived he had accomplished for the Longhorns and to adopt the same system.[2]

In fact, they did a great deal more. Possibly because they had better initial stock to breed from, the Collings succeeded in beating their master at his own game. It came to pass that it was the Shorthorn as fashioned by Charles and Robert Colling that drove the Longhorn, both improved and unimproved, from the meadow lands of England. The game itself, however, remained Bakewell's game, 'systematic principles of breeding, as opposed to the chance mating of nobody's son with everybody's daughter'.[3]

Incest in cattle became – not merely permissible – but customary in bull-breeding herds. The basis of the business was a bull as near perfection as possible in himself who would leave offspring stamped with his individual excellence, a property called prepotency. The first essential was to find such a bull and many a bull-breeder of the late eighteenth and early nineteenth centuries spent half a lifetime in finding one. In almost every cattle breed there arose a breeder or family of breeders – for the breeding of cattle, like forestry, is a business which may outspan a human lifetime – who had the knowledge, the instinct or some would have it, the plain good fortune to find an outstanding and prepotent bull to sire his herd. Such breeders, of as distinctive a character as the bulls they bred, are remembered in the history of every cattle breed of the present day. Many of these breeders remained single all their lives as though in some dimly reminiscent way they had come to a monastic worship of the bulls they owned. Thus James Sinclair in his *History of Shorthorn Cattle*,[4] wrote:

By the way, can anyone explain how it is that so many of our first-class breeders of cattle have been bachelors. There was Bakewell, to begin with,

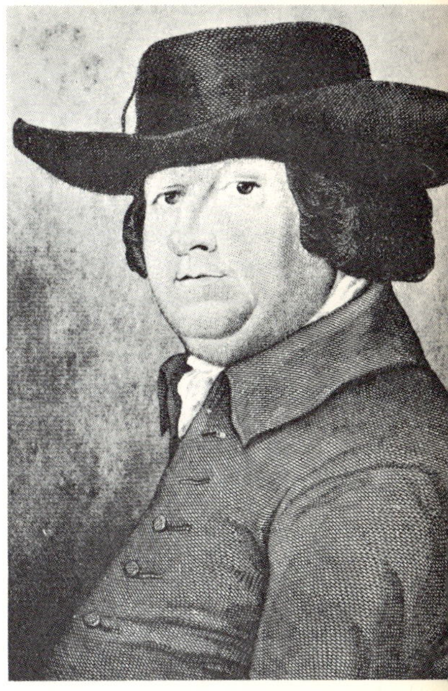

Robert Bakewell (1725–95), from an engraving by F. Englehart, 1842. Bakewell, of the farm of Dishley Grange, Leicestershire, achieved fame through the improvement of animal productivity by introducing deliberate in-breeding among cattle.

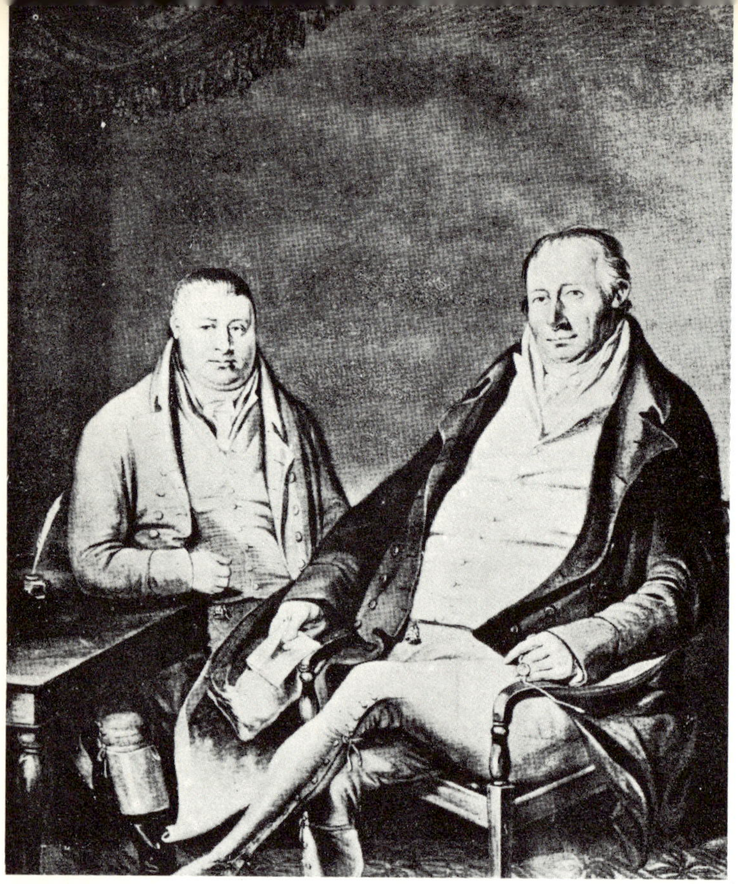

The Colling brothers, Charles (1750–1836) and Robert (1749–1820). Sons of Charles Colling sen. of Ketton Hall, near Darlington, these brothers shared in the development of the breed of Shorthorn cattle and greatly improved the stock. Charles Colling jun. farmed at Ketton Hall, while Robert occupied a farm at nearby Brampton.

Robert Colling, Thomas Bates, Mason of Chilton, Richard Booth, Wilkinson of Lenton and Torr – almost all the old masters, in fact.

These were the master breeders of the Shorthorn breed, famous in their day and generation. Similarly in other breeds there was Tomkins in the Herefords, Hugh Watson of Keillor and William M'Combie of Tillyfour in the Aberdeen-Angus breed, Francis Quartly of the 'Red Ruby' Devons. These were the men who, using the Bakewell recipe of selection followed by close in-breeding, were shaping their breeds towards the beef ideal. Men of similar type were diverting their breeds towards milk production.

To follow the history of each breed in too much detail would be a monotonous procedure. It must suffice here to select one for more detailed description and since the first successful application of Bakewell's breeding recipe to cattle began with the Shorthorn, let us follow the Shorthorn. The early breeders were men of North England, farming mainly around Darlington in Yorkshire, and the Colling brothers, after sitting at the feet of Bakewell, were two of the first. To demonstrate their success they advertised their cattle by showing them at the 'Cattle Shows', at that time in their infancy, and by sending them for exhibition through the countryside. There was Charles Colling's 'Durham Ox' and Robert Colling's 'The White Heifer that Travelled', both sired by a bull appropriately named 'Favourite'. The success of the Collings

116

in breeding Shorthorns was proved at the Ketton dispersion where Charles Colling sold his stock bull 'Comet' for one thousand guineas. In an age when guineas were still golden – the date of the dispersion was 1810 – a thousand guineas, besides being a record price for a bull, was a considerable amount of money.

A Mr Thornton, one of the numerous authors who combined to establish a perfect library of Shorthorn history and legend, wrote in his article on 'Ancient Shorthorns' that when this great bull 'Comet' died he was buried in the centre of the paddock, three miles from Darlington, where he had been put to grass and that a chestnut tree was planted on his grave. 'The paddock is known as Comet's garth to this day.'[5] There is more than a suggestion of a dying flicker of the

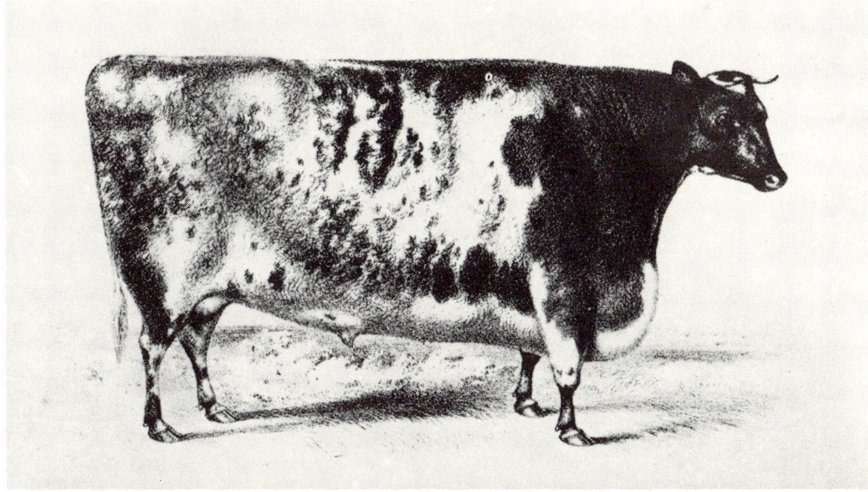

Above: Charles Colling's 'Durham Ox'.

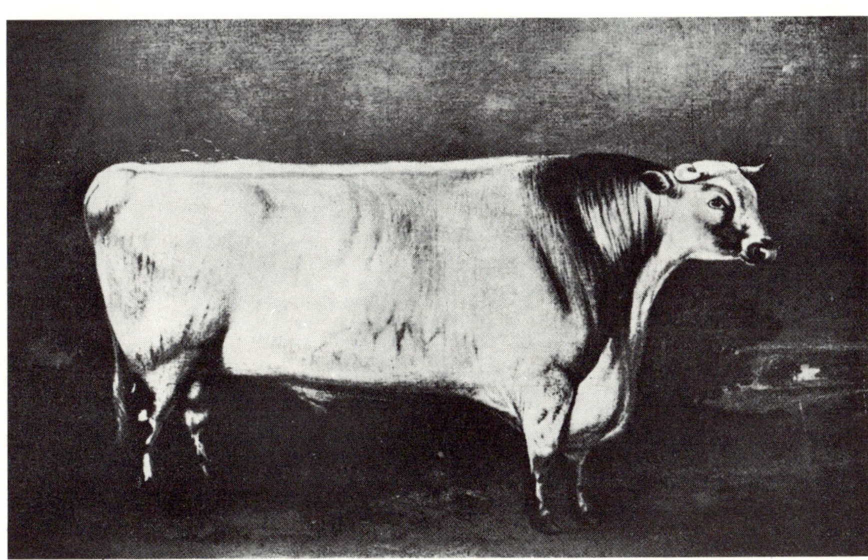

Below: 'Comet', Charles Colling's famous stock bull sold for 1,000 guineas in 1810.

bull cult here. Better still had an oak tree rather than a chestnut marked Comet's grave!

After the Colling brothers, Charles and Robert, had had their day, the breeding work they had begun was carried on by a farming family called Booth on the one hand, and a bachelor called Bates on the other, and a curious yet bitter rivalry arose between them. The venom was mostly on Bates's side. He was a pious man, nicknamed 'Bible Bates', but he never learnt to love his neighbour's cattle as his own.

It was about this time, in 1812 or so, that a Mr George Coates, himself an enthusiastic but not particularly successful breeder of Shorthorns, conceived the idea of recording the pedigree of this now fashionable breed. He proceeded to do so in imitation of the Stud-Book already devoted to the lineage of the thoroughbred horse. He published the first Shorthorn Herd Book as a private venture in 1822, and it has been known as Coates's Herd Book ever since, although taken over by the Shorthorn Society of Great Britain in 1872. Not every breeder of his time agreed altogether with the pedigrees he provided for their cattle. Some, indeed, asserted that George Coates had his preferences and that should a breeder get on the wrong side of him he was liable to find his best stock bull falsely labelled a bastard.

Neither then nor since was the pedigree of livestock quite as reliable and accurate as it claimed to be. Just as all human pedigree depends upon a woman's word, so in cattle it depends upon the herdsman's word. A titled character of Oscar Wilde's play, *A Woman of No Importance* put the matter very neatly when he said, 'You should study the Peerage, Gerald. . . . It is the best thing in fiction the English have ever done.'

Nevertheless, pedigree in Shorthorn cattle became almost a fetish for a time, so much so that very poor cattle with impressive pedigree sometimes sold for very high prices, and excellent unpedigreed breeding cattle made little or nothing at all. The export market for Shorthorns, expanding throughout the nineteenth century, encouraged the pedigree cult, as importing countries such as those of North and South America insisted on the production of adequately certified pedigrees before permitting importation. Incidentally, practically all the other breeds of livestock in Britain – were they cart-horses, cattle, sheep or pigs – followed the example George Coates had set. Stud books, herd books, flock books, with their annual additions of yet another volume, overcrowded the bookshelves of all agricultural libraries.

While the early Shorthorn breeders were mainly North of England men, the evolution of that type of Shorthorn known as the 'Beef Shorthorn' or 'Scotch Shorthorn' was, as the name suggests, the work of Scotsmen.

Captain Barclay of Urie, an estate beside the then little fishing

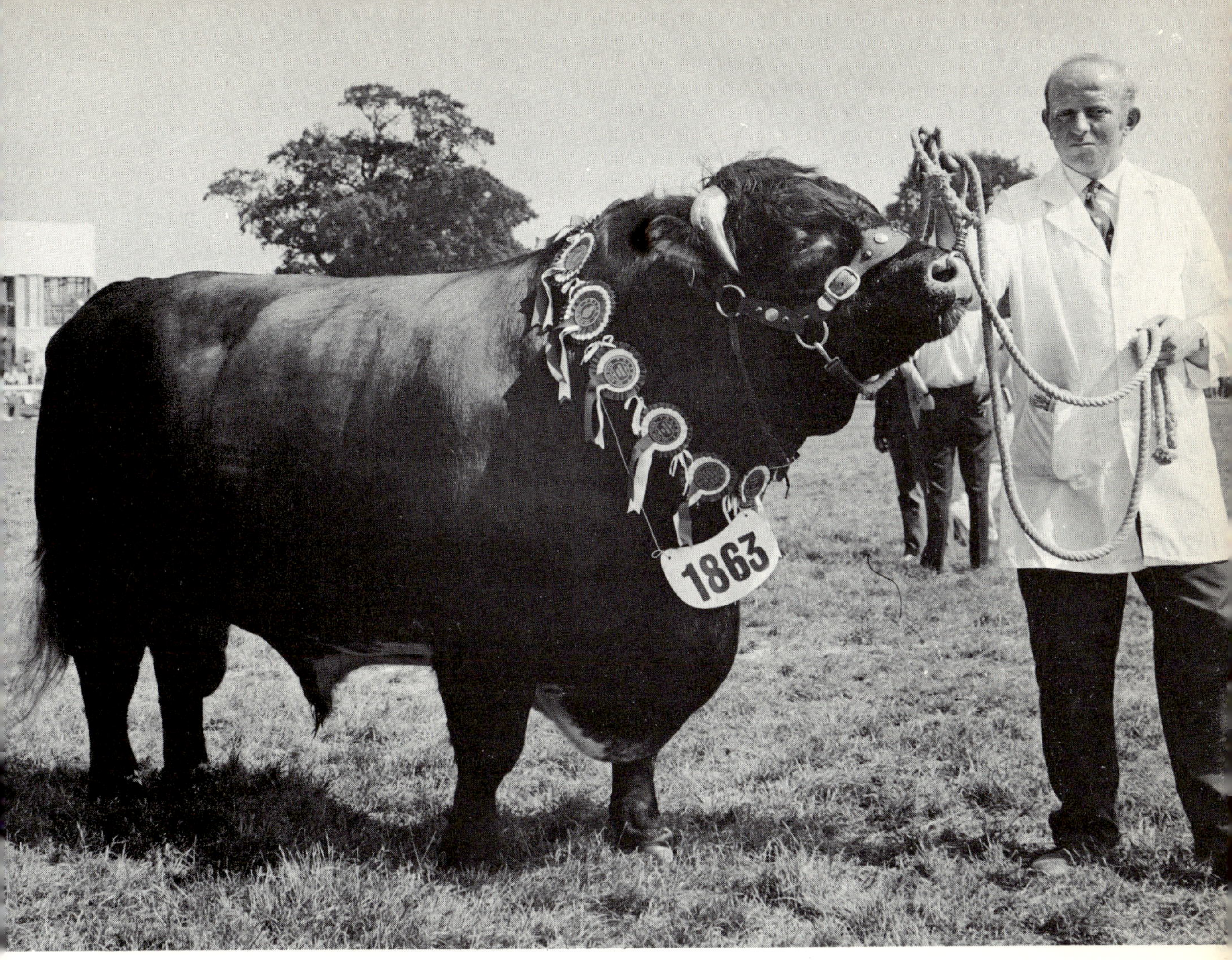

village of Stonehaven, in the county of Kincardine, was one of the first Shorthorn breeders in the north-east of Scotland. An extraordinary man was this Captain Barclay of Urie: gentleman, sportsman, athlete, farmer, eccentric; who trained pugilists; walked a thousand miles in as many hours; drove the London coach, 'The Defiance', when the mood was on him; was so strong that he once threw a donkey over a wall; and in his more serious moments founded a Shorthorn herd. From time to time he appears to have tired of such tame cattle and he dispersed his herd twice. His dispersals were important because his sales were not widely advertised and therefore mainly local. By thus twice dispersing his herd chiefly amongst local buyers, he distributed the best type of the Shorthorn cattle of his time among the tenant farmers of Aberdeenshire. They could not have fallen into more capable hands because that county had already begun to achieve its great reputation for breeding and feeding cattle of the highest beef quality.

Champion Beef Shorthorn bull 'Upper Mill Pagan' at the 1971 Royal Show. The Shorthorn breeders were the first to adopt wholeheartedly and successfully the principles of rigorous selection and the closest possible in-breeding of the select in establishing a separate and distinct breed of cattle. (*Fox Photos*)

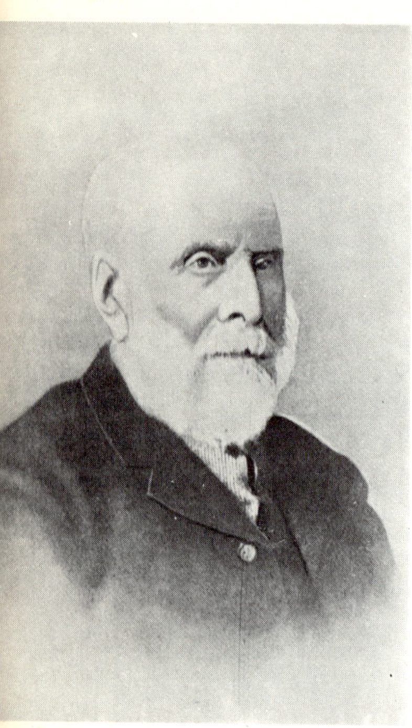

Amos Cruikshank (1808–95), 'the herdsman of Aberdeenshire'. Amos was the real founder of the Shorthorn breed, and the last surviving partner of the original firm of 'A. & A. Cruikshank', owners of the Sittyton herd of Shorthorns.

As a result of these fortunate dispersions there came to be developed what was essentially a new breed, the Beef Shorthorn or the Scottish Shorthorn, bred specially for beef production with the dairy an unimportant side issue.

Amos Cruickshank, of the farm of Sittyton within easy riding distance of the town of Aberdeen, was the real founder of the breed. This quiet old Quaker bachelor was in partnership with his brother, a glovemaker in Aberdeen, but it was Amos who managed the cattle. In the year 1852 he had been touring the Shorthorn herds in England and visited the farm of Lenton in Nottinghamshire tenanted by one John Wilkinson. Amos was greatly impressed with this herd, so much so that six years later, a picture of the Lenton herd still in his mind, he wrote to John Wilkinson asking whether he had a good red-coloured young bull he might be willing to sell. Wilkinson replied that he was unable to oblige but offered Amos an aged red bull – he was eight years old – at bargain price. After the canny hesitation proverbial in his native county, Amos accepted the offer. The bull called 'Lancaster Comet' duly arrived. Amos was thoroughly disappointed with the appearance of his purchase and Sinclair thus describes his reaction:

The bull was forwarded in November, 1858. Mr Housman has told how Amos Cruickshank rode down to the railway to meet the new arrival, and how he felt when he saw the great head and horns lowering upon him over the side of the truck. One earnest look sufficed, and he turned away. Like the Laird of Cockpen, 'Dumfoundered he was, but no sigh did he gie' – or more probably he did give a sigh, perhaps even a groan. The remarks of those neighbours who first saw the beast were not encouraging. 'If you wanted a Highland bull,' said one sarcastic friend, 'you might have got one nearer home.' It was therefore thought injudicious to use the animal freely, so Lancaster Comet was relegated to the Clyne farm, to hide his horns there. . . .[6]

This farm of Clyne was a subsidiary to Sittyton and not the choicest part of the land Amos rented. It was bleak, cold land and poor pasture. Lancaster Comet was there allotted a small group of shy breeding cows, those, in fact, that had failed to settle to the Sittyton stud bulls. The fate of Lancaster Comet makes rather a sad story. Unaccustomed to a harsh northern climate after eight years in the milder more fertile plains of England, he developed rheumatism, he caught cold and he died. He had, however, proved his virility before his decease. He had overcome the shyness of one particular cow called 'Virtue by Plantagenet' for she was in calf to him. This mating was an event important, not only to the fortunes of Amos and the reputation of the Sittyton herd, but to the world's developing beef cattle industry. For as the result of this almost accidental conception there was born, in the autumn of the year 1859, a bull calf which Amos rather strangely and perhaps prophetically called 'Champion of England'. He could, as subsequent history proved, have called him 'Champion of both Americas' for such, in the event, he proved to be.

Commander T.B. Marston, writing about the 'Scotch Shorthorn' almost a hundred years later described what the birth of this bull calf meant to the subsequent development of the Beef Shorthorn breed:

At Sittyton, Lancaster Comet sired Champion of England (17526) out of Virtue by Plantagenet (57868). This deep-bodied short-legged roan (calved November 29, 1859) was remarkable for his covering of natural flesh and abundant coat of hair, and proved one of the greatest Shorthorn characters that ever lived for he consolidated Sittyton and founded a world dynasty. His prepotency was great, his daughters being as good as his sons, of whom fourteen were used at Sittyton, and in addition, grandsons and great grandsons.[7]

Aberdeenshire, with its cold, wet summers, its frozen winters and the superb husbandry of its cattlemen, was a fitting cradle for a hardy breed. In a climate once described as 'nine months winter and three months bad weather' no weakling was likely to survive. Like Scotsmen themselves, and for a similar reason, the Scotch Shorthorn, stabilised at Sittyton by close in-breeding, colonised well.

. . . American buyers gave the new type a trial, it throve on the prairies, and the buyers came back for more, and then for more again. Meantime new herds, destined to be almost as famous as the Sittyton one itself, were being built up with Cruickshank blood in Aberdeenshire – by Marr of Uppermill, Duthie of Collynie, and many others.[8]

Duthie of Collynie, a name to conjure with some fifty years ago! In the year 1919, at the conclusion of the First World War, the Beef Shorthorn herd of Mr William Duthie, graduate of Aberdeen University, local banker in the village of Tarves and master breeder, held complete supremacy in the Shorthorn world. Thus, 'in 1919, twenty-four Collynie bull calves averaged £1,400.8.9. with a top price of £5,655'[9] – big prices indeed, in those distant days.

It was a remarkable experience to visit Collynie, a typical Aberdeenshire tenant's farm, with its limited acreage and unpretentious farmhouse and steading; to see there the cattle that millionaires at that time would have given half their fortune to possess; to scan the visitors' book inscribed with the names of all the greatest cattle-breeders in the world; to meet in such a bleak out-of-the-way corner of rural Scotland, buyers from the Argentine, from Uruguay, from America, from Canada and the Australias, who offered something of the same reverence to the Aberdeenshire farm of Collynie as Mohammedans give to their prophet's birthplace in Mecca.

The export trade for the Scotch Shorthorn, necessarily and completely interrupted between 1914 and 1919, flourished anew when exportation became feasible once again, and continued with the normal fluctuations until the outbreak of the Second World War in 1939. Once more there was a cessation from then until 1946, a complete interruption of seven years. Many people imagined that after such a long gap, the Argentinians, Americans, Canadians and Australians would have no further interest in Scotland nor in her Shorthorn bulls.

It proved quite otherwise:

The eighty-second Show and Sale of Shorthorns bulls at Perth in February of the year 1946 will long be remembered for the record prices realised. There were 39 transactions of 1,000 guineas and over, and the 417 animals sold realised £182,755, 14s with an overall average of £438. Some 100 bulls and 20 females were brought for export at a cost of upwards of £80,000. Five bulls from the Pittodrie herd, all sired by Bapton Upright (316211) realised 35,700 guineas, an average per head of £7,497, and the Kirkton herd's Female Champion made 3,000 guineas.[10]

For the better part of a century, therefore, the pick of Scottish Shorthorn bulls had been bought at high prices to go abroad. Why? That was a question which puzzled the agricultural scientist for many a long year. To the geneticist it was obvious that the best genetic or breeding material had already reached all the newer pastoral countries in sufficient abundance. Were Scottish stockmanship responsible for the assumed superiority of Scottish Shorthorn bulls the stockmen would have cost far less than the cattle. The explanation put forward by Scottish cattlemen themselves, although that explanation was completely opposed to biological theory, was that once the Scottish Shorthorn left its native heath it tended to lose type. It was said of the Argentine particularly, that after a few generations in that country the Scottish Shorthorn tended to grow more leggy and rangy, losing the low-set, blocky and massive beef conformation of the original breed. If the breed were to retain its excellence abroad, it was essential, therefore, to return periodically to the source, the fountainhead, as it were, to prevent deterioration. Similar claims have been put forward by many other British societies interested in exporting their stock. The possibility of such claims being made in defence of vested interests is too obvious to merit further discussion. In the case of the Scotch Shorthorn breed the claims appeared to be better supported by the evidence than in most others. Yet, despite that evidence the claim can no longer be made. For, within more recent years, the Scottish Shorthorn founded by Amos Cruickshank and his 'Champion of England' away back in the middle of last century has faltered and failed. At the traditional Perth Bull Sales, held in February of each year – apart from the interruptions due to wars – for over a hundred years, the Shorthorn was first sent to the rear of a competing breed, the Aberdeen-Angus, and has now shrunk to a mere remnant supported by a dwindling number of the faithful few.

What then of the main competitor – the Aberdeen-Angus? Its

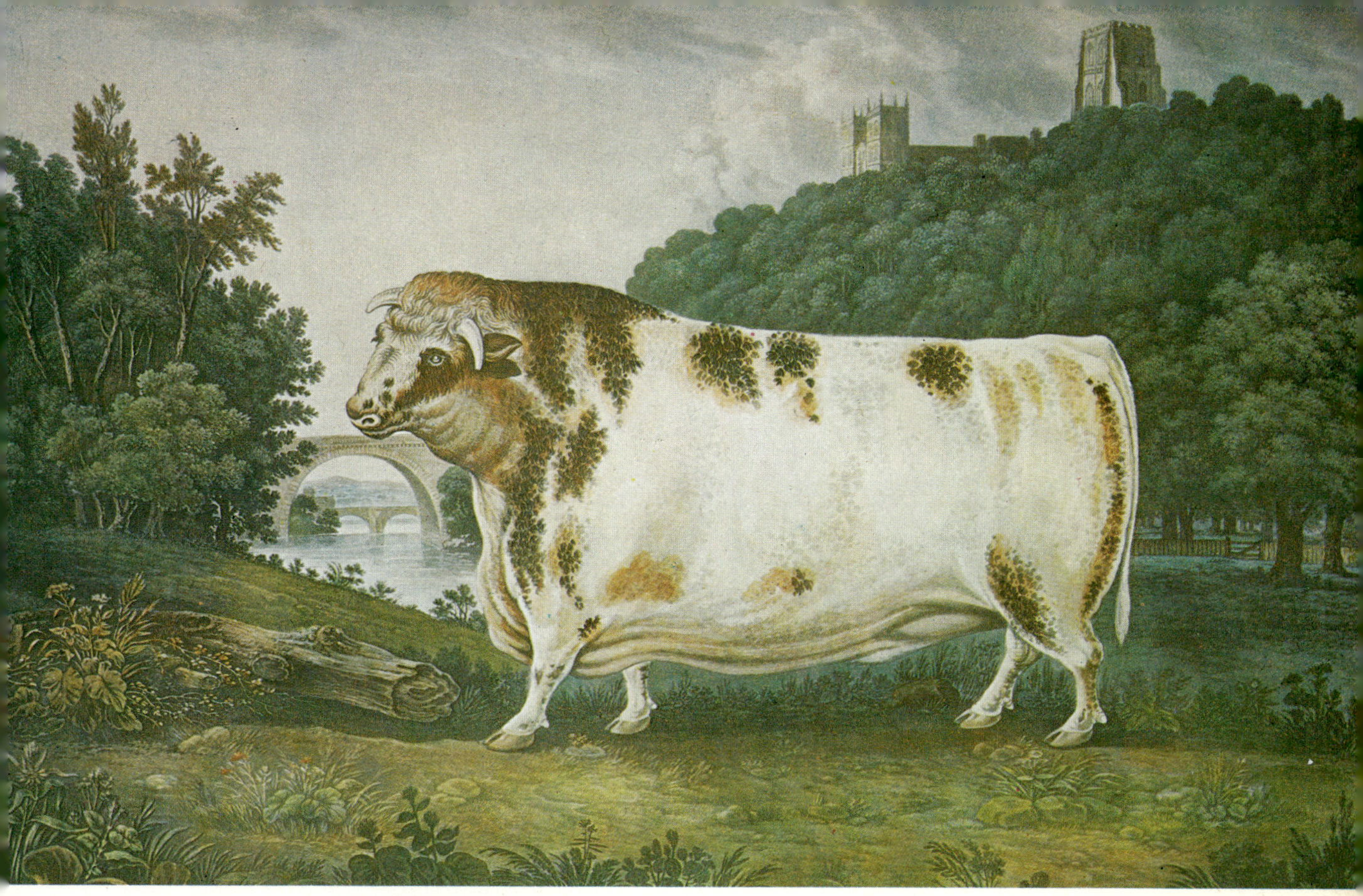

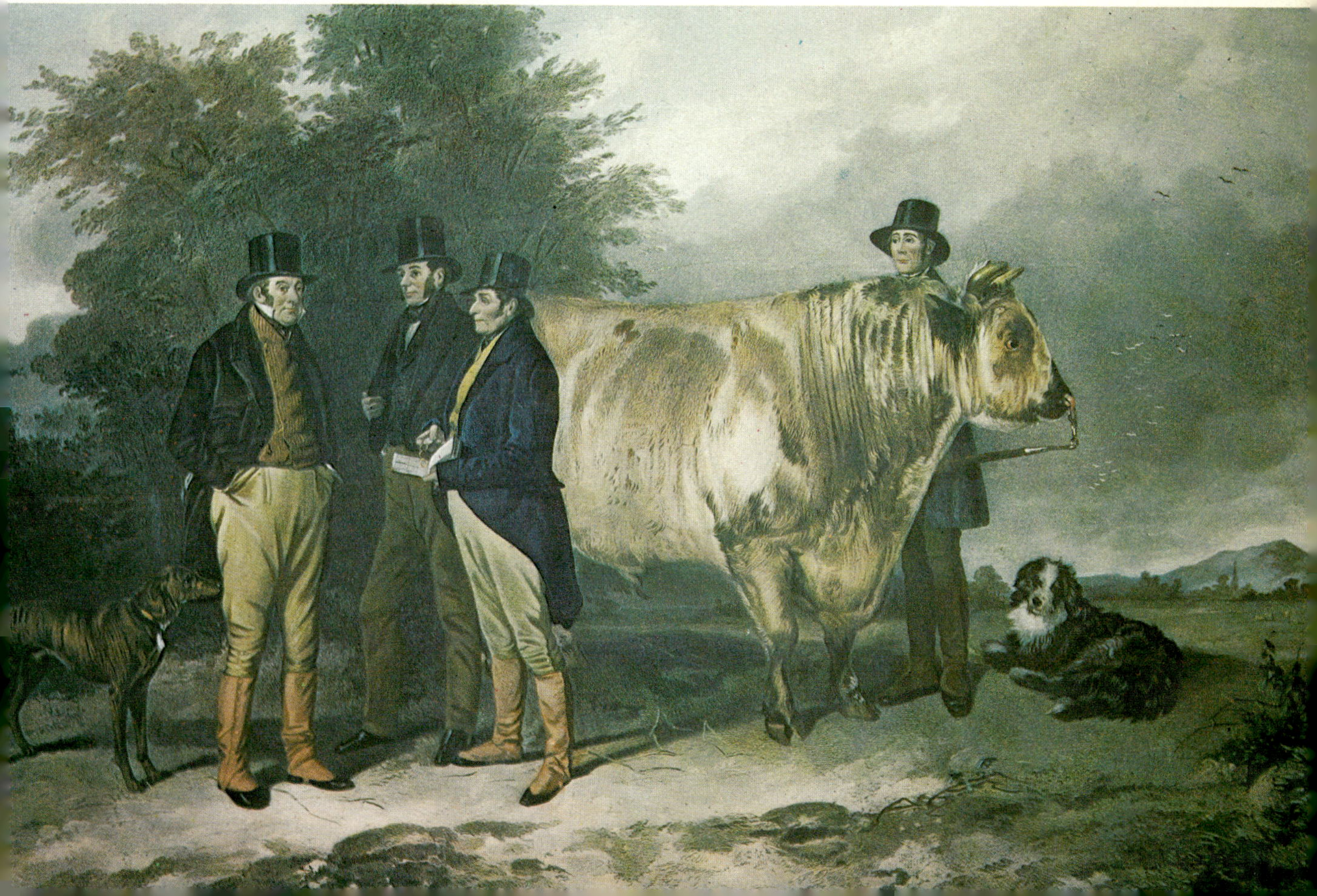

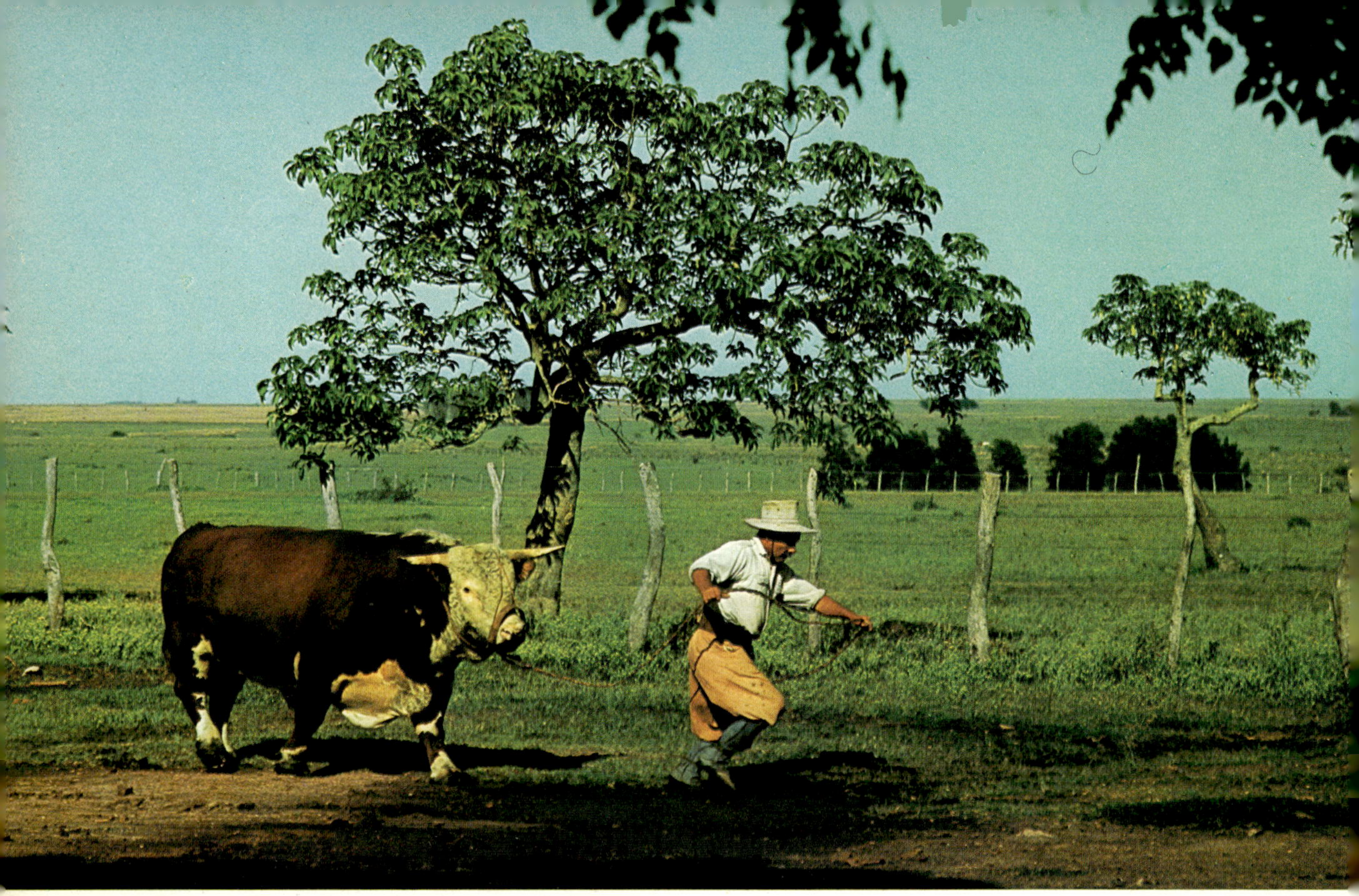

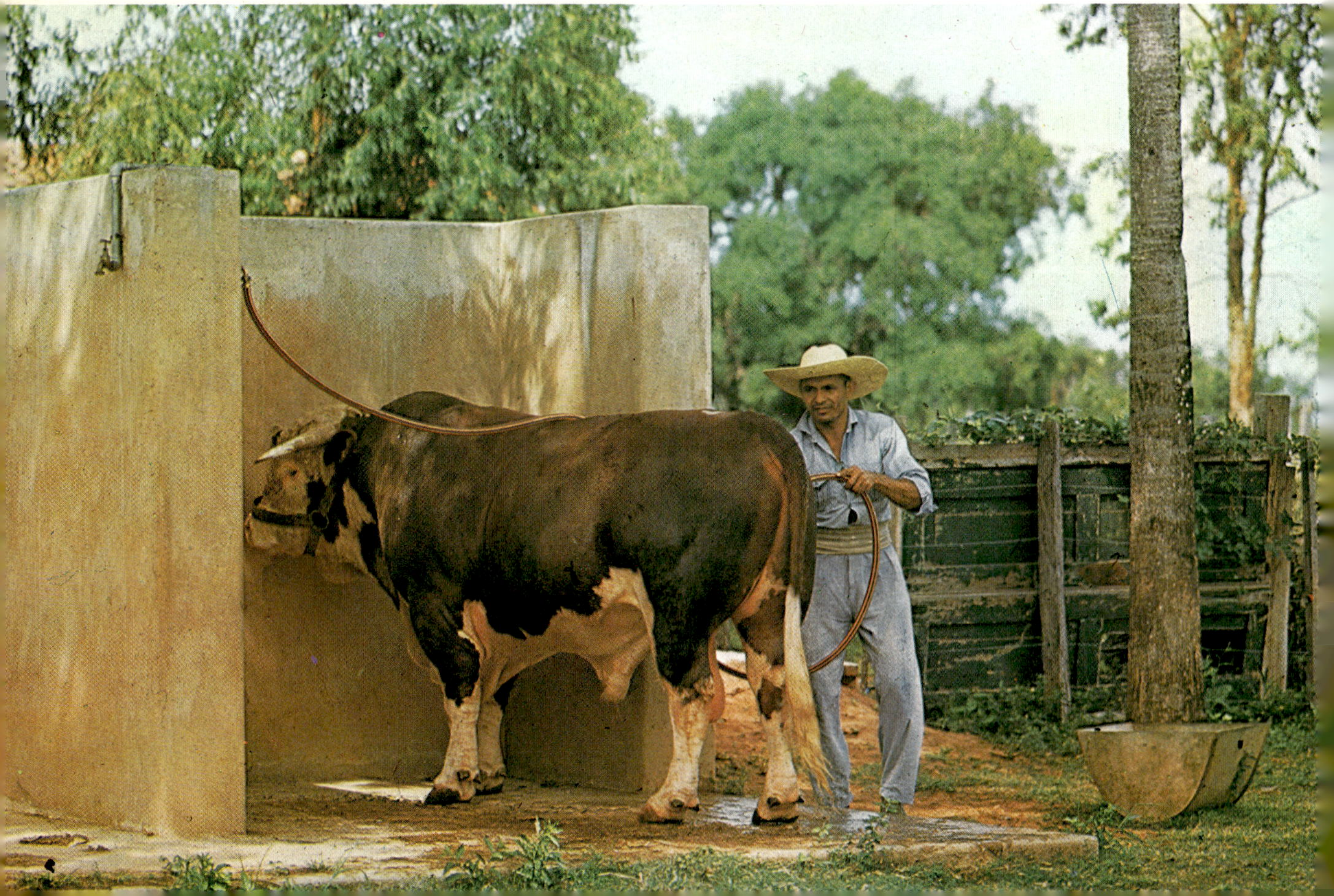

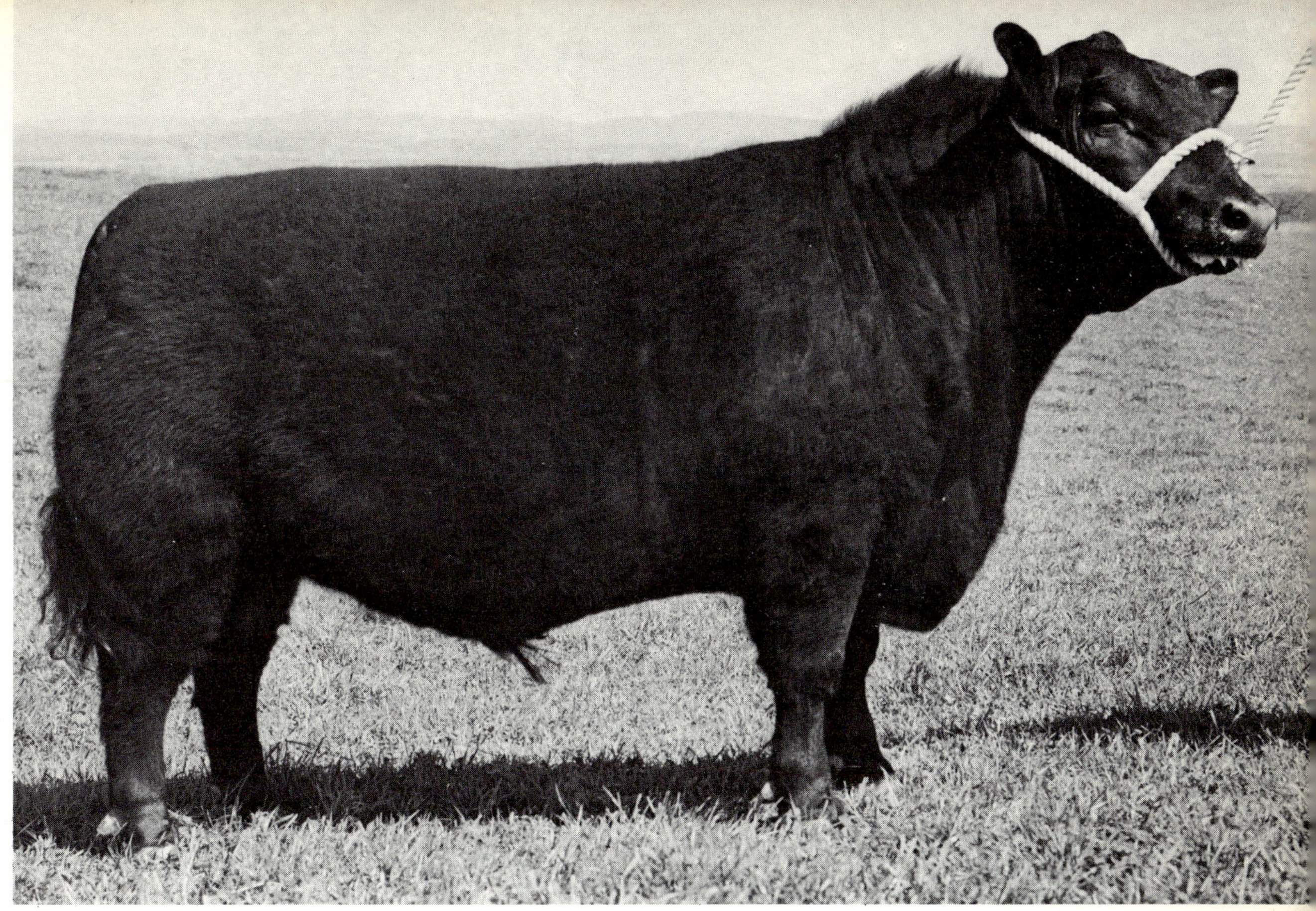

reign was shorter. Shooting up to a record price of £60,000 for a bull in the 1960s, its decline has been almost as rapid as its rise and there are those who fear it may follow its closest rival into relative obscurity. Yet it never quite acquired the prestige of the Shorthorn. Indeed, it may be doubted whether any breed of cattle will ever again attain the proud position the Shorthorn once held in England, in Scotland and abroad. So much has been said, written and published about Shorthorns that the results of specialised Shorthorn documentation and research would crowd the shelves of a capacious library. At times, the breeding of Shorthorns threatened a divorce from commercial stock husbandry in becoming a cult. As Trow-Smith wrote in a memorable and revealing passage:

... a passion for pedigrees ran mad through the world of Shorthorn breeders; shelf upon shelf of books analysing and recording ancestries were written and published; tribes and families were regarded with a devotion little short of that paid to the divinity or the monarch, and sometimes with more; and Coates' Herd Book joined the Bible and the Book of Martyrs upon many a farmhouse table.[11]

Until the 1880s the British farmer held a virtual monopoly of the beef market and was better able to indulge his passion for pedigree, fancy and expensive cattle. Ship refrigeration and the return of the

The Aberdeen-Angus. There had always been black, polled cattle in Aberdeen and in Angus – and by selecting these from the somewhat motley herds of earlier times, two breeders of distinction, Hugh Watson of Keillor in Forfarshire (1789–1865) and William M'Combie of Tillyfour in Aberdeenshire (1805–80) united to form a distinct breed. (*Photo: Alex C. Cowper*)

Opposite, above: Argentina. Champion Hereford bull being led away for his daily scrub down. (*Erich Hartmann/Magnum*)

Opposite, below: the Argentinian Hereford receiving much care and attention. (*Erich Hartmann/Magnum*)

progeny of exported bulls in the form of frozen and later chilled carcases broke both the monopoly and the market. 'From 1880 onwards the increasing costs of production and the appearance of overseas meat in the British market in increasing quantities began to affect the British cattle industry.'[12] 'Concentration on the pedigrees rather than the individual merits of animals continued until the disastrous farming year of 1879; this year marked a beginning of the decline in Shorthorn breeding as a business, a hobby or a fancy.'[13]

This decline in the prestige of the Shorthorn recorded by Stewart applied mainly to England where the breed had flirted between beef and milk for the better part of a century. In Scotland, where breeders had concentrated on beef and beef alone, ever since the days of Amos Cruickshank and his bull 'Champion of England' the 'business, a hobby or a fancy', persisted much longer, right up to 1950 or so. It was, admittedly, sometimes difficult to decide whether it was a business, a hobby, or a fancy! Undoubtedly the leading bull-breeding herds made money, on occasions a modest fortune for their owners. Yet the reputation of some of the leading herds was remarkably short-lived, and there were those sufficiently uncharitable and sceptical to suggest that reputation might fade with a change of herdsman. In other words that the 'bringing out' of the bulls was as important as their breeding. Certainly skill in husbandry and salesmanship counted for a great deal. Showmanship on occasion descended to faking. A weakness never bred out of the breed was a tendency to uneven distribution and patchiness about the tail-head. Although of relatively small practical importance it was considered a serious fault by show judges. Consequently a delicate and skilful operation called 'lifting' was introduced, by which subcutaneous dissection succeeded where breeding had failed. Again, the shape, curvature, texture and colour of the bull's horns were deemed important and precise rules were laid down by the Breeding Society on these trifling points. To bring reality into conformity with regulation, special horn-training implements were employed to guide, as it were, nature into the realms of fiction.

Nevertheless, notwithstanding all artificial aids to achieve perfection, the acceptable and outstanding Shorthorn bull remained a rarity, which explains, perhaps, the seemingly quite uneconomic prices paid for particular bulls at the leading bull sales. It was not that one bull was worth many thousands of pounds more than his full brother, so much as that two particularly wealthy buyers happened to fancy the same bull.

The words 'fancy' or 'hobby' were certainly inapplicable at the close of the eighteenth century when the breeding of pedigreed Shorthorns began. They were, however, amply justified by the close of the next century. The majority of pedigreed Shorthorn herds were quite unprofitable. The average pedigreed Shorthorn bull was sold at a loss. Why, then, did so many farmers in Britain continue to breed them? Partly, no doubt, because, just as in football pools and premium bonds today, there was always an outside chance of a quick fortune, although it is much more difficult to breed a good bull than to fill in a coupon. Partly in the hope of attracting agents for the export trade or foreign buyers, because these paid at least a reasonable price for what they were getting. Nevertheless, the average pedigreed bull was produced at a loss. Why, then, once again, did so many breed them?

Because, at least in Scotland, it brought a certain prestige both to farm and to farmer. To be 'in the Shorthorn set' was to have stolen a march on the Joneses or the MacTavishes. There was, of course, a certain snob value in owning pedigreed livestock of any variety, were they cattle, sheep, ponies or pigs. In northern Scotland, however – was it because of the dependence on cattle-rearing of not-so-very-remote ancestors? – it had to be cattle, and for preference, Shorthorn cattle. There was even a period when the owner of a Shorthorn herd felt slightly superior to the owner of the competing breed – the black Aberdeen-Angus. On occasion, it was a matter more of pedigree than of cattle. Many a flourishing farm with excellent crops and thriving 'commercial' livestock maintained a small herd of pedigreed Shorthorns to be proudly displayed to visitors on a Sunday afternoon's farm-walk, although casual inspection suggested that apart from pedigree they were hardly worth their salt.

The pedigree cattle business was, at times, as much cult as commerce. The cash value of a bull or cow depended so greatly upon its pedigree that once the reliability of its ancestral history was questioned or discredited, the stock became relatively worthless.

Certain families within the Shorthorn breed were, at times, especially fashionable and therefore particularly valuable. One particular breeder was doing very well for himself by selling a number of such a family, but he sold one too many to an Irish breeder. On checking up the pedigree of his fashionable purchases, the unfortunate Irishman discovered that, according to the book, certain cows had apparently given birth to two calves – not twins – within the space of one year. Now no cow – not even a pedigree cow – can do that, and the Irishman raised a considerable uproar. The final upshot was that the miraculous creator of two calvings within a year was expelled from the Society and the whole fashionable family lost their pedigree prestige and pedigree premium and were sold at give-away prices for crossing stock. Yet from the point of view of beef production they were exactly the same cattle, equally productive and just as valuable.

The emphasis on pedigree in cattle-breeding, although first established in the Shorthorn breed, became fashionable in all others. Yet it was never quite the same. The Shorthorn breeder, often a bachelor, at times seemed in love with his cattle. It was the custom to

AGRICULTURE.

Long Horned Bull.

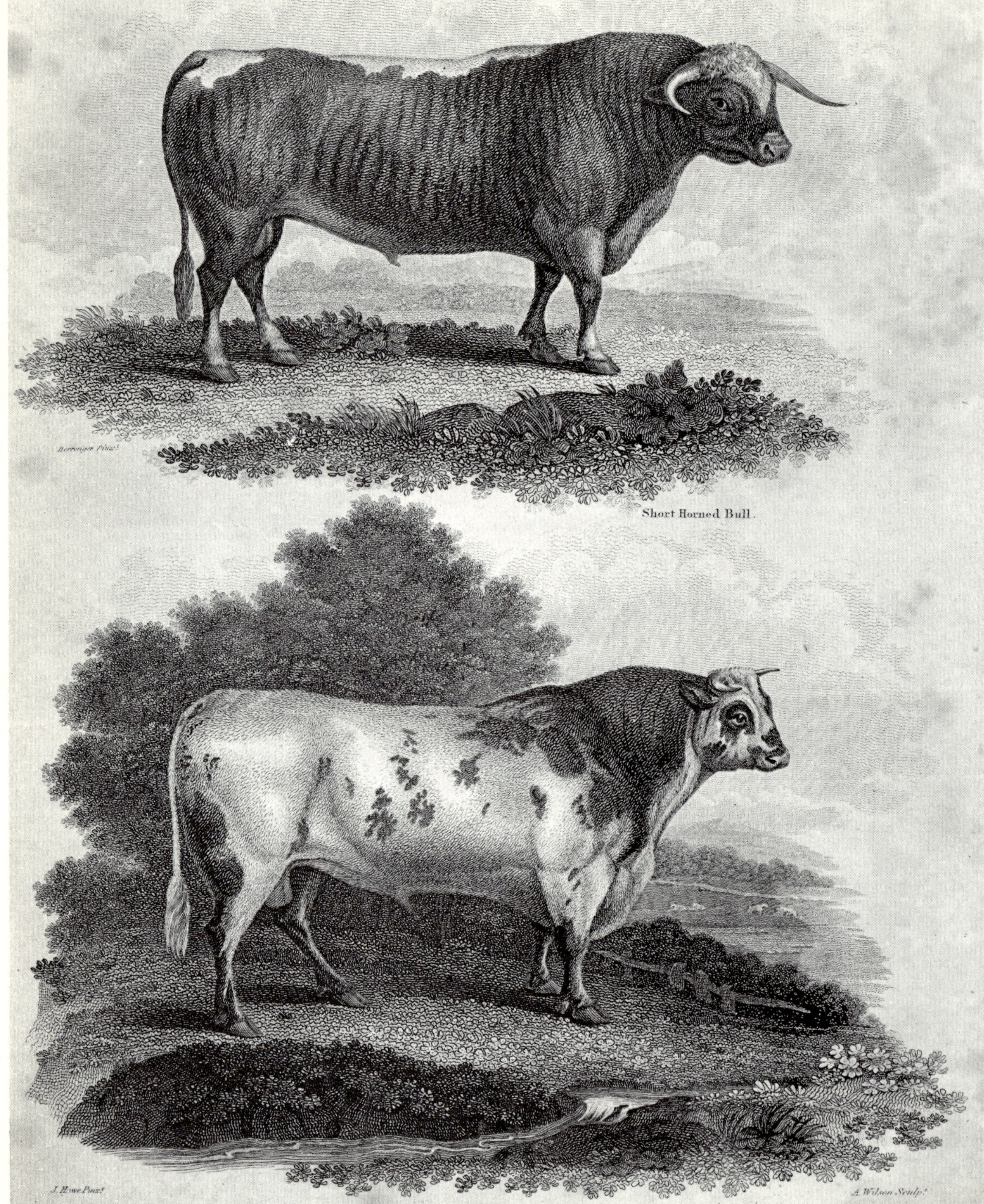

Short Horned Bull.

Published by A. Constable & C.o 1815.

split up the herd, often sired by the same or closely related bulls, according to the names of cows and the names chosen by the breeder were at times quite poetical – Red Rose, Blossom, Bright Eyes, Strawberry, Moss Rose, Wild Eyes, Clipper, Lavender, Nonpareil, Orange Blossom. One of the most famous families in Shorthorn history was that of the Duchesses bred by Thomas Bates. He thought so highly of them that he kept them, admired them, idealised them, although they failed to fulfil the chief purpose of a cow, which is to breed calves. It is recorded that of the fifty-eight cows of the Duchess family that Bates reared to breeding age, twenty-four never bore a calf.

The Shorthorn breeders gave resounding names to their bulls as well as to their cows. Far back in early Shorthorn history there was Hubback and Comet, Young Phoenix and Favourite, Foljambe and Bolingbroke. There was Hamlet, Mussulman, The Duke of Northumberland. And there was, of course, also Champion of England. Nobody dreamt in those distant and different days that bulls and their breeders were doomed to lose their individuality and to become computer fodder in an age of numbers.

Early nineteenth-century engraving of pedigree bulls. Above, a 'Long Horned' bull; below, a 'Short Horned' bull. (*Mansell Collection*)

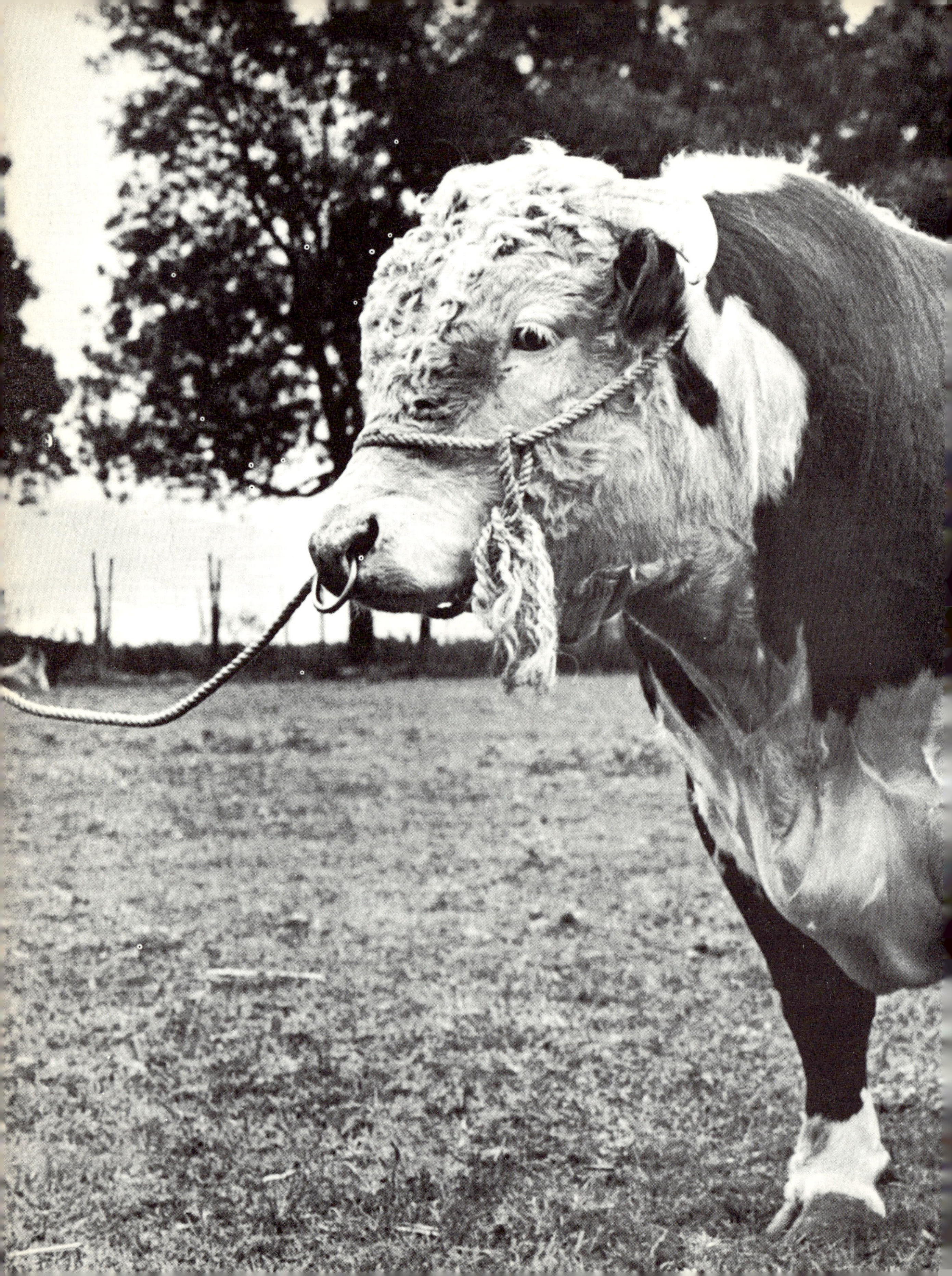

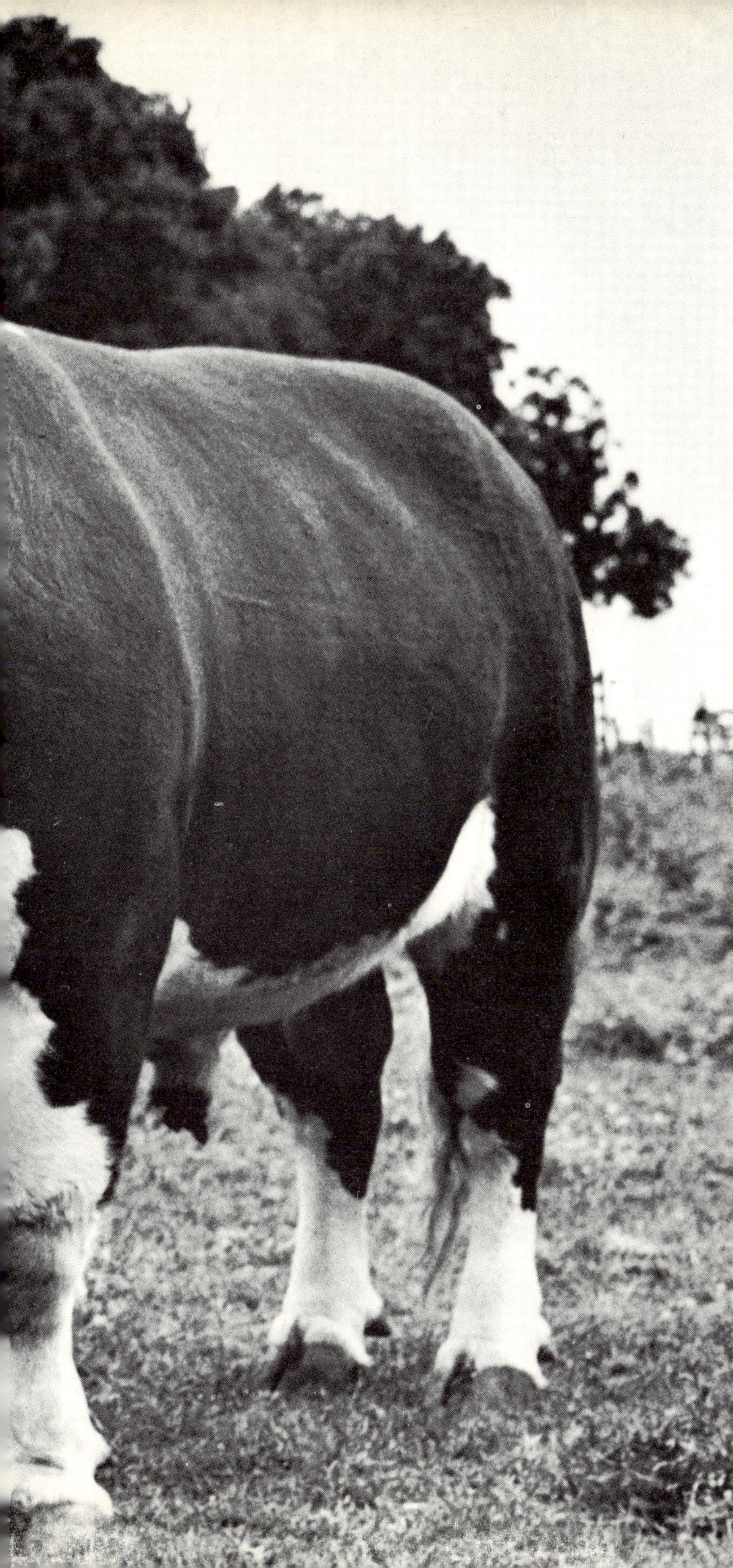

7
The Bull
in
Farming

Uruguayan Hereford bull.
(*Erich Hartmann/Magnum*)

§ The Shorthorn breeders were the first to adopt, wholeheartedly and successfully, the principles of rigorous selection and the closest possible in-breeding of the select in establishing a separate and distinct breed of cattle. It is the principle always associated with the name of Robert Bakewell, although other eighteenth-century cattle-breeders with less publicity worked along similar lines.

The Hereford followed closely on the heels of the Shorthorn. This 'is not only one of the most valuable and best known, but, owing to uniformity of colour and markings, one of the most picturesque of British breeds'.[1]

These colourings as stabilised in the breed today are indeed attractive, and the spectacle of the Hereford bulls on parade at the Royal Agricultural Show of England in bright sunshine is one that can never be forgotten by anyone with an eye for cattle or for animal beauty. The background on the bull is a deep rich red colour relieved by white markings. The face is white, so also is the crest, throat, dewlap, underside, socks and tail brush. All the rest of the body is red-brown. Before the 'improvers' guided its white-socked feet into the way of beef, the Hereford was famous in old England for its prowess in the plough. The eight-team ox-plough of medieval times was the motive power in cultivation, and for heavy land the Hereford oxen had few rivals and no masters. Of the cattle of Hereford at the beginning of last century, one John Duncomb wrote:

The cattle of Herefordshire have long been esteemed superior to most if not all the other breeds in the island. Those of Devonshire and Sussex approach nearest to them in general appearance. Large size, athletic form, and unusual neatness characterise the true sort; the prevailing colour is a reddish brown with white face. The rearing of oxen for the purposes of agriculture prevails universally, nearly half the ploughing being performed by them, and they take an equal share in the labours of the harvest. They are shod with iron in situations which frequently require their exertions on hard roads, but it has already been noted that grazing is not generally pursued except for provincial consumption. The show of oxen in thriving condition at the Michaelmas Fair in Hereford cannot be exceeded by any similar collection in England; on this occasion they are generally sold to the principal graziers in the countries near the metropolis, and there perfected for the London market.

During the eighteenth century, therefore, and indeed for some time afterwards, beef was a by-product of draught oxen, the main purpose for which Hereford cattle were then kept.

Towards the end of that century selective breeding on Bakewell's principles began.

One, Richard Tomkins of New House, King's Pyon, Herefordshire, yeoman, who died in 1723, left to his son Benjamin in his duly attested Will, 'the cow Silver with her calf'. Benjamin made good use of the

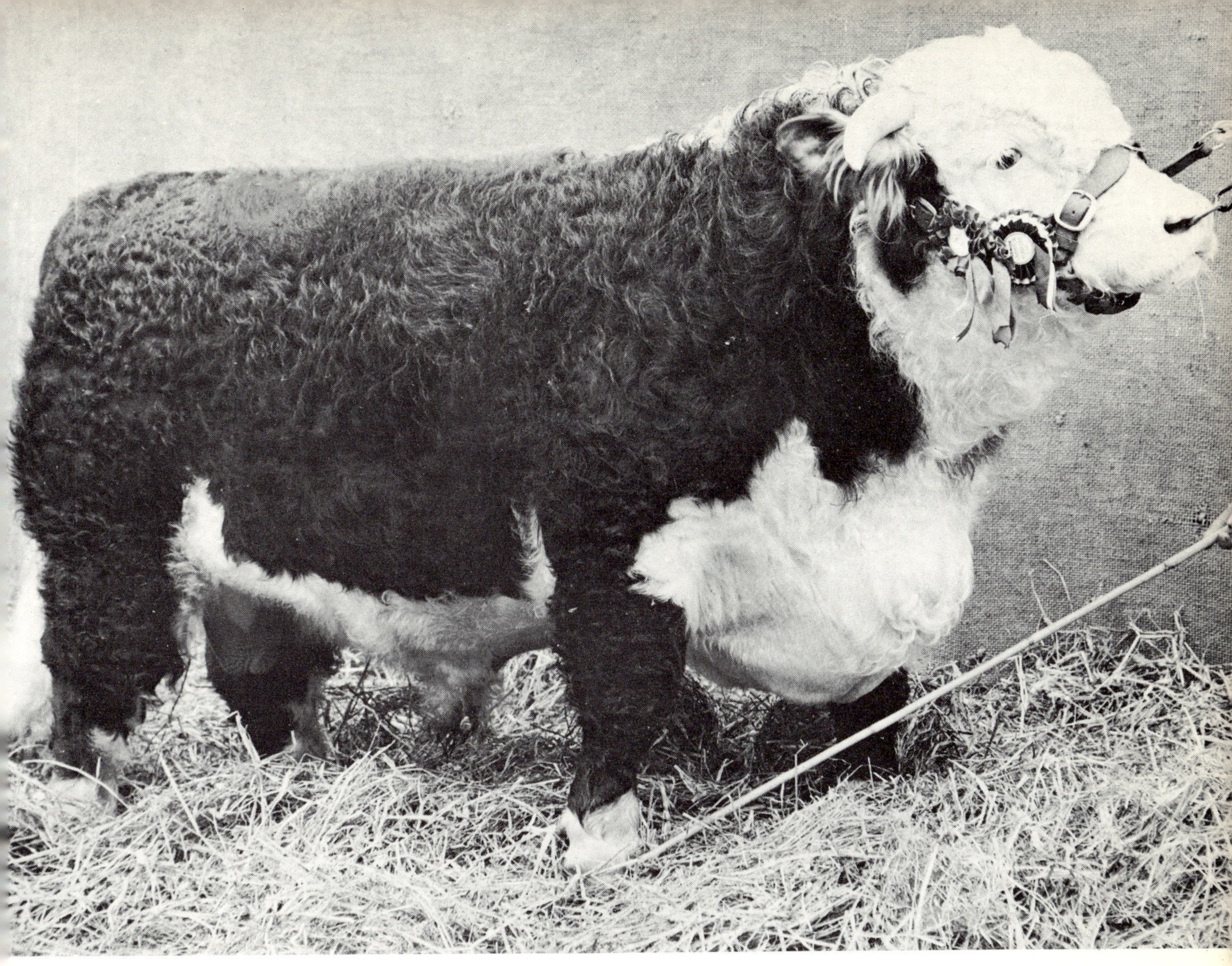

legacy. She and her descendants followed and shared in the fortunes of the Tomkins family, father and two sons farming over eight hundred acres between them. The younger of the two sons considered that the first big improvement – 'break-through' would be the term used today – was due to the bull called 'Silver Bull'. He had the red coat and white face of the true Hereford breed and was said to be descended from the very cow 'Silver' mentioned in the will of old Richard. Other Hereford breeders, many of them titled and distinguished, carried on the work the Tomkins family and 'Silver Bull' had begun. The Hereford Herd Book, in imitation of Coates's Shorthorn Herd Book, was begun by T. C. Eyton, Donnerville, Salop in 1846. Just as Coates's Herd Book was purchased and taken over by the Shorthorn Society in 1872, so the Hereford Herd Book Society in 1876 acquired the Hereford Herd Book that Eyton had founded.

There were famous bulls among Herefords that shaped the early history of the breed – Sir David, Sir Benjamin, Lord Wilton, Horace,

Champion Hereford bull. The Hereford is not only one of the most valuable and best known, but, owing to the uniformity of colour and markings, one of the most picturesque of British breeds. (*Barnaby's Picture Library*)

Sir Roger, Sir Thomas. The old Hereford breeders seem to have conferred birthday honours on their bulls!

The Hereford started its world career slightly later than the Shorthorn but soon caught up with it and in numbers at least, surpassed its rival. The export demand, reached its peak in the year 1883, when the bull 'Lord Wilton' went overseas at the price of 3800 guineas.

[The Hereford] established itself in many of the most important pastoral regions of the world as a breed of primary rank. From all quarters comes a unanimous verdict of praise. The magnificent build and vigorous constitution of the animal enable it to face a wide variety of climates and to fatten on the natural herbage of almost any grass-growing country. The procreative potency of the bull and the gentle and maternal instincts of the cow are the subject of universal panegyric.[2]

Today it is the most numerous and widely distributed breed of cattle of English origin. This is fairly evident to anyone watching Wild West films. The red-brown skin and the white markings of the Hereford are as distinctive of this form of popular entertainment as are the stetson hats and the sheriff's badge. In the ranching state of Texas for example, the Hereford has it all its own way.

Closely related to the Hereford is the Devon, nicknamed 'Red Rubies' because of their beautiful red-brown coat. Like their cousin the Hereford, the Devon, to mix metaphors, gained its spurs in the plough. The Reverend W. Quartly of Molland, North Devon maintained, some time towards the close of the eighteenth century, that a pair of Devon oxen could plough an acre of stiff land in a day. One, John Lawrence by name, in his book *A General Treatise on Cattle etc.*, published in 1796, wrote that '. . . the fashionable substitution of horses has made no progress in the district of these cattle' and that 'the Devons are the speediest working oxen in England, and will trot well in harness'.

It was Francis Quartly of Great Champson, in Molland, North Devon (of the same family as the Reverend Vicar of that name), who 'filled the position in the history of North Devon cattle which the Collings did among Shorthorns and Tomkins among Herefords'.[3]

These early 'improvers' all worked to the Bakewell pattern – find a fine bull – mate him with his mother, his sister, his female cousins and his aunts – choose the best of the progeny, scrapping the rest – and found an improved breed.

The Sussex, nearly related to the Devon, left the plough at a later date and still shows its origin in weight and strength of shoulders. There were teams of Sussex oxen ploughing the heavy clay of the Sussex Weald at the beginning of this century. Edward Cane of Berwick Court was the most prominent improver of the Sussex breed.

Now, these three fairly closely related breeds, the Hereford, the Devon and the Sussex, all established a reputation as plough oxen before cattle breeders began to specialise towards meat or milk.

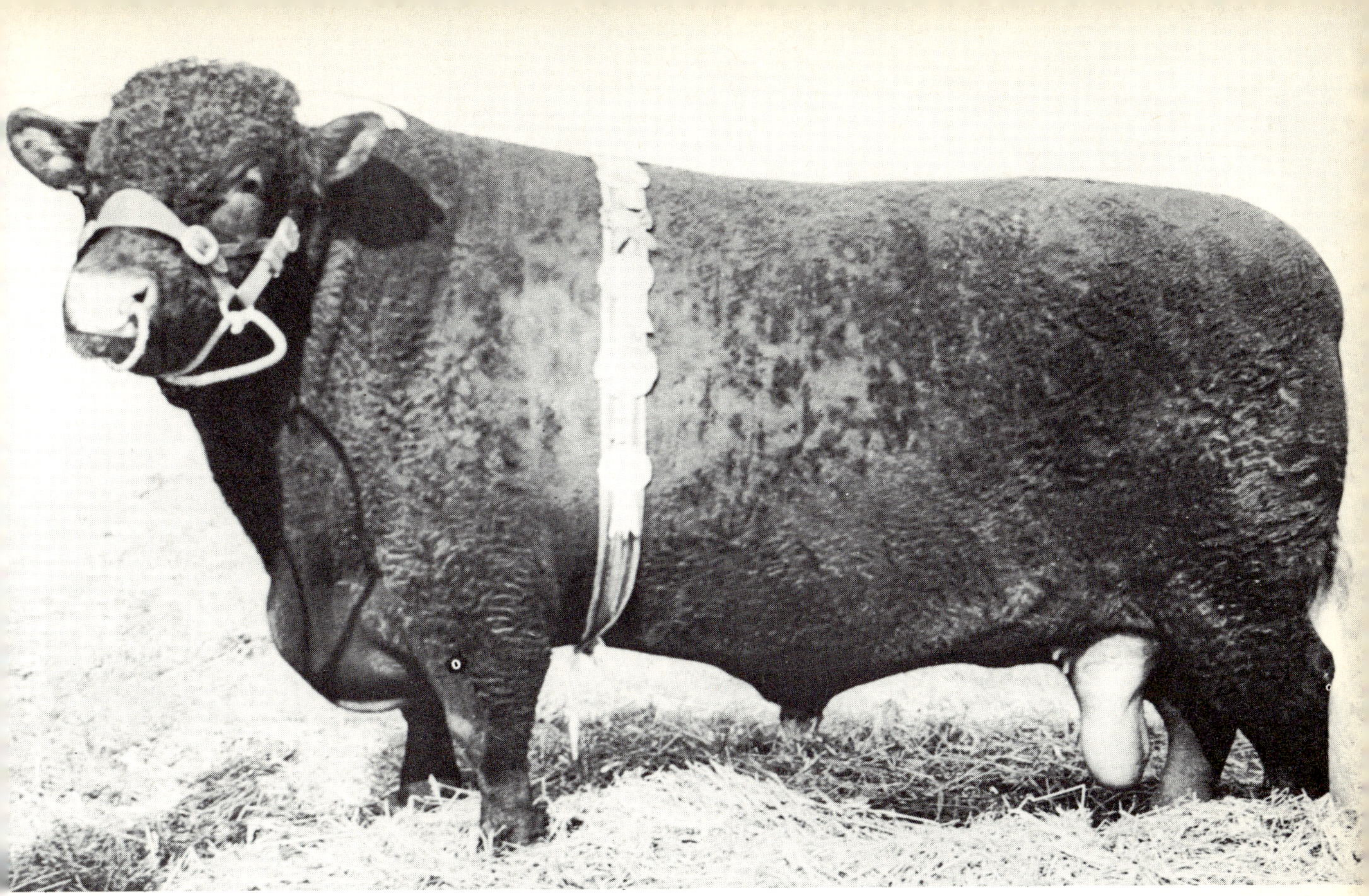

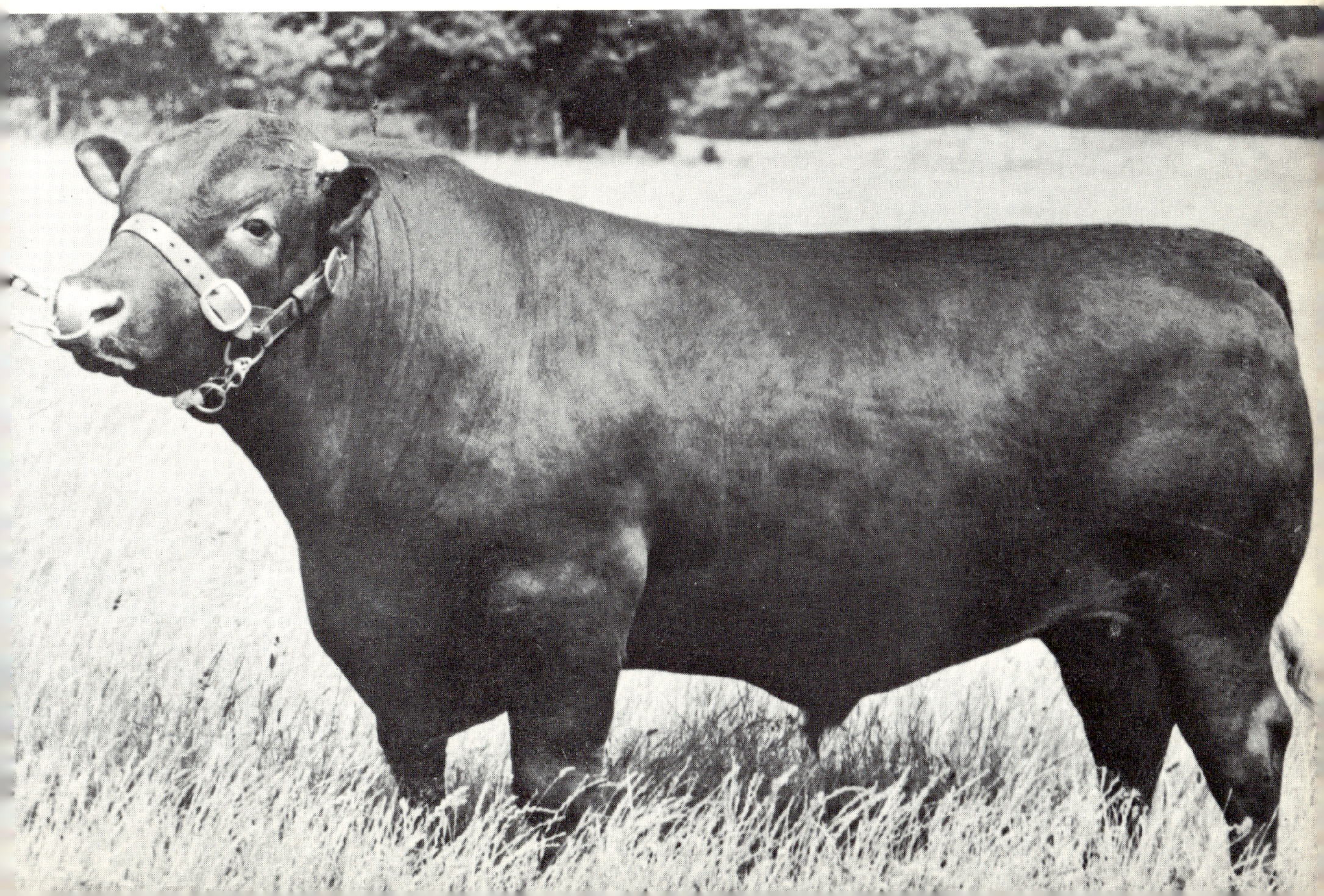

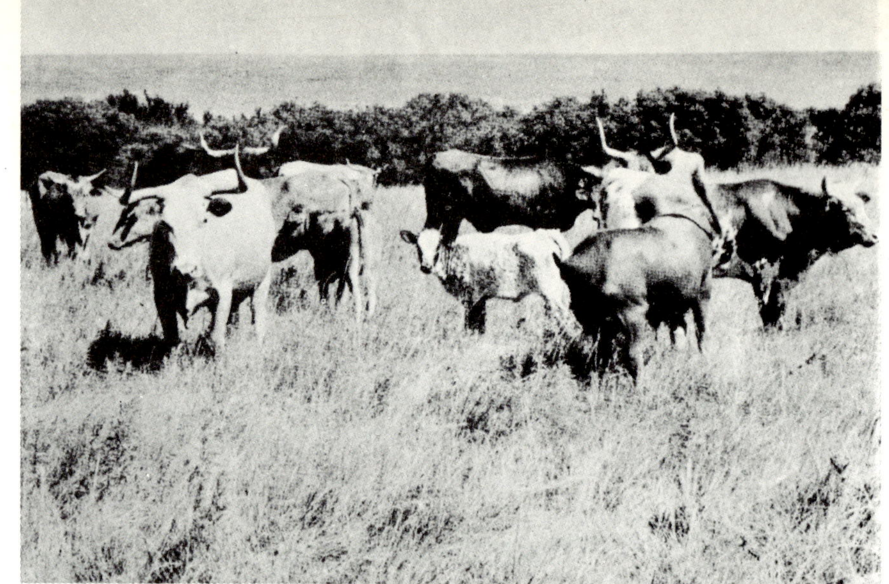

A herd of Longhorn steers and cows on the trail, Texas. Photograph taken in 1897. Longhorn bulls were essentially of the type seen today in the bullrings of Mexico and Spain. Now practically extinct in the United States, there were the predominant breed on the Western Ranges until about 1880, when the Hereford began to displace them.

These breeds were raw material for the breeders, using the Bakewell code, who planned to breed their cattle towards beef. Cattle bred for the plough required muscle for strength, and muscle alive is lean meat when dead. The basic material was already there and the Tomkinses and the Quartlys and the Canes made good use of it.

In the course of the nineteenth century the Shorthorn and the Hereford between them colonised the developing countries of the pastoral world. Particularly on the prairies of North America and the pampas of the Argentine the colour insignia of these two breeds, the red, white and roan of the Shorthorn, the white face and rich red brown of the Hereford, spread like a flock of locusts over the grazing lands.

In South America and the Southern United States they found cattle before them, the Longhorned Spanish breed, small, thin cattle that the *conquistadores* had brought with them from Spain. The change-over to Shorthorn and Hereford was performed by a breeder's technique called 'top-crossing' in which the part played by the bull was of paramount importance. Shorthorn and Hereford bulls were crossed with what were termed the 'scrub' cattle. The females of this first cross were mated with Shorthorn and Hereford bulls and so on until the fourth or fifth generation, when by repeated mating with bulls of one or other of these two British breeds, the whole vast herds of cattle were practically pure-bred, if not always pedigreed, Shorthorn or Hereford in appearance and performance. This 'top-crossing' programme was the foundation and main support of the specialised and pedigreed bull-breeding herds in their country of origin.

The Shorthorn and the Hereford shared the profit and the glory between them almost unopposed until a third breed of specialised beef cattle came out of north-eastern Scotland to voice a challenge. This was the Aberdeen-Angus, often called 'The Blacks' for short.

'The Aberdeen-Angus was the last of the three great Beef Breeds to become established in this country and in consequence was the last to enter the ring in beef production abroad.'[4] There had always been black, polled cattle in Aberdeen and in Angus and by selecting these from the somewhat motley herds of earlier times, two breeders of distinction, Hugh Watson (1789–1865) of Keillor in Forfarshire and William M'Combie (1805–80) of Tillyfour in Aberdeenshire, united to form a distinct breed on the Bakewell pattern. Hugh Watson started with Shorthorns, was an associate of the eccentric Captain Barclay of Urie; and from Shorthorn breeders acquired the knowledge of what Bakewell principles had done for that breed. It seems to have occurred to Hugh Watson, who was only nineteen at the time, to use these methods in establishing a new breed of his own out of the cattle of his native county of Forfarshire, then called Angus. He chose black, polled individuals, bulls and heifers, to found this breed and he was exceedingly fortunate in his initial choice. For, as was later proved in the early application of Mendelian genetics to cattle-breeding, both black coat colour and the polled (hornless) head are what are termed dominant characters. This means that if you mate a black bull with cows of any other colour, the calves born are black. Again, should you choose to mate a polled bull with a horned cow of any breed, the calves are born polled. Granted that, in the second generation when these calves, grown to maturity, are in-bred, complete dominance tends to fade, and the odd red or horned calf appears again in a certain proportion. Nevertheless, 'The task of breed formation that Hugh Watson undertook must have been made much easier through the fact that two of the most striking characters he bred for, namely, a uniformly black coat and a polled head, happen to be strongly dominant in inheritance, so that at least a superficial uniformity was quite readily achieved.'[5]

But if it was Hugh Watson who first established the breed in Angus, it was William M'Combie in Aberdeenshire who both saved and popularised it.

In the county of Aberdeen, the outstanding personality in the establishment of the breed was William M'Combie, Tillyfour, who, taking up the mantle of Hugh Watson, was successful in raising the Aberdeen-Angus from a local to that of a national and international breed, and it is his name that is most closely associated with its evolution, if not, indeed, its rescue from entire extinction as the result of the craze for crossing which followed the introduction of the Teeswater or Shorthorn cattle into the North of Scotland, about the years 1830–40.[6]

M'Combie of Tillyfour, like Duthie of Collynie, went to Aberdeen University as a student, but it didn't suit him. Instead of demonstrating to change the University according to the dictates of his adolescent fancy as so many of its students do today, young M'Combie adopted a better plan. He left the place! He went cattle-dealing with his father, an adventurous and arduous enough job in those distant days, when roads were tracks and railways non-existent. He learnt much about cattle, a great deal about mankind and above all, the value of showing livestock at the right place at the right time and to the best advantage. What he had learnt in his youth in forays from Caithness to Falkirk he put to good use in his maturity. He exhibited the black, polled cattle bred at Tillyfour at Smithfield in London and at the French International Exhibitions in Paris. He won all along the cattle lines.

M'Combie's last fat stock victory in Paris was won at the International of 1878, when, with a group consisting of the bull Paris and the females Gaily, Pride of Aberdeen 9th, Sybil 2nd, Halt 2nd, and Witch of Endor, which twelve out of fourteen judges had already selected for the Prize of Honour for the best group for breeding purposes in the Exhibition, he secured, by twenty-four votes to seven, the prize for the best group of animals for beef-producing purposes. He won from 1,314 French and 370 non-French cattle, and of his six cattle only Gaily was more than twenty-five months old.[7]

M'Combie was his own P.R.O. Note how he christened his bull 'Paris' as a compliment to France where his greatest honours were won! He cultivated, if not captivated Royalty. From the massive carcase of his celebrated steer Black Prince, supreme champion of both Birmingham and Smithfield Fat Stock Shows, he sent, at his own expense, a baron of beef – the two sirloins left uncut at the backbone – in humble homage to Her Gracious Majesty Queen Victoria, then resident at Windsor.

It would seem that Her Majesty appreciated the prime Aberdeen-Angus steak presented by her loyal subject who, like all cattle-dealers of distinction, was very well able to look after himself. For the Great Queen, while resident at Balmoral on Deeside, visited M'Combie at his farm of Tillyfour, in the adjacent valley of the Don, specially to view his internationally famous, prize-winning black, polled cattle on their native heath. A legend records how the International Showman, equally great in his own more domestic sphere, staged a really Royal Show, by having the cattle led in endless succession round and round the house, while the Queen, seated in the porch, marvelled at the number of cattle he possessed!

That, then, was the great M'Combie!

After his sojourn at Aberdeen University, where he did not stay long enough to secure a degree, and his escape to the more adventurous occupation of cattle droving and cattle dealing, in which his father was already well established, he underwent a thorough apprenticeship to the store cattle trade – probably the most highly skilled branch in the whole of cattle farming.

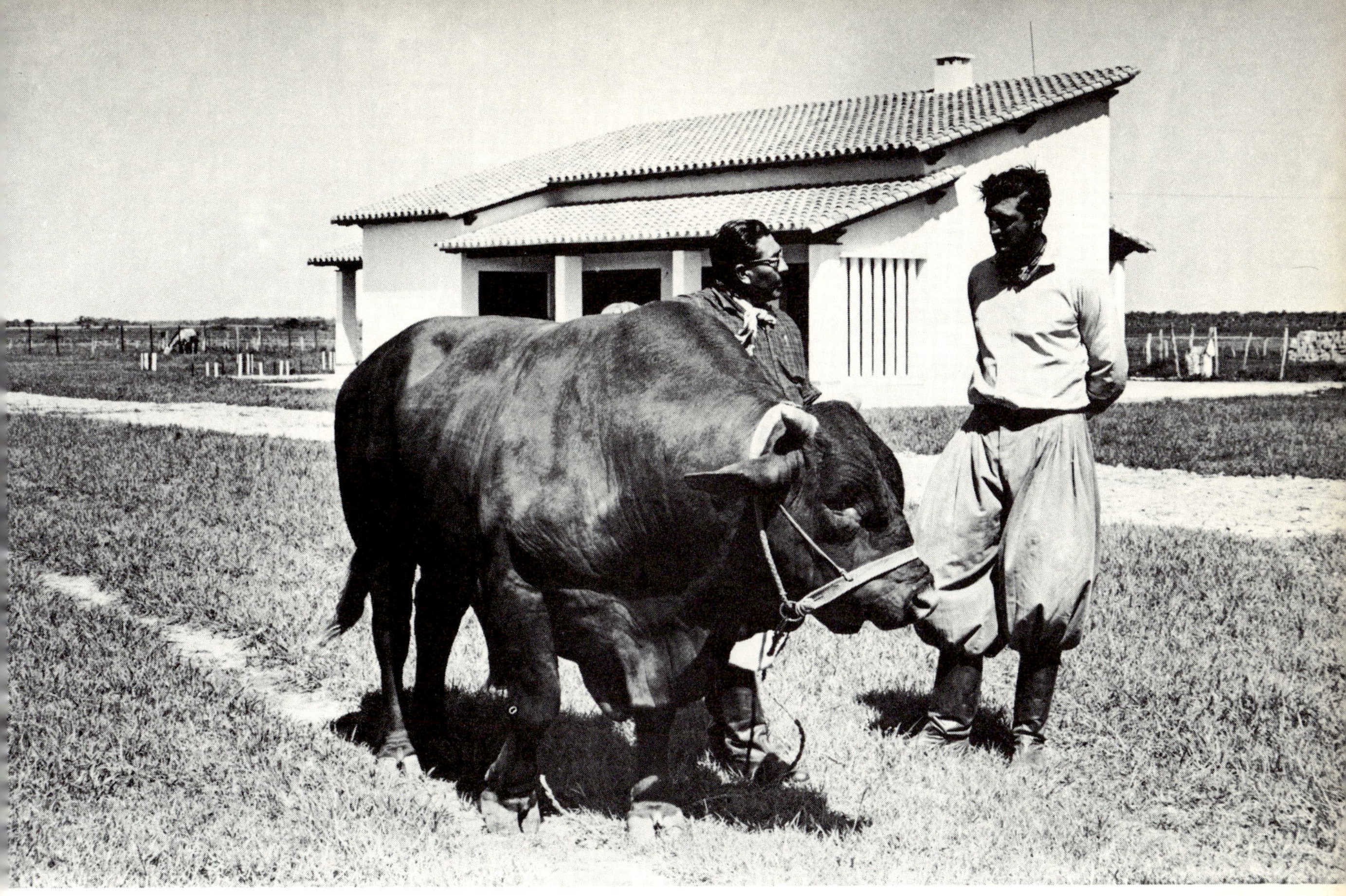

M'Combie then turned to cattle feeding and, finally, to the breeding of his Black Polls. Possibly no man ever had a finer and more thorough training in cattle husbandry. Probably no man who ever lived knew more about beef cattle, and in his volume of memoirs – *Cattle and Cattle Breeders* – he has passed on some of the wisdom based on experience for the benefit of posterity. He learnt how to breed for beef, how to select individual beasts that would make beef, and finally, and not least important, how to feed for beef. His early training in dealing helped him to display and advertise his chosen breed to the best advantage.[8]

M'Combie, in his latter years, turned to politics and became an M.P. It seems rather a waste of a good man. During his brave cattle days he was greatly aided by his cattleman John Benzies who, when preparing cattle for the Fat Stock Shows, was wont to visit his beasts at dusk, at midnight, and again before dawn to induce them to eat the little bit extra that added to their weight. He had his reward. Of one champion he brought out, he remarked proudly in his native idiom that he was 'beef tae the reets o' his lugs' – which, translated into English meant that he was beef to the roots of his ears.

Like Shorthorn and Hereford, the Aberdeen-Angus spread to all pastoral countries, to America, to Canada, to the Argentine, New Zealand and Australia. Coming somewhat later, looking to those

Santa Gertrudis bull on the Estancia Yacaré, Paraguay. The breed was developed by crossing Brahman beef-type bulls on beef-type Shorthorns. A bull with the name of 'Monkey' is credited with being the foundation sire of the herd. Several other breeds – Beefmaster, Brangus and Charbray – were developed on similar lines by crossing the Brahman bull with Shorthorn and Hereford cows (Beefmaster), Aberdeen-Angus cows (Brangus) and with French Charolais cows (Charbray). (*Erich Hartmann/Magnum*)

Overleaf: Hereford and cross-bred steers being rounded up for classification on an *estancia* in Argentina. (*Erich Hartmann/Magnum*)

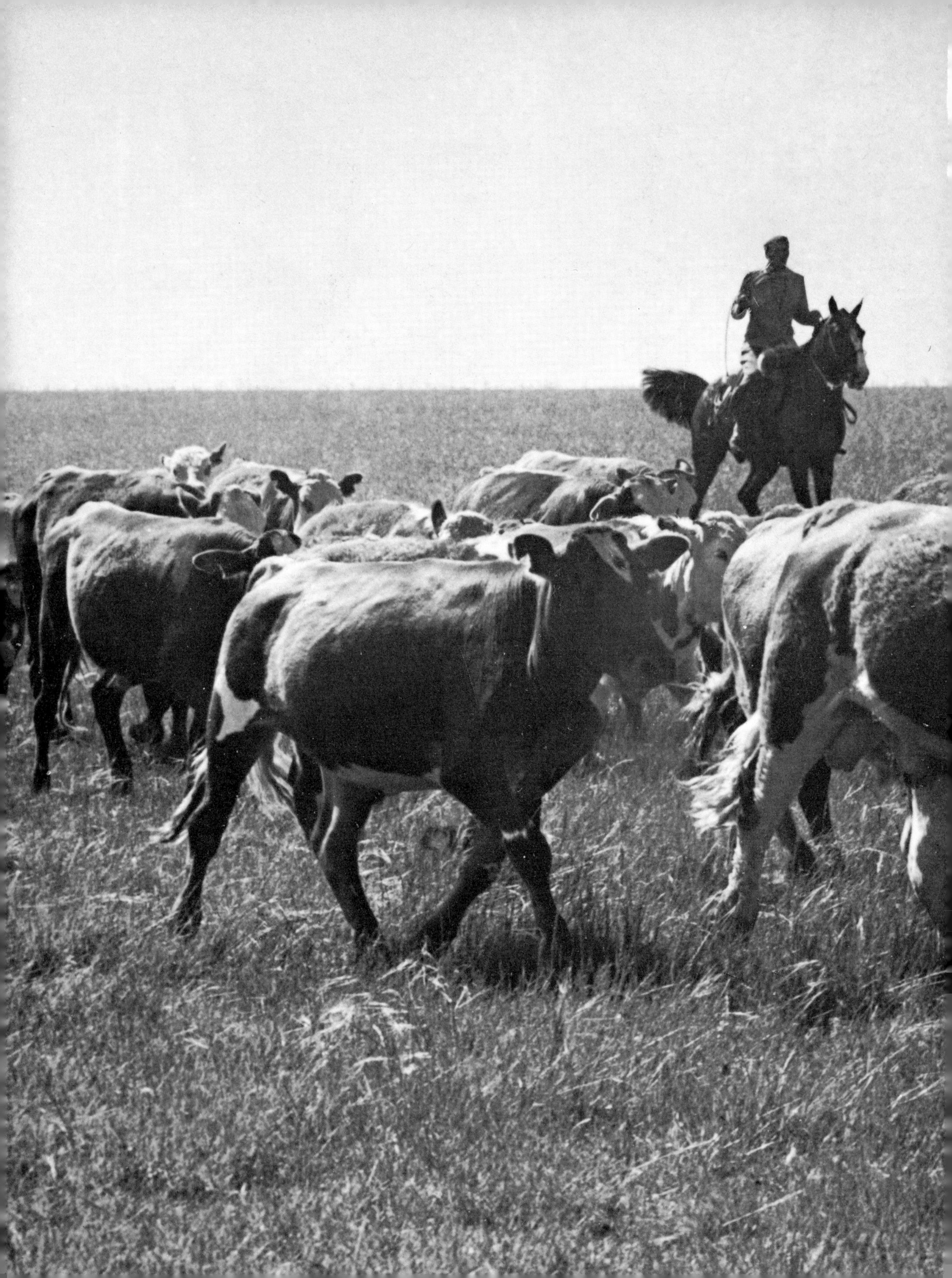

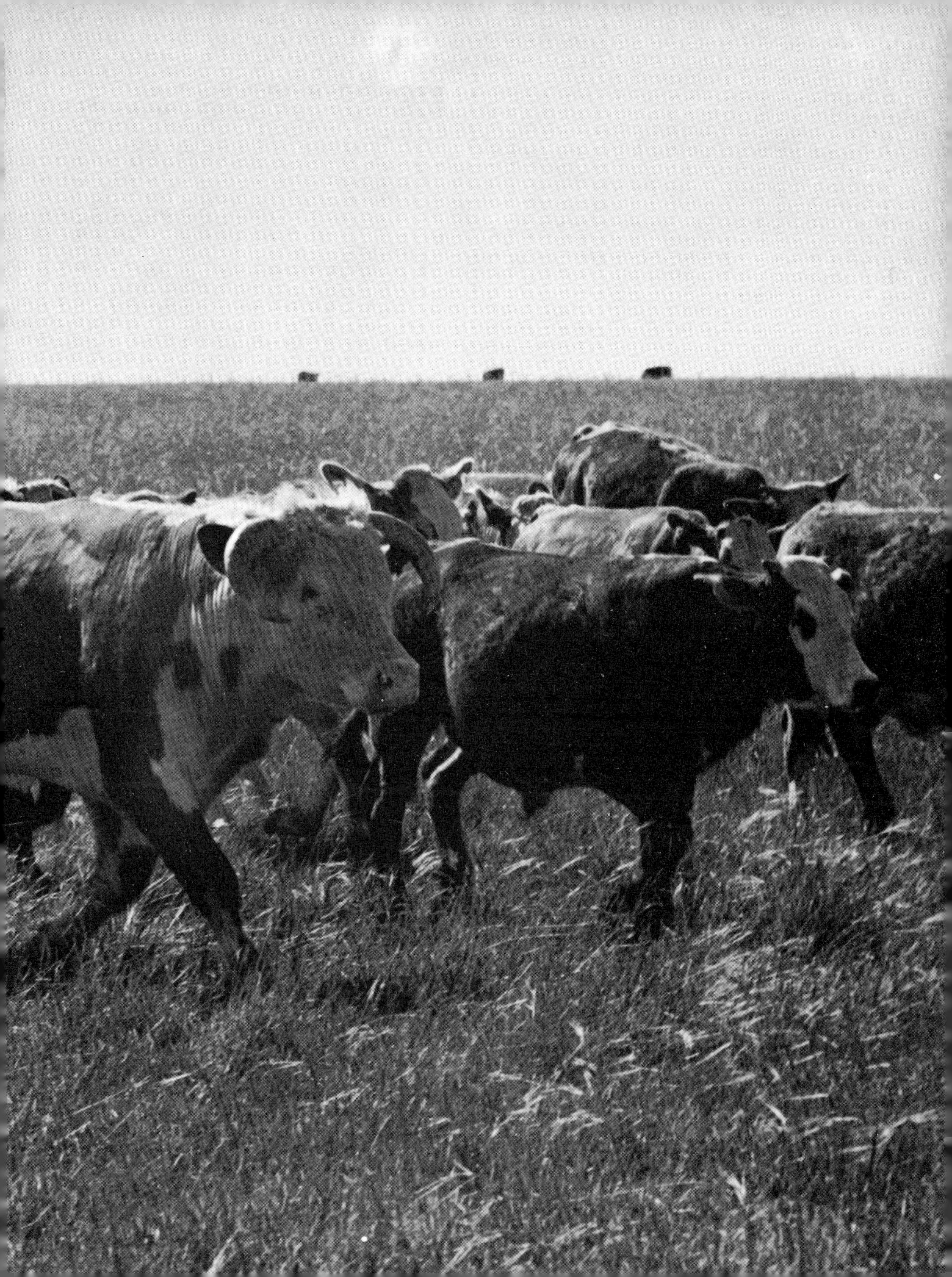

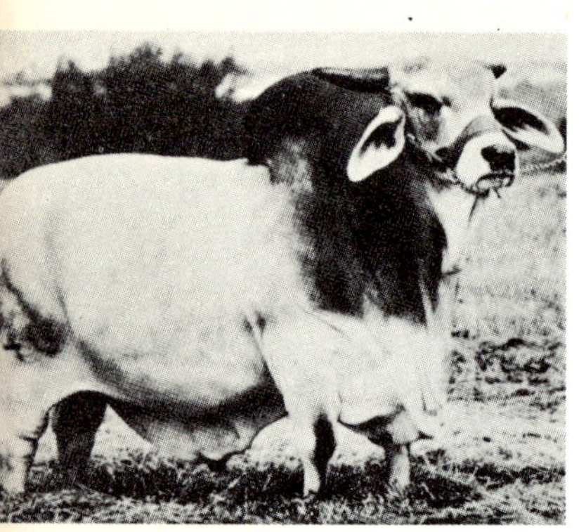

Brahman bull. Several breeds of beef cattle have been developed in the United States. All these breeds were developed by using Brahman crosses on European breeds. The Brahman or Zebu is Indian in origin, hump-backed, and more heat-resistant in semi-tropical climates.

accustomed to other breeds rather like the bull in mourning for its horns, it received a chilly reception: 'The first Aberdeen-Angus bull arrived in the Argentine in 1876, and its appearance, black without horns, created a sensation that did not seem to presage any very satisfactory future for the incomer.'[9] However, these early prejudices were quickly overcome and the breed, particularly at Fat Stock Shows such as Smithfield and Chicago, continued on its winning way.

Britain gave three great breeds of cattle to the beef industry of the world – the Shorthorn, the Hereford, the Aberdeen-Angus. In the specialised dairy breeds, her success and reputation were never quite as high, unless, indeed, the Channel Islands be regarded as a part of Britain. Perhaps because the task of forming a new or improved breed on the Bakewell system is much more difficult in breeding for milk than in breeding for beef. The bull is the great problem. For whereas a beef bull shows in his own body what beef he can lay on, nobody can hope to guess what quantity and quality of milk a dairy bull might have yielded had he been a cow. Yet, from the point of view of dairy-breeding policy, the unfathomable bull is half the herd. The only feasible method of assessing the productive value of a dairy bull is to judge him on the quantity and quality of milk his daughters yield. Not at all a simple thing to do, as the agricultural boffins discovered when, in the United States of America, they first began to intrude upon the farmyard. The average dairy farmer hadn't a clue as to the individual milk yield of his cows. That started the boffins off on Milk Recording which at the beginning led to serious conflict with certain farmers. It was found that the majority of dairymen had a favourite cow, it might be Molly, or Daisy, or Buttercup that, against all the evidence of weights and measures, they persisted in proclaiming as being their best cow as well as their favourite cow. Yet the boffins proved ruthless. In the course of time they persuaded the dairy farmer that the graceful and affectionate creature that nuzzled his overalls at milking time might yield very little, whereas the plain Jane that preferred his hired man yielded double the amount of milk and better milk at that.

Unfortunately that wasn't the only, nor the most difficult problem requiring solution. Milk yield in cows is very variable, being influenced by a whole host of environmental factors such as age, season, climate, health, and above all food. An improvement in feeding will almost certainly raise the milk yield of any herd and should a new stock bull happen to coincide with improvement in pasture or compound cattle cake, what was due to the feeding might be credited to the bull. Then, again, cattle are such slow-growing creatures that young cows – heifers they are called – may be over two years old before they have their first calf and come into lactation. Considering all these difficulties it is really remarkable that specialised breeds of dairy cattle ever arose. However, the breeders learnt from experience – and it was often a bitter one – that subsequent to the purchase, possibly at a high price, of a young, handsome and pedigreed bull, the milk yield of the entire herd might suffer a disastrous reduction. On the other hand they might be lucky, the new stock bull might prove a winner and the herd milk yield rise. By this slow profiting by experience, with the market grapevine spreading the sad or glad tidings, the milk-sheep became separated off from the milk-goats, the herds producing bulls that left profitable daughters held to the advantage by in-breeding, and other breeders competed for the surplus in-bred stock. That, presumably was how it happened in the beginning when breeds were being formed and the boffins were still at rest. What these have done, or claim to have done since, with the introduction of Artificial Insemination, Progeny Testing, Statistics and other techno-logical aids, sometimes requires to be believed to be seen!

Although some pedigree breeders concentrated on beef and others on milk, in England, particularly, the ordinary farmer preferred to make the best of both worlds, fattening his bullocks and milking his cows. These cattle were labelled dual-purpose. For very many years the dual-purpose Shorthorn as distinct from the specialised Scotch beef type, was the standard dairy cow on English farms.

During the last century [the nineteenth] the dual purpose cow was almost universal in England. Its popularity was due to a large and regular demand by city and suburban dairies for cows in their prime [just commencing their third or fourth lactation] which would fatten readily as their milk yield declined.

Gradually, however, the decline in the city dairies, the importation of beef from abroad, and the increasing importance of milk induced farmers to give more attention to breeding for milk, with less emphasis on the ultimate beef value. The movement was away from the lower yielding type of dual-purpose herd towards better milking strains and single purpose dairy breeds and their crosses.[10]

In sympathy with this drift towards milk, the Dairy Shorthorn (Coates's Herd Book) Association was founded in 1905. The objects of this new association – a breed society within a breed society – was to maintain the position of the Shorthorn as a dairy cow. Some felt that, partly because of the importation of Scotch Shorthorn bulls, the whole Shorthorn breed was tending too nearly to beef. Had its founders been able to see far enough ahead they might have thought differently, because fifty years later importation of beef was so much reduced that the British Government offered progressively higher incentives to encourage home-produced beef. Possibly in the interval the Dairy Shorthorn had moved too far towards milk, because when faced with the challenge of a new milk breed, the British Friesian, it had lost some of its beef without a compensatory increase in milk. The British

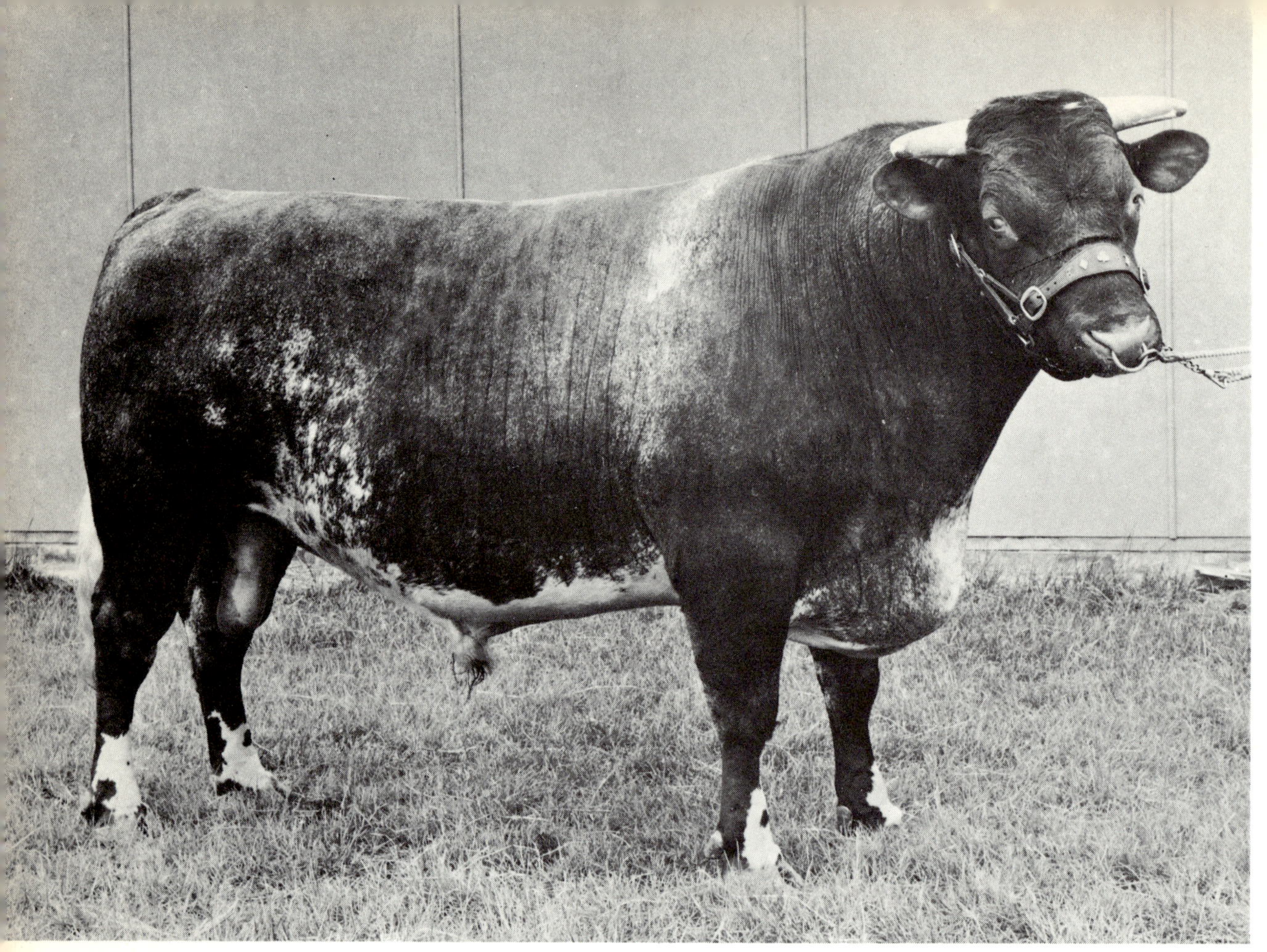

The Dairy Shorthorn – a dual-purpose breed for meat and milk. During the last century this dual-purpose cow was almost universal on the dairy farms of England. (*British Farmer & Stockbreeder*)

Friesian beat it first in milk yield and then strangely enough, itself became dual-purpose in fact if not in name, producing both milk and beef in large quantity if not especially high quality and, in a progressively more utilitarian age, reaping the benefits of both.

The Friesian takes its name from the Dutch province of Friesland, which forms the corner of land lying north-east of the Zuider Zee. Predominantly black and white in colour with a characteristic colour pattern, and of pronounced dairy type, the Friesian is probably the most important as it is certainly the most highly improved of the Dutch breeds. . . .[11]

During the second half of the nineteenth century there were considerable importations of black and white cattle, mainly unpedigreed Friesians, out of Holland to the British market. From 1860 onwards large numbers of these Dutch cattle began to come to this country and found a ready sale. A proportion were milking and breeding cattle; all were cows or heifers. No bulls came in. The British Friesian Cattle Society, founded in 1909, went about breed-formation in a rather novel way. It had to select animals deemed worthy of registration in its Herd Book by inspection of the somewhat motley population of black and white cattle domiciled in Britain as a result of sporadic

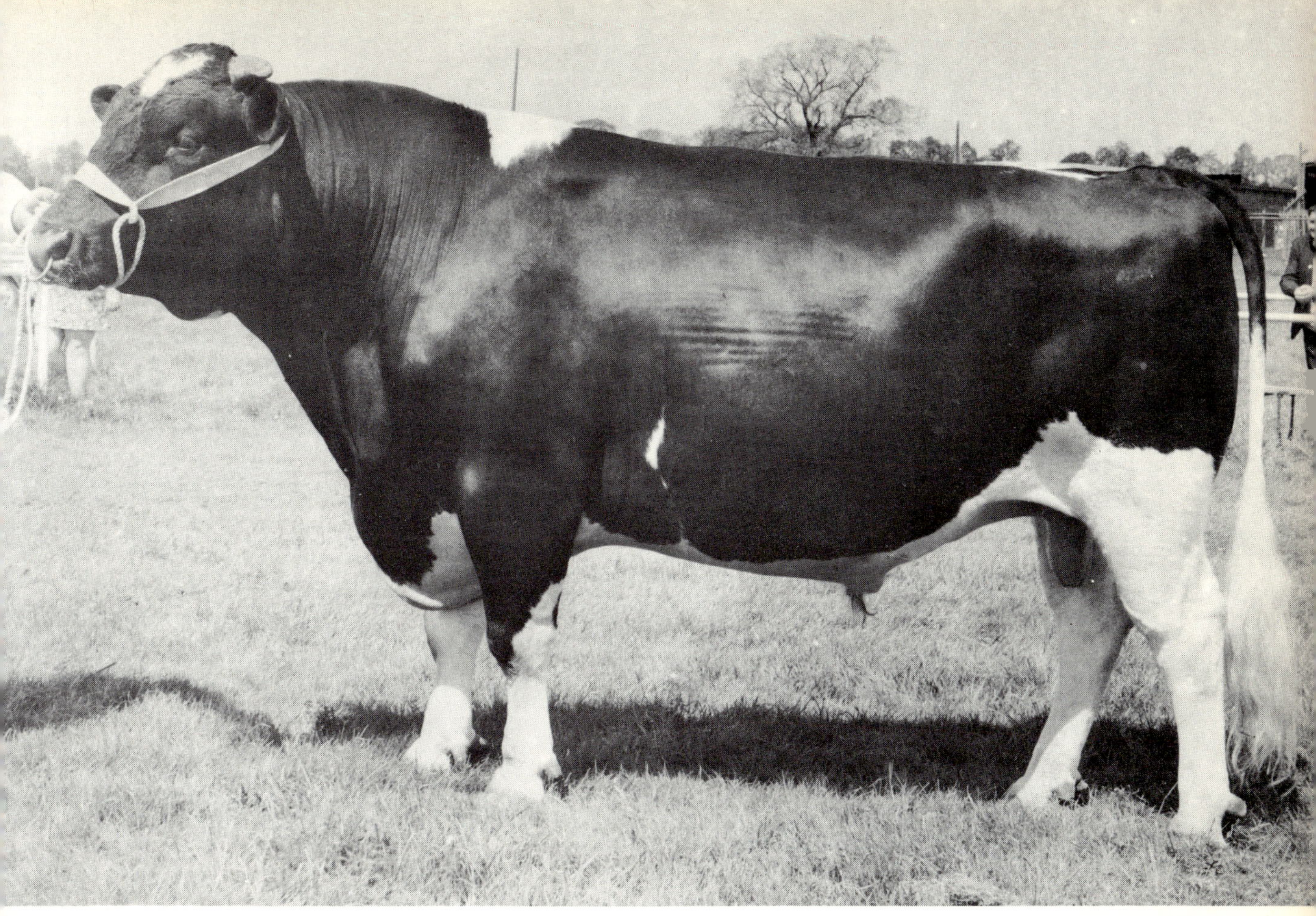

importations of unpedigreed cattle of Dutch origin. This undertaking, although both unusual and courageous, could hardly have proved an outstanding success since only five years later, in 1914, the Society imported sixty pedigreed Friesian cattle from Holland, of which forty were bulls. This importation was followed at the conclusion of the First World War, in the year 1922, by one of pedigreed Dutch Friesians from South Africa, a direct importation from Holland being out of the question at that time, because of the prevalence of foot-and-mouth disease on the Continent.

This importation from South Africa really founded the British Friesian breed as it exists today because it brought together an outstanding bull, a yearling named Harlens Marthus, bred in 1921 by the Golden Valley Citrus Estates in Natal, with an English breeder of genius, Gerald Strutt of Terling in Essex, who knew how to use him. Under the new name of Terling Marthus he became more famous than any other bull in the history of the British Friesian breed, before or since. The geneticists Robertson and Asker wrote of him as being the breed's

... most important member. Although of South African stock, all the lines in his pedigree trace back to animals in Holland around 1910 ...

Champion British Friesian. The Friesian takes its name from the Dutch province of Friesland, and is now the predominant – and in some districts the exclusive – dairy breed of Britain. (*British Friesian Cattle Society*)

and though his influence was small in 1931 it increased rapidly during the thirties and was accelerated by the sale of some of his inbred sons out of his own daughters. He now contributes [in the year 1951] 6 per cent of the genes in the breed and is therefore virtually the great-great-grandfather of the breed.[12]

George Odlum, another Friesian breeder of note, wrote this of the Terling herd (Terling Marthus was 'the great bull of the 1922 importation' that he refers to):

The Terling herd appears to have started with more or less the usual lot of pre-society animals, entered by inspection. Some of them remarkably good animals. But by using a series of superior bulls, it has reached a standard that is the envy of all. Just how they managed to select all those good bulls is somewhat a mystery. Particularly how they picked the great bull of the 1922 importation, and one of the few great females of that same importation.

The Terling management has never said anything about testing bulls by progeny, and perhaps does not test exactly as I did; that is, by using a little and then keeping idle for a long period. But that, in some way, they measure the bulls by early progeny is very evident. One only has to note the great usage of some of the best, and the disappearance of some others.[13]

If the great bull, Terling Marthus, is mainly responsible for the quality of the British Friesian breed, it was the Second World War that established its quantity. Every official encouragement was accorded to liquid milk production; payment was on gallonage without regard to the solids, butter-fat and solids-not-fat each gallon contained, a system that favoured the Friesian in competition with other breeds. The greater carcase weight of the Friesian steer or discarded cow was a further advantage in a time of meat scarcity.

As a result the Friesian achieved a dramatic expansion during the war years. To quote J. K. Stanford in his book *British Friesians*, 'The war, in fact, did not hit the Society very hard. Prices of Friesians went up 600 per cent, their membership rose to 5,500 [it was only 1,879 in 1939] and their invested funds to £70,000. Their herds rose astronomically.'

The expansion of the breed was possibly a shade too rapid to sustain the highest quality. Rapid multiplication without strict selection is a danger to any breed of livestock. In any event there were two further importations soon after the war, in 1945 from Canada, in 1950 from the fountainhead of the breed in Holland. Were those who travelled far from Britain to make the purchases seeking for another Terling Marthus? Perhaps he *was* there, had a master-breeder like Gerald Strutt been there to find him!

For many years the Friesian's main competitor both at Shows and in the dairy was the Scottish breed, the Ayrshire, native to that county. Compared with the Friesian its milk yield is lower although its milk quality is higher, and its suitability for beef production distinctly

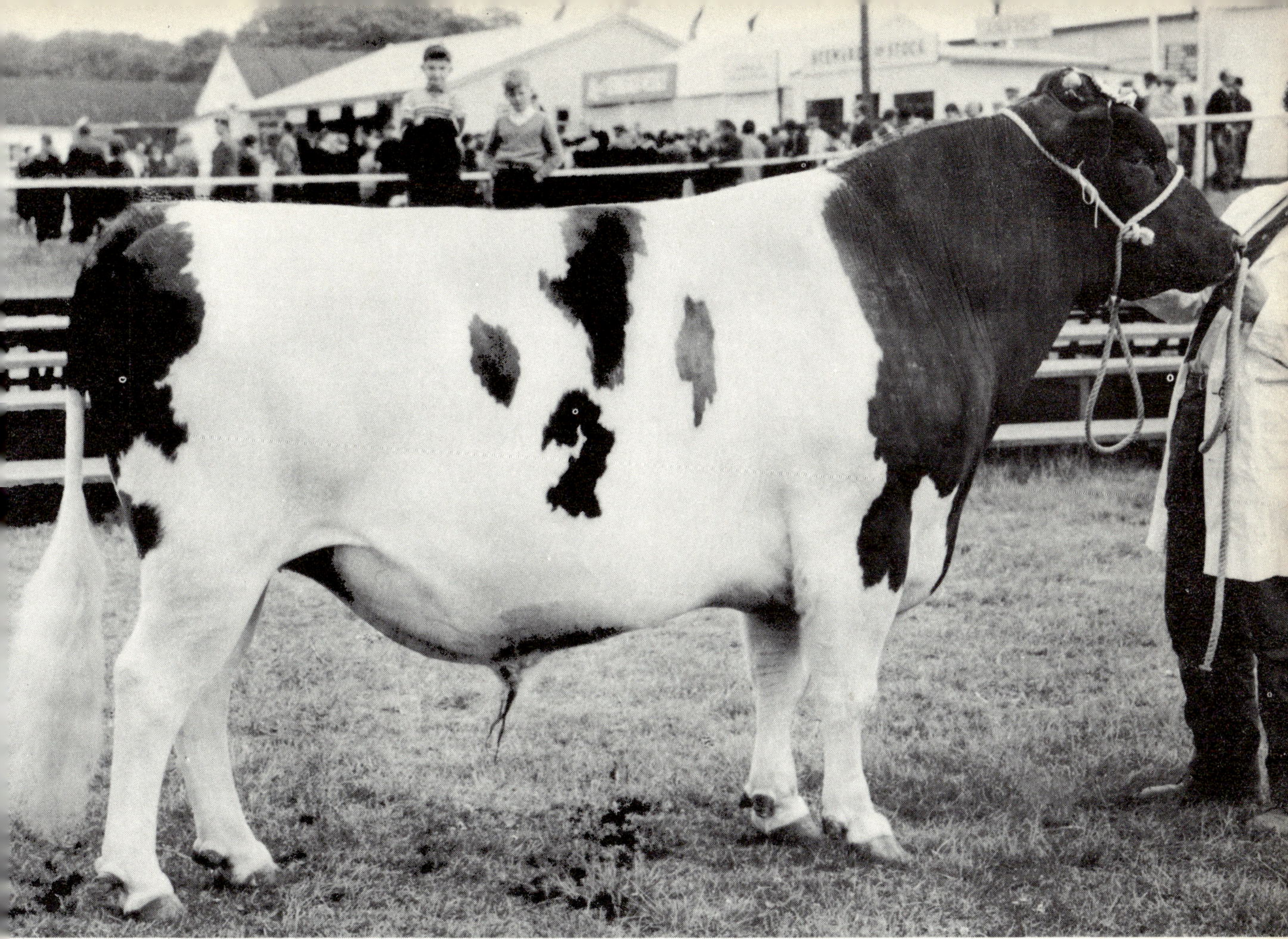

poorer. It fought a brave battle for supremacy but eventually failed.

The Ayrshire is a breed influenced in its early days by the introduction of Channel Island blood. It gives milk of good quality, thanks to Jersey and Guernsey, and small fat globules best suited for cheese-making. It is noted for the early introduction of milk recording and for being the first breed association to attempt the eradication of tubercular disease from its herds. Cheese-making was the speciality both of the breed and of its country of origin. So much so that in the old days when the great bulk of cheese was farmhouse cheese, fat women were reputedly in demand as wives since their weight on the cheese vats resulted in a swifter separation of the whey which was fed to the pigs!

In more modern times the improvement of the Ayrshire in many useful points is linked with the name of a bull-breeding family called Howie and with a bull-breeding farm called Bargower. Yet the breed has at times suffered from the dangers of the Show-ring and in-breeding. At one time the leading breeders became so obsessed with beautiful udders on their cows that the teats, although symmetrically placed, were so neat, short and tidy, that they wouldn't fit into the cups of a

Ayrshire. Native to that Scottish county, the Ayrshire has for many years been the main competitor with the Friesian both at show and on the dairy farm. Recently it has lost ground mainly because of the superior beefing quality of the Friesian. (*Ayrshire Cattle Society*)

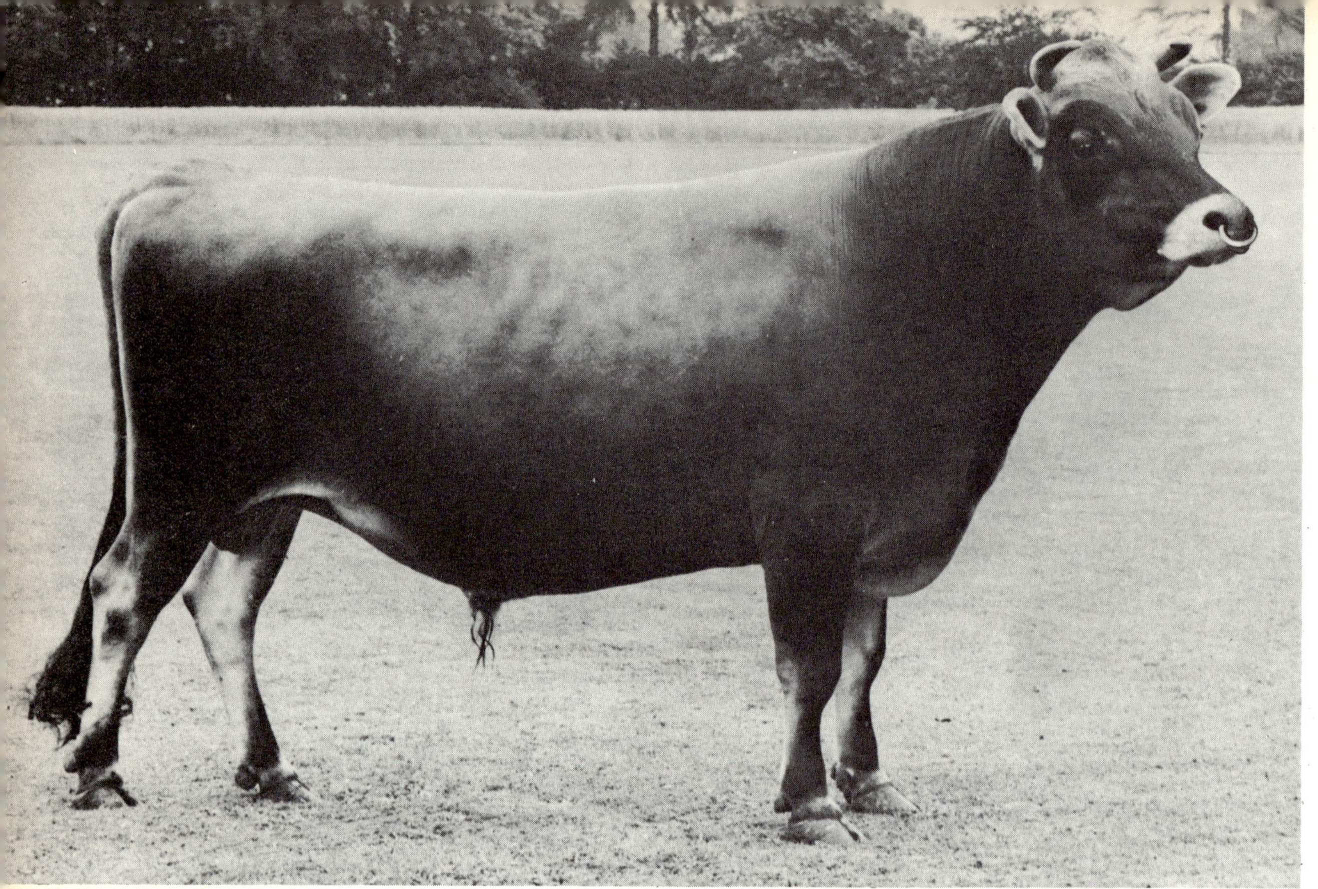

Jersey bull, 'Dreaming Prince'. Native to that island, the Jersey produces the richest milk of all dairy breeds. The bulls, although small, are reputed to be the most dangerous among dairy cattle. (*Jersey Cattle Society*)

Opposite, above: Herding young Hereford bulls on the Estancia Yacaré, Paraguay. (*Erich Hartmann/Magnum*)

Opposite, below: Brahman bull, Paraguay. (*Erich Hartmann/Magnum*)

Overleaf: Crossbred Zebu cattle on a ranch in Rhodesia. (*Erich Hartmann/Magnum*)

milking machine. The long, curved, sharply pointed horns were a danger to both man and beast until de-horning became the rule. The bulls are inclined to be rather hasty and, especially if confined, at times dangerous. The risks of in-breeding was emphasised by the history of a very famous Ayrshire bull that left excellent daughters, giving abundant milk of good quality. Unfortunately, tucked away in what geneticists call his genotype, was a recessive factor for abnormal and monstrous calves. This only came to light after he was mated with his own daughters when abnormal calves were so frequently born as to cause genuine alarm. It was a simple enough problem in genetics which the Edinburgh Institute of Animal Breeding soon sorted out. Unfortunately the recessive gene had by that time been rather widely distributed throughout the breed through the use of fashionable bulls, and it took some time finally to clear the matter up. The scientific approach has certain definite advantages because in olden days, when monstrous calves appeared in a herd, some poor old hag, accused of bewitching it, was burnt at the stake.

Finally, those bewitching Channel Island cattle, Jerseys and Guernseys, in which the secondary sex characters are so decisive that, while the bulls are little devils, the cows are perfect pets. Strange, in a way, that such a distinctive breed as the Jersey, native to such a small island, should have spread throughout the world.

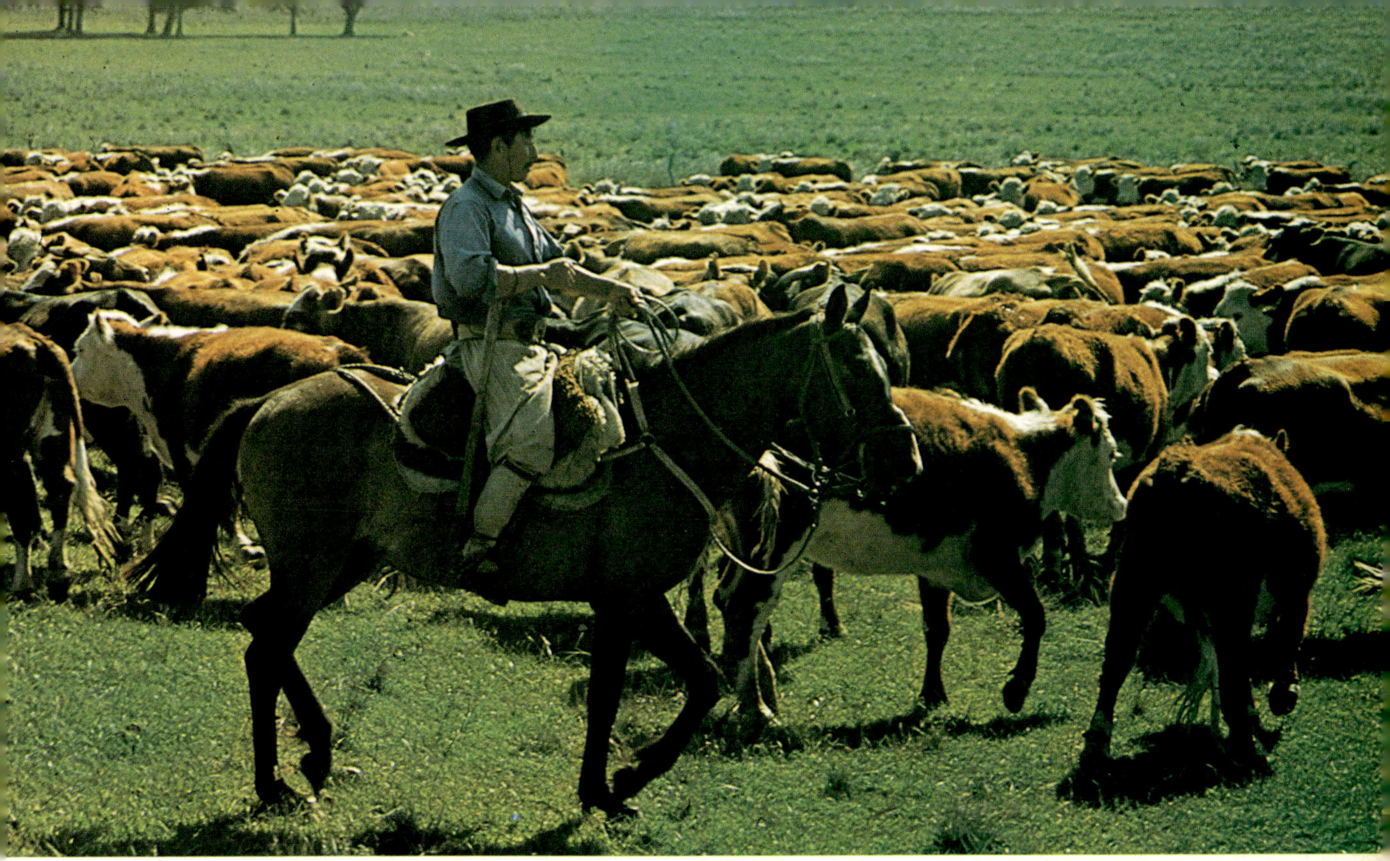

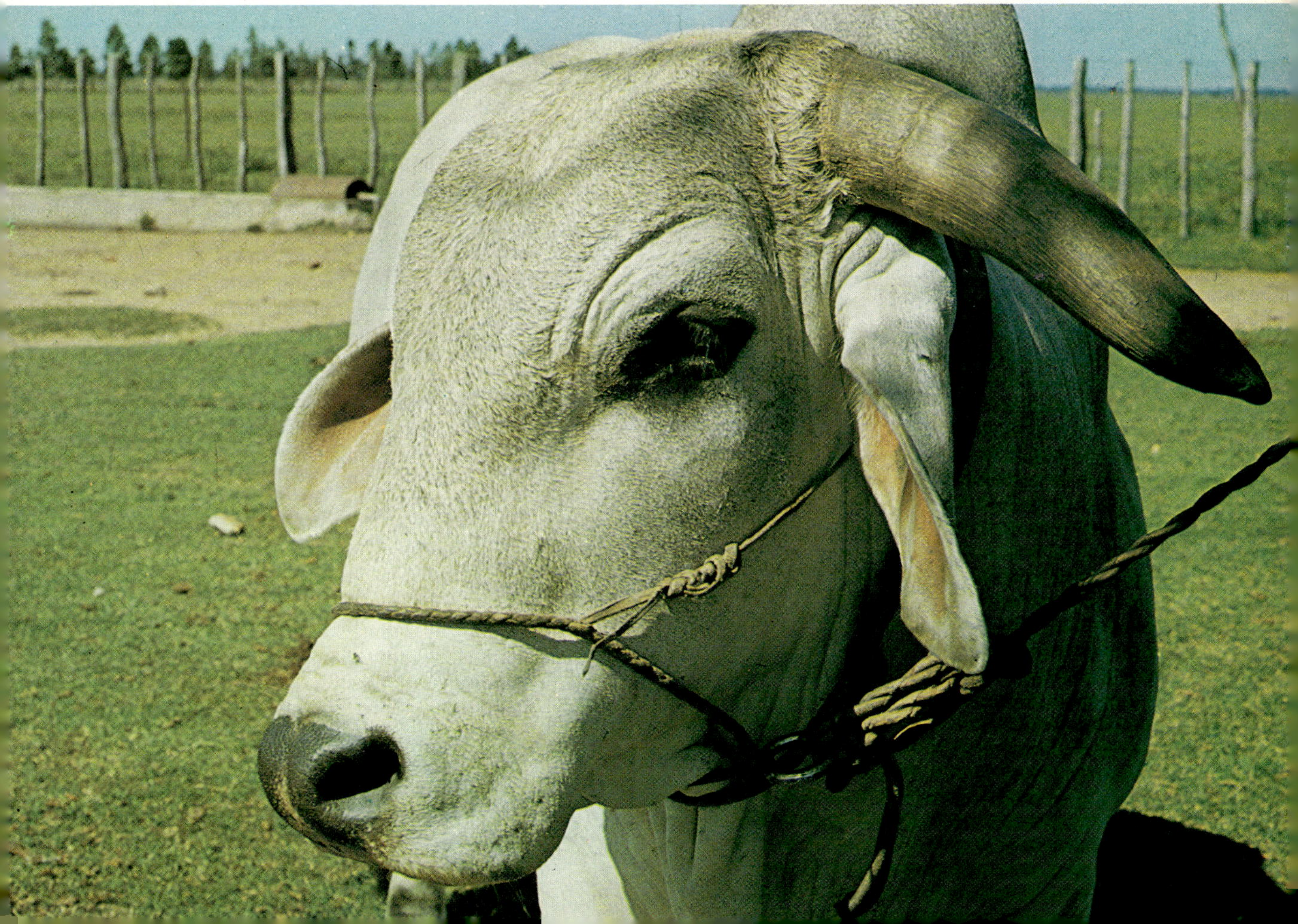

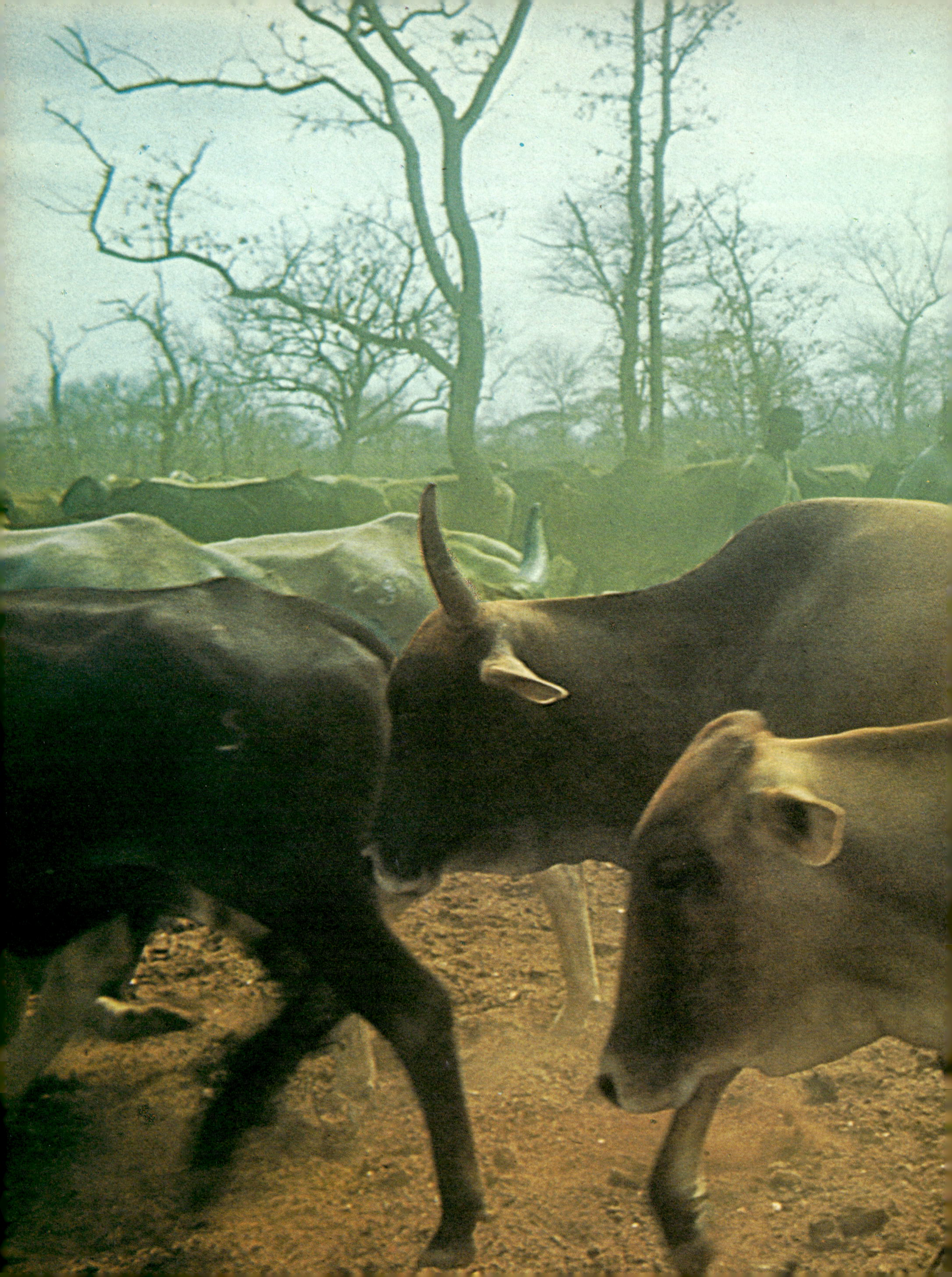

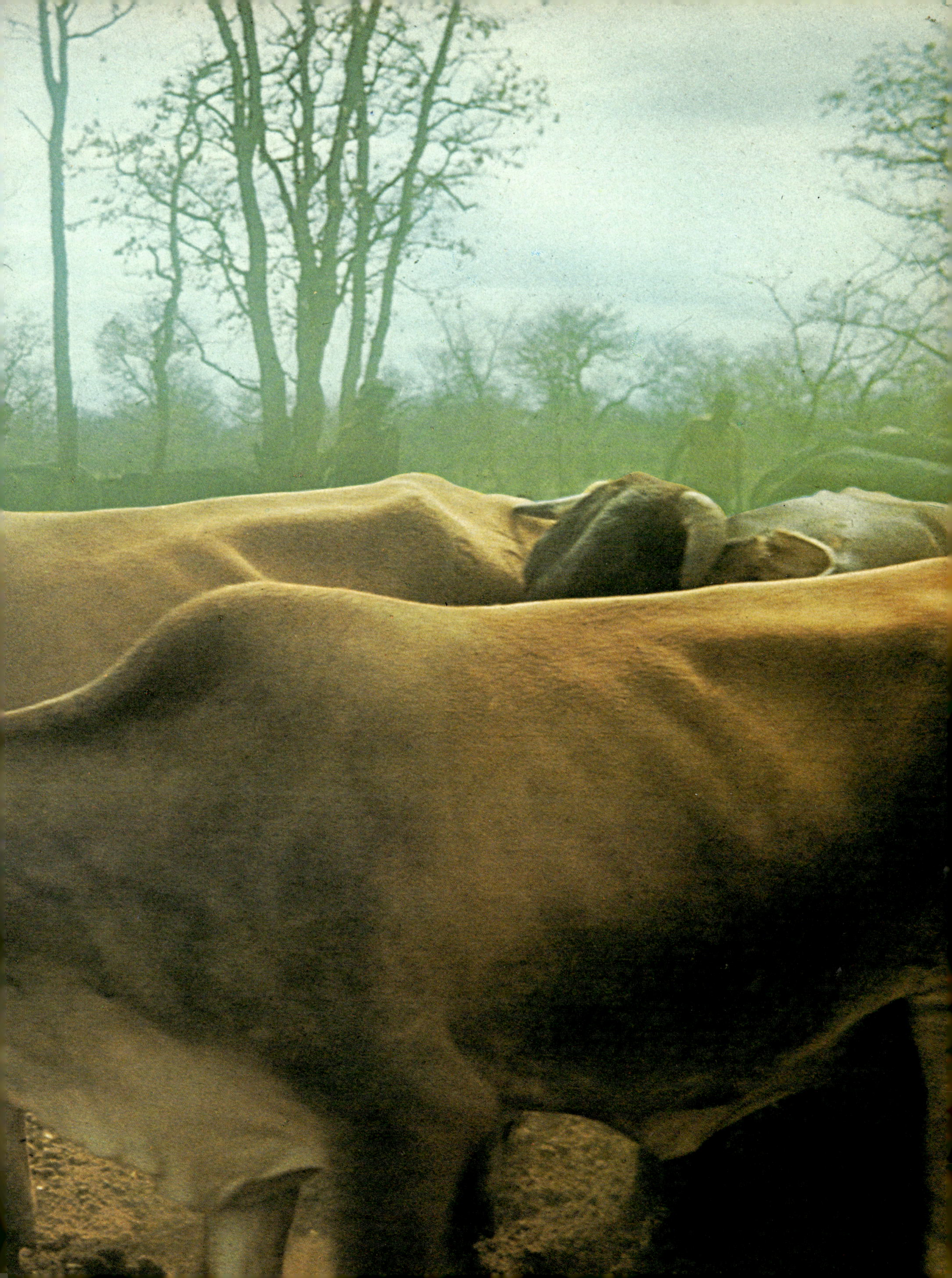

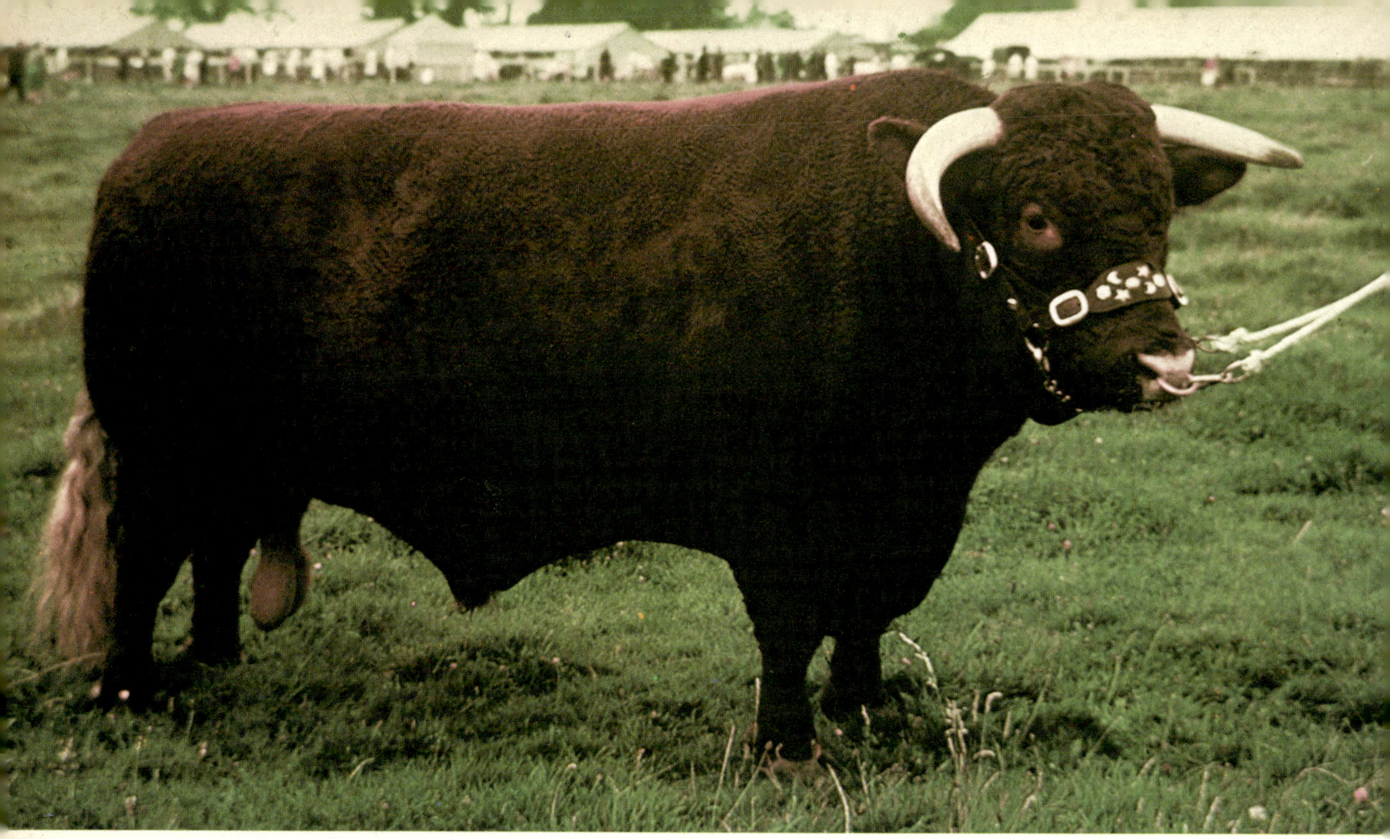

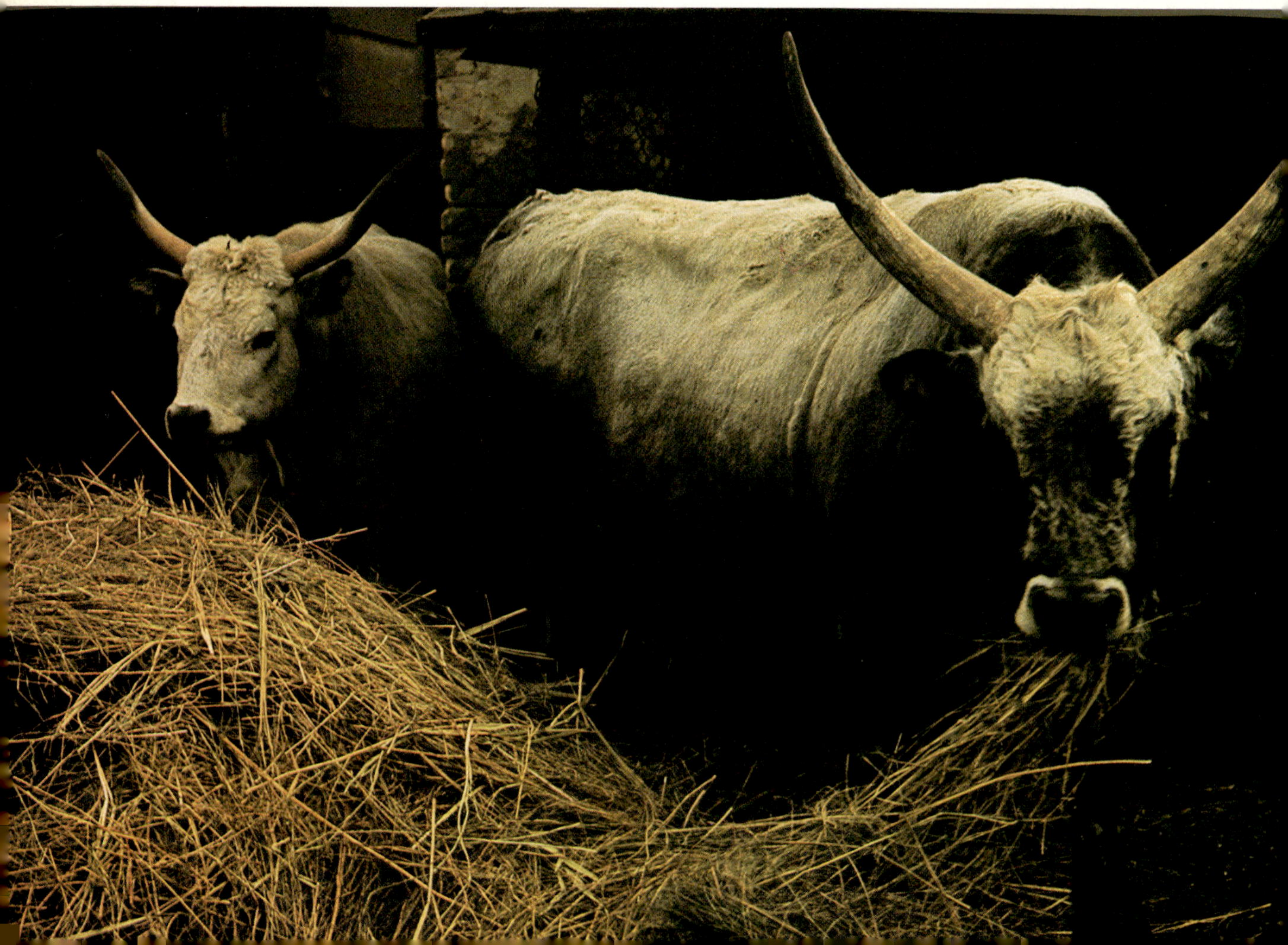

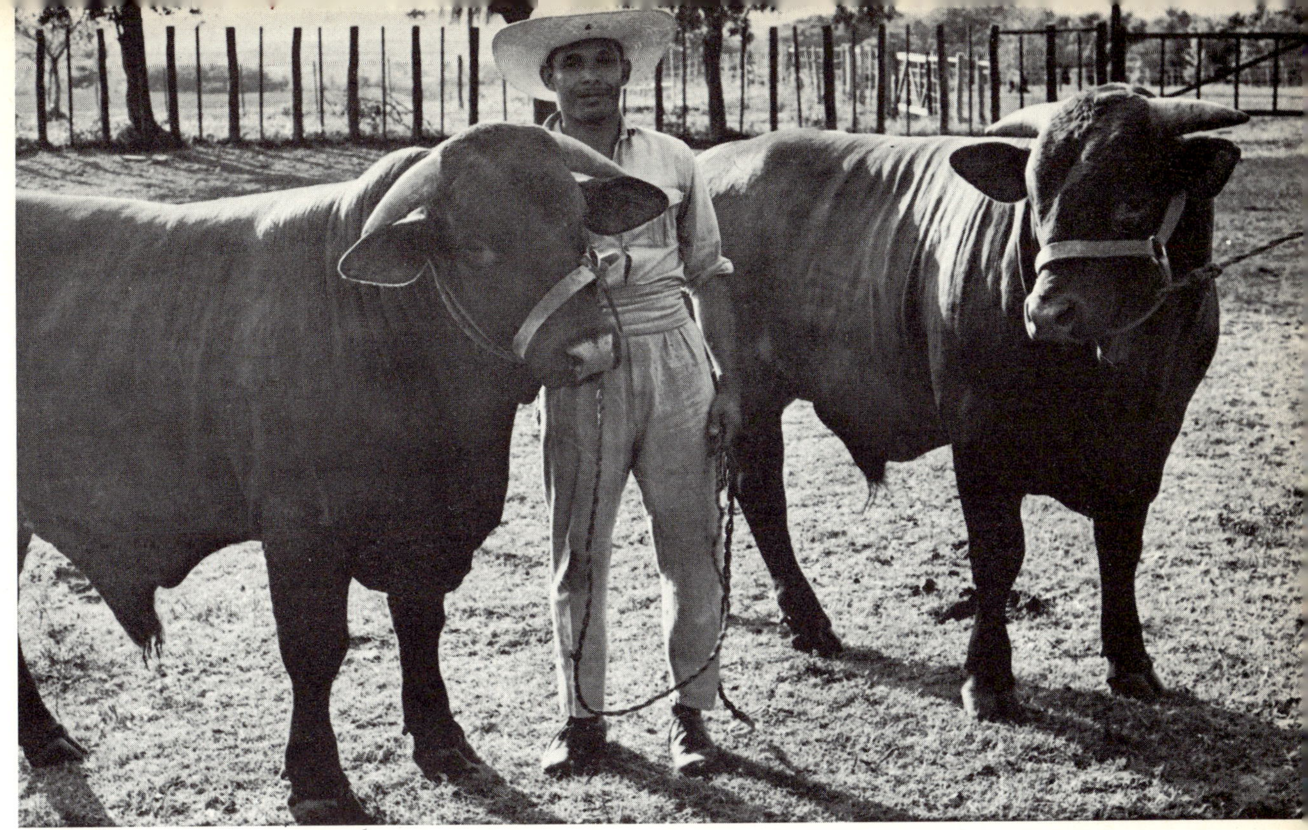

Young Santa Gertrudis bulls, Paraguay. (*Erich Hartmann/Magnum*)

Wherever butter is the main dairy product, as in New Zealand, the Jersey cow prevails. In quality, cream content and colour, Jersey milk is unrivalled. One of the modern uses of the breed in Britain is the addition of one or two Jersey cows to a Friesian herd. To add their milk to that of the Friesians is the most speedy, most sensible and most economic method of ensuring that Friesian milk reaches a satisfactory butter-fat standard.

There is a certain air of superior breeding in the Jersey, perhaps because of early aristocratic patronage.

'Many have taken part in the work as breeders, but the two grand old men of Jersey cattle fame are Colonel le Couteur and, following him, Colonel le Cornu whose far-seeing wisdom and untiring devotion to the best interests of the breed have done so much to secure its present enviable position in competition with other dairy cattle.'[15] Were these old Colonels who did so much for their cattle half in love with their cows? This is how Colonel le Couteur described a Jersey cow: 'she possessed the head of a fawn, a soft eye, an elegant crumpled horn, small ears, yellow within, a clean neck and throat, fine bones, a fine tail' – and then, almost as an unpoetical afterthought – 'above all, a well-formed, capacious udder, with large swelling milk veins'.[16]

That, then, is the story of the Bull on the Farm, in every breed and in every bull-breeding herd chosen and honoured for the productive value of his get, although sometimes sailing away into the cloud-cuckoo land of dubious pedigree and fancy points judged beautiful.

Opposite, above: Devon bull. (*Devon Cattle Breeders' Society*)

Below: Hungarian bulls. (*B. Kapadia*)

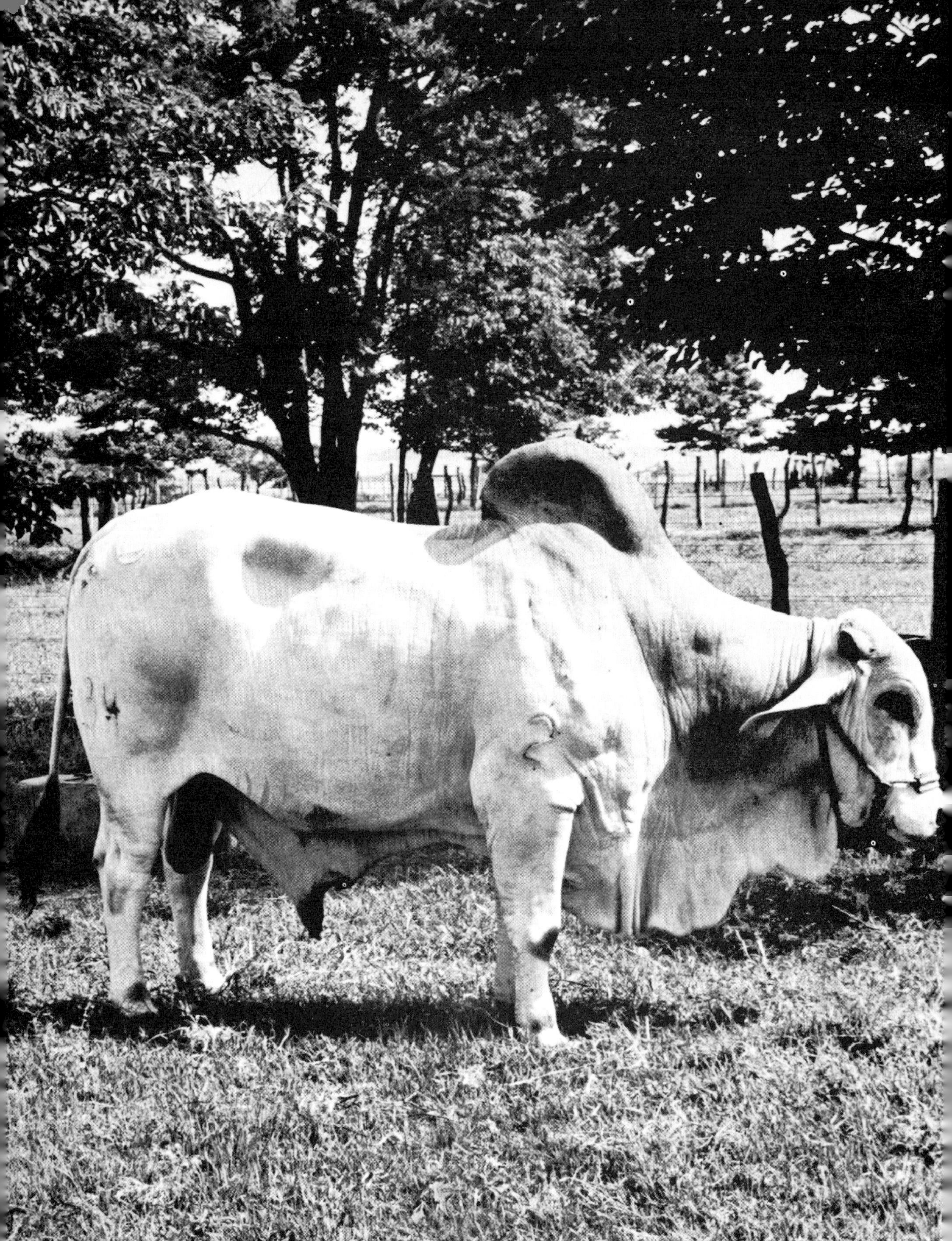

They were the pride, the joy, and occasionally the fortune of those quaint old master-breeders, who used few tools in their breeding methods save common sense and observation. Let us, for the moment, in the words of Ecclesiasticus, praise famous men as well as great bulls. These old master-breeders were rather like the cave-men artists of Lascaux. They made fine things simply. How was it done? In writing of sheep I once posed this question – mainly to myself but also to my readers:

How did men who knew nothing of genetical science, of nutritional science, of veterinary science, with pastures unimproved, roots non-existent, and cake undreamt of, produce breeds that have stamped an English seal on the faces of sheep of three continents, so that the fame of their counties of origin, of Leicester, of Lincoln, of Romney Marsh, have been carried to distant corners of the farthest Antipodes?[17]

The Bull on the Farm and the Cow on the Farm! The bull, respected and cared for as the father of the herd, respected also and often feared for his strength, his courage, his masculinity and his forcefulness. The cow, in her appealing femininity creating an affection sometimes almost akin to love. The Bull on the Farm being led to his mating with the herd, his proud virility, strength and evident sexual desire the heroic poetry of the male. The Cow on the Farm, a long line of leisurely matrons in the cool dusk of evening, their full udders swinging, coming home to the milking. Peace – and a peace, indeed, that passes all understanding. The pride of Paganism, the peace of Christ, brought together on an English farm.

Brahman bull, Argentina.
(*Erich Hartmann/Magnum*)

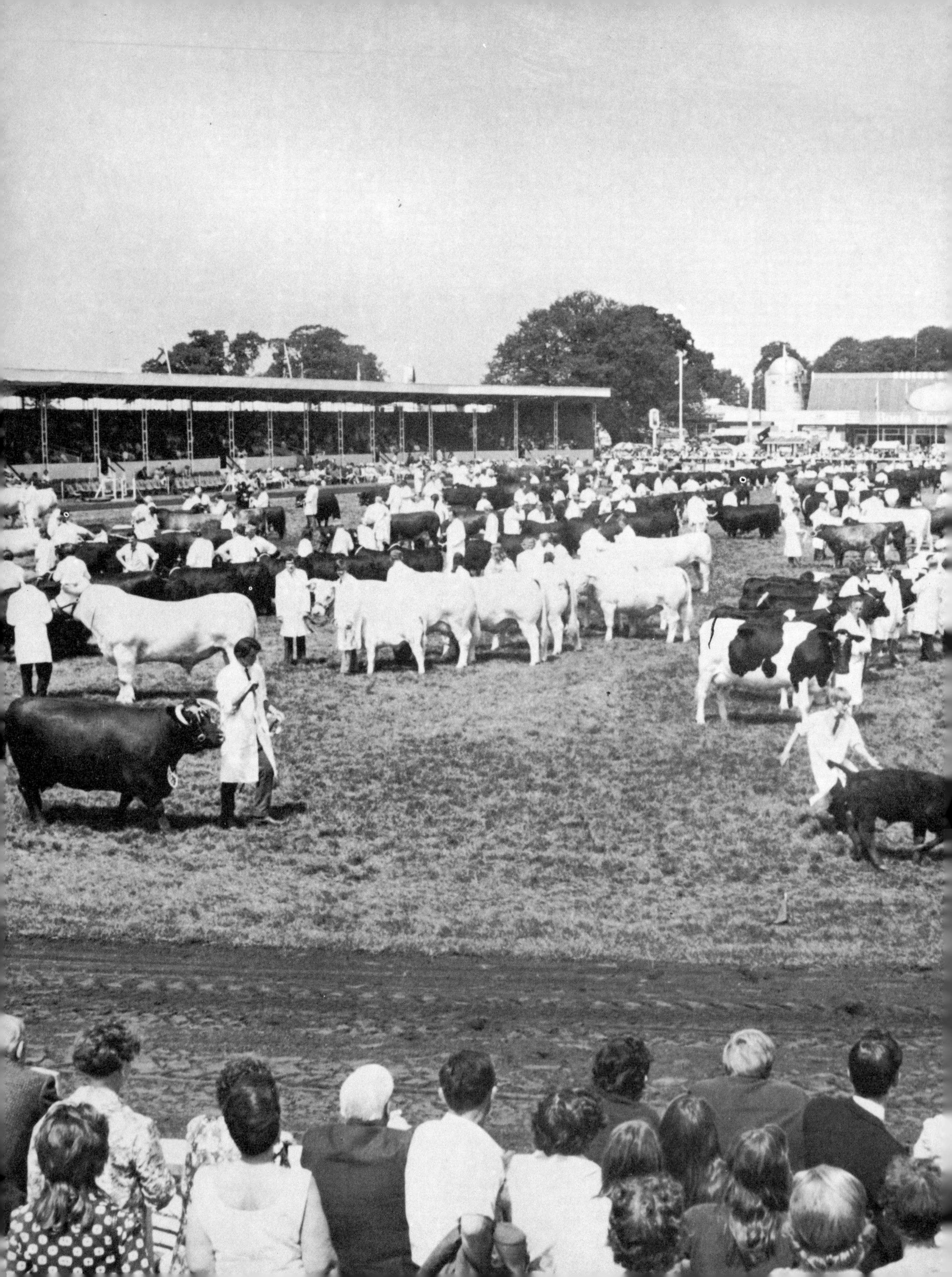

8

The Bull in Technology

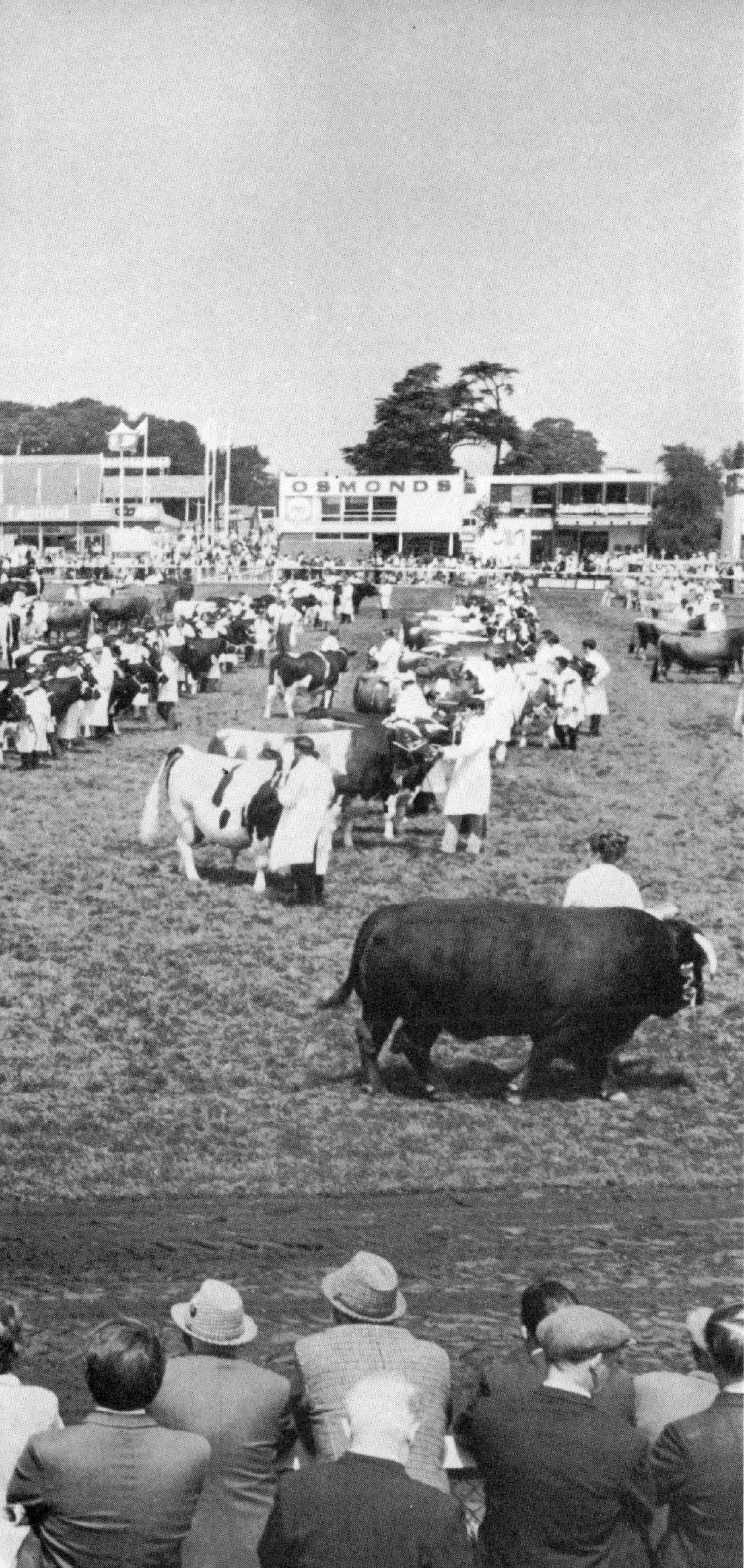

Cattle Parade at the Royal Show (1971). The parade of cattle in progress in the Main Ring of the Royal Show in the grounds of Stoneleigh Abbey, Kenilworth, Warwickshire. (*Fox Photos*)

§ The conventional farm with its flocks and herds, and the green grass growing, geared to the slow progress of the seasons, is beginning to bear a somewhat old-fashioned appearance. Farming is being drawn, gradually but it would seem inevitably, into the urbanised pattern of industrial production. The change has proceeded – one dare not use the word 'progressed' – farthest in the poultry industry where the hen, confined from hatching to slaughter in overcrowded floors and battery cages, never sees daylight or breathes the open air; where economists and animal husbandry experts compete with one another as to how many birds can be crammed without an uneconomical death-rate into the smallest possible area of floor-space. The hen battery egg and the broiler-house chicken are its cut-price products. A similar industrial, modernised, unaesthetic revolution is overtaking and is likely to engulf all other branches of animal production whether from poultry, pigs, cattle or sheep. In cattle, already, veal calves are penned from birth to early slaughter in dark boxes in which they are unable to turn round. Such developments are called modern advances or modern developments and are characteristic of what is termed 'The Age of Technology'. Some people take a pride in it, but it is improbable that farm animals do, certainly not the bull. Admittedly, ever since domestication, the bull, like the males of all livestock, has had to suffer the pain, discomfort and indignity of castration without anaesthesia. It would cost too much in anaesthetics and man hours to make the elimination of pain an economic proposition. Consequently, since there have always been far more bulls born than were required for reproduction in a polygamous species, the scorpion of the Mithraic bull sacrifice has been replaced, first by the crushing stones, then by the knife, most recently by elastic rubber rings which encircle and compress the blood and nerve supply to the testicles until they rot and drop off. Nowadays, even the bull permitted to remain a bull hasn't much of a life of it, incited to masturbation on a dummy at intervals not necessarily convenient to himself but to the current demand for semen.

Nevertheless, unpleasant though discussion of castration may be, it is certainly neither modern nor does it require any advanced technology. It is as old as domestication itself because for so many purposes the castrate, whether it be the eunuch to guard the harem in mankind or the ox to draw the plough or to fatten for beef, proved so much more trustworthy than the entire male. Castration, also, when applied selectively, provided a greater opportunity of closer selection of breeding stock in the specialisation of livestock, generally termed animal improvement.

In cattle, as in all mammals, the sexes are born in equal numbers – one bull calf for every heifer calf. The bull produces two types of germ cells, spermatozoa, or seed as the ancients frequently and quite appropriately used to call them, and he produces them in equal numbers. One type, call it type A, when it meets with and fertilises the microscopic egg or ovum within the genital passage of the cow, results in a bull calf. The second type, call it type B, results in a heifer calf. As regards sex determination, the eggs or ova of cows are all similar, and it being purely a matter of chance whether they meet the one or the other type of spermatozoa, the sexes are born in equal number. The sex of all cattle is thus predetermined at their conception and it is nine months following conception before the calf is born.

When a bull calf is born he may be slaughtered for veal shortly after birth, which is the fate of many in the milking breeds, or he may be castrated at an early age to be finally slaughtered for beef. Either for breeding purposes or bull beef production he may be left entire.

The castrated bull is called, variously, a steer, an ox or a bullock. The term used in America is almost invariably 'steer' and is now widely used in Britain. The term 'ox' is practically obsolete. Castration implies the removal or destruction, by a variety of methods, of the two testicles or testes which are supported in the scrotum or bag of the bull. It must be one of the oldest surgical procedures in history because in every language there is one word for the entire male and another for the castrate. In the English language a human castrate is called a eunuch, a castrated ram a wedder, a castrated boar a hog, a castrated cock a capon, a castrated bull a steer. There are many profound differences between bull and steer in both physical and mental characteristics.

The six main results of castration are: permanent sterility; sexual impotence; under-development of what are termed secondary sexual characters, which distinguish male from female; a change in the development of body structure; alteration in body composition; greater docility and tractability.

It is important to distinguish between fertility and potency because the two characters, usually co-ordinated but on occasion totally distinct, are and have been frequently confused. Sterility means, in the male, that, although he may be powerfully potent he is incapable of leaving offspring because of failure of production or abnormality of his spermatozoa. Impotency in the male means that although he may be producing perfect spermatozoa in abundance within his testicles he is physically or psychologically incapable of conveying them to the female's genital tract during copulation. It is particularly important to distinguish between the fertility and potency in the bull, because they are often confused today and, on the evidence of mythology, were even more frequently misinterpreted in the past.

Failure to produce sperm does occur occasionally in bulls as in all male mammals. Before Artificial Insemination was introduced into animal husbandry, the proof of sterility in a bull had to await the evidence of a failure of conception in the cows he had served. It is

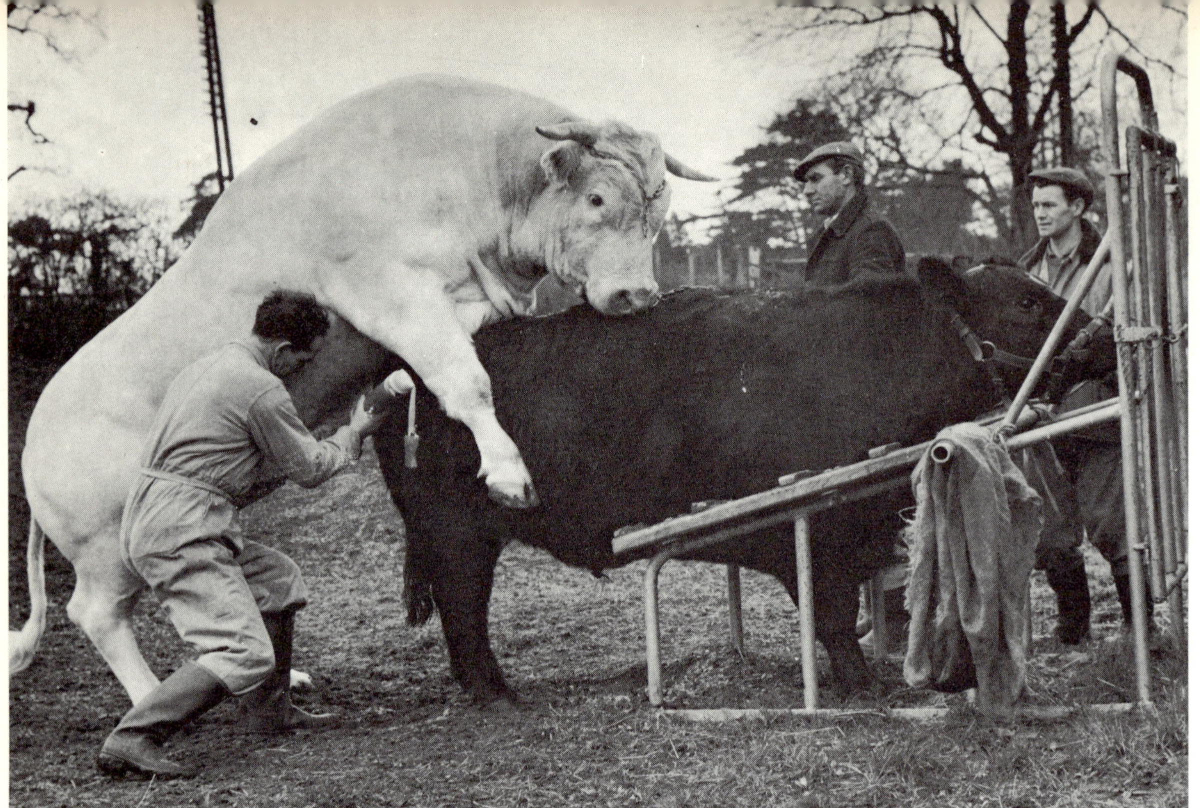

Collecting semen by the use
of the artificial vagina.
(*Milk Marketing Board*)

now possible, using A.I. techniques, to examine the semen of a bull
before he is put into service at all and determine by microscopic
examination and other tests whether he is likely to be fully fertile,
imperfectly fertile or completely sterile.

A sterile bull may be perfectly potent and not only able to serve
cows but sometimes particularly eager and active in doing so. The
strength of the sex urge or 'libido' as it is usually called is not necessarily
correlated or connected with high fertility at all. A striking illustration
of this fact was given by Professor W. C. Miller of the Animal Health
Trust in describing differences of mating behaviour of thoroughbred
stallions:

The 1927 Derby winner, 'Call Boy', when at stud, was a most vigorous
performer, at times almost uncontrollable. Indeed, it took two to three men
to hold him. On entering the covering yard, he would make a wild plunge
forwards, 'roaring like a bull' leap upon the mare, perhaps driving her
forwards on to her knees, perhaps scattering mare, men, grooms and himself
in a tangle of threshing hooves on the straw of the yard. When he did serve
the mare it was a most vigorous service. 'Call Boy' remained at stud for
several years, but only three or four foals could be credited to him during
the whole of his stud career. Examination of semen had been made on many
occasions, but no defects could be detected.

As a contrast, a stallion with one of the most consistently high fertility
records for many years is the twenty-year-old 'Hyperion', Derby winner in
1933. He is a perfect gentleman and a complete artist in covering his mares,
never putting a foot wrong and under perfect control throughout.[1]

160

The occasional lack of perfect correlation between fertility and potency in stallions, bulls and other male mammals is owing, basically, to the dual function and compound structure of the testicles.

Their first and most important physiological function is the production of spermatozoa, which are formed in long, coiled tubes called seminiferous tubules. Fertility depends upon the healthy functioning of these tubules. The second testicular function is the manufacture of the male sex hormone, testosterone, produced in what is called the interstitial tissue, separating and filling in the spaces between the seminiferous tubules. This hormone passes directly into the blood stream regulating male behaviour (including sex drive or 'libido') and all of what are termed the secondary sex characters of the male. In the bull, the strong muscular development of shoulders and neck, the greater bodily size and deep voice, are examples of these bodily secondary sex characters. His sex drive or libido, his combativeness and courage are examples of his psychological sex characters.

There is a congenital abnormality which occurs sporadically in all male mammals including cattle and which illustrates clearly and neatly the dual function of the testicles. The abnormality is called cryptorchidism, meaning hidden testicles, whereby, instead of the testicles descending into the scrotum as they normally do, they are retained within the abdominal cavity. The temperature of the body in general is slightly higher than that of the scrotum. Consequently, the seminiferous tubules cannot develop or function there. The bilateral cryptorchid (with both testicles undescended) is, therefore, totally and permanently sterile. The interstitial tissue, however, in contrast to the seminiferous tubules, is less sensitive to higher temperature and develops fully although retained. As a result, the double cryptorchid, apart from his sterility, shows all the characters of the complete male, both in behaviour and in development of the secondary sex characters appropriate to his species.

When a bull calf is castrated and both testicles removed or destroyed he is deprived of both testicular functions. He becomes, as it were at the stroke of the knife, a mere steer, permanently sterile and impotent. He does not develop in full any of the secondary sex characters that the hormone testosterone causes to develop in the bull. Physically he is smaller, lighter and far weaker. His neck and shoulder muscles are under-developed, his voice does not break and he lacks the deep, rumbling roar of the bull. Mentally, he is uninterested in females, he lacks pugnacity and courage, he is relatively placid in temperament and easily controlled. The effect of castration is shown even in the intimate composition of his body. His flesh contains less lean meat and more fat. His rate of growth is slower, his appetite less keen and his utilisation of food not so economical. This gulf between bull and steer in both body and mind is due to a hormone of relatively simple chemical composition – a steroid which has been artificially synthesised – a hormone formed naturally in the interstitial tissue of the testicles of the bull. In certain mythologies it was believed that the essence of the bull, its strength and virility, was centred in its horns. 'As in Crete, so in Greece, the horns of the bull were considered to be the seat and focus of his strength.'[2] Possibly, certain of the ancients had a clearer knowledge. In the rites associated with the Greek god Attis of Aegean origin that spread throughout the Roman Empire and in which, like the similar cults of Mithra and Dionysus, bulls were sacrificed, 'the testicles as well as the blood of the bull played an important part in the ceremonies'.[3] Since the object of these ceremonies was to endue the devotees with the admired characters of the bull – his strength, courage and fertility – the followers of Attis were scientifically correct. It is the testicle that makes the bull. It is the absence of testicles that forms the steer.

Since one bull, in natural conditions can serve, on an average, no more than fifty to one hundred cows in the course of a year, it was always necessary to maintain at least two out of every hundred male calves born, entire and uncastrated. The extension of technology into farming practice, however, has already reduced that percentage and with the improvement and extension of Artificial Insemination techniques is likely to reduce it still further in the future. Technology has already made a sharp impact upon the pedigree bull-breeding business, despite all its glamour and prestige.

An ambitious breeder of Scotch Shorthorn bulls, on being introduced to that great scientist, farmer and gentleman the late Sir John Hammond, said bluntly, 'You are the man who has ruined my business.' That accusation, although rude, contained an element of truth because the impersonal scientific approach to animal production in general and to animal breeding in particular which Sir John Hammond typified was inevitably a serious threat to the pedigree breeder, particularly to the breeder of Shorthorn cattle.

One of the earliest contributions of Mendelian genetics to cattle-breeding was in the elucidation of coat colour inheritance resulting in the development of what is termed 'colour marking' of calves. Suppose you want to breed a useful beef calf out of a dairy cow of any breed. If you use a Hereford bull the calf is born with a white face so that its paternity is manifest to all. Again, if you use an Aberdeen-Angus bull the calf is born black, and once more, its paternity is proved. Consequently, both Hereford and Aberdeen-Angus are termed colour-marking breeds. On the contrary a Shorthorn bull leaves no certain colour mark to confirm paternity, and for long, and largely owing to the insistence of Sir John Hammond, preference in calf subsidy was accorded to colour-marked beef calves out of dairy cows and the Beef Shorthorn was left out in the unsubsidised cold.

A further and quite revolutionary contribution of scientific technology to animal husbandry was the development and extraordinarily rapid expansion of Artificial Insemination, for convenience commonly contracted to the simple initials A.I. Its definition is a very simple one. *A.I. is the placing of spermatozoa in the female genital tract by means other than by natural service.* Accepting that definition, A.I. has a very ancient history. It is known that the Arabs, as far back as 1322 were using a primitive technique in the breeding of their incomparable horses. Stallions of exceptional value were mated naturally with a mare in heat and a proportion of its semen removed manually from the vagina of that mare and inserted, again manually, into the vagina of other mares also in heat.

An Italian physiologist, Spallanzani in 1780 did something of the same thing with dogs and Hunter, in 1799, succeeded in securing conception in a woman by her fertile although impotent husband. Ivanoff, a Russian physiologist, began a study of A.I. in farm animals as early as 1899, established a laboratory for further investigation in 1909, and encouraged by Soviet enthusiasm initiated large-scale investigations and the practical application of his findings in 1922. It is really to the scientists of the USSR that the main advances in A.I. are due. Developments in England came rather later and were to a certain extent a repetition of what had already been achieved in the Soviet Union.

Sir John Hammond and his collaborator, biochemist Dr Walton, gave the first public demonstration of A.I. techniques at Cambridge in the year 1934.

Artificial Insemination, now so widely practised – as far as the bull is concerned – is merely induced masturbation. In the year 1931 the Russian Milovanov, invented a simple enough instrument called the artificial vagina, consisting essentially of a lubricated thick rubber tube surrounded by a water jacket at appropriate temperature and pressure. The bull's erected phallus is guided manually into this tube and ejaculation occurs, the semen being collected in a sterile glass phial at the tube's extremity. After dilution, storage and possibly deep freezing, a small quantity is inserted into the vagina of a cow in heat. Both the collection and insertion of semen present few difficulties. On the contrary the preservation of semen outside the animal body has necessitated a great deal of advanced biochemical research.

To maintain spermatozoa alive outside the male body was, indeed, a triumph of technology. Provided the semen is transferred to the female genital tract immediately after ejaculation, as was the method used with Arab stallions, no great difficulty arises. But left to themselves the spermatozoa soon become first immobile and then die. To keep them both alive and capable of fertilisation requires precise control of temperature, acidity, and the provision of soluble food to give the

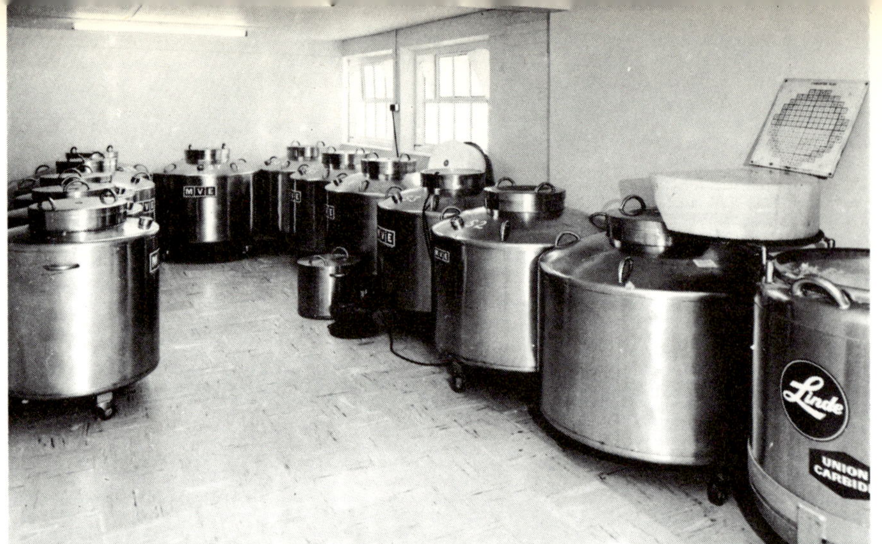

Once collected, the semen is stored in liquid nitrogen in deep freeze units at minus 193 degrees centigrade, where it can remain indefinitely. Recently, on a farm in Buckinghamshire, a pedigree Guernsey calf was born whose sire died sixteen years ago. The semen of prize Guernsey bull 'Murrell Prince', who had sired more than 15,000 offspring, was discovered at one of the Milk Marketing Board's A.I. centres. (*Milk Marketing Board*)

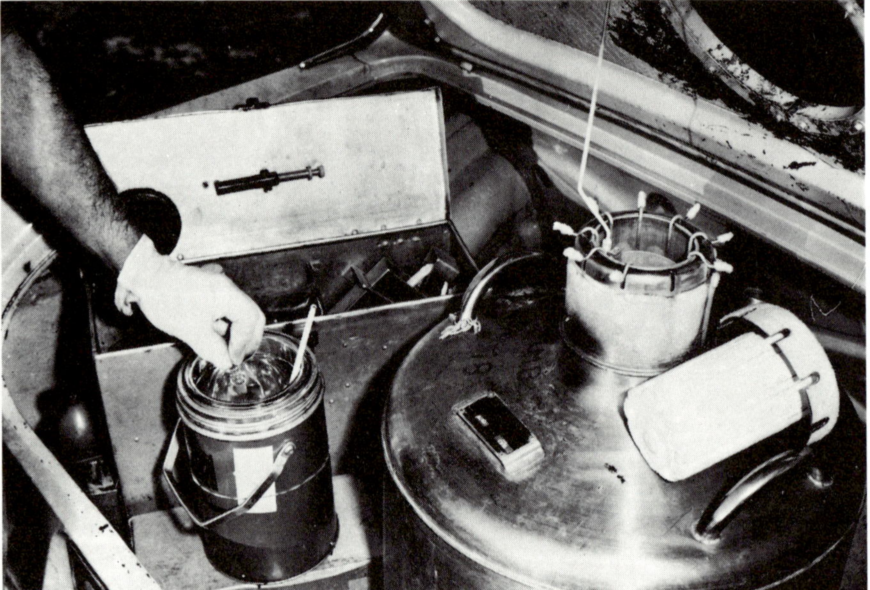

Thawing an ampoule of semen which has just been taken from the liquid nitrogen flask. (*Milk Marketing Board*)

energy they need for survival.

In order to preserve spermatozoa outside the body they must be kept at a low temperature to slow down their movement and prolong their life. By gradually reducing the temperature to the lowest obtainable limit, using liquid nitrogen as freezing agent, the sperm, like trout in an arctic river, freezes solid; just like the trout, it regains its vitality and mobility when thawed out again. This is called the deep-freeze method of preserving semen. Semen can be kept in the deep freeze indefinitely and the breeding value of an outstanding bull maintained for decades. Close in-breeding to conserve the qualities of an outstanding bull is no longer necessary. More directly and efficiently the semen banked in his lifetime can be drawn upon long after his death – conferring upon him a species of technological immortality.

The success of the A.I. technique is proved by its wide practical application, particularly to dairy cows. In certain countries, in Sweden for example, well over 90 per cent of cows conceive in this manner. Dr Joseph Edwards was the pioneer of the practical application of A.I. in England. In 1942, supported by several influential breeders of dairy cattle, he established – appropriately at Cambridge – the first A.I. centre in Britain.

To start with there was a distinct resistance by many practical cattle breeders to this revolutionary method of producing calves. The practice was deemed unnatural, which by simple definition it certainly is. It was suggested that calves conceived in this manner would lack the vitality of those conceived by natural service. This anxiety, in the event, proved unfounded. Breeders of pedigree bulls feared it would damage and eventually destroy their business and, what to many was of greater importance, their influence and prestige. In this case, their fears were justified. It is by now evident that the elaborate and at times quite pictorial edifice that arose on the basis of pedigree registration – specialised bull-breeding herds, bull sales of international repute and so on – has lost much of its authority and with it, the imponderable prestige, aesthetic pleasure and interest which gave so much satisfaction to the majority of breeders producing pedigree bulls at a loss. The bull of today faces a less colourful, more utilitarian future.

Since one bull, by A.I., can sire very many thousands of calves during his lifetime it is clearly evident that he must be a well-tested and proven bull, producing calves best fitted for their purpose whether that purpose be milk or beef. To put the semen of a bull leaving inferior progeny into wide circulation would be disastrous. Consequently, around the sun of A.I. many planets nowadays revolve. These, called progeny testing, sire performance tests and so forth are all designed to ensure that bulls selected for A.I. are the best available for production purposes – and very rightly so. In the days (one is almost tempted to write 'the good old days') of pedigree breeding, it was commonly said that the bull was half the herd; with the invention of A.I. the bull can very easily become half the breed.

Although breeders of pedigree bulls in general distrusted and at times opposed A.I., there were at least three other groups who welcomed and encouraged its development. First, and perhaps most important, the ordinary dairy farmer selling milk for his living. At the time of A.I.'s first introduction – in the 1940s – the average dairy herd was in general a small commercial unit, the average herd number in England being no more than 10 to 20 head of cattle. In order to put his cows in calf – and a cow must have a calf before she comes into lactation – he had to own or borrow a bull. That involved keeping at least one less cow, lowering his milk production between 5 and 10 per cent. He could not afford a good bull unless he was lucky enough to secure a cheap bull which proved a good breeder as sometimes occurs.

The liquid nitrogen
technique for freezing
semen means that farmers
can have the benefit of
service from the best bulls in
the Milk Board's A.I. stud.
Semen is stored in straws in
the liquid nitrogen. (*Milk
Marketing Board*)

Artificial insemination being
carried out. An inseminator
inseminates a cow. (*Milk
Marketing Board*)

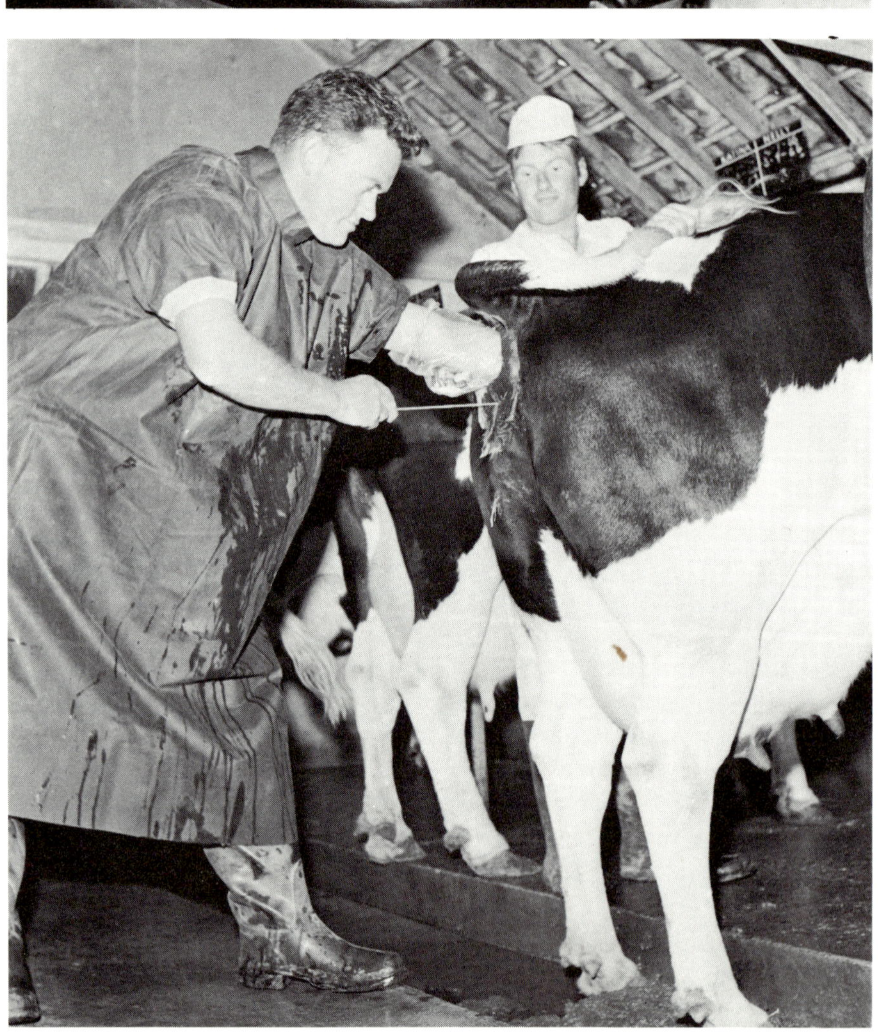

He had to maintain, for the sole purpose of serving a score or half-score of cows, a large, expensive and potentially dangerous creature, often in unsuitable buildings, a continual menace to his family and to himself.

Secondly, it was an encouragement to the scientist – the geneticist, the biochemist, the statistician, generically called the boffin – because without their specialised knowledge and sophisticated techniques the business of artificial insemination could never have arrived at its present perfection.

For some time the agricultural scientists had been sniping at the Breed Societies firmly entrenched behind ever-mounting piles of Stud Books, Herd Books, Flock Books, in which the occasionally somewhat dubious ancestry of pedigree livestock was piously recorded. A.I. provided the boffin with a most powerful artillery barrage to breach the breeders' voluminous defences. It had, for example, long been a custom of the breeder to hold an annual summer parade – a sort of demonstration in force – at first called 'The Cattle Show' and later 'The Agricultural Show'. At these shows, spectacular and altogether delightful were the weather propitious, beef and dairy bulls of various recognised breeds paraded before the shrewd eyes of the judges selected by the exhibitors themselves. To judge dairy bulls in a useful way with some reference to commercial reality is no easy task. For whereas a Beef Bull has unmistakable evidence of some beef about him, no Dairy Bull ever gave a drop of milk in its life on which the quantity and quality of his milk potential could be assessed. The only means of judging Dairy Bulls in a useful manner is to find out what sort of female progeny he has left: whether they were beautiful creatures showing all the breed points of coat coloration, horn curvature and so forth in perfection although possibly lamentable performers in the pail; or whether although a shade less picturesque they produced milk in abundance with butter fat to spare. Armed with the powerful weapon A.I. provided, the boffins proceeded to probe this indelicate question using the lance of Progeny Testing, which in addition to A.I. required milk recording, butter-fat testing and statistical analysis of data as essential auxiliary weapons. The results of this inquiry were not altogether favourable to the breeders' assertions nor to the judges reputations. Certain Dairy Bulls of magnificent appearance, outstanding Show performance and impeccable pedigree were found, when progeny tested, to have left quite unprofitable daughters. Other bulls of the same breed that had never caught the judges' eye were shown, on occasion, to have left daughters that were far more profitable and productive. The prestige attached to pedigree was severely shaken. Certain boffins pressed the pursuit just a little too hard in concluding that the Breed Societies with their entrenched vested interests, their elaborate pedigrees, their livestock shows, challenge cups, garlands and prize certificates were so much hocus-pocus. After all, it was the breeder, not the boffin, who had established the breeds. It was the breeder, not the boffin, who had directed useful productivity in cattle, on the one hand towards milk, on the other towards beef. It was the breeder, not the boffin, who ever since the Industrial Revolution had succeeded in providing the vastly swollen industrial proletariat with beef and milk.

Nevertheless, following upon the extension of A.I. and the separation of semen from the bull that carried it, the position of the boffin was so greatly enhanced that the breeder, nowadays, in cattle-breeding, comes to the boffin for guidance and advice and may even elect one chairman of an annual conference!

The fairest judgement of the result of this wordy battle about bulls is that the breeder did the best he could do – and his achievement was far from negligible – while working by candle-light. The boffin of today, however, with novel resources ranging from the artificial vagina to the computer, can do more, and do it more swiftly. The old candle served its turn, but modern electricity gives clearer vision, providing that the more powerful beam is cast in the right direction.

Thirdly, veterinarians, particularly in Europe, welcomed the innovation as a means of controlling V.D. in cattle. It is sometimes assumed that venereal disease is a problem in humanity alone. That is not so. There are at least four cattle diseases which may be conveyed during copulation from bull to cow or vice versa. One of these, brucellosis, is of medical interest since it may cause relapsing fever in mankind. Vibrio foetus is another. By the avoidance of direct contact between bull and cow it was assumed, with justice, that at least one path of infection would be eliminated.

As far as the bull is concerned, the introduction of A.I. has meant that the number of breeding bulls used in agriculture has decreased and will further decrease. It may result eventually in only a small, selected, carefully investigated group of male cattle avoiding castration.

On the other hand, certain further modern developments in beef production may render castration in male cattle intended for slaughter less universal than it has hitherto been.

Until recently, at least in the UK, any bull beef coming into the meat market has been that from discarded breeding bulls of advanced age. That has inevitably given bull beef a bad reputation among butchers and meat traders. Beef from old bulls is poor quality beef, tough, strongly flavoured and dark in colour. Nobody would buy it except at a give-away price. In fairness to bull beef, however, it should be added that beef from aged steers has much the same failings. In medieval times most of the 'roast beef of old England' came from discarded work oxen of anything up to a dozen or more years of age and that beef, like the beef of aged and discarded bulls, must also have been tough, and dark in colour although without the unpleasant 'bull

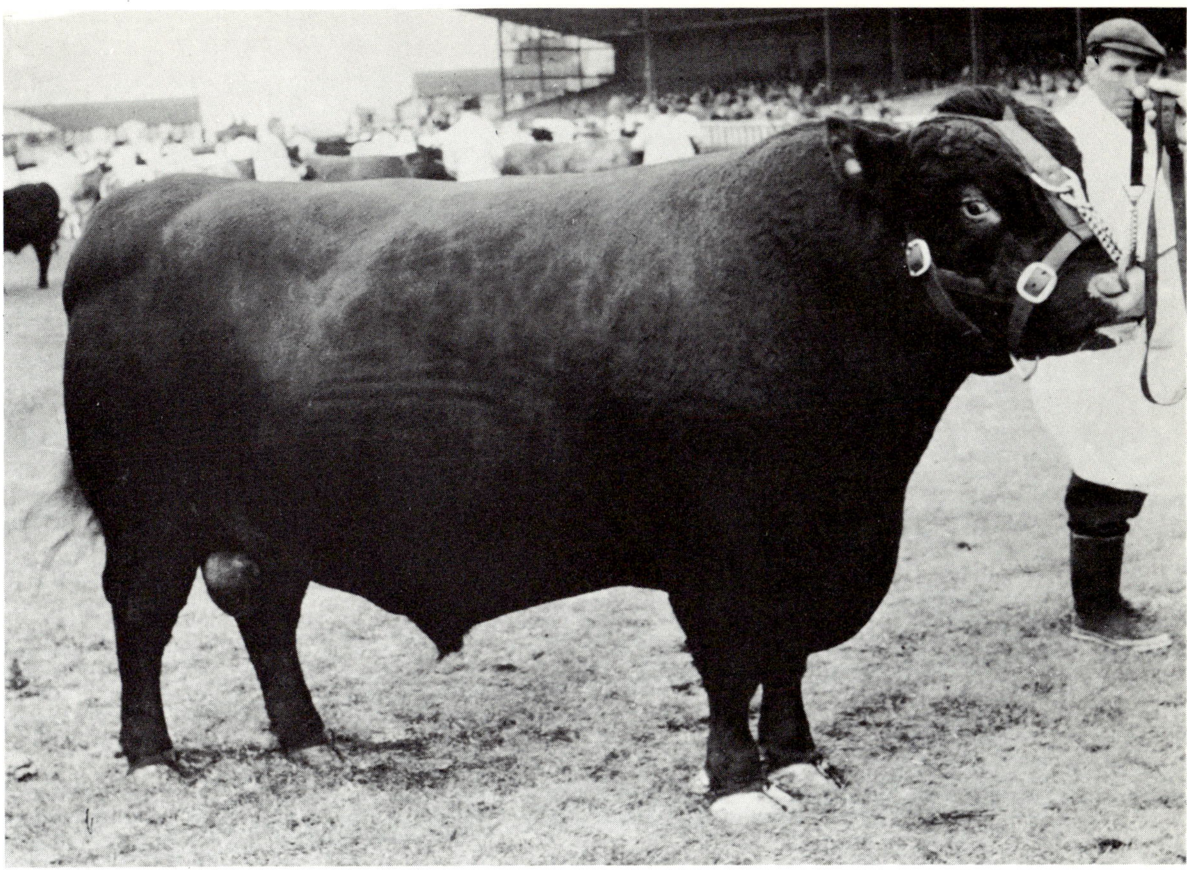

'Wenhaston Red Dawn', Red Poll Bull. Semen from this champion of breed bull at the Royal Show of 1960 has been exported to South America, and his progeny born there have been show champions in Colombia. (*Red Poll Cattle Society*)

taint' which may give mature bull beef its undesirable flavour.

Today cattle are slaughtered for beef at a much younger age. Even twenty years ago many, probably the majority of steers were three or four years old when killed. Today the average age of slaughter is two years or less. Under the 'factory-farming' systems of animal production that have developed in recent years, cattle are slaughtered at $1\frac{1}{2}$ years or younger. Now, beef from bulls at that age is neither tough nor dark coloured. Nor is there risk of bull taint or flavour. Provided that bulls are slaughtered for beef while still immature, the undesirable qualities hitherto associated with bull beef are no longer a serious disadvantage. At the same time young bulls offer certain clearly proved advantages over young steers in the economical production of beef.

In the UK serious consideration of bull beef production began in the 1960s. Already there had been comparative feeding trials conducted both in the US and in Europe. Beef from young bulls had become fully acceptable in Germany and Sweden. Fairly large imports of bull beef from Yugoslavia found a ready market in Britain. Consequently, further research was undertaken on the subject in this country. It was proved conclusively that bulls grow faster than steers; that they make

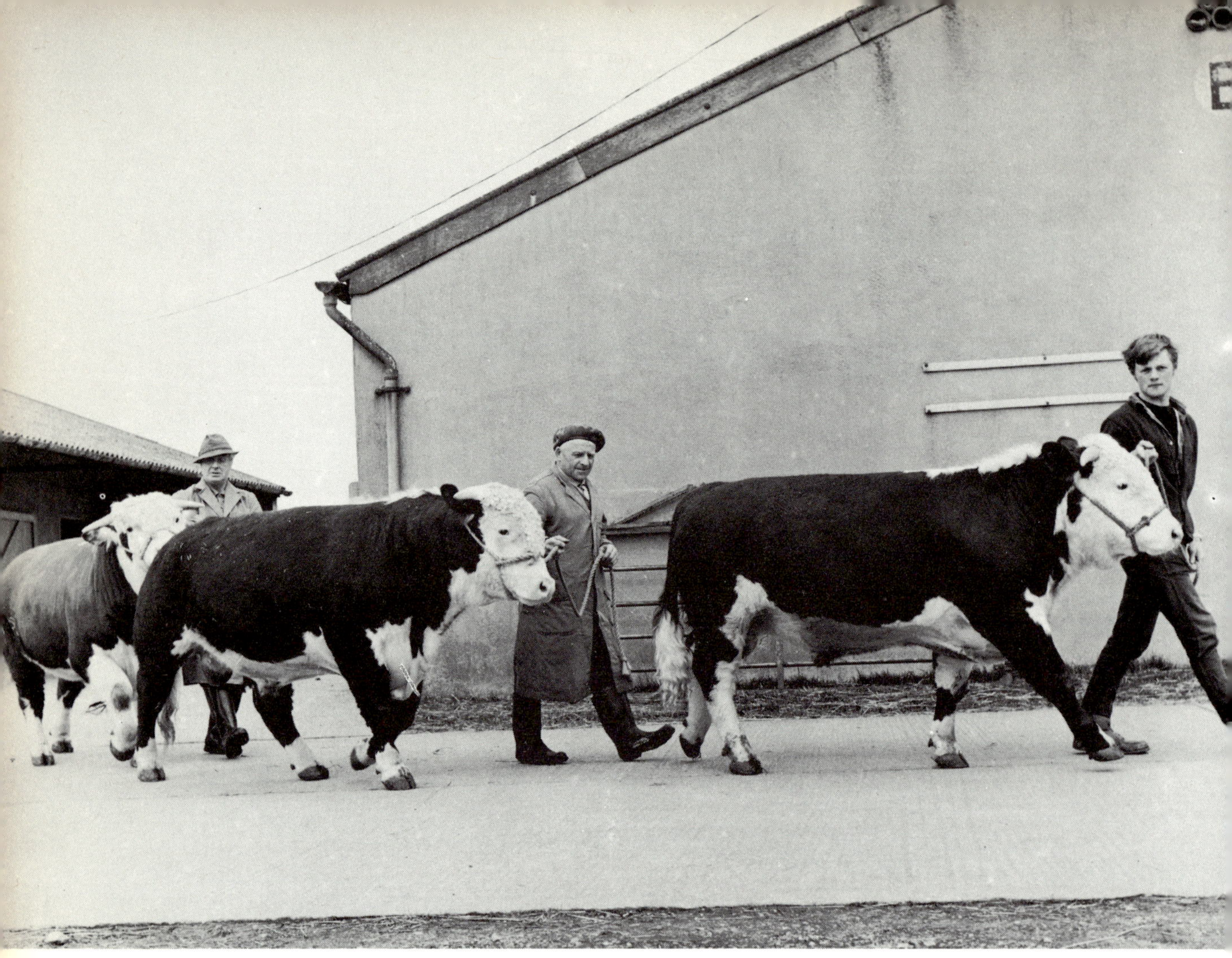

Stockmen handling show bulls. Technology has made a sharp impact upon the pedigree bull-breeding business, despite all its glamour and prestige.

better use of their food and that their carcases contain more lean meat. To add definite figures to these general statements, their advantage in growth rate is 11·8 per cent and in food conversion efficiency 14 per cent. There is, therefore, a definite possibility that at least a substantial fraction of the world's future beef supplies may come from uncastrated bulls rather than from castrated steers.

How do the young bulls behave compared with steers? Both masturbation and homosexual riding may prove troublesome and energy-wasting. Some of the weaker bulls may be badly abused and even injured. They are inclined to fight each other as might be expected.

Are they dangerous to stockmen? That has been argued about and the answer seems to be that the degree of danger depends upon the conditions under which they are kept and the ability of stockmen to control them. Where, under systems of intensive beef production, bulls are confined in buildings, possibly tied up individually, the risk of accident is much reduced. Even then, there is inevitably an element of danger incurred. Otherwise the regulations imposed by our Ministry

170

of Agriculture would be meaningless. These regulations require that bulls must be securely housed under conditions that enable feeding and cleaning to be carried out without the stockmen having to enter the pens.

The question of danger to stockmen is an interesting one. Familiarity is said to breed contempt but it also instils confidence and in our bull-breeding herds the techniques of experienced stockmen are a lesson in animal management. The late Gordon Blackstock, until his untimely death, manager of the famous 'Bapton' herd of Shorthorns at Cairnbrogie in Aberdeenshire, was a delight to watch. When demonstrating bulls in his pleasing Irish brogue he seemed to anticipate every movement, indeed every change of mood in the bull he handled.

Ayrshire bulls are more kittle cattle than Shorthorns yet an expert bull-breeder such as one of the Howie family on a farm walk could lead a party through fields stocked with young bulls safely grazing without as much as a bellow to disturb his leisured conversation. These men handled bulls and some that were dangerous bulls all through their lives, yet were not killed by their bulls. Undoubtedly any man who has the ambition to work with bulls should have a natural courage that can match the animal's. A timid man is useless. Big game hunters assert that dangerous game, such as the African buffalo, can smell fear. Very probably bulls can do the same, and a nervous man can be attacked where a more stolid type would go unscathed. K. B. Jones, after wide experience of producing bull beef on the intensive system (he actually fattened 1500 of them!) wrote 'that there is no danger at all from bulls'.[4] That is clearly an exaggeration contradicted by centuries of experience in cattle husbandry. In this kind of exercise not everybody would wish to keep up with the Joneses.

As stockmen, Jones preferred young men who had had no experience of handling steers. That advice is certainly sound. The animals are different and the handling technique must differ accordingly.

It is, of course, possible to make too much of the danger element in bull beef production. No occupation is without its occupational risks and already in both Germany and Sweden the majority of male cattle destined to be slaughtered for beef are left uncastrated.

The future existence of bulls depends, then, upon the continuance of the bullfight in Latin countries in competition with other sporting spectacles, particularly football; and on the persistence of dairy produce and beef in human dietary. There are many alternative spectacular events to bullfighting; dairy produce can and has been obtained from domestic ruminants other than cattle, such as sheep, goat and water-buffalo. Beef, on the contrary, can be had from cattle and from cattle alone. Because of the proven superiority of bulls over steers in rate of growth and economy of feed utilisation, much future beef may well be bull beef.

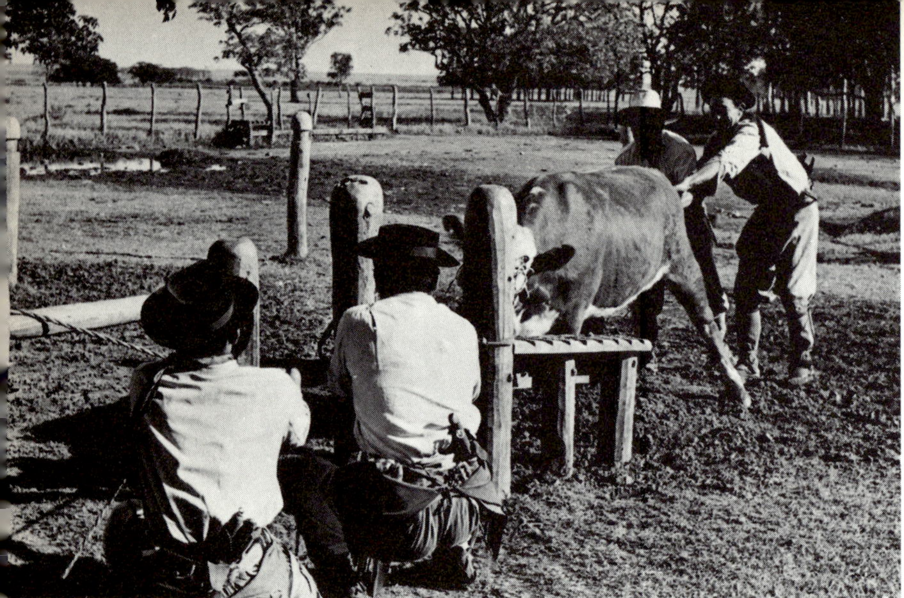

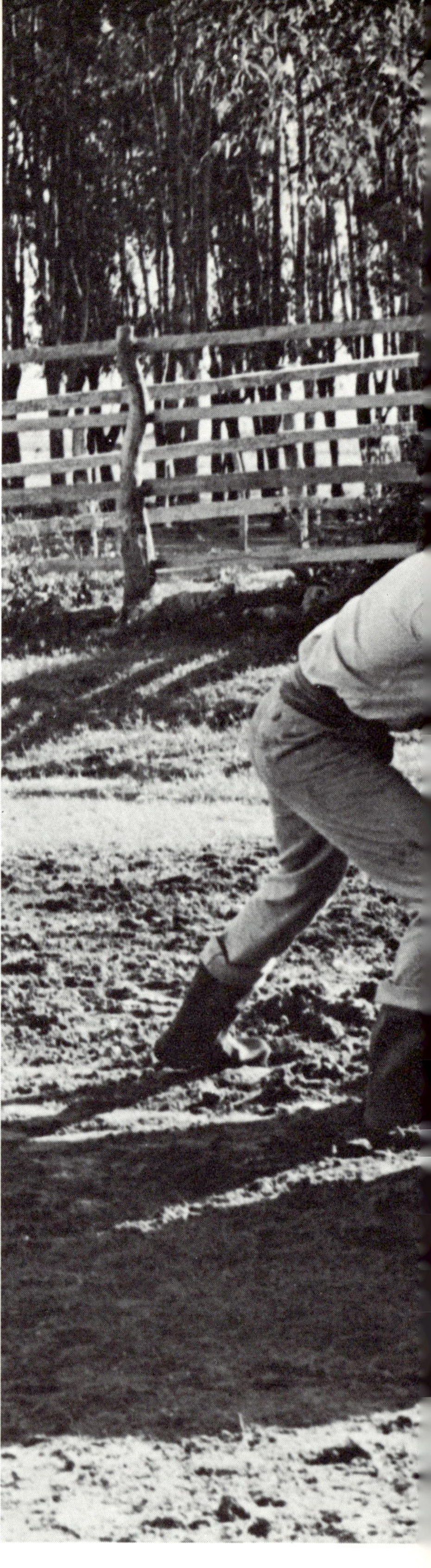

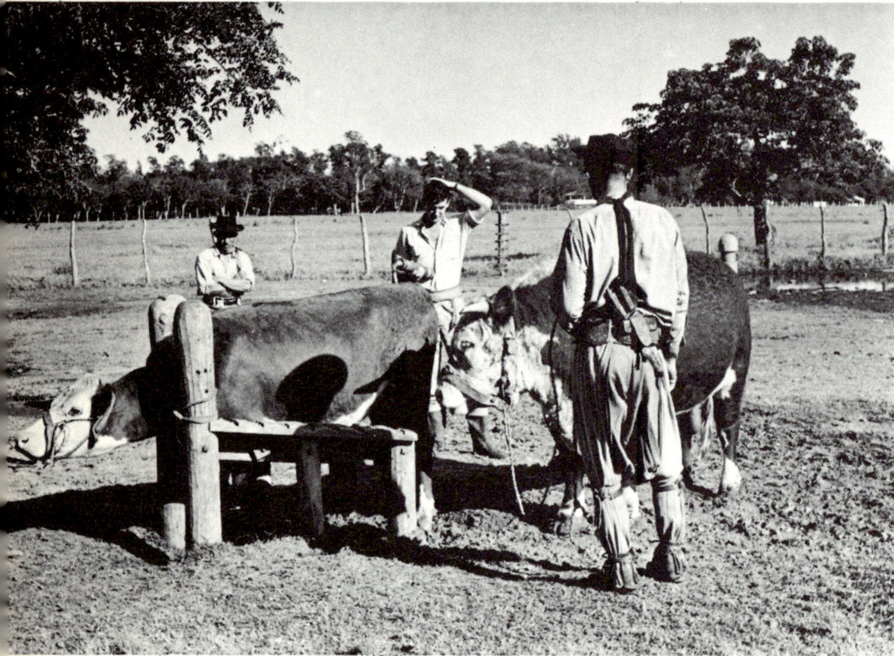

Artificial insemination in Argentina: 1. Hereford cow is driven into a stall by peons and tethered. (*Erich Hartmann/Magnum*)

Argentina: 2. A champion breed bull is brought to the tethered cow. (*Erich Hartmann/Magnum*)

Argentina: 3. Semen from the bull is collected in an artificial vagina as quickly as possible. (*Erich Hartmann/Magnum*)

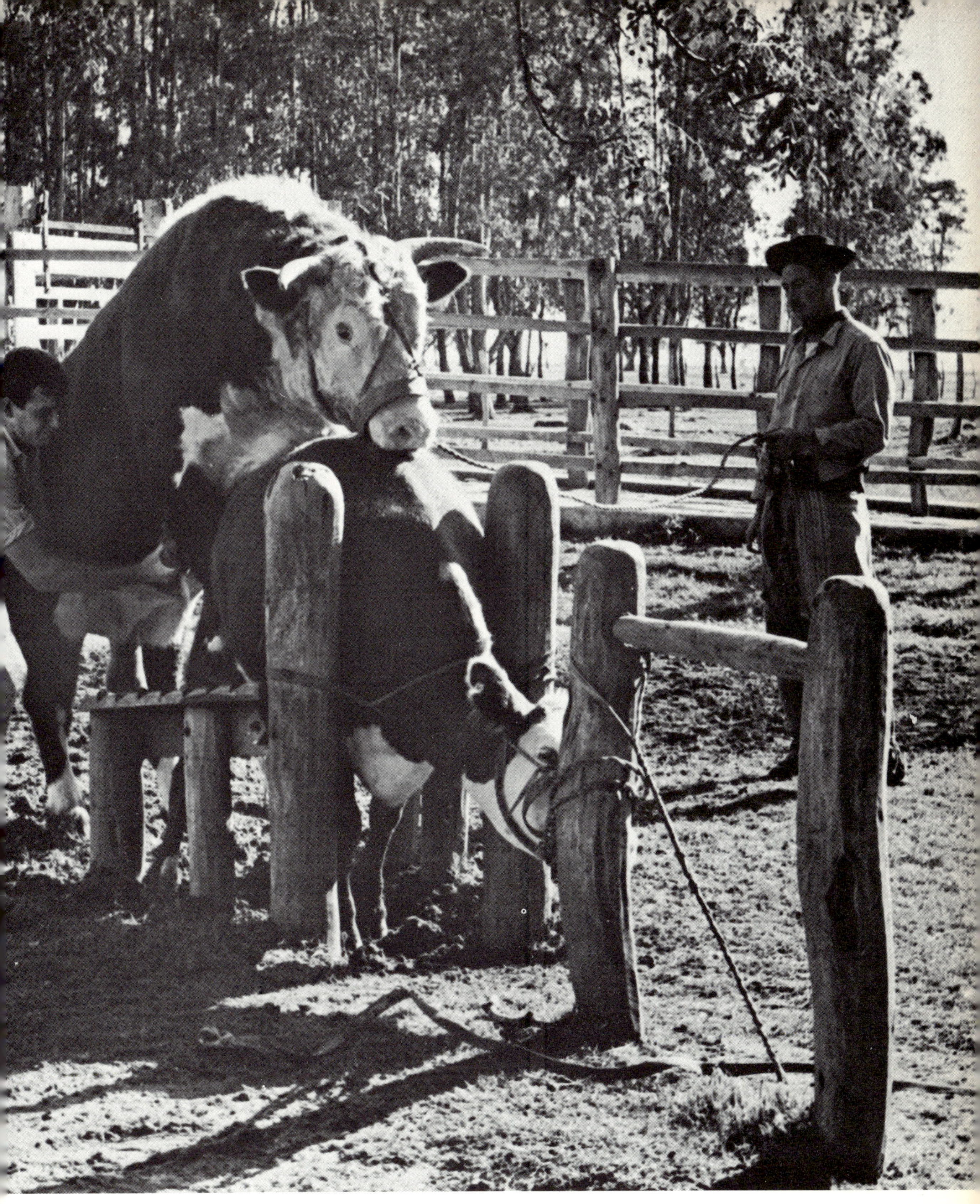

Now, beef has always been and still is a slow and expensive meat to produce. The leisurely rate of multiplication (one calf per cow per year), the slow growth rate (at its best some 3 lb [13·5 kg] added daily to a beast weighing up to 10 cwt [508 kg]), means that in comparison with other types of meat, be it pork, mutton, lamb, veal, chicken or turkey, beef will always be relatively costly.

There is no scientific evidence that beef, whether it be from bulls or steers, is, in the dietary sense, in any way superior to other meat. Nevertheless, despite the relatively high cost of production, beef remains by far the most popular type where consumers can afford it. Why? Most people will reply that it is because of its superior flavour. That is certainly the most obvious answer. Yet there are certain difficulties in accepting this superficial explanation. Now that the majority of people depend upon dentures rather than natural teeth for mastication, taste sensitivity has been markedly reduced, owing to the fact that a considerable area of taste buds on the palate are occluded by the upper denture. Moreover, since the masticating power of dentures is only a fraction of that of natural teeth, tenderness as opposed to flavour has become the most important quality in meat consumer preferences. This patent fact that tenderness is of greater import than flavour has been demonstrated in every meat consumer research survey conducted within recent years. Since there are so many alternatives to beef that are generally very much more tender, lamb and chicken for example, it is in a way surprising to discover in the same consumer surveys, a strongly marked preference for beef.

Is it not possible, in view of the persistent and well-nigh universal bull cult the pages of this book disclose, that, latent in the modern consumers' preference for beef, there remain traces of the reverence for the qualities of the species from which beef is derived?

In every religion that man through the ages has come to adopt, the element of sacrifice recurs like an orchestral theme. Whether in actuality or symbolically, the eating of the flesh and the drinking of the blood of the sacrificial victim is one of the most solemn rites a priesthood ordains. Clearly the belief immanent in such rites is that by the eating of the flesh and the drinking of the blood, the most-admired qualities of whatever is sacrificed are imparted in some measure to those partaking of the sacrament.

In more primitive peoples the sacrificial element in belief may be omitted where men believe that the qualities of an admired animal may be transmitted to mankind simply by devouring that animal's flesh. Thus, in discussing what anthropologists term the homoeopathic magic of flesh diet, Frazer cites as an example how, 'the Abipones of Paraguay ate the flesh of jaguars in order to acquire the courage of the beast . . . and with a like intent they eagerly devoured the flesh of bulls, stags, boars and ant-bears, being persuaded that by frequently partaking of such food they increased their strength, activity and courage'.[5]

A similar idea was developed by Sir Walter Scott in *The Fair Maid of Perth* in excusing the panic flight of Conachar from the historic Battle of the Clans in Perth because having 'drunk the milk of the white doe' he became a coward.

The same thing occurs in proverbial sayings such as 'chicken-hearted' or more obviously 'a milk and water youth'.

On the contrary, beef-steak is commonly regarded as the ideal food for red-blooded he-men. The belief is evident in the Shakespearean play, *Henry V*, when the Constable of France spoke thus of English soldiers on the eve of Agincourt: 'give them great meals of beef, and iron and steel, they will eat like wolves and fight like devils'.[6]

Would they have fought less fiercely on a diet of chicken and lamb?

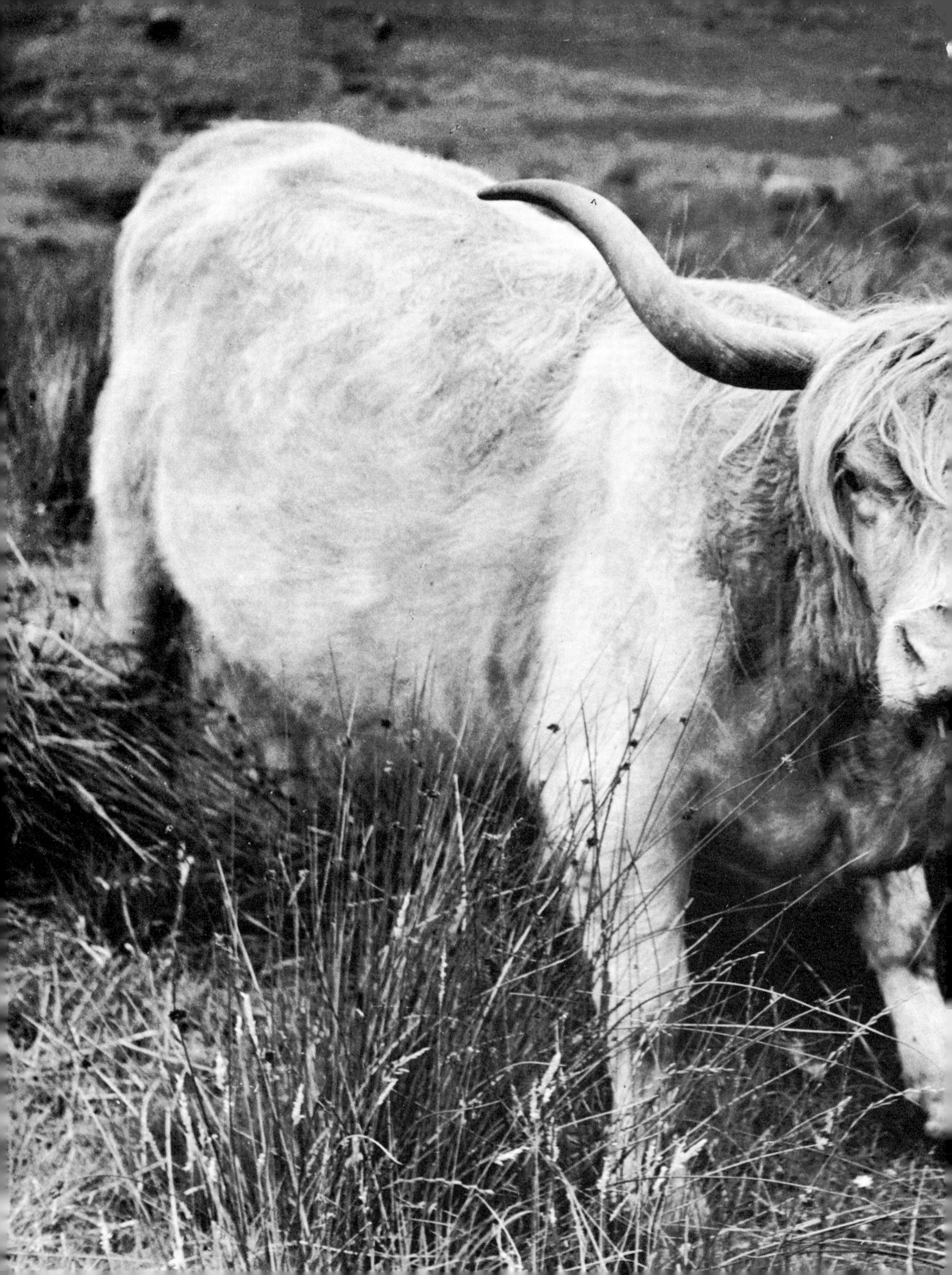

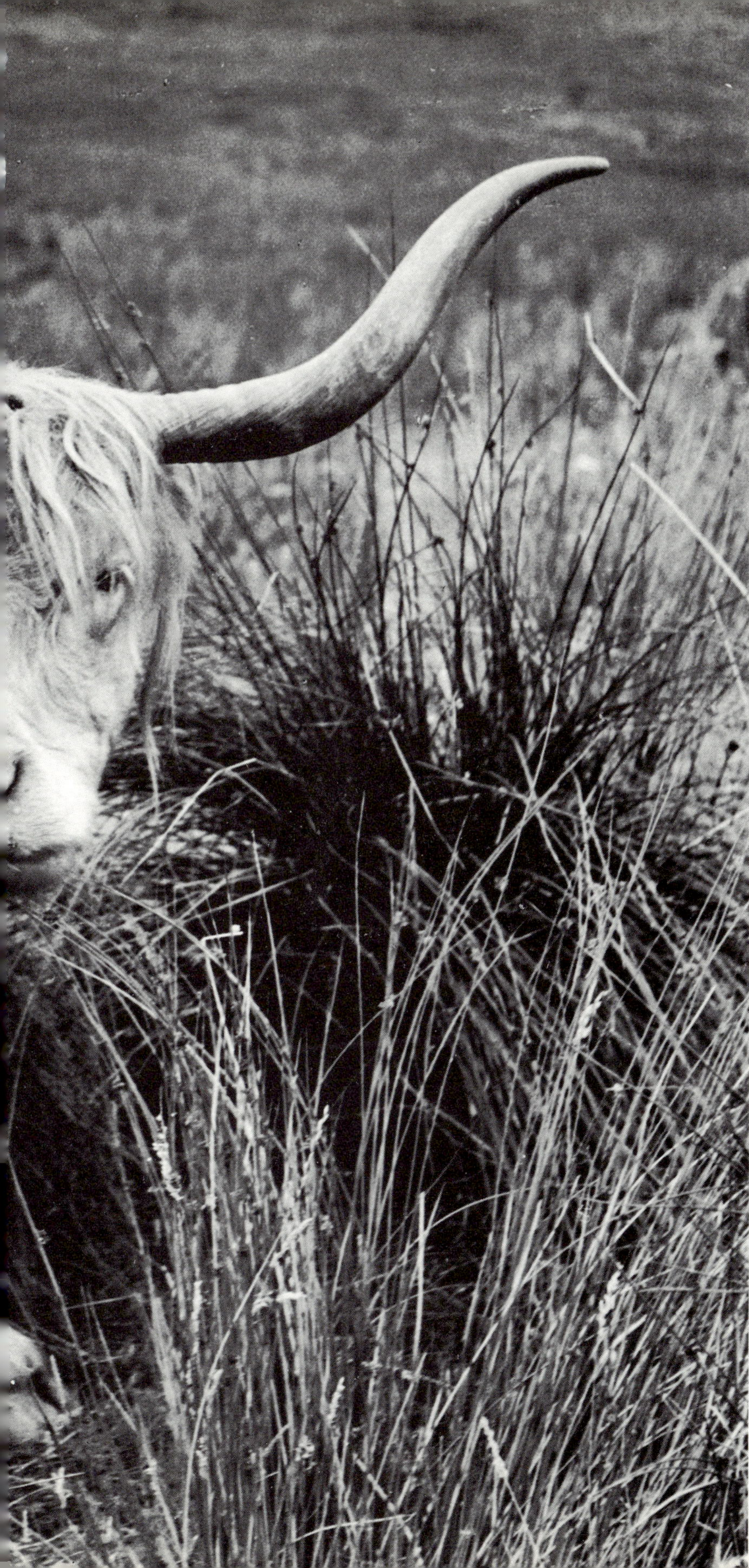

9

The Bull in Review

Highland steer, Argyllshire.
(*Barnaby's Picture Library*)

§ 'The Bull, which to the primitive herdsman is the most natural type of the procreative energies . . .' This quotation from Sir James Frazer's *Golden Bough* is the clue to the strange involvement of mankind with the bull, with man's mythology and his sacrifices, an involvement dating from prehistoric times and flowing over India to Persia, through the whole Middle East to Europe and the British Isles, until the last wavelets of an ebbing tide beat against the shores of superstition in the Outer Hebrides.

A pastoral people, concerned mainly with cattle, counting their wealth by head of cattle, gaining their living by the produce of cattle and, in the end, becoming emotionally involved with cattle! It is easy enough, with some knowledge of the way of living of pastoral peoples, to understand why and in what manner the strange intimacy arose between humanity and cattle, between man and beast.

Without doubt, the caveman hunter came to know, to admire and to fear, the king bull of the wild aurochs herd which was one of the objects of the chase. The testimony is written on the cave walls of

The bull as the zodiacal sign of Taurus. From the sixteenth-century *Das Grosse Planeten Buch*. (*Radio Times Hulton Picture Library*)

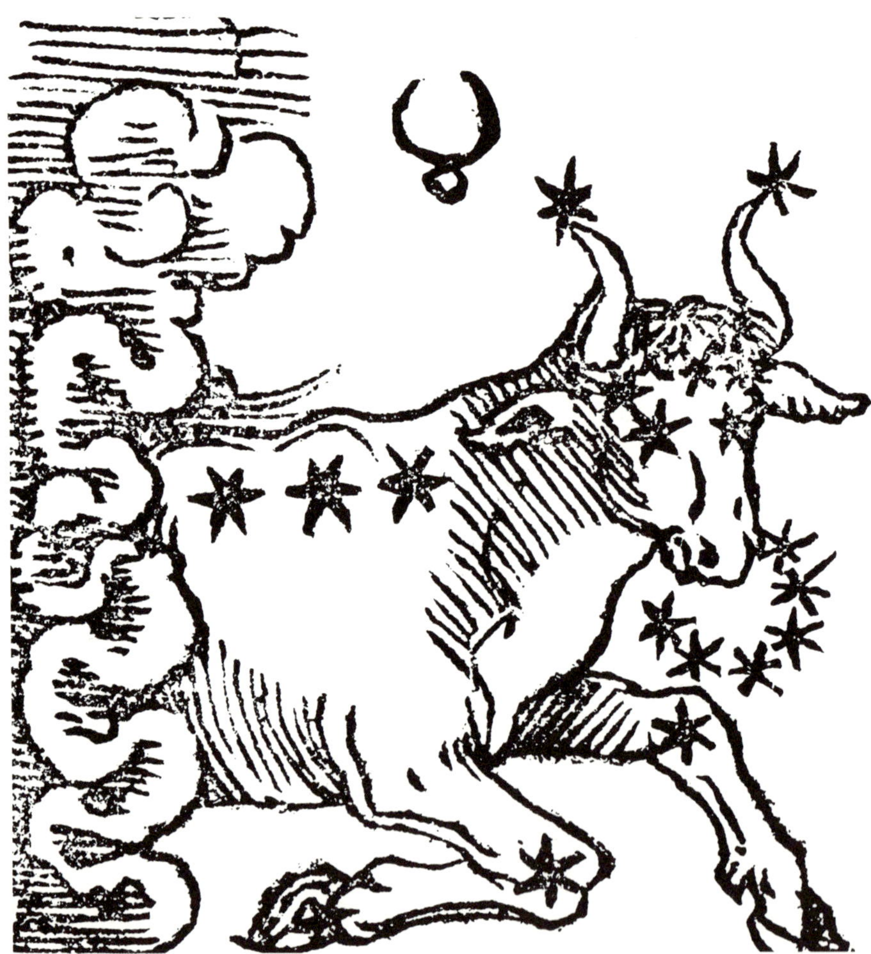

Opposite:
'Avon Priam', champion Beef Hereford bull and winner of the Burke Trophy at the Royal Show 1971. (*Fox Photos*)

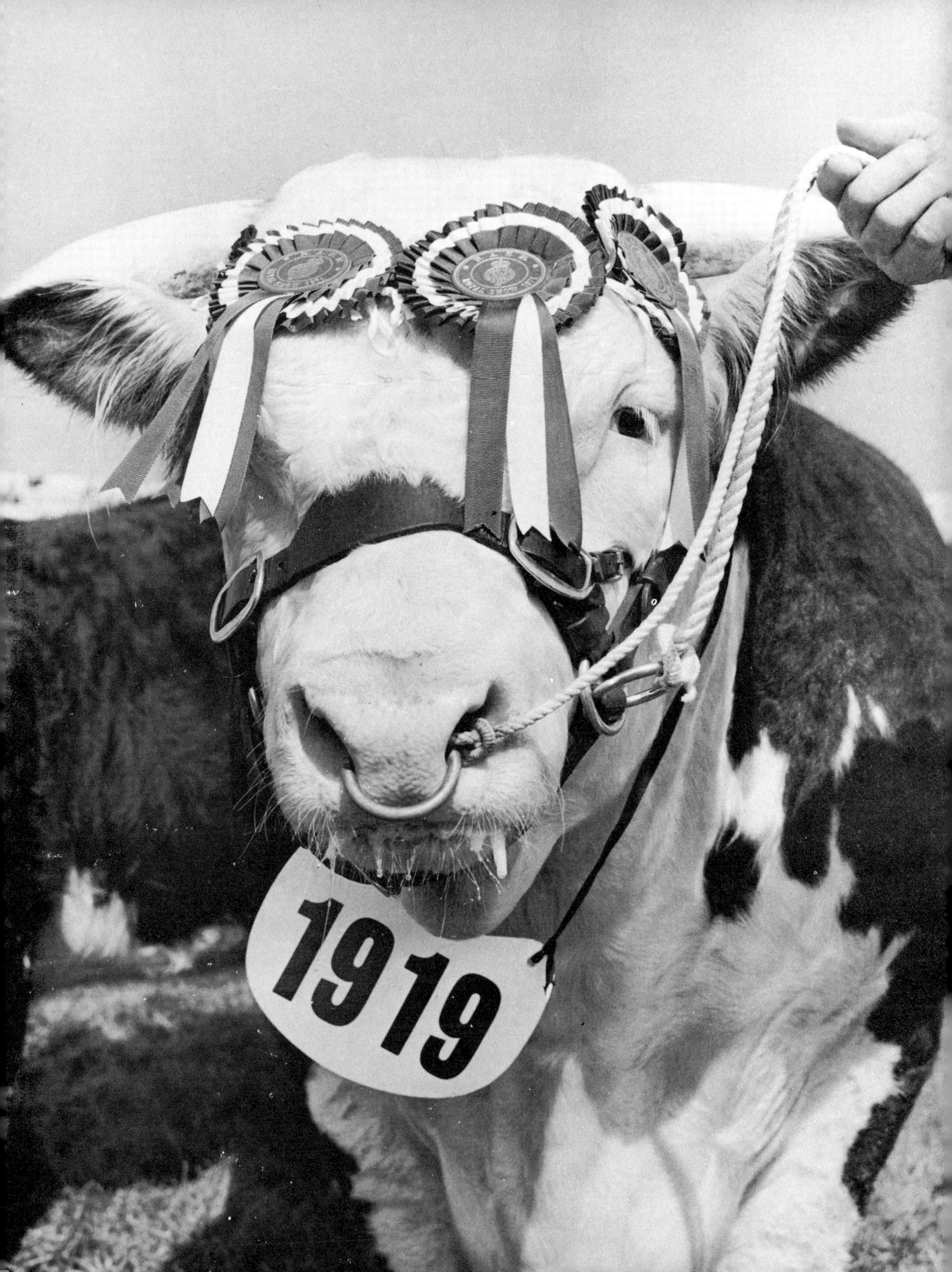
1919

Lascaux. Yet wild cattle were one, and only one, of the many species pursued in his hunting forays. In the pages of the Abbé Breuil's *Four Hundred Centuries of Cave Art* there are illustrations of so many other animals besides the bull – the rhinoceros, the bison, mammoth, deer, horse, boar and bear. Only at Lascaux does the bull predominate. Taken in all, in the series of caves that the Abbé describes, there are probably a dozen bison to every one bull. Why, then, has the bison no place in the world's mythologies, whereas from India to Scotland's Moray Firth the image of the bull keeps recurring, cropping up in unexpected places, in Mycenae in Greece, in Crete in the Mediterranean, in Germany, in France, in excavated rubble of the City of London. In Europe the bison outlived the aurochs, yet there are no records of frescoes, rhytons, bricks or intaglios with bisons portrayed.

It seems reasonable to suppose, then, that the bull cult began with the domestication of cattle. Let it be confessed that the date and manner of the domestication of cattle, as of all other domestic animals, is an enigma; that even the precise nature of their wild progenitors is often in question; that authorities are still at war over the origin of the dog and the domestic fowl, some asserting that they were derived from one wild species, others maintaining that they arose from several. Certainly the domestication of cattle, as of all domestic animals, occurred long before written history, and as to how it first arose, that can only be a guess.

The most plausible suggestion is that, in that transitional period of prehistory when man the hunter was changing into man the pastoralist, the hunter from time to time brought home to his cave or his encampment the young of the species he slew. Perhaps he had killed a hind and then came by accident upon her hidden fawn; or upon a wild cow and then met her trusting calf come tottering to meet him. He possibly thought them too small and useless for meat and hide if slain, or was touched by pity which, like cruelty, is a part of every man, and faced with a creature so confiding and so helpless, he may have held his hand and ready weapon. Most probably, he thought of his own children, for prehistoric man must have experienced bouts of paternal affection, or else none of us would be alive today. He may have lifted up the fawn or calf and carried it home as a plaything for his brood. The reception there may well have been a mixed one, for a child may be either cruel or loving to an animal pet, according to its upbringing, its nature or its mood. Some prehistoric children must, of necessity, have been kindly, or this theory of domestication falls to the ground, like Adam beset by original sin.

If this hypothesis contains an element of truth, why, then, did the calf abide with a human family and become the useful cow, or the reindeer fawn grow up to serve the Lapp as a beast of burden, to yield hides and venison and milk, while so many other animals the

hunter followed – the bison, the bear, the mammoth, the rhinoceros –
have left no domesticated descendants in the service of man?

A Dutch geneticist, Hagedoorn, perhaps more popular than profound, elaborated the theory that certain species of wild animal –
and, obviously, he had to include all those species supposed to have
left domesticated descendants – were tameable by nature, by their
genetic constitution. On the other hand the majority were by nature
untameable and, therefore, could never submit to domestication.
He advanced as evidence in support of his contention the fact that,
while the known and distinct species of wild mammals in the world
number over three thousand, only nineteen, less than one per cent, have
ever been domesticated.

There may be something in Hagedoorn's theory or there may not.
In his enthusiasm for the science of genetics he was, like so many
other and more academic geneticists, inclined to marshal facts to
suit his theory, ignoring those refusing to fall into line. For example,
Hagedoorn maintained that if you take the litter of a wild rabbit and
foster them on a tame rabbit doe, the young wild rabbits are wild
from the very beginning and remain wild. Yet if, as Hagedoorn
presumed, the wild rabbit is genetically untameable where did the
tame rabbit come from? Out of a conjurer's hat?

Another geneticist, of greater academic status than Hagedoorn, an
American called Lush of the highest international reputation, confessed that 'Literally nothing is known about how domestication was
first accomplished.' Yet accomplished it was and through domestication cattle among pastoral peoples dependent on their livestock came
into daily, intimate contact with the people who tended them from
childhood to old age.

Of the customs and habits of prehistoric cattlemen we can hope to
learn very little, but the dependence of people on cattle – call it cattle
culture – survived until quite recent times. The native Irish were such
a cattle-culture people until Queen Elizabeth, Cromwell and William
of Orange ground them down to potatoes and pigs. The Scottish
Highlanders were such another, for a further half-century until
Cumberland stole the cattle and butchered the men.

These people lived under the same roof as their cattle. To a child
growing up in such a closely linked community, the soft lowing of a
cow would have been a sound as familiar as its mother's lullaby;
the angry bellow of the bull as customary and infinitely more menacing
and terrifying than its father's outbursts of anger. As soon as the child
could walk it was out on the hillside, its childish duty to keep the
cows from the corn. Before the days of compulsory school education
in 1872, and indeed quite often for some time afterwards, the Highland
crofters' children were herding the cattle from dawn to dusk, and they
were watching them.

Published in 1822 under the title of 'Oxen, etc', these engravings are the work of
Charles Towne, an artist of the early 1800s who specialized in painting landscapes
and animals.
Opposite, above: a wild bull.
Below, and opposite below: Galloway cow and bull.
Although Towne's impression of a wild bull may not perhaps be the most accurate
record of this close relation to the very first 'aurochs', from which all domesticated
cattle are said to be derived, one cannot fail to be aware of the proud virility,
strength and stamina which lie beneath this bull's shaggy hide. The Galloway bull
and cow show a pleasing contrast between the dominant master and the appealingly
feminine and submissive matron. (*Mansell Collection*)

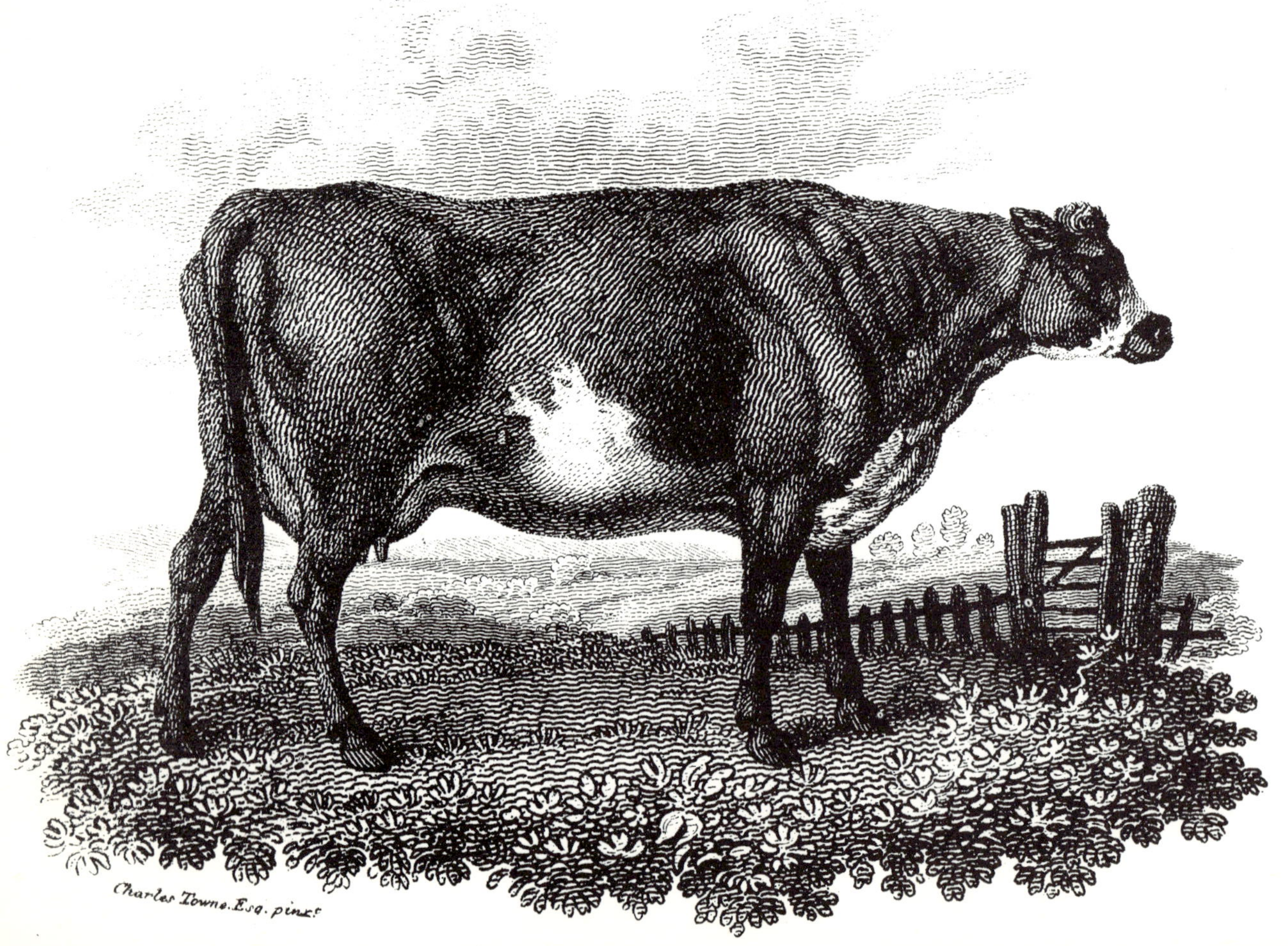

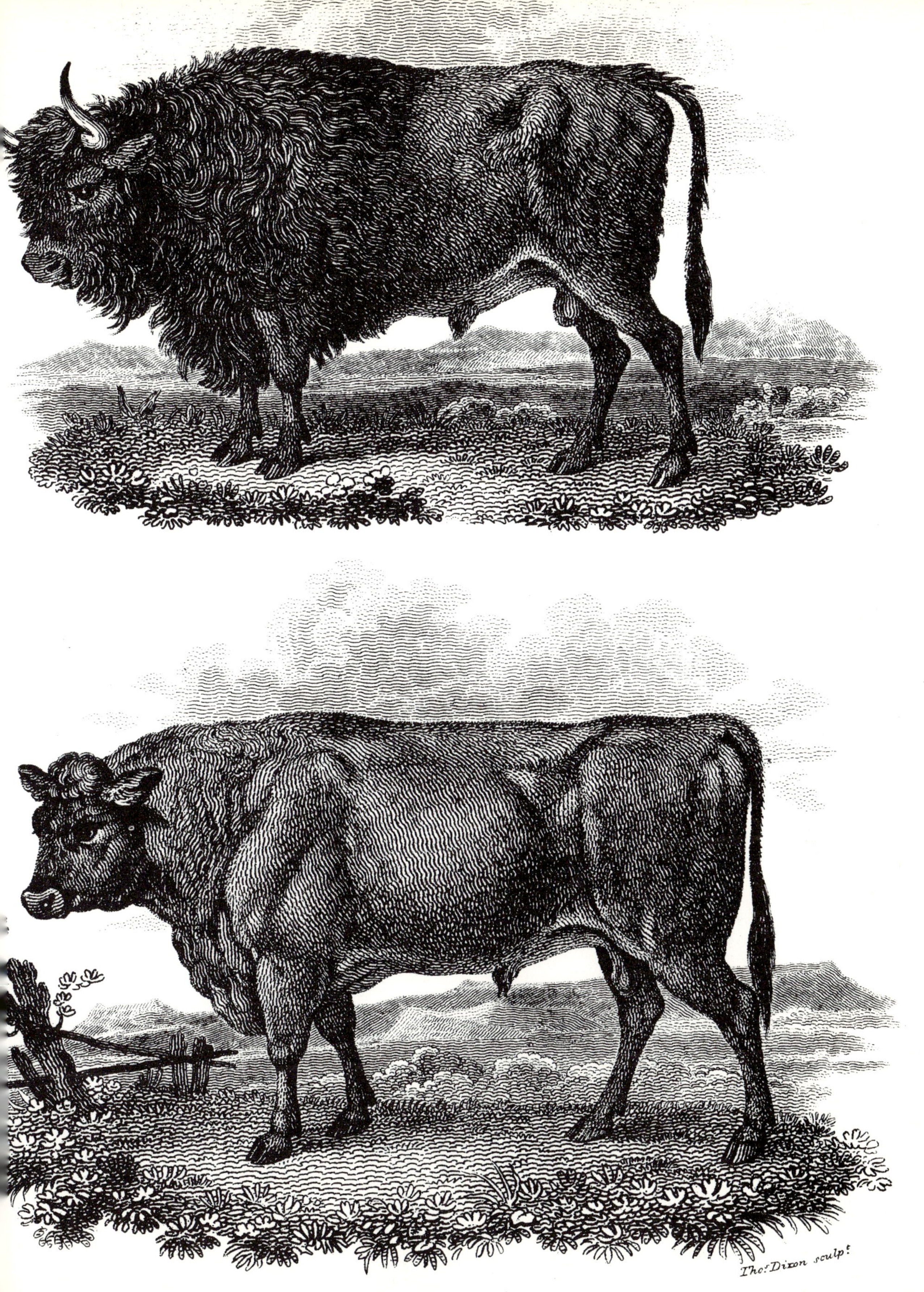
Tho.s Dixon sculp.t

It was then they learnt about what are nowadays called 'the facts of life' and they learnt them from watching cattle. As Colin MacDonald, the Gaelic-speaking crofter's son who became a civil servant and an author, wrote in his *Highland Journey*, 'For us there were no storks or angels about births or deaths; just an intelligent understanding and sensible acceptance of natural happenings.'

For the crofters' children of those days there was no necessity or possible danger in viewing controversial educational films. Indeed, the necessity may seem rather questionable today, when any observant child with greater economy both of time and space can see as much or more of physical sex in any urban park on a Sunday afternoon. Yet, among cattle-raising people it must have been the sexual behaviour of cattle that first came to their notice and, without doubt, the strength and masculinity of the bull excited their curiosity, admiration and respect. They lived, as it were, in the shadow of the bull overshadowing the cow. The bull was the most powerful and the most masculine object of the limited vision of their pastoral world. They

The breed of Highland Cattle, sometimes called the 'West Highland' or 'Kyloe', is descended from the native breed of the Scottish Highlands. (*Barnaby's Picture Library*)

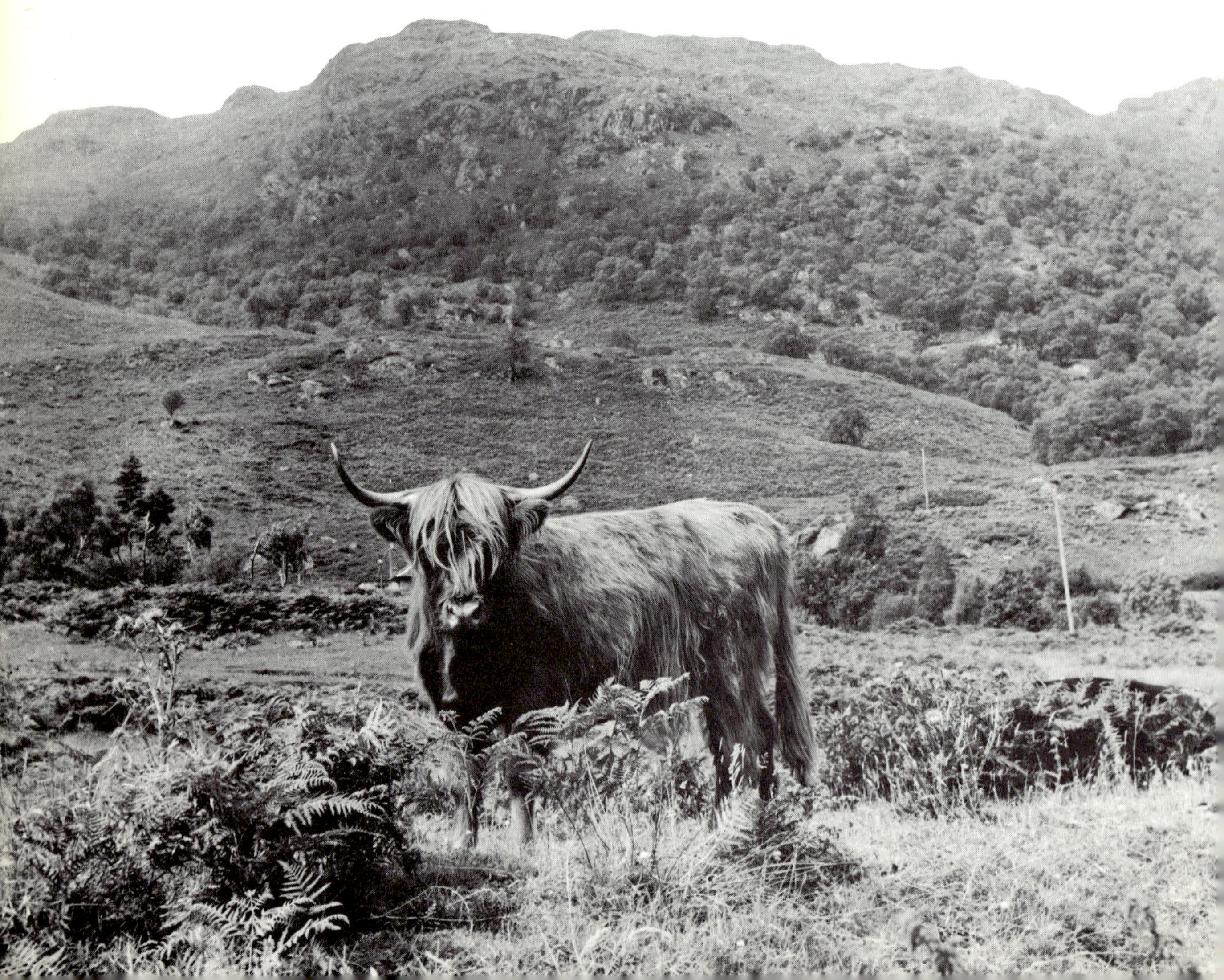

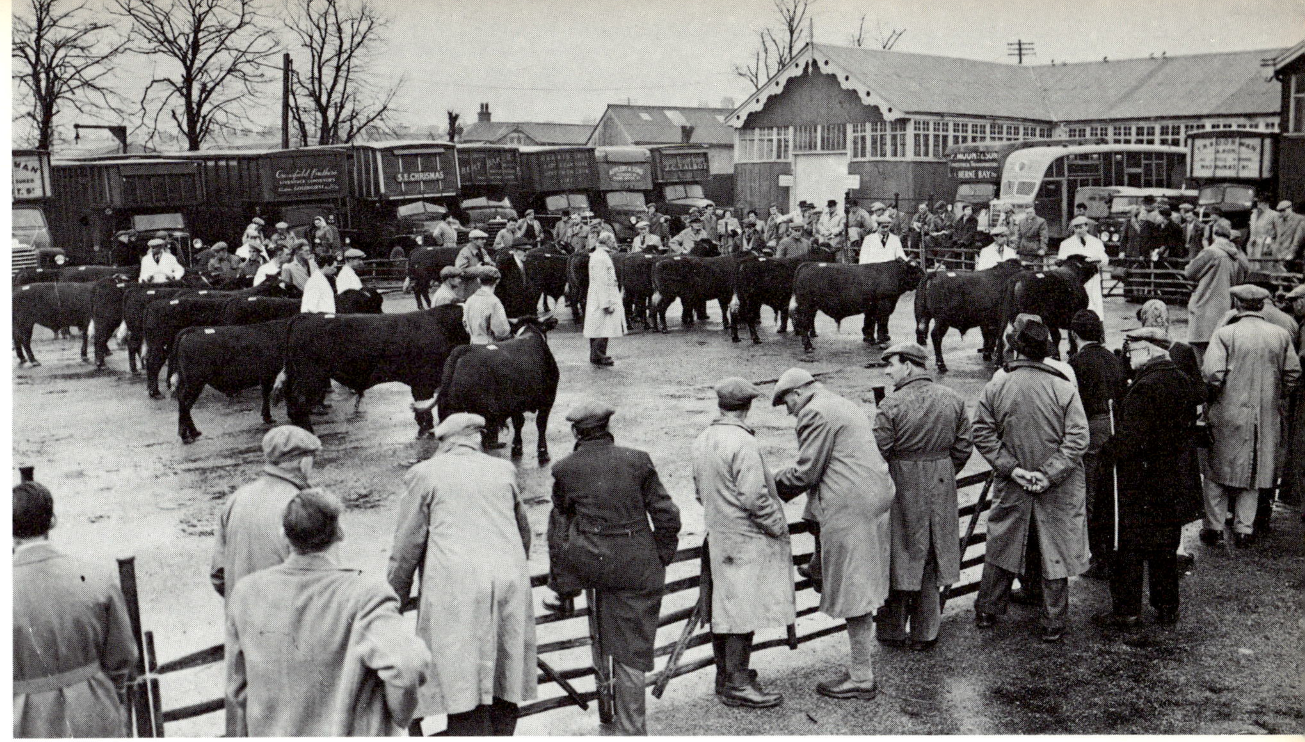

learnt the way of a bull with a cow and that without it there could be neither calves nor milk.

So also in adult years the strange intimacy and sympathy with cattle continued. As Colin MacDonald wrote,

Judging in progress at the Sussex Bull Spring Show and Sale at Ashford, Kent, 1955. (*Photo: John Topham*)

> We of the crofts did not regard our livestock merely as commercial possessions to be ruthlessly bartered for gain. True we did sell off each year the lambs and stirks and an occasional foal; but these had not yet attained to that degree of warm affection with which we regarded the permanent stock. Bho Ruadh (Red Cow) and Bho Bhan (White Cow) and Maggie-the-Mare were more or less members of the family, all doing their utmost for the common good. Consequently when Anno Domini did at last compel a severance with one of these, there was gloom in the household for several days.

In the golden days of high summer, when the people went to the huts called 'shielings' on the mountain pastures, the cattle, the old friends of the family, went with them too and the children, boys and girls, were out on the heather all day, herding them and preventing them straying. Again, the cattle were with them and they watched their ways, 'all doing their utmost for the common good'.

'A warm affection' may go deeper and develop into a feeling not far removed from love. There is no need to elaborate on the subject of bestiality, although without question it must on occasion have occurred. Many a dairyman has had his favourite heifer, many a Bedouin his special goat and the Spanish shepherd in his lonely summer pilgrimage to the mountains his particular bell-wether to relieve the lonely watches of the night. Such things occur but do not mean so very much; much more significant is what goes on in the mind. Many

185

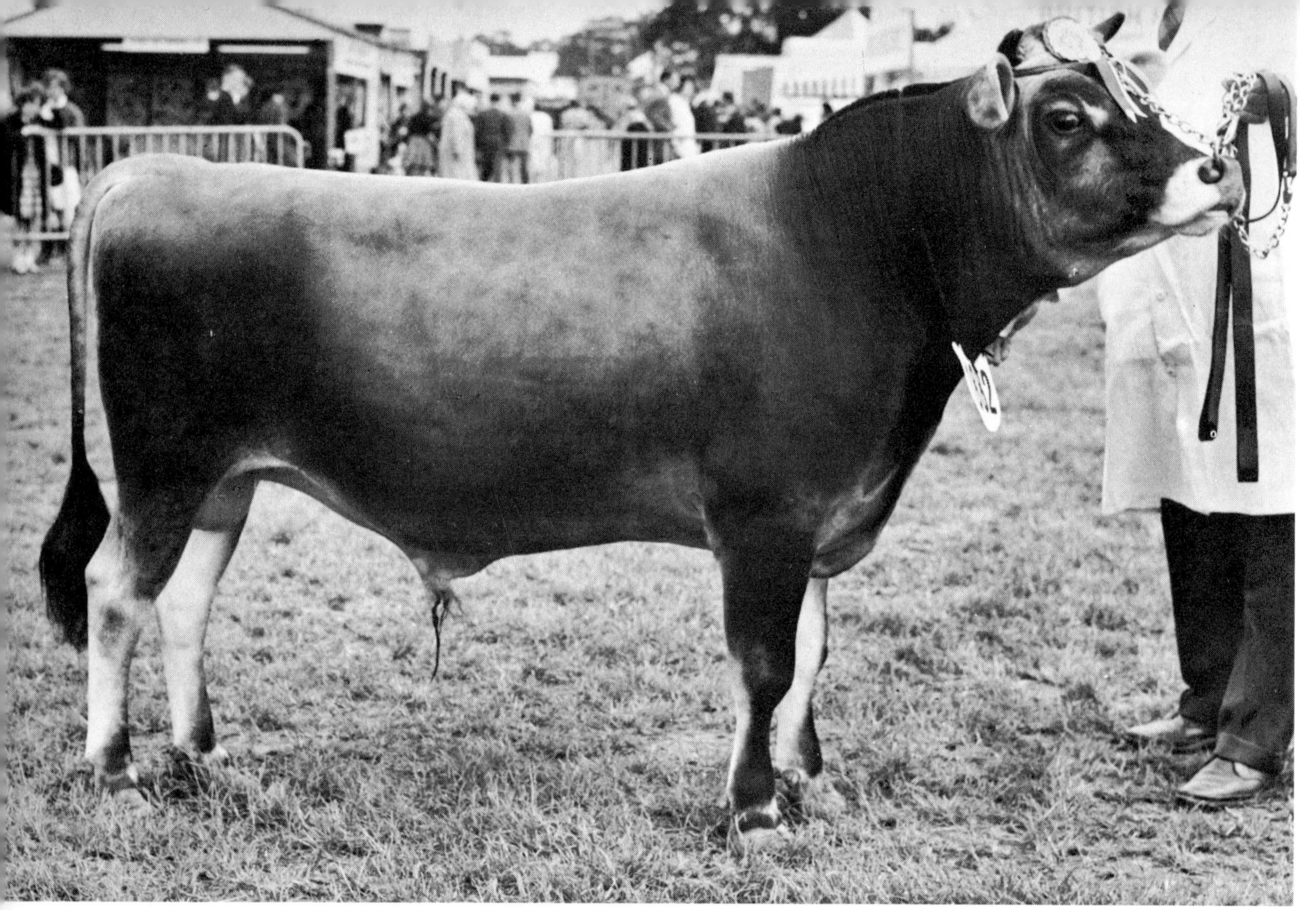

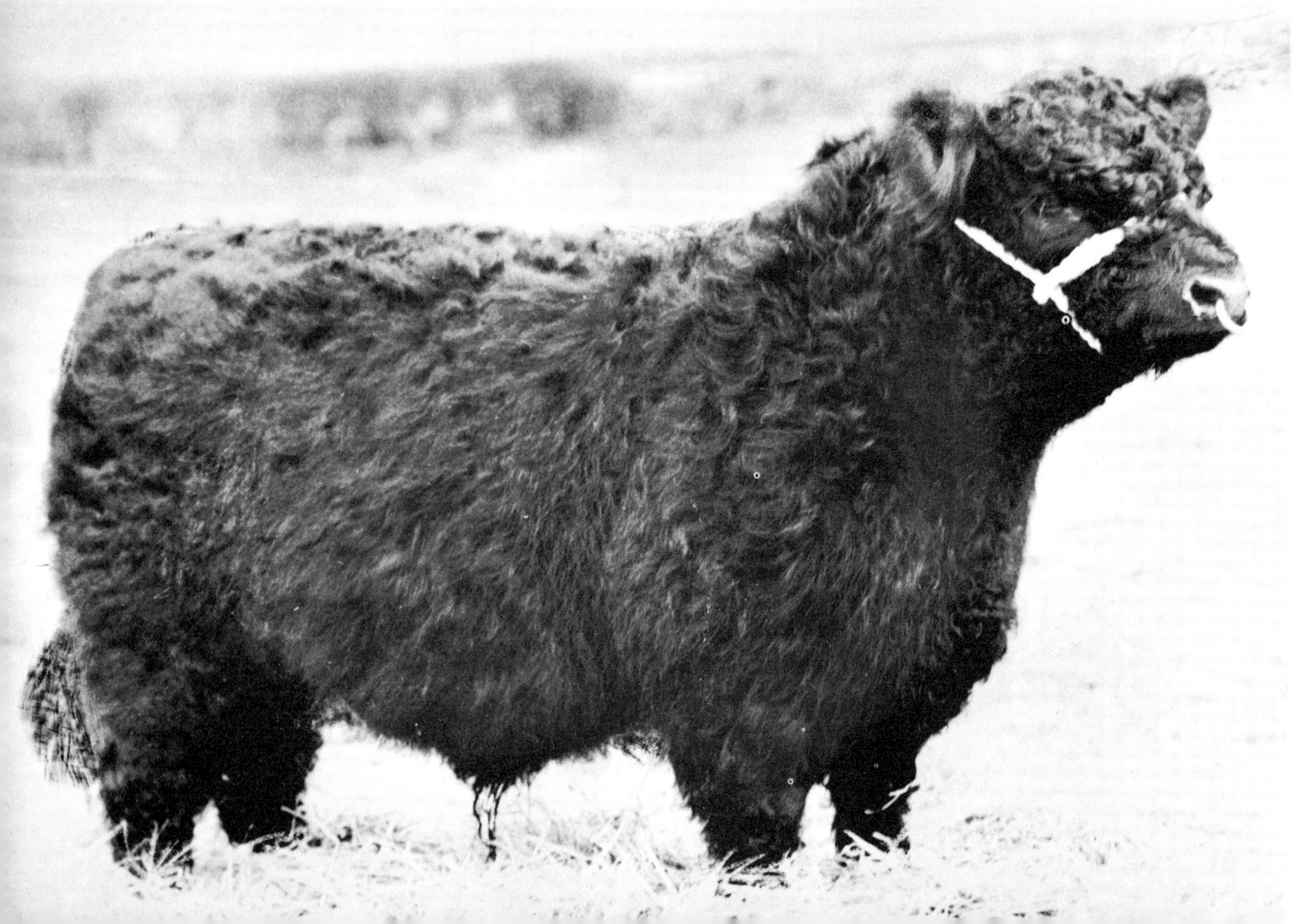

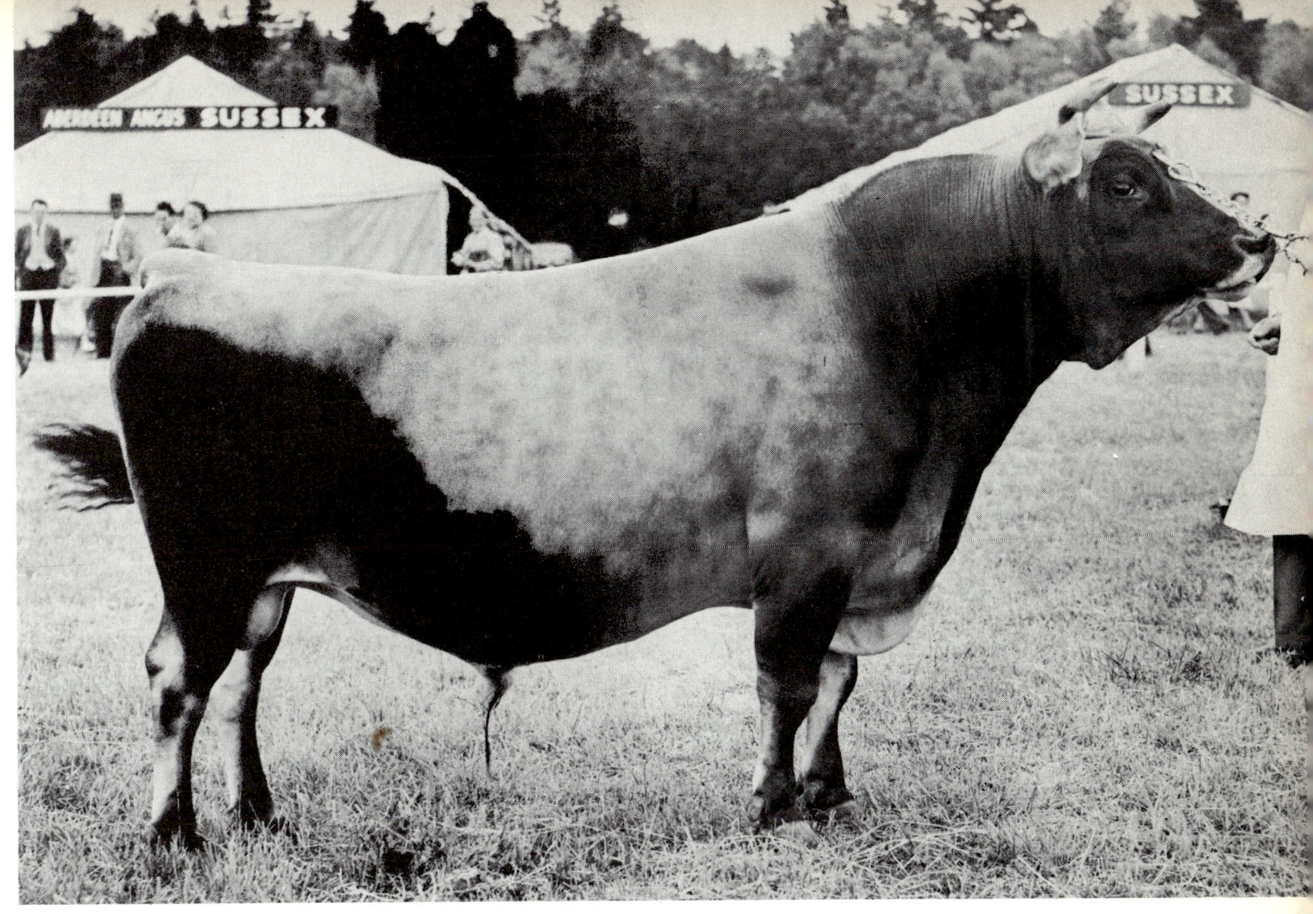

a boy watching the bull in service of the cow must have envied and admired the bull, wishing for the time and opportunity when, without seeking to be a bull himself, he might come to emulate it in lustful strength and masculinity. Again, although it might have required the genius of a Daedalus to assuage the unnatural yearning of Queen Pasiphaë, there may have been women, burdened perhaps with weak, feeble or impotent husbands who, in their secret hearts, came to envy the cow her satisfaction by the bull. Or a shy and bashful maiden, closeted in dreams, may have sighed for the lover with the strength, courage, and sex-assurance of the masterful bull.

The virtues of the bull are all masculine virtues. His secondary sex characters are more strongly developed than in most other species. Fearless, powerful, combative, proudly potent – these are the characters that most men hope for, the characters in men that most women admire and the want of which they find it hard to excuse.

From sex to religion is only a step. The two things are so closely intermingled that it is sometimes difficult to distinguish where one begins and the other ends. The religious revivals that used to occur periodically in Scottish fishing villages, were sincere expressions of genuine religious emotion. But in those days before conveniences such as pills and abortion had eliminated the penance from modern per-

Royal Counties Show at Poole, Bournemouth, 1956. The Jersey bull 'Bramley Zeno's Dreamer' was first in the classes of best bull and best of breed. (*Sport & General*)

Opposite, above: H.M. The Queen's Jersey bull 'Browney's Louise Sparkler' at the 1963 Royal Show at Stoneleigh, Warwickshire. (*Sport & General*)

Opposite, below: 'Plascow Norseman', Galloway bull sold for 13,500 gns. The Galloway's early popularity and fame followed closely on the union of the crowns of Scotland and England, and the subsequent demand from Norfolk and south-eastern counties for cattle for breeding purposes. (*Galloway Cattle Society*)

missiveness, the local doctors were most infernally busy with simultaneous confinements some nine months afterwards. Mythology proves, moreover, how in more distant times religious observances and festivals were very apt to conclude in some sort of free-for-all orgy with sex unbridled.

So the bull, admired and perhaps idealised both by men and women for his strength, courage and sexual vigour, was easily drawn into the realms of idolatry and even up into heaven. Only in the Hittite mythology, apparently, was the bull elevated to a full and complete divinity. In other faiths, as in Mithraism, he more frequently became the companion or symbol of a god.

Admired, then worshipped because of his power and potency, the bull became also the god or symbol of both animal and plant fertility. At first sight a symbol, somewhat hard to interpret, because cattle as a species are far from highly fertile. One calf a cow each year, and the bull under natural or range conditions fit for no more than fifty cows, is no great achievement. Why, in this respect cattle are completely eclipsed by the rabbit or rat, and the boar, compared with the bull, makes a mockery of him. Admittedly with the aid of Artificial

The President of the Hereford Breed Society (*left*) holds the Burke Trophy for the Inter-bred Supreme Championship of the Royal Show 1971, which he has just received from H.R.H. the Duchess of Gloucester. The animals are the Hereford heifer 'Wenlock Oyster' and the Hereford bull 'Avon Priam'. (*Fox Photos*)

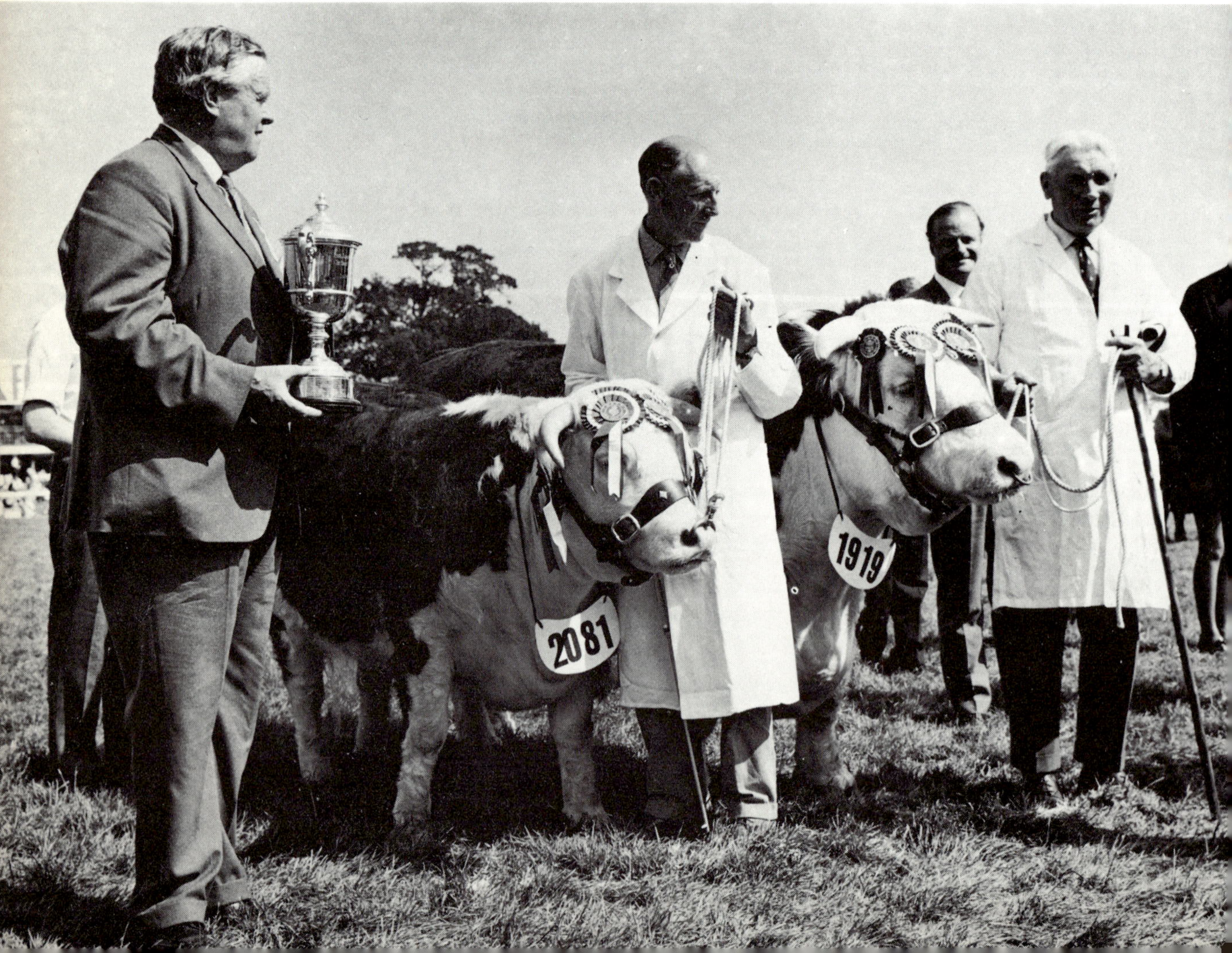

Insemination and the periodical tapping of the hidden wells of his latent fertility, one bull may sire many thousands of calves. Some have sired thirty thousand calves and that is fertility indeed. But the ancient peoples who initiated the cult of the bull knew nothing of A.I., at least in its modern and sophisticated developments. Nevertheless, to a predominantly pastoral people the bull may well have become a symbol of fertility as well as of courage and strength. In a community dependent on cattle, the death, illness, impotence, sterility or temporary incapacity of the bull must have meant disaster in no small measure. Without the bull in full service there could have been no calf crop and even the partial failure of the calf crop would lessen herd population over several years. To the pastoralist, fertility, therefore, became yet another quality admired in the bull.

Now, it has often been said, and mythologies confirm the statement, that the gods may become jealous of mankind. Conversely, at times, mankind appears to have grown jealous of the gods. At least it must have been so in the case of the bull. For, very frequently men killed the bull, hoping that by drinking its blood and eating its flesh, even by wrapping themselves in its reeking hide, they might imbibe, at least in some small measure, his strength, his courage, his readiness to fight, his lust and potency – even his assumed fertility. There was a time when the young Hindu bride was set down on the hard leather cushion of a bull's hide before her husband's door in the pious hope that, by so doing, her marriage might prove the more fruitful.

Again, the bull, although a demi-god in his own right, was frequently a victim of sacrifice to gods of a superior divinity. This is not a fitting occasion to attempt to elaborate or pontificate upon the mysticism of sacrifice. In brief, its essence was to curry favour with a god or gods – to encourage the beneficence of a god in kindly mood or to propitiate his anger when inclined to vengeance. What was dearest to a man's innermost heart was most likely to encourage or to pacify the god he revered. And what more dear to him than his first-born son? Yet it must have seemed to him, at times, that the sacrifice, although most holy, was almost beyond the power of his endurance. He may have faltered or the god relented, feeling perhaps in his omnipotence that this was too much to ask of any man. The Great God would consent to accept an animal substitute instead. It is all written down in that very moving passage of Genesis, in its beautiful and sonorous Jacobean prose:

So they went both of them together, and they came to the place which God had told him of; and Abraham built an altar there, and laid the wood in order, and bound his son, Isaac, and laid him on the altar upon the wood, and Abraham stretched forth his hand, and took the knife to slay his son. And the Angel of the Lord called upon him out of heaven, and said, 'Abraham, Abraham!' and he said, 'Here am I.' And he said, 'Lay not thy hand upon the lad, neither do thou anything unto him; for now I know that thou fearest God, seeing thou hast not withheld thy son, thine only son from me.' And Abraham lifted up his eyes and looked, and behold behind him a ram caught in a thicket by his horns; and Abraham went and took the ram, and offered him up for a burnt offering in the stead of his son.

On the high mountain summit where Abraham had been bidden to go, the ram was the appropriate sacrificial substitute for an only son. Among the peoples of the cattle culture it was the bull, the possession most honoured, most treasured and, after his own kindred, the nearest to his heart. So the bull came to take precedence over heifers, rams, goats and doves in the organised sacrifice of established ritual. In the Third Book of Moses called Leviticus it is all described in elaborate detail – the varieties of sacrifice, the burnt offering, the heave offering, the wave offering, the division of the carcase when, to those cynical of priestcraft, it would seem that the choicest cuts were always the prerogative of the officiating priest.

In Mithraism, the organised religion of the bull cult, the sacrificed bull became something more than a gift to the gods. The mythical bull that Mithra slew gave rise to all the crops and livestock useful to mankind. From the flesh and blood of the dying bull sprang all the crops that men might harvest and from its semen all the livestock useful to mankind. Even greater benefits followed, for in the words of Cumont 'the life-giving blood of the bull became the pledge of immortality'.

The suppression of Mithraism and the triumph of Christianity led to the fading away of the bull cult of pastoral peoples. Was that triumph in part due to the fact that the central sacrifice was greater? Mithra was said to have come down to earth as mediator between gods and man. He was also a Redeemer, saving the souls of mankind and granting them the promise of immortality through the ceremonial partaking of the flesh and blood of the sacrificed bull. In the worship of Christ, the sacrament was similar, but the sacrifice, the only Son of God come down to earth in human form, was something beyond.

Possibly because cattle culture continued to linger and survive in lonely and outlandish districts among peasantries, the bull cult, hidden from the prying eyes of the clergy and the law, tended to survive in secret places. Sometimes it hid its head under Christianity's cloak, at times it joined the goat and ram in celebration of a witches' Sabbath. In the end it became a mere survival, a superstition, a New Year's play-acting that had lost its meaning or as in the *corrida* of Spain a lure to tourists seeking after new sensations. Sometimes it reached the dregs of degradation as in bull-baiting or in 'running the bull' when, like fox-hunting and other blood sports, it descended to mere blood lust and cruelty without the saving grace of godly sanction.

Yet, wherever cattle were kept in intimate association with people, something of the true tenderness and beauty of the cattle cult survived. The crofter's wife, rearing calves with the dedication she gave to her own children; the old master-breeders, planning the mating of their herd with absorbed attention, watching its progress with a solicitude that was half paternal; the stock bull of promise or achievement receiving some of the admiration and respect accorded to the divine bulls of pagan eras. When the bull was led to the herd in the field or to the expectant cow in the covering yard, he was still the embodiment of the masculine virtues most men admire, proudly irresistible in his strength, courage and sexual potency.

And now technology has broken an ancient link that, for many ages and among many peoples, for good and for ill, bound the bull and mankind so closely together. The great body of the full-grown bull has become a mere encumbrance. His strength, his courage, his potency are no longer required. Fertility has become divorced from

Overleaf: Herding cattle on an *estancia* in Argentina. (*Erich Hartmann/Magnum*)

Champion Shorthorn bull, South of England Show, 1971. (*Barnaby's Picture Library*)

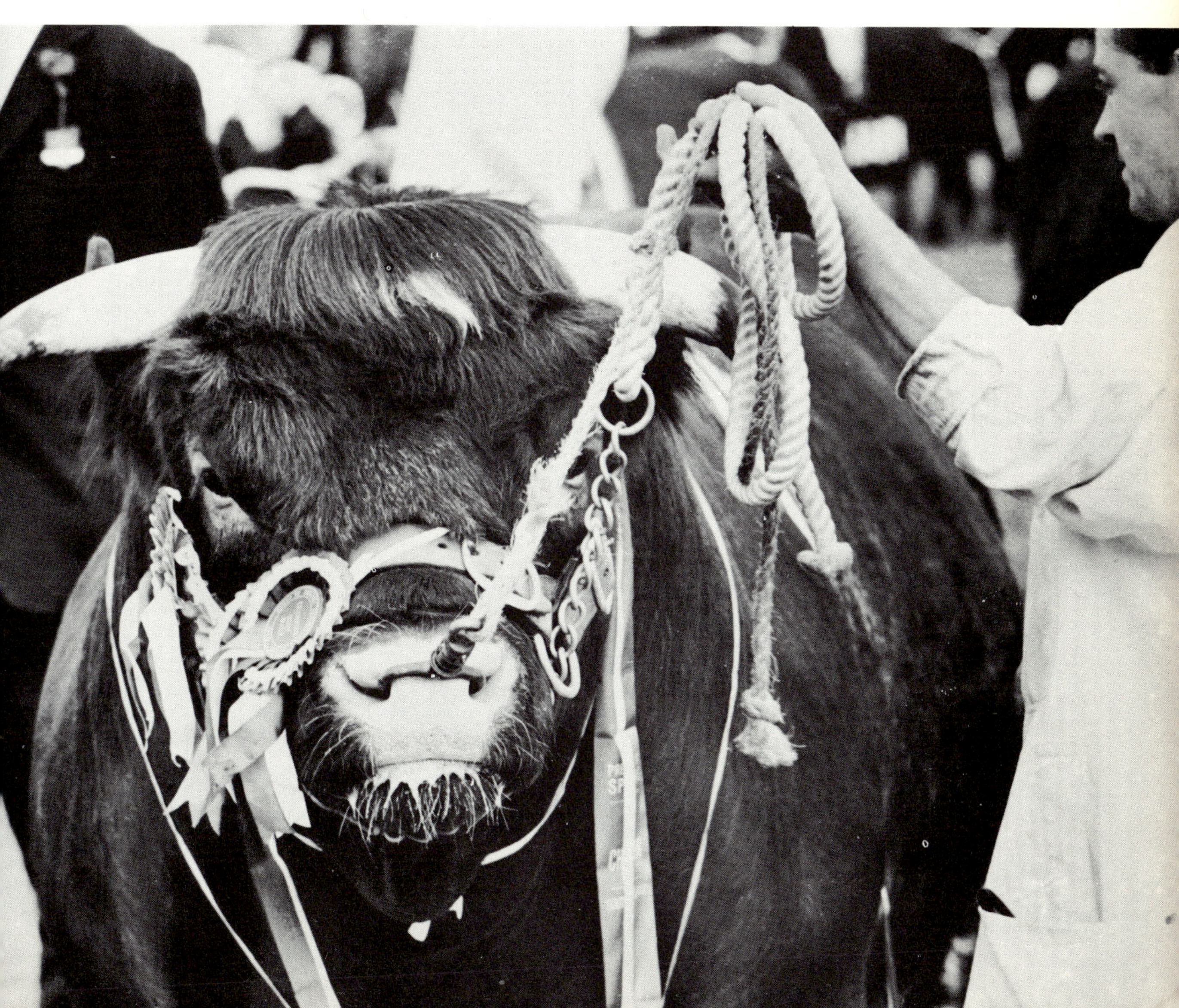

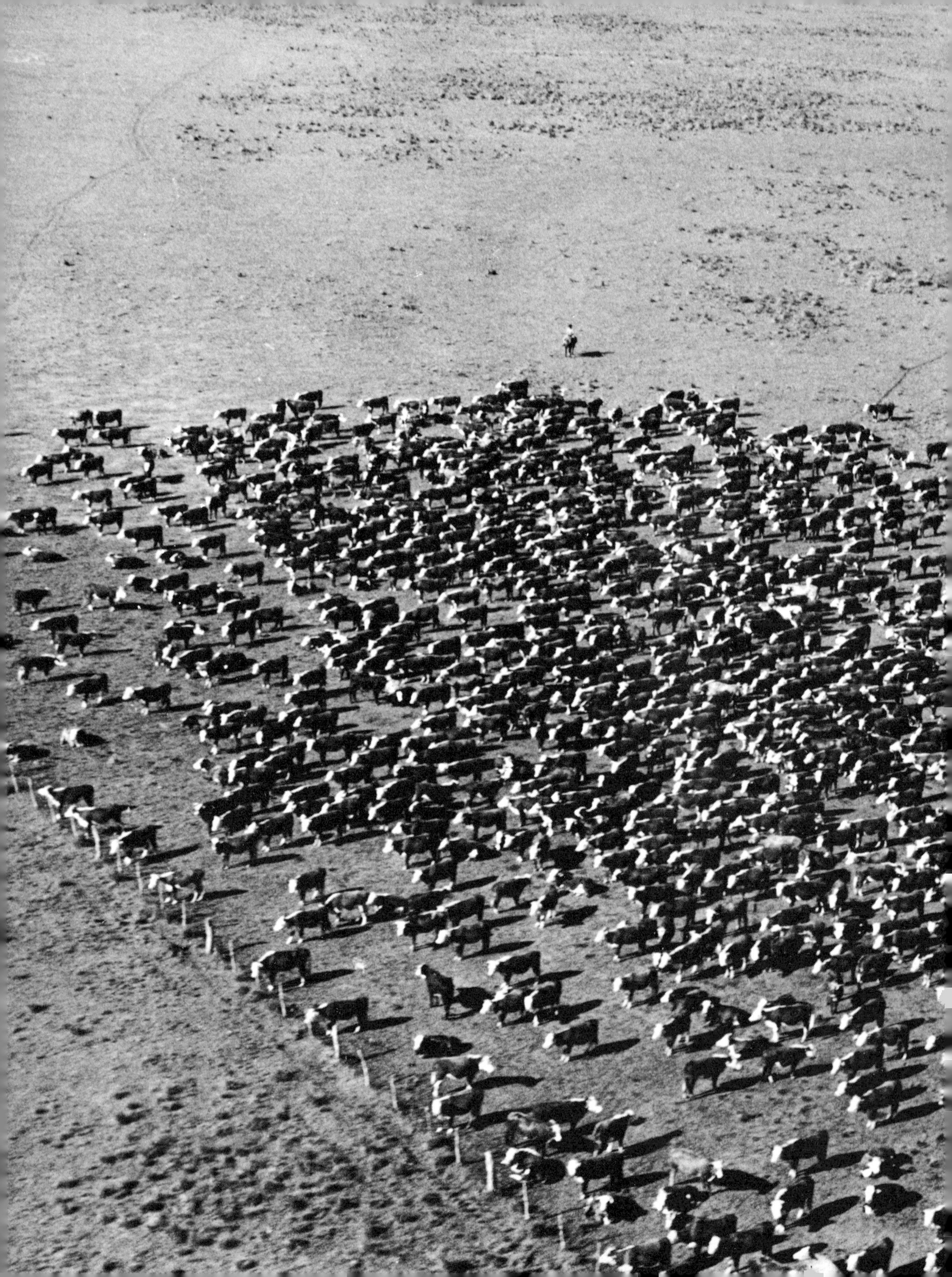

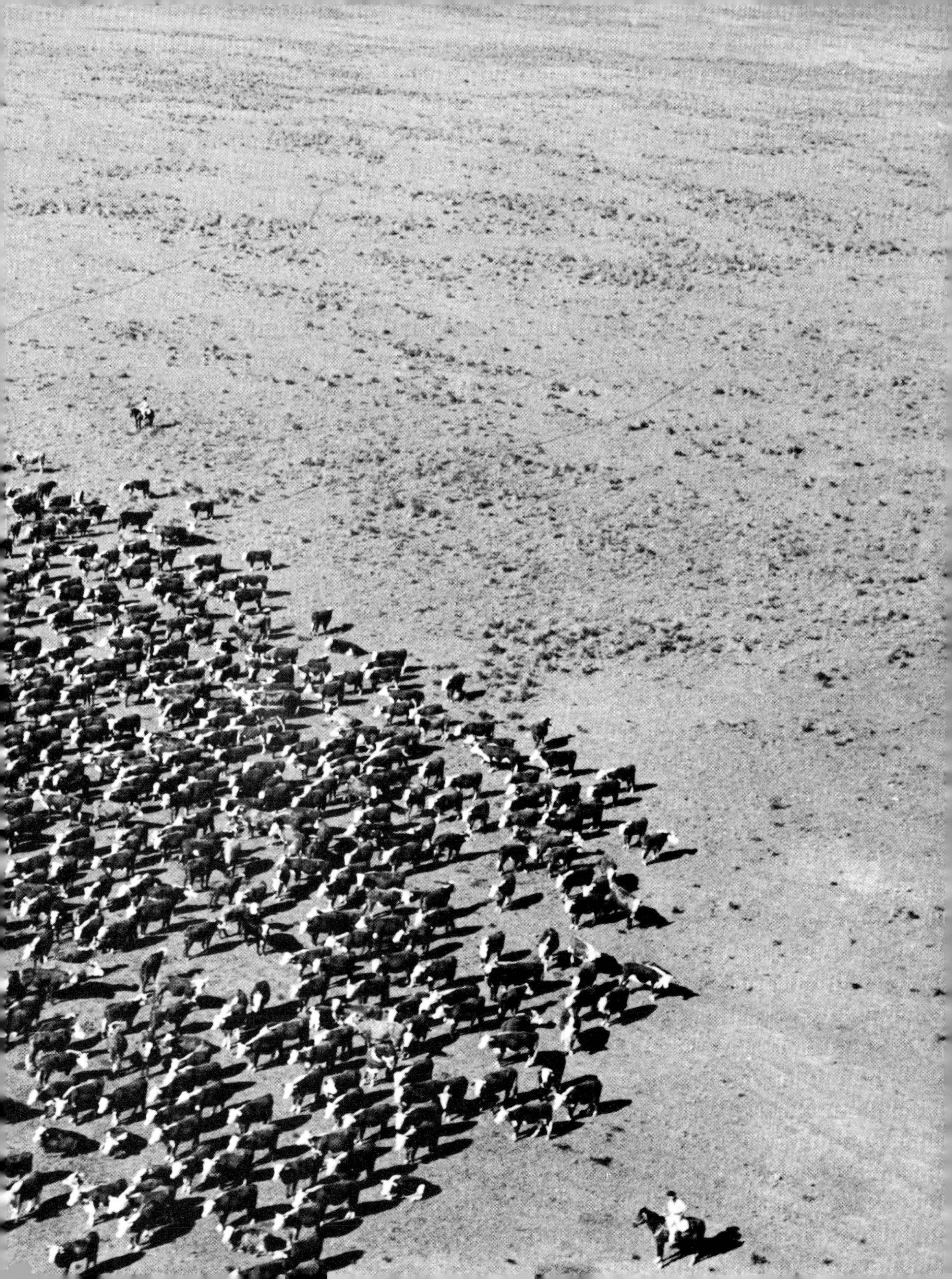

valour, potency prostituted to unnatural usage. Fewer and fewer bulls ever meet with a cow. To ensure the burden of conception a cow must suffer the intrusion of a plastic straw bearing a mere half cubic centimetre of deep-frozen bull's semen from an unseen donor. She is denied everything in sex that people clamour for, bearing the unwanted and unasked offspring without the pleasure copulation provides. Mankind caught up in the slave chains of technology is fast converting the helpless animals he exploits into the image of machines, sacrificed in the service of a modern idolatry. Cattle, both bull and cow, are fast losing all pride of breed, all individuality, all that ever gave a measure of meaning to their enjoyment of life. The bull of proud title, the cow with poetical name – they are doomed to become mere numbers on a filing card system. Man, in his sacrifice to Technology, has degraded his sacrificial substitutes, the cow and the bull; the cow to the level of a mere incubating test-tube; the bull to that of a masturbating machine. Must man, himself, follow as the supreme sacrifice? Or will it so happen that in a revolt of nature and in the shadow of a fading cross, the bull with head down and dewlap sweeping the ground, may charge and bellow again? After all is said and done it may not always be the meek who inherit the earth.

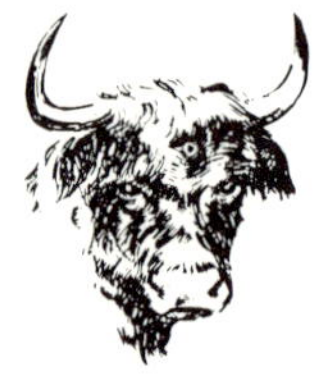

References

CHAPTER 1

1. G. K. Whitehead, *The Ancient White Cattle of Britain, and Their Descendants*, pp. 28, 29, Faber & Faber, 1953.
2. Lydekker's translation of Julius Caesar's *De Bello Gallico*, Book 6, Chapter 29, quoted by Whitehead, ibid, p. 29.
3. Pliny, quoted by Whitehead, ibid, p. 29.
4. F. E. Zeuner, *A History of Domesticated Animals*, p. 226, Hutchinson, London, 1963.
5. Whitehead, ibid, p. 31.
6. Zeuner, ibid, p. 203.
7. Ibid, p. 204.
8. M. S. Garretson, *The American Bison*, New York, 1938.
9. Whitehead, ibid, p. 28.
10. Ibid, p. 43.
11. Pliny, *Natural History* v. 30, p. 13, quoted by T. D. Kendrick in *The Druids*, p. 90, Methuen, London, 1927.
12. Ibid, p. 89.
13. L. Spence, *The History and Origins of Druidism*, p. 116, London, 1951.

CHAPTER 2

1. Sir James Frazer, *The Golden Bough*, v. 4, p. 71, Macmillan, London, 1932.
2. J. R. Conrad, *The Horn and The Sword*, p. 75, E. P. Dutton, New York, 1957.
3. R. Graves in *Larousse Encyclopedia of Mythology*, 6th impr., p. vii, Paul Hamlyn, London, 1965.
4. Frazer, ibid, v. 7, p. 368.
5. Ibid, v. 5, p. 132.
6. Conrad, ibid, p. 97.
7. Frazer, ibid, v. 4, p. 111.
8. Ibib, v. 6, p. 164.
9. Conrad, ibid, p. 125.
10. F. E. Zeuner, *A History of Domesticated Animals*, p. 229, Hutchinson, London, 1963.
11. Zeuner, ibid, p. 229.
12. Ibid, p. 233.
13. Frazer, ibid, v. 4, p. 71.
14. J. A. MacCulloch, *The Religion of the Ancient Celts*, p. 140, T. & T. Clark, Edinburgh, 1911.
15. Ibid, p. 280.
16. Ibid, p. 139.
17. Ibid, p. 128.
18. Ibid, p. 140.
19. Frazer, ibid, v. 6, p. 246.

20. Ibid, v. 7, p. 288.
21. Ibid, v. 6, p. 15, n2.
22. Ibid, v. 6, p. 191.
23. Ibid, v. 6, p. 95.
24. F. Cumont, *The Mysteries of Mithra*, p. 181, Kegan Paul, London, 1903.
25. Frazer, ibid, v. 5, p. 274.
26. Ibid, v. 5, p. 276.
27. Ibid, v. 7, p. 14.
28. A. Mitchell, *The Past in the Present*, pp. 274–5, David Douglas, Edinburgh, 1880.
29. Ibid, p. 274.
30. MacCulloch, ibid, p. 243.
31. A. Carmichael, *Carmina Gadelica*, v. 1, p. 149, Constable, Edinburgh, 1900.
32. Frazer, ibid, v. 9, p. 216.

CHAPTER 3

1. F. Cumont, *The Mysteries of Mithra*, p. 1, Kegan Paul, London, 1903.
2. M. J. Vermaseren, *Mithras, The Secret God*, p. 75, Chatto & Windus, London, 1963.
3. Ibid, p. 67.
4. Cumont, ibid, p. 3.
5. Ibid, pp. 134, 135.
6. Ibid, p. 137.
7. H. Stewart Jones, *Encyclopedia of Religion and Ethics*, v. 8, pp. 752–9, ed. James Hastings, T. & T. Clark, Edinburgh, 1915.
8. Cumont, ibid, p. 146.
9. Ibid, p. 143.
10. Ibid, p. 43.
11. Ibid, p. 52.
12. Ibid, p. 57.
13. *Firmicius Maternus* (fourth century), quoted by Vermaseren, ibid, p. 38.
14. Jones, ibid, p. 757.
15. Cumont, ibid, p. 137.
16. Vermaseren, ibid, p. 65.
17. Quoted by Vermaseren, ibid, p. 17.
18. Vermaseren, ibid, pp. 131–3.
19. Cumont, ibid, p. 198.
20. Jones, ibid, p. 759.
21. Vermaseren, ibid, p. 103.
22. Ibid, p. 102.
23. Jones, ibid, p. 753.
24. Cumont, ibid, p. 142.
25. Ibid, p. 193.
26. Ibid, p. 149.
27. J. Romilly Allen, *The Early Christian Monuments of Scotland*, pp. 119–24, Society of Antiquaries of Scotland, 1903.

CHAPTER 4

1. Abbé H. Breuil, *Four Hundred Centuries of Cave Art* (English trans.), p. 22, Centres d'Etudes et de Documentation Préhistoriques, Montignac, Dordogne.
2. Ibid, p. 23.
3. Ibid, p. 107.
4. Ibid, p. 45.
5. Sir Arthur Evans, *The Palace of Minos at Knossos*, v. 3, p. 223, Macmillan, London, 1921.
6. Ibid, p. 212.
7. Ibid, p. 172.
8. Ibid.
9. Ibid, v. 2, p. 527.
10. Ibid, p. 530.
11. Ibid.
12. L. Cottrell, *The Bull of Minos*, p. 161, Evans Bros., London, 1953.
13. Evans, ibid, v. 2, pt. 2, p. 530.
14. Ibid, v. 3, p. 108.
15. Ibid, v. 3, p. 218.
16. F. Cumont, *The Mysteries of Mithra*, p. 209, Kegan Paul, London, 1903.
17. Ibid, p. 210.
18. Ibid, p. 216.
19. Ibid, p. 228.
20. *A Selection of Engravings on Wood by Thomas Bewick*, p. 20, King Penguin Books, London and New York, 1947.
21. J. Rothenstein, *The Tate Gallery*, p. 54, Thames & Hudson, London, 1958.
22. W. J. Turner (ed.), *Aspects of British Art*, p. 167, Collins, London, 1947.
23. W. Gaunt, *A Concise History of English Painting*, p. 152, Thames & Hudson, London, 1964.
24. *Goya – Engravings and Lithographs*, v. 2, pp. 311–63, Tomas Harris, Bruno Cassirer, Oxford.
25. M. Raynal, *Picasso* (trans. J. Emmons), p. 99, Skiro, Geneva, 1953.
26. Ibid, p. 100.
27. Sir James Frazer, *The Golden Bough*, v. 7, p. 3, Macmillan, London, 1932.

CHAPTER 5

1. E. Hemingway, *Death in the Afternoon*, p. 111, Cape, London, 1932.
2. Ibid, p. 220.
3. Ibid, p. 197.
4. Ibid, p. 196.
5. J. Marks, *To The Bullfight*, 2nd ed., p. 12, Derek Verschoyle, London, 1953.
6. Ibid, p. 12.
7. Hemingway, ibid, p. 69.
8. Marks, ibid, p. 15.

9. R. C. Conrad, *The Horn and the Sword*, E. P. Dutton, New York, 1957.

10. Hemingway, ibid, p. 104.

11. Ibid, p. 114.

12. Ibid, p. 69.

13. Marks, ibid, p. 24.

14. Hemingway, ibid, p. 70.

15. Ibid, p. 108.

16. Ibid, p. 121.

17. Ibid, p. 106.

18. Marks, ibid, p. 46.

19. Ibid, p. 6.

20. Ibid, p. 26.

21. Ibid, p. 58.

22. Ibid, p. 71.

23. Hemingway, ibid, p. 121.

24. Ibid, p. 253.

25. Marks, ibid, p. 8.

26. Ibid, p. 8.

27. G. K. Whitehead, *The Ancient White Cattle of Britain, and Their Descendants*, p. 51, Faber & Faber, London, 1953.

28. C. Hole, *English Sports and Pastimes*, p. 104, Batsford, London, 1949.

29. Ibid, p. 104.

30. D. Brailsford, *Sport and Society – Elizabeth to Anne*, p. 206, Routledge & Kegan Paul, London, 1969.

31. Hole, ibid, p. 105.

32. Quoted by Brailsford, ibid, p. 166.

33. Hole, ibid, p. 105.

34. Ibid, p. 106.

35. Ibid, p. 106.

CHAPTER 6

1. A. Fraser, *Animal Husbandry Heresies*, p. 18, Crosby Lockwood, London, 1960.

2. J. Sinclair, *History of Shorthorn Cattle*, p. 25, Vinton, London, 1907.

3. A. Fraser, *Beef Cattle Husbandry*, 2nd ed., p. 44, Crosby Lockwood, London, 1959.

4. Sinclair, ibid, p. 395.

5. R. Wallace, *Farm Livestock of Great Britain*, 4th ed., p. 166, Oliver & Boyd, Edinburgh, 1907.

6. Sinclair, ibid, p. 410.

7. T. B. Marston, *The Scotch Shorthorn*, British Agricultural Bulletin, III, 3, 1950.

8. J. A. S. Watson and M. E. Hobbs, *Great Farmers*, 2nd ed., p. 147, London, 1951.

9. Marston, ibid, p. 6.

10. Marston, ibid, p. 7.

11. R. Trow-Smith, *A History of British Livestock Husbandry, 1700–1900*, p. 235,

Routledge & Kegan Paul, London, 1959.
12. A. Stewart, *The Development of the Dairy Shorthorn in Britain*, Journal of the Royal Agricultural Society of England, III, 63, 1950.
13. Stewart, ibid, p. 65.

CHAPTER 7

1. J. A. Wallace, *Farm Livestock of Great Britain*, 5th edn., p. 103, Oliver & Boyd, Edinburgh, 1923.
2. Ibid, p. 112.
3. Ibid, p. 127.
4. Memorandum on Aberdeen-Angus Cattle Breed Society Publication, p. 1.
5. A. Fraser, *Beef Cattle Husbandry*, 2nd edn., p. 65, Crosby Lockwood, London, 1959.
6. Aberdeen-Angus Review, 1919, v. 1, p. 5.
7. Aberdeen-Angus Breed Society Handbook, p. 6.
8. Fraser, ibid, pp. 65, 66.
9. *British Pedigreed Cattle*, p. 4.
10. J. Macintosh, British Dairy Farmers' Association, September 1945.
11. Wallace, ibid, p. 218.
12. A. Robertson and A. A. Asker, *The Genetic History and Breed Structure of British Friesian Cattle*, Empire Journal, Experimental Agriculture, 19, pp. 118–27.
13. G. M. Odlum, *An Analysis of the Manningford Herd of British Friesians*, p. 73.
14. J. K. Stanford, *British Friesians, A History of the Breed*, p. 156, Max Parrish, London, 1956.
15. Wallace, ibid, p. 229.
16. Ibid.
17. A. Fraser and J. T. Stamp, *Sheep Husbandry and Diseases*, 5th edn., p. 48, Crosby Lockwood, London, 1968.

CHAPTER 8

1. W. C. Miller, *Variations in Male Sex Behaviour*, pp. 14–24, Proceedings of the British Society of Animals Production, 1950–1.
2. J. R. Conrad, *The Horn and the Sword*, p. 143, E. P. Dutton, New York, 1957.
3. Sir James Frazer, *The Golden Bough*, v. 5, p. 276, Macmillan, London, 1932.
4. K. B. Jones, *Meat Production from Entire Male Animals*, p. 179, ed. Rhodes, A. N. Churchill, London, 1969.
5. Frazer, ibid, v. 8, p. 140.
6. Shakespeare, *Henry V*, Act III, Scene 7.

Index

(Page numbers in italic refer to illustration captions)

Aberdeen-Angus beef bulls 98, 116, 122, *125*, 127, 136, 142, 162
breeding of 137–42
A General Treatise on Cattle etc. (Lawrence) 134
Ahriman (Mithraic equivalent of Satan) 57
Amenemhet, tomb of, bull painting in *16*
'Ancient White Cattle of Britain and their Descendants' 16, 23
Ancient White Cattle of Cadzow 16–20
Animal Health Trust 160
Apis, sacred bull of Egypt 29
bronze statue of *29*
Argentinian Hereford bull *125*
Ariadne, statuette of *72*
Artificial Insemination 143, 159–60, 162–8, *166*, 189
in Argentina *172*
art, the bull in 11, 69–87
Asker 145
Assur-nasir-pal, palace of winged man-headed bull from *67*
Attis, ritual of 40
aurochs 10–23, 97
Caesar's description of 13
painting of *15*
Pliny's description of 13
paintings of in the caves of Lascaux *13*, 70
status of the king 10–11
Zeuner's description of 14
see also bull
'Avon Priam' (Hereford bull) *178*
Ayrshire bulls 146–7, *147*, 148, 171

Bakewell, Robert 114, *115*, 134
breeding techniques of 115, 116, 132, 136, 137
Bantu mythology, bull in 40
'Bapton' herd of Shorthorns 171
Barclay of Urie, Captain 118–19, 137
Bates, Thomas 116, 118, 129
beef cattle 171–4
Beef Shorthorn 118, *119*, 120, 121, 162, 167
Beilby 103
Benzies, John 139
Bewick, Thomas 81, *81*, 103
Biggar, Andrew 19
Blackstock, Gordon 171
Book of Leinster 37
Book of the Dun Cow 37
Booth, Richard 116, 118
Bos indicus (aurochs) 11
primigenius 11, 70
taurus 11
Brahman bull *142*, *148*, *155*
beef-type *139*
pottery *97*
'Bramley Zeno's Dreamer' (Jersey bull) *187*
breeding procedure of pedigree cattle 114–29
Breeding Society 126
breed societies 167
Breuil, Abbé H. 11, 70, 180
British Friesian bull *82*, *97*, 143–4, *145*
British Friesian Cattle Society 144
British Friesians (Stanford) 146
Brown Bull of Cuailgne 37

'Browney's Louise Sparkler' (Jersey
  bull) *187*
Brown, Professor Baldwin 72, 73
Buchis, mythological bull 29
bull
  anatomy of the fighting 98–9
  as a zodiacal sign *178*
  breeding and training of the
    fighting 100–3
  castration of 114, 158–9, 161
  compared to the Devil 79
  congenital abnormality in 161
  copper bulls at Tell-el-Obeid *66*
  Cretan 30–1, 72, 98
  depicted on an ostrakon *16*
  fertility and potency of 159–61
  figure of Minoan acrobat and *77*
  figure of (Larsa Dynasty) *78*
  in ancient Egypt 27–30
  in art 69–87
  in Bantu mythology 40
  in Celtic mythology 34, 37
  in farming 131–55
  in Greek mythology 30–4, 40, 41
  in mythology 25–44
  in Persian mythology 48
  in religion 47–66
  in Scottish mythology 42–4
  in sport 89–110
  in technology 157–75
  interpretation of Mithra's
    sacrifice of the 57–8
  king 10–11, 20
  mural of (Ishtar Gate) *19*, 65
  pedigree 113–29
  sacrifice of 30, 34, 40–2, 47, *65*,
    101–2
  Spanish fighting 16, 39
  statue of a sacred Indian *25*
  terracotta figure of *71*
  winged man-headed *67*
  see also aurochs, Longhorn *and*
    Shorthorn bulls
bullbaiting
  in England 103, 107, *108*
  in Portugal *110*
bullfighting
  described 97
  eighteenth-century Spanish *90*
  first in Mexico (1529) 90
  in Barcelona *89*
  in Mexico *92*
  in Portugal 102

  of the Spanish Moors 83
  Roman *99*
  Spanish 97
bull-leaping (or grappling) 77, *77*
  acrobats 77
  described 72–3
  fresco (Knossos) *19*, 30, *31*, 72–3
  on Vapheio cups 76–7
bullrunning in England 103, 107
  at Stamford 108–10, *110*
Bulls Fighting (Ward) 82
brucellosis (V.D. in cattle) 168

cabestros (trained steers) 101
Caesar's description of the aurochs
  13, 98
Cane, Edward 134
Capua, grotto at 59–60
Carmichael, Alexander 42–4
Cattle and Cattle Breeders (M'Combie)
  139
cattle, domestication of 181
Cattle Parade at the Royal Show
  1971 *157*
Celtic mythology, bull in 34, 37
'Champion of England' bull 120–1,
  122, 126
Charolais bull *97*
Chartley Park, Ancient White
  cattle of *19*
Chillingham Park, wild white cattle
  of 16–20, *20*
  bull of 81, *81*
  hunting 103
Christianity, triumph over
  Mithraism 53, 59, 63, 79, 190
Coates, George 118
Coates's Herd Book 118, 133
Colling, Charles 115, 116, *116*, 117,
  117, 118
Colling, Robert 115, 116, *116*, 118
Collynie bull 121
'Comet' stock Shorthorn bull 117, *117*
corrida 90, 100, 103, 190
Cottrell 74
cow, dual purpose 143
Cretan bulls 30–1, 72, 98
'Cretan Bull, The' (Greek cup) *78*
Crete, bull worship and sacrifice in
  30–1
Cruickshank, Amos 120, *120*, 122,
  126

Crystal Cave, The (Stewart) 49, 52
'Cúchulainn Cycle' 37
Culley, George 115
Cumont, Franz 49, 55, 65
    interpretation of the sacrifice of
        the bull 57–9, 60

Daedalus, legend of 33–4, 187
Dairy Shorthorn *144*
Dairy Shorthorn Association 143
Devon bulls 134, *134, 153*
Dionysus (Bacchus)
    in the form of a bull *44*
    rites of 41
Duncomb, John 132
'Durham Ox' (Shorthorn bull) 116,
    117
Dutch Friesian cattle 145
Duthie, William 121, 137

*Early Christian Monuments of Scotland,
    The* 66
Echoes of the Glen (MacDonald) 41
Edinburgh Institute of Animal
    Breeding 148
Edwards, Dr Joseph 165
Egypt
    cult of the bull and the Dead 65
    the bull in ancient 27–30
Europa, rape of 32–3, *32*
Evans, Sir Arthur 30, 71, 73, 74, 75,
    76
Eyton, T. C. 133

farming, the bull in 131–55
Farquharson, Joseph 74
'Favourite', Durham Shorthorn bull
    122
fire-darts, used in bull fighting 101
Four Hundred Centuries of Cave Art
    (Breuil) 11, 180
Frazer, Sir James 34, 87, 174, 178

Galloway bull *182, 187*
Galloway, sacrifice of a bull in 41–2
Garretson, M. S. 14
Gilleron, E. 72
Gill, John 122
Golden Bough, The (Frazer) 34, 178

Gordale scar (*The Bull* by Ward) 82,
    92
Goya, Francisco de 82, 83, *83*, 86,
    103
Graves, Robert 26
Greek mythology, bull in 30–4, 40,
    41
Guernica (Picasso) 86, *87*
Guernsey cattle 148

Hagedoorn (Dutch geneticist) 181
Hammond, Sir John 162, 163
Heck, Heinz and Lutz 15
Hemmingway, Ernest 83, 90, 97
    description of the fighting bull 98,
        99, 101, 102
Heracles and the Cretan bull (relief)
    37
Hereford bulls 142, *148*, 162, *188*
    Argentinian *125, 139*
    breeding of 132–6
    Champion *133*
    Uruguayan *131*
Hereford Herd Book 133
Hereford Herd Book Society 133
Herrera, Matador Paco *104*
Highland bull *184*
Highland Journey (MacDonald) 184
Highland steer *177*
History and Origins of Druidism, The
    (Spence) 23
History of Quadrupeds (Beilby) 103
History of Shorthorn Cattle (Sinclair) 115
Howie (bull breeding family) 147,
    171
Hungarian bull *153*

Ivanoff (Russian physiologist) 163

Jersey
    bull 148, *148, 187*
    cow 153
Jones, K. B. 171

Knossos, palace of
    excavations at 75
    frescoes at *19*, 30, *31*, 72–3
Kom el Shugafa, sarcophagus from
    65

INDEX

'Kyloe' cattle *184*

Lascaux, cave paintings of 11, *13*, 14, 15, 65, 155, 180
La Tauromaquia (bullfighting by Goya) 82, *83*
Lawrence, John 134
le Cornu, Colonel 153
le Couteur, Colonel 153
Lenton herd 120
Longhorn
  bulls *113*
  steers *136*
'Long Horned' bull *129*
Longhorned Spanish breed 136
Lush (American geneticist) 181
Lydekker 13

MacCulloch 37, 42
MacDonald, Colin 41, 184, 185
Marks, J. 97, 99, 103
Marston, Commander T. B. 121
M'Combie, William 116, *125*, 137
  cattle-dealing of 138
  cattle feeding 139
metroön (temple of Cybele) 60
Michelangelo 79
Milovanov 163
milk yield recording 142–3
Miller, Professor W. C. 160
Minoan bull-grapplers 77
Minos, legend of 33–4, 78
Minotaur, legend of 33–4
Mitchell 41–2
Mithra 78, 79
  and the capture of the bull 48–55
  sacrifice of the bull 57–8, 62
Mithraeum
  at Dura-Europos 63
  from beneath the Church of San Clemente *61*
  in London 55–6, *55*
  in Ostia, Italy *34*, 55, *56*, 60
  paintings in the grotto of Capua 59–60
Mithraic rites 58–60
  grades of initiation 61–2
Mithraic shrines 48, 55–6, 57, 79
  rituals of worship in 58–9, 60
Mithraism 53–66

struggle against Christianity 59, 63, 79, 190
Mycenae, palace of
  excavations at 74–5
mythology, the bull in 25–44

Nandi, bull-mount of Siva *51*
Nietzsche 59

Odlum, George 146
Ox and its Kindred, The (Lydekker) 13
'Oxen' engraving *181*

Palace of Minos at Knossos, The (Evans) 74
Pasiphaë, myth of 33–4, *33*, 187
pedigree bulls 113–29
Persian mythology, the bull in 48
Picasso 86, 87, *87*
Piper, John 81
'Plascow Norseman' (Galloway bull) *187*
Pliny the Elder 22
  description of bulls by 13
Plutarch 53
Potter, Paul *69*, 82
progency testing 143, 167

Quartly, Francis 134
Quartly, Rev. W. 134

Raphael 79, *81*
Red Poll bull *169*
'Red Ruby' Devon bulls 116, 134
religion, the bull in 47–66
Renault, Mary 73
rhytons 74
  from Hagia Triada 77
  in form of a bull 74
  in form of a humped bull 75
Robertson 41, 145
Romano, Giulio *33*

sacrifice rituals with bulls *22*, 30, 34, 40–2, *47*, 65, *110*
salteadores 103

Santa Gertrudis bull *82, 139,* 153
Schliemann, Heinrich 71
   excavations of 74–5, 76
Scotland
   bull sacrifice in 41–2
   mythology of the bull in 42–4,
     65–6
'Scotch Shorthorn' 118, 120, 121,
   143, 162
semen
   collection of *160, 164, 166, 172*
   deep freezing method 164
Shorthorn bulls *113,* 115, 125, 126,
   127, 136, 142, 143, *191*
   breeding of 116–27, 132
   export of 121–2
   model head of *97*
   see also 'Comet', 'Durham Ox',
     'Favourite' and 'Wiseton'
'Short Horned' bull *129*
Shorthorn Herd Book 118
Shorthorn Society of Great Britain
   118, 133
'Silver Bull' Hereford breed 133
Sinclair, James 115, 120
Sittyton, close in-breeding at 121
Smith, Hamilton 14
Sol, Sun-God 49, 53, 62
Spain, fighting bulls of 16, 39
Spallanzani (Italian physiologist)
   163
Spanish Moors, bullfighting of 83
Spence, Lewis 23
Stanford, J. K.
steer, age of slaughter of 169
Stewart 126
Stewart, Mary 49, 52
Strutt, Gerald 145, 146
Stubbs 81
Sussex bulls 134, *134*
Sussex Bull Spring Show *185*

Táin Bó Cuailgne (the Cattle Raid
   of Cooley) 37
'Taureador Frescoes, The' 73, 77
Taurobolium, ceremony of the 40, 60
technology, the bull in 157–75

Tell-el-Obeid, copper bulls at *66*
'Terling Marthus' (Friesian bull)
   145, 146
The King Must Die (Renault) 73
The Past in the Present (Mitchell) 41–2
Theseus and the slain Minotaur *34*
Theseus slaying the Minotaur *43*
Theseus with the Marathon Bull *39*
Thornton 117
Tomlin, Benjamin 132–3
Tomkins, Richard 116, 132–3
Trow-Smith 125

Ur ar-en-ptah, bull from mastaba
   of *54*
Uri *see* aurochs
Uruguayan Hereford bull *131*

Vapheio tomb, gold cups from 76,
   92
Vibrio foetus (V.D. in Cattle) 168
V.D. in cattle 168
Vision of Ezekiel, The (Raphael) 79,
   81

Ward, James 81, 82, *92*
Watson, Hugh 116, *125,* 137
'Wenhaston Red Dawn' (Red Poll
   bull) *169*
'West Highland' cattle *184*
Whitehead, G. K. 15, 16, 19, 23
'White Heifer that Travelled' bull
   116
Wild White cattle 20, 103
Wilkinson, John 116, 120
'Wiseton' (Shorthorn bull) *122*

Young Bull, The (Potter) 69, 82

Zeuner, F. E. 30–1
   description of aurochs 14
Zebu cattle *148*
Zeus, disguised as a bull 32–3, *32*

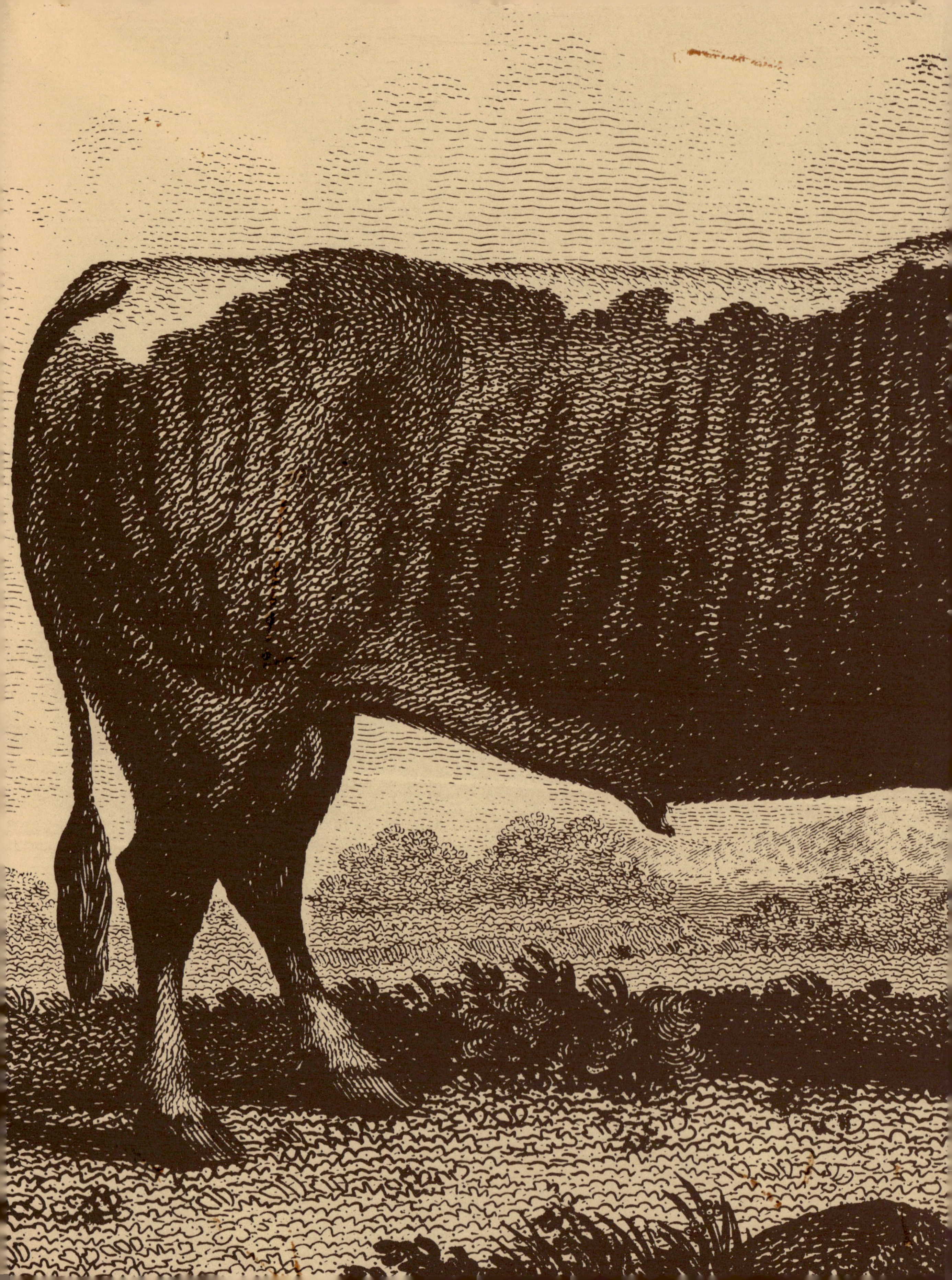